INTRODUCTORY READINGS
IN PHILOSOPHY

INTRODUCTORY READINGS IN PHILOSOPHY

edited by

Marcus G. Singer
University of Wisconsin

and

Robert R. Ammerman
University of Wisconsin

CHARLES SCRIBNER'S SONS · NEW YORK

For
Carl Bögholt
who inspired it

PREFACE

I

A substantial part of this volume consists of the reading materials used by most of the instructors of Philosophy 1, Introduction to Philosophy, at the University of Wisconsin. To this core a number of other selections have been added, in order to give the book greater balance and versatility. Some of the selections are relatively complete, but most have been internally edited, and some are no more than excerpts. The main criterion for including a selection has been whether it would actually be used in the course, and this, where it has operated, has also been the criterion for determining whether and to what extent a selection should be edited. But an attempt has also been made to keep the selections relatively simple, so that they would be intelligible and interesting to beginners. There are, nevertheless, gradations of difficulty and variations in interest and intelligibility, and some selections are relatively difficult. There is undoubtedly more material included here than could possibly be used in any single semester. There is enough for several courses. It is hoped that selections that meet the needs of so many different instructors at one large university will also meet the needs of a variety of instructors at other institutions.

The selections have been divided into a number of groups, according to the branches of philosophy they seem best to fit, although admittedly some selections could easily have gone in more than one place. It was thought best to keep the number of section headings to a minimum. Within each grouping the arrangement has been dictated solely by the chronology of the authors. This arrangement has been adopted in order to counter to some extent the influence of the editors' own views and preferences. The philosophical connections between various selections scattered in various parts of the book, which this arrangement might otherwise obscure, have been indicated by a number of cross references to be found in the footnotes.

Editorial omissions are indicated by the usual ellipses, and editorial additions by the usual brackets. All footnotes are editorial, except those that are numbered. The sources of the selections have been indicated in the appropriate places, as have acknowledgments, where required.

The editors wish to thank Professors William H. Hay, Eugene F. Kaelin, and Julius R. Weinberg, of the University of Wisconsin Philosophy

Department, for their advice and assistance in editing the selections they chose for inclusion, and Professors Hay and Weinberg for the translations they prepared especially for this volume.

A preliminary edition of this book, for local use, was published in 1960 by the Wm. C. Brown Book Company of Dubuque, Iowa. The experience gained in using this preliminary edition has proved invaluable. The editors would also like to thank Professors William Baumer, Monroe Beardsley, C. J. Ducasse, Vergil Dykstra, A. C. Garnett, Ernest Nagel, Glenn Riddle, Calvin Rollins, and Herbert Spiegelberg, who examined the preliminary edition of this book and offered various comments and suggestions. Some of these suggestions we were able to adopt. Only limitations of space have prevented us from adopting more.

II

How to Use This Book

After considerable deliberation, it was decided not to include any body of introductory and teaching apparatus in this collection. Such matter is often extraneous, and misleads students into raising issues irrelevant to the selections they are reading. Moreover, since the core of the book consists of materials selected and actually used by five different instructors, there is no single plan of selection or theme around which the arrangement is constructed. However, there are a number of interconnections among the selections included, which are not brought out by their arrangement in the book (though most of them are indicated in special footnotes), and it seems desirable to say a few words about them.

One obviously connected set of materials consists of selections 14 (Clifford), 33 and 34 (James), and 37 (Cohen). These were intended to be read together, but the selections are included in different parts of the book because, although they discuss a common problem, they emphasize different aspects of it.

Similarly, selections 23 and 24 (Mill), 25 (Engels), 26 (Darrow), and 28 (Campbell) each discuss facets of the problems of free will and determinism. They have been included under Metaphysics because, although the problems have significance for ethics, religion, and science, the question of the nature of man and the world in which he lives seems preeminently a metaphysical one. The chronological arrangement adopted precluded their being set together.

Some selections might appear to overlap but such duplication is only apparent. Selections 26 (Darrow) and 23 (Mill), for example, cover much the same material, but the Darrow piece is an extreme and provocative statement of a position that the Mill selection modifies almost to the point of reversal. By the same token, although selections 6 (Cohen and Nagel) and 13 (Peirce) deal with the same subject, the Peirce selection is overloaded with irony, and partly for this reason is often obscure on crucial issues. Cohen and Nagel are clearer and more precise. The two pieces supplement rather than duplicate each other, for the Peirce is useful as a stimulus for discussion, while the Cohen and Nagel helps to clarify thought on the subject.

Some of the selections were included mainly because they are useful as stimuli for discussion; for example, Part I of selection 7 (Somerville), and selections 8 (Black), 16 (Joad), 26 (Darrow), and 51 (de Tocqueville) seldom fail to excite interest and discussion among beginning students.

Some reference should be made to the paucity of materials on aesthetics. Space limitations have prevented the inclusion of more than selections 45 (Santayana) and 48 (Beardsley). These pieces, however, go nicely together and they should serve as an introduction to that subject.

The reader should not suppose that the selections in this volume offer a reliable guide to the philosophies of the authors included. The selections have been chosen as vehicles for the presentation and discussion of certain philosophical problems, and not as keys to the philosophies of the authors. Those readers who are interested in ascertaining the views of a particular author will find reference to many of his important works in the Biographical Notes.

It may be useful to sketch two possible ways of using the materials of this book in a course of semester length. One such arrangement, used by one of the editors, is the following. Begin with problems of logic and the theory of knowledge, using selections 16 (Joad) and 11 (Descartes). Then take up as one related group selections 13 (Peirce), 6 (Cohen and Nagel), and 51 (de Tocqueville). Then proceed to selections 12 (Hume) and 17 (Murphy), together with 9 (Copi) and 8 (Black). The nature of science could be dealt with by reading 7 (Somerville) and 10 (Copi). The questions about causality and the establishment of empirical laws that arise here are an obvious bridge to the second part of the course, on the free will problem, the reading consisting of selections 26 (Darrow), 25 (Engels), and 23 and 24 (Mill). One could also include here selection 28 (Campbell).

Questions about belief and evidence arising in the first part of the course provide a useful transition to Part III of the course, dealing with the ethics of belief, using selections 14 (Clifford), 33 and 34 (James), and 37 (Cohen). This then leads to questions of ethics, where selections 40 (Hume) and 47 (Murphy) are obvious foils for each other. The consideration of ethical questions would lead, if time permitted, to political philosophy, where selections 50 (Calhoun), 54 (Broad), and 53 (Tawney) go well together. One could end with any of the selections in Part I that seem suitable.

It should be noticed that in the course just outlined each part begins with some selection that presents a skeptical position on the matter under discussion. This is a good way for beginners to be introduced to philosophical problems, because it challenges customary ideas. But there are other arrangements.

An alternate way of arranging a course would be to begin with a general description of the nature of philosophy. Selection 2 (Rogers) should be useful for this purpose. One might then introduce the students to some of the questions of ethics, a subject in which most beginning students are already interested. One might, for example, read selections 46 (Stace), 42 (Bentham), 41 (Kant), 44 (Dewey), and Part III of selection 32 (d'Holbach). The latter selection, concerned as it is with both ethics and religion, provides a natural bridge to the problems of the philosophy of religion. Here various proofs for God's existence can be considered, using selections 29 (Anselm), 30 (Aquinas), and 31 (Hume), as well as the problem of justifying believing in God on faith. Selections 14 (Clifford), 33 and 34 (James), and 37 (Cohen) provide a well-rounded discussion of that subject. Part II of selection 31 (Hume), dealing as it does with the problem of evil, brings up the problem of free will which allows for a passage from philosophy of religion to pure metaphysics. Selections 26 (Darrow), 23 and 24 (Mill), and 28 (Campbell) provide excellent grounds for discussion of that topic. The transition to the problems of philosophy of science is easily effected after a discussion of the doctrine of Determinism. Selections 5 (Mill) and 10 (Copi) could be used to introduce the student to some of the problems in that area. The final assignments might be selections 1 (Whitehead) and 3 (Ducasse), which deal with the nature of wisdom and the relation of philosophy to life.

Neither of these two possible courses, naturally, finds a use for all of the materials included here, and they have, admittedly, considerable overlap. Yet they should serve to bring out the flexibility inherent in the book. Many more arrangements are possible, perhaps some of them better.

III

How to Read Philosophy

All philosophical reading should be directed by a plan. This is especially true of the material contained in this book. The student should not attempt to read it without guidance. "Books are tools, which wise men use to suit their own ends," it has been said, and this book is pre-eminently a tool for teaching. Nevertheless, some general advice on how to read philosophical writings can be given in this place.

One of the difficulties beginners have is that they do not know how to approach the reading of a philosophical essay. Philosophical writings should always be read with certain questions in mind, and they almost always should be read more than once, for a single reading will seldom bring them into focus. "In all . . . philosophical studies," according to Professor G. E. Moore (perhaps with some exaggeration), "the difficulties and disagreements, of which its history is full, are mainly due to a very simple cause: namely to the attempt to answer questions, without first discovering precisely what question it is which you desire to answer." Of course, to discover just what problem a philosopher is trying to solve is not always easy.

In studying philosophy, the student is not usually expected to absorb and memorize large amounts of material. This deadens the capacity for reflection, and leaves no zest for it. And reflection here is of the essence. The student should read a selection carefully and thoroughly, several times, asking himself the following questions:

(1) What question is this philosopher trying to answer?
(2) How did the question arise? *i.e.*, Why is he trying to answer this question?
(3) What answer does he give?
(4) Why does he give this answer instead of some other one? *i.e.*, What reasons does he have for the answer at which he arrives?
(5) Is the answer he gives a good one—does it really answer the question?

In other words, one should always try first to determine the *point* of a selection, to decide *what* the author is trying to prove. Then one should consider *why* he is trying to prove that point. Thirdly, one should ask: How does he go about proving it? i.e., What reasons or arguments does he give? What evidence does he present? Finally one may raise the critical questions: Are his reasons good ones? Does he really prove his point? Has he met all the objections that might bear the other way? Has he overlooked any facts he should have considered?

One should therefore first read through an assignment fairly rapidly in an attempt to get a general picture of what it is about, not worrying on first reading about details. Then one should read it again, more slowly, attempting to fit the details into the general picture. Reading a philosophical essay intelligently is analogous to the procedure involved in solving a jigsaw puzzle: it is much easier to put the separate pieces together if you have an idea of what the picture is about. The student ought not to feel discouraged if at first it seems difficult. It often is difficult. But nothing really worthwhile comes easy. Lewis Carroll once said:

> When you come to any passage you don't understand, *read it again*; if you still don't understand it, *read it again*; if you fail, even after *three* readings, very likely your brain is getting a little tired. In that case, put the book away, and take to other occupations, and next day, when you come to it fresh, you will very likely find that it is quite easy.

It is remarkable how often a procedure like this works. However, the student will be well advised not to allow himself to be stopped by *just one* passage. If you come to a passage you don't understand, read on a bit; maybe the context will make it clear.

The above remarks provide merely some general hints to help the student with his reading. They will not take the place of the student's own reflection. Nor will they take the place of discussion, which is often invaluable in clearing up a point and helping one settle one's own ideas.

M.G.S.

R.R.A.

Madison, Wisconsin
October 31, 1961

TABLE OF CONTENTS

PART I

THE NATURE AND USES
OF PHILOSOPHY

• I •

WISDOM *

Alfred North Whitehead (1861–1947)

The fading of ideals is sad evidence of the defeat of human endeavor. In the schools of antiquity philosophers aspired to impart wisdom, in modern colleges our humbler aim is to teach subjects. The drop from the divine wisdom, which was the goal of the ancients, to text-book knowledge of subjects, which is achieved by the moderns, marks an educational failure, sustained through the ages. I am not maintaining that in the practice of education the ancients were more successful than ourselves. You have only to read Lucian, and to note his satiric dramatizations of the pretentious claims of philosophers, to see that in this respect the ancients can boast over us no superiority. My point is that, at the dawn of our European civilisation, men started with the full ideals which should inspire education, and that gradually our ideals have sunk to square with our practice.

But when ideals have sunk to the level of practice, the result is stagnation. In particular, so long as we conceive intellectual education as merely consisting in the acquirement of mechanical mental aptitudes, and of formulated statements of useful truths, there can be no progress; though there will be much activity, amid aimless re-arrangement of syllabuses, in the fruitless endeavour to dodge the inevitable lack of time. We must take it as an unavoidable fact, that God has so made the world that there are more topics desirable for knowledge than any one person can possibly acquire. It is hopeless to approach the problem by the way of the enumeration of subjects which every one ought to have mastered. There are too many of them, all with excellent title-deeds. Perhaps, after all, this plethora of material is fortunate; for the world is made interesting by a delightful ignorance of important truths. . . . Though knowledge is one chief aim of intellectual education, there is another ingredient, vaguer but greater, and more dominating in its importance. The ancients called it "wisdom." You cannot be wise without some basis of knowledge; but you may easily acquire knowledge and remain bare of wisdom.

* Excerpted from chapter 3 of *The Aims of Education;* copyright 1929 by The Macmillan Company, renewed 1957. Used by permission of The Macmillan Company, New York, and Ernest Benn Limited, London. The title of this selection has been supplied by the editors. Compare with selection 3.

Now wisdom is the way in which knowledge is held. It concerns the handling of knowledge, its selection for the determination of relevant issues, its employment to add value to our immediate experience. This mastery of knowledge, which is wisdom, is the most intimate freedom obtainable. The ancients saw clearly—more clearly than we do—the necessity for dominating knowledge by wisdom. But, in the pursuit of wisdom in the region of practical education, they erred sadly. To put the matter simply, their popular practice assumed that wisdom could be imparted to the young by procuring philosophers to spout at them. Hence the crop of shady philosophers in the schools of the ancient world. The only avenue towards wisdom is by freedom in the presence of knowledge. But the only avenue towards knowledge is by discipline in the acquirement of ordered fact. . . .

The importance of knowledge lies in its use, in our active mastery of it —that is to say, it lies in wisdom. It is a convention to speak of mere knowledge, apart from wisdom, as of itself imparting a peculiar dignity to its possessor. I do not share in this reverence for knowledge as such. It all depends on who has the knowledge and what he does with it. That knowledge which adds greatness to character is knowledge so handled as to transform every phase of immediate experience. It is in respect to the activity of knowledge that an over-vigorous discipline in education is so harmful. The habit of active thought, with freshness, can only be generated by adequate freedom. Undiscriminating discipline defeats its own objects by dulling the mind. If you have much to do with the young as they emerge from school and from the university, you soon note the dulled minds of those whose education has consisted in the acquirement of inert knowledge. . . . Furthermore, this overhaste to impart mere knowledge defeats itself. The human mind rejects knowledge imparted in this way. The craving for expansion, for activity, inherent in youth is disgusted by a dry imposition of disciplined knowledge. The discipline, when it comes, should satisfy a natural craving for the wisdom which adds value to bare experience. . . .

In my own work at universities I have been much struck by the paralysis of thought induced in pupils by the aimless accumulation of precise knowledge, inert and unutilised. It should be the chief aim of a university professor to exhibit himself in his own true character—that is, as an ignorant man thinking, actively utilising this small share of knowledge. In a sense, knowledge shrinks as wisdom grows: for details are swallowed up in principles. The details of knowledge which are important will be picked up *ad hoc* in each avocation of life, but the habit of the active utilisation of well-understood principles is the final possession of wisdom. . . .

• 2 •

PHILOSOPHY *

Arthur Kenyon Rogers (1868–1936)

No man who is able to learn from experience at all, can live very long in the world without finding himself continually passing judgment, in one way or another, on the meaning and the value of life. At the very least there will be some things which it will seem to him to be worth the while to do, and other things, again, which will fail to interest him, and which by implication therefore he will condemn; but besides such fragmentary and instinctive judgments, he also, if he reflects at all, can hardly help but ask himself at times whether life has not some meaning as a whole, which would serve to throw light on the scattered and chaotic fragments of his everyday experience, and bring them into some degree of unity. Now philosophy, apart from technicalities of definition, is nothing but an attempt, in a reasoned and comprehensive way, to answer this question, What is the meaning of life? Every one, therefore, in so far as he adopts a certain general attitude towards the problems that meet him, looks at them from a certain point of view, and does not simply let himself drift from one experience to another without any purpose or unity to connect them, is taking the standpoint of philosophy. Such an attitude we call his philosophy of life, and if he is more or less clearly conscious of what this attitude is, and is able to express it in a unified and consistent way, we say in a popular sense that he is a philosopher. Technical philosophy differs from this only in the fact that it tries to do thoroughly, and in full consciousness of itself, what in popular thinking we do in a loose and unsystematic fashion. Instead of picking out those factors in life which appeal to us more personally and directly, it tries to set individual prejudices and limitations aside, and to include, as impartially as it can, all the elements which experience presents. It is true that in doing this it frequently gets far enough from what seem to be living interests; but back of all technical discussions, there is still the underlying conviction that by this path, and this alone, can we get at the vital and essential meaning of the world, or else we have no longer philosophy, but mere pedantry and hair-splitting. It is natural, then, that we should find the definitions which men have given of

* From the Introduction to A Brief Introduction to Modern Philosophy (New York: The Macmillan Company, 1899). The title of this selection has been supplied by the editors.

5

philosophy at different times are not by any means the same. They are not
the same because, under different circumstances, men's interests are
directed to different points, now to the importance of conduct, now to the
nature of the external world, now to the existence of supersensible realities. But to say that their interest lies at one point or another, is only to
say in other words that here they find the value of life; this is the test that
can always be applied, the real motive, if not the apparent one. So we can
speak of the philosophy of any pursuit whatever in which men can engage,
or of any subject which can occupy them, of science, of history, of the
technical arts. Between science and the philosophy of science, history and
the philosophy of history, there is indeed no hard and fast separation; but
what in the one case we are specially concerned with is the positive nature
and the laws of a certain group of facts, which have been selected out
from the rest of the world to be studied by themselves, while in the other
we restore that connection with the whole which for the time being we
had set aside, and try to look at our facts in the light of the meaning which
they have for life in its entirety.

Even when it is stated in this preliminary way, the definition which has
been given of philosophy will be seen to have a bearing on the disputes
which have been common about the value of the study, and the very unequal estimation in which it has been held. There are many people to
whom the pursuit of philosophy has seemed to be, at best, of very doubtful
utility. Sometimes it is one who, like Matthew Arnold, is so impressed
with the concrete values of art and conduct that the world of the philosopher seems to him abstract and barren in comparison. More often it is the
man of science, who feels that he has got hold of reality so immediately
and palpably in the world of matter, and of reality which is so far-reaching
in its significance, that he has no interest left to give the supersensuous and
very doubtful world which he understands that philosophy is trying to construct by merely thinking about it. Now the answer to be made the scientist is this, that he is not getting along without philosophy, as he supposes,
but only is adopting one particular kind of philosophy, whose implications,
however, he does not try to understand. And he can hardly hold that this
refusal to examine into the presuppositions of his thinking is, in opposition
to the metaphysician's course, a highly meritorious thing, without stultify-
ing his whole scientific procedure. He may, indeed, as a scientist, merely
devote himself to the discovery of facts; but unless he is prepared to say
that the bare objective fact is everything, and its meaning, its value for us,
is nothing (which is very like a contradiction in terms), he cannot avoid en-
croaching on the philosopher's field. In reality he always does bring with
him his own interpretation of the facts of science, and they differentiate the

way in which he looks at the world from the way in which other men look at it; the only question is as to whether this should be conscious and thoroughgoing, or whether it should be unconscious, and unaware of the possible difficulties that may be involved. In any case the mere facts of the objective world, as objective, cannot exhaust the problems which arise, and arise necessarily, for this external world would not exist, for us, if it did not have a value as coming within our conscious life, and so it forms but a part of experience, not the whole. Whatever it may be in itself, for human interest at least the objective fact or law as such cannot possibly be a final and sufficient goal. Even the man who thinks that it is so, must have some reason why the search for objective truth appeals to him; its simple existence in itself does not explain why he should want to know it. It may of course be that, in the end, one might be driven to admit that no vital relation to human life could be discovered; in that case science at once would cease to be pursued. But answerable or not, at least it cannot be said that when the problems go beyond mere scientific matter of fact they cease to have any *interest* for us; knowing the chemical composition of water will not satisfy us in face of the larger question, What is this world of which our lives form a part? what is its meaning and destiny? And it is through philosophy, not through science, that this latter question must receive an answer, if it is answered at all.

Nevertheless there is some justification for this contemptuous attitude which science is apt to adopt towards philosophy, and which grows out of the true feeling that any value which is really worth our consideration must attach to the actual world in which we live, not to some far-away abstract world, which only can be got at by the occasional philosopher, and through the colorless medium of thought. What we are after is the meaning of life as we live it, and if we come out at the end with something that finds no place for the concrete values with which we are familiar, then certainly a large factor in the problem has without any justification been juggled out of sight. So that we have to insist, in the second place, that the data which the philosopher uses are not something which, by a pure act of intellectual creation, he spins out of his own head, but the same facts with which science, and history, and everyday living, deal. In this sense, therefore, the philosopher is dependent on the scientist; he cannot go his own way and construct his world *a priori*, but he must continually be falling back upon the concrete knowledge which science represents. So, also, philosophy does not "give us God, freedom, immortality," if by this we mean that it some-how puts us in possession of values which we had not before suspected. Religion, morality, the social life, all come before philosophy, and are pre-supposed by it; and philosophy, in turn, in so far as it is only a bare recogni-

tion of truths, and not a vital appreciation of them, in so far as it stops
with itself as mere knowing, and does not hand back the material which
it has been elaborating intellectually, to the immediate experience in which
this originated, is forgetting its place as the handmaid of life, and so is
rendering itself barren and formal. All that philosophy can do is to take the
actual values which come to us in experience, work out their implications
and their mutual relationships, and, it may be, get at some unitary point
of view, from which each element can be looked at, and have full justice
done it. But by this very process it will be making a positive addition to the
value of experience itself, not by creating truths which are entirely new,
but by clearing up and throwing new light upon the meaning which already has been present in our lives, and so making it more real to us.

And this will also serve to indicate the answer to a very common com-
plaint against philosophy, in which it is set over against feeling, as something quite opposed. It is common to hear people say, After all, it is
feeling truth, not reasoning about it, which is the important thing; and
philosophy, by translating everything over into the cold and impersonal
medium of thought, and by introducing all sorts of doubts and limitations,
is a foe to that immediate enjoyment of truth which alone is worth the
having. Whether this is true or not depends entirely on what we mean by
it. If we mean by feeling unintelligent, blind feeling, just the mere confused sense of satisfaction, it is not true at all. But this is not what we mean
when we speak of feeling as it is aroused by poetry or art: that is equivalent
rather to insight, intelligent appreciation. It is, therefore, not something
which is opposed to reason, but its highest, most immediate exercise. But
here again we shall be doing an injustice if we oppose immediacy too
sharply to the more laborious and reflective work of thought. It is not
philosophy which comes in to spoil the fineness of the enjoyment we get
in immediate feeling, but it is the fact that feeling breaks down, and will no
longer satisfy us, that compels us to betake ourselves to thought. Feelings
are sure to clash, and then they possess no criterion within themselves
which shall say whether this feeling or that one is the truer; merely as
feeling they cannot tell us whether they are valid objectively, or whether
we are only deluding ourselves with subjective emotions. To compare
their values, and to bring them to the test of their consonancy with the
whole of life, thought is needed; but that does not mean that we pass from
immediate experience to something higher, thought; it means that,
through thought, we get from an immediacy which is limited and partial,
to one which is truer, richer, and more inclusive.

Now systems of philosophy are simply attempts to get at a unified way
of looking at things. . . . In a general way we may say that they all of

them have to do with a few very simple-looking assumptions, which every one is accustomed to make, and which are so natural that when our attention is first called to them we hardly see how anybody can be so foolish as to bring them into question. We all feel very sure, that is, that out there in space a lot of things exist,—trees, stones, houses,—which we know are there because we see them when we open our eyes, and touch them when we stretch out our hands. To be sure, we are not looking at them all the time, but that makes no difference to the things themselves; they still are there, whether we see them or not. Then again we are sure that we ourselves exist. If we were asked to define this "self," we might indeed have difficulty in determining just in what it consisted, but in general it is that which thinks and feels, has sensations and desires, and acts according to conscious purposes, none of which attributes are we ready to suppose belong to things in the external world. Finally, it is not only my own self that I believe in, but I am just as firmly convinced of the existence of other selves, with whom I am continually in communication. These three assumptions it never enters into the head of the ordinary man to doubt.

Now in these beliefs, on which every one, including the philosopher himself, continually is acting, there are involved the various problems of philosophy, even the most abstract. This world of men and things which we assume seems clear and unambiguous in its nature only so long as we refrain from thinking about it; a very little consideration shows the necessity of defining more exactly in what the reality of these things consists, how they are to be thought. In so far as philosophy has this problem, of determining the true nature of the real, it is called Ontology. If we start by assuming the separation between mind and matter, we must ask precisely what it is we mean by these two terms, and then the more they seem to differ from and exclude each other, the more insistent becomes the problem as to how that still more basal form of reality is to be conceived, which shall restore the unity of which philosophy is in search. But things not only exist, they have a history; and this brings us into still more evident contact with the practical values of experience. For any inquiry into the laws which govern the history of the material world, into the nature and connection of the world processes, raises at once and inevitably the question, what relation these have to our own conscious lives and purposes, whether they are mechanical merely, and indifferent to human interests, or whether something in the nature of meaning and aim can be detected in them. This in general is the field of Cosmology. But now the fact that we started with individuals more or less distinct from the world, gives rise to a third set of problems. It is soon apparent that we cannot talk about the nature of reality, without also giving some account of the source from

which we get our knowledge, a problem which again becomes more difficult, the more we insist upon the separation between the knower and the
object which is known. An answer to this question, What is the nature of
knowledge? or How is knowledge possible? constitutes Epistemology.

Of course it would be a mistake to suppose that these three provinces
of philosophy deal with problems that are in any strict sense distinct; in
reality it is all the while a single problem which we are approaching from
different sides. That problem is, to get some way of looking at things as a
whole, some unitary conception which shall find a place for the actual facts
of life, and by reference to which we may have some reasonable ground for
believing that these facts possess real validity and worth. Philosophical
systems are simply the most general points of view from which this unity
has been sought. . . .

• 3 •

THE GUIDE OF LIFE *

C. J. Ducasse (1881–)

In *The History of Phi Beta Kappa* by Oscar M. Voorhees we read that
Philosophia Biou Kubernetes, the Greek phrase that gives the Society its
name, was "formed and adopted" by John Heath, a student of Greek
classics at the College of William and Mary, on whose initiative the Phi
Beta Kappa Society was founded in 1776. This phrase—philosophy, or
love of wisdom, the guide of life—and the Latin phrase *Societas Philoso-
phiae,* the initials of which appear on the reverse of the Phi Beta Kappa key,
express the five founders' conviction about the right role of philosophy in
life.

But although taking philosophy as one's guide through life seemed to
John Heath and his fellow-students an eminently wise resolve, today the
perspective in which educated people view human life is different from
that of 1776; and members of Phi Beta Kappa may find themselves challenged to give reasons for adopting philosophy as the guide of life in
preference to religion or to science, either of which today enjoys far more
general prestige than does philosophy. I propose to consider those reasons
here.

* From an address originally given to initiates of The Trinity College Chapter of Phi
Beta Kappa which was printed in *The Key Reporter,* Vol. XXIII, No. 2, January 1958.
Reproduced here by kind permission of Phi Beta Kappa. Compare with selection 1.

WHY NOT SCIENCE AS GUIDE?

At the time of the founding of Phi Beta Kappa any suggestion that man should take science rather than philosophy as his guide in the conduct of his life would have been hardly intelligible. The investigation of puzzling natural phenomena was not commonly thought to be a potential source of counsels for living. The justification, if any, for studying the mysteries of nature was held to lie only in such gratification of idle curiosity as it might yield to the few impractical persons who engaged in that study. The attitude then prevalent towards their research is well exemplified by the reaction that greeted the first observations of electric current, made about 1786 by Luigi Galvani, then professor of physiology at the University of Bologna.

The story is that his wife was ill with tuberculosis; and her physician having prescribed a broth made with frogs' legs to give her strength, Galvani was getting some ready for cooking one day, sitting on his balcony. As he proceeded he suspended each pair of legs from the balcony's railing by a copper hook; and he noticed that whenever any of the legs so suspended happened to touch the iron uprights, the leg muscles contracted sharply.

This curious little fact, however, had no discernible utility, nor did it fit in with the scientific knowledge possessed in his day. Hence nobody took seriously what he reported. "I am attacked," he complained in 1792, "by two quite opposite sects—the learned and the ignorant. The ones and the others laugh at me and call me the frogs' dancing master. Yet I know that I have discovered one of the forces of nature."

Other reports of facts or theories belying what W. F. G. Swann has called "the common sense of a given epoch" have encountered a similar attitude, which has been a persistent feature of the history of science. Nevertheless science developed rapidly during the nineteenth century and has continued to do so at an even faster pace in the twentieth. The result of this has been, in the words of Sir William Dampier, that "the whole conception of the natural Universe has been changed by the recognition that man, subject to the same physical laws and processes as the world around him, cannot be considered separately from that world, and that scientific methods of observation, induction, deduction and experiment are applicable, not only to the original subject matter of pure science, but to nearly all the many and varied fields of human thought and activity."

Furthermore, the fruits of pure scientific research have in many cases turned out to be applicable to the solution of concrete practical problems; and in civilized countries these practical applications have immeasurably improved the material conditions of human life. That science has put into the hands of man power undreamed of before over the processes of nature, and enabled him to utilize her forces for attainment of his purposes, is today evident to everybody, and accounts for the enormous prestige science now enjoys.

On the other hand, the fact is now becoming all too evident that the ledger of scientific progress has a debit as well as a credit side. The power that scientific knowledge brings has indeed made possible the cure or prevention of many diseases; it has provided new and highly efficient means of production, communication, and transportation; and it has given man all the convenient gadgets on which he is today so dependent. But at the same time it has complicated his life, robbed it in large measure of the joy of craftsmanship, multiplied its needs, and brought it new diseases and ghastly perils. The natural sciences and the might they have brought to man are in themselves wholly neutral as regards values; they lend themselves equally to the efficient implementation of good and of evil purposes.

But whereas in the last hundred years the natural sciences have made more progress than in the preceding thousands, the soul of man, on the contrary, has during that time undergone no great change. Some customs and institutions have altered, but the passions that are the mainsprings of human conduct have remained much the same. Men are better informed today but probably not much more intelligent than before; their economic standard of living has risen; but when occasion offers, they exhibit a nature hardly less selfish or brutal or greedy than of old. They are not fundamentally much more self-disciplined, honest, kindly, or wise than in earlier ages. Measured in terms of spiritual maturity, the average man today is still a child. And it is in the hands of that child that the natural sciences, almost overnight, have placed powers that in their magnitude and possibilities of evil, no less than of good, are to those man had earlier as dynamite is to the strength of bare hands. Great nations have risen in the past only to fall victim to destructive forces within them. But today it is the whole of life on earth, or even the very earth itself, the continued existence of which is in danger.

Obviously, then, if man is to be saved, what he now needs is not more of the power the natural sciences bring, but more wisdom wherewith to direct the use he makes of the powers he already has.

WHY NOT RELIGION AS GUIDE?

For such direction, and for the serenity that obedience to it brings, men have traditionally turned to religion. But to many people nowadays religion no longer carries the authority it did in earlier times.

A number of factors are responsible for this. As a result of efficient means of communication and transportation, men—and especially educated men —are better acquainted than in earlier times with the religions of mankind other than their own. A person with the wider perspective of such acquaintance sees that the dogmas of the other religions are different from, and sometimes irreconcilable with, those of his own; and yet that the needs that turn men to religion are on the whole satisfied by the other religions for their devotees as effectively as they are satisfied for him by his own.

Furthermore, he realizes that if he had been born and brought up in a different part of the world, his religion would almost automatically have been the one that happened to prevail in that particular region. And this thrusts upon him the question whether the location of a man's birthplace determines not merely which religion he *will believe*, but also its *truth or falsity*. And of course merely to ask this question is virtually to answer it, especially in an epoch when so many of the traditional religious teachings about the place of the earth in the universe, the age and history of the earth, and the origin of life and of man, have been conclusively disproved by the knowledge that science has produced in lieu of mere creeds, pious opinions, and crude cosmological or biological fancies handed down by the religious traditions.

In the light of these and similar considerations, the articles of faith of the various religions—of one's own as well as of the others—are seen to be not statements known to be true or false, but essentially *psychological tools*: instruments mankind has automatically devised for performance of certain important social and personal functions. For religious dogmas to influence the conduct, the feelings, and the attitudes of men, they need not be true but need only be firmly *believed*.

Like other tools, moreover, they can be used otherwise than in the beneficent manner that gives them worth. As we know only too well, bigoted men who were ignorant, stupid, arrogant, sadistic or perverse, and who happened to have power over their fellows, have too often interpreted the dogmas of their religion as warranting the wars, persecutions, and senseless cruelties that stain the histories of even the monotheistic, self-styled higher religions. This forces on modern man's attention the fact that the religions, like the sciences, are ambivalent and have a dark side; and hence that the teachings contained in their various sacred books or promulgated by their officials cannot be uncritically assumed to supply ready-made the wise guidance that man so direly needs. Rather, those teachings have to be carefully sifted and the wisdom or folly of each intelligently appraised.

How about Philosophy?

And this brings us back to philosophy. Does it offer a better prospect than either science or religion of furnishing man with the wisdom he needs?

In the popular opinion at least, hardly so. For philosophy is commonly reputed to be nearly the most nebulous and impractical thing there is. Yet if philosophy were really so remote from practical affairs, it would be hard to understand either the execration or the veneration in which various philosophers have at times been held. Why, for instance, should Socrates, Hypatia, and Giordano Bruno have been put to death, Plato sold into slavery, and Campanella imprisoned, for voicing the philosophical opinions they held? On the other side of the picture, why should the same Plato have sometimes been referred to as "the divine Plato," and Kant as "the immortal Kant"? Why have their writings and those of other great philosophers continued to be read and prized through the centuries?

The answer, I believe, lies in the fact that philosophy, despite the seeming idleness of some of its technicalities, really has practical import and indeed in this respect may ultimately outrank most things of more obvious utility.

The nature of the practical value peculiar to philosophy will become evident if we try to gain a clearer conception than is common of what philosophy and philosophical reflection in fact are.

Philosophical reflection is not an activity indulged in only by specialists called philosophers who allegedly live in architectural monstrosities known as ivory towers. Just as each of us at times engages casually in horticulture or medicine or carpentry without special training, so practically all of us on certain occasions spontaneously occupy ourselves with philosophical questions.

We may, for example, read in the newspapers of a child born hopelessly malformed and defective, but who, if operated upon at once, might nonetheless be kept alive. And we may read further that the physician in charge realizing that the child's life could not be other than a grievous burden to himself, to his parents, and to society, refrained from operating and allowed the child to die. Then, in letters from readers to the editors of newspapers all over the country, controversy rages about whether the physician's action was morally right or morally wrong. And even if we do not ourselves take active part in them, we too form opinions of the question.

In such a controversy the participants do not merely state their moral appraisal of the physician's course. They also give reasons of one kind or another to support the validity of their judgment. And if these reasons are in turn challenged, each participant brings forth considerations he believes adequate to vindicate the validity of his reasons.

The reasons, and the reasons for the reasons, that are thus appealed to as grounds for endorsing or condemning the physician's action, constitute a moral philosophy, or at least a fragment of one. And the mental activity of searching for those reasons, and of then so editing them as to purge them of the inconsistencies or exaggerations or errors that opponents were able to point out, constitute philosophizing, or philosophical reflection.

In this example the issue is a moral one, and the philosophy constructed on the spur of the occasion by a participant is therefore, as far as it goes, a moral philosophy: that is, a theory of the nature of the difference between moral right and wrong, and of the nature of the situations to which appraisal in terms of morality and immorality is congruous. But similar controversies, or indeed doubts within one person's mind, arise about issues of other kinds: about the merits of certain works of art for example, or about educational issues, or about the sufficiency of the evidence offered as basis for a given assertion, and so on. The fragmentary philosophies similarly improvised on such occasions are then a philosophy of art, a philosophy of education or a philosophy of knowledge. And there can be no doubt that on the occasions impelling us to engage in such reflection, a judgment shaped by the conclusions reached in that reflective manner is likely to be wiser than would be one made without it. . . .

If one engages in philosophical reflection under pressure of immediate need to solve a particular practical problem of appraisal, such reflection will inevitably be hasty and relatively uncritical. But the persons called philosophers make it their life work to reflect on the meaning of the various value-predicates and on the kind of subject that is alone congruously appraisable in terms of each. They attempt to purge such reflection of the narrowness and imprecision that are the unavoidable defects of the extempore philosophical reflection we all undertake as occasion compels. Not only does the philosopher strive to carry on his reflections in a thoroughly methodical manner; he also strives to make them comprehensive rather than particularistic. That is, his business as a philosopher is not to solve himself the many practical problems of appraisal. It is on the one hand to clarify . . . the various value-concepts that enter into the formulation of the problems; and on the other, to specify the kinds of empirical knowledge that must be obtained in order to discern whether or not a given appraisal is valid in a given case. Actually to obtain that empirical knowledge is not the business of the philosopher; it is the business of the particular person who is confronted with a particular practical problem of appraisal.

Clarification of the meaning of terms, however, whether in general or in the particular case of terms of appraisal, is a semantic task. Consequently the question immediately suggests itself whether philosophical reflection, in undertaking it, is not concerning itself with mere words, and therefore, presumably, with something of no great importance.

The answer is that to speak of "mere words" is much like speaking of "mere dynamite." For although words do not in themselves control the processes of inanimate nature, they do control the thoughts, the feelings, and the acts of men—initiating and shaping them, or inhibiting them. In men's dealings with one another and in the individual's dealings with himself words are analogous in function and in importance to the insignificant-looking switches that govern the operations of giant machines in industry.

Hence it is of the greatest moment for man to know just where the psychological wires lead from the verbal switches; for the terrible thing about words is that to a great extent they cause and shape the acts of men, whether or not they really fit the things to which men apply them, and whether or not men understand their meaning correctly. Common sayings such as "Give a dog a bad name, and you can hang him," or "Slander on, some of it always sticks," testify to this fact. Among us today, for example, to call a man a Communist is to damage his reputation even if it is not true that he is a Communist, and even if the persons who hear him so called have but the vaguest idea of what communism is. And, similarly, the most potent of the weapons Communists have employed is perversion of the meaning of words: calling "liberation" what is in fact enslavement, for example.

Thus when the words we use do not fit or are ill-understood, the feelings, the beliefs, and the courses of action they nonetheless generate cheat our aims and stultify us. This is especially true when the words concerned are value-predicates, for a man's course is shaped at innumerable points by evaluative statements. Whether he formulates these for himself or accepts them from others ready-made, they determine the basic policies, the tactics, and the strategic decisions of his life. This vast power of language is what gives outstanding practical importance to clear, analytical knowledge of just which things our substantives denote and just what characters our adjectives predicate of the things to which we apply them.

LOVE OF WISDOM AS THE GUIDE OF LIFE

In conclusion let us consider briefly the term "wisdom" and note the light that philosophical analysis of its meaning throws on Phi Beta Kappa's counsel to take philosophy—that is, love of wisdom—as the guide of life.

What exactly, then, is wisdom? It consists in *knowledge of what in given circumstances would on the whole be the best thing for a person with given equipment to do.*

Thus the counsel to make love of wisdom the guide of one's life packs together four distinct recommendations, which may be separately stated. One is that when a person attempts to reach a wise decision about a difficult practical problem, he should inform himself as accurately and completely as is practicable about its *objective circumstances.*

Another is that with similar care he should take stock of *the powers at his disposal:* on the one hand, of the diverse means he happens to have, any one of which would enable him to achieve a particular end he might decide on; and on the other, of the diverse ends, any one of which he could achieve with the particular stock of means he commands.

The third recommendation is that he should then consider *the various kinds of value*—positive and negative, intrinsic and instrumental—which, for the persons who would be affected, would follow from each of the courses of action open to him in the circumstances of the case with only the particular powers he has.

And the fourth recommendation is that when he has thus considered as well as he can all the values at stake, he should then choose the course of action that *on the whole is best,* or *least bad:* the course that *everything considered,* will probably yield the maximum total positive value, or the minimum total negative value.

Needless to say, this choice will in many cases be anything but easy or confident. And the person who makes it may well come eventually to judge it to have been mistaken. But this will be the judgment of the wiser person he will then have become by learning from his mistakes. At the time a decision has to be made, however, no way exists for any man to make a wiser one than by the procedure just described. For "wisdom"—so much of it as in practice happens to be obtainable by a given person at a given time—*means* what emerges out of that procedure.

Finally, under the shelter of the preceding elucidations I shall venture to state as a sharp choice what I take to be the gist of Phi Beta Kappa's advice to its initiates. And to formulate it I shall borrow the sharp words of the title of a book on a somewhat similar theme written by an Australian journalist.

That sharp choice so sharply worded is *Think—or be damned!*

PART II

LOGIC AND PHILOSOPHY
OF SCIENCE

• 4 •

SCIENTIFIC KNOWLEDGE *
Aristotle (384–322 B.C.)

1. . . . As regards syllogism and demonstration, the definition of, and
the conditions required to produce each of them, are now clear, and with
that also the definition of, and the conditions required to produce, demonstrative knowledge, since it is the same as demonstration. As to the basic
premisses, how they become known and what is the developed state of
knowledge of them is made clear by raising some preliminary problems.

We have already said that scientific knowledge through demonstration
is impossible unless a man knows the primary immediate premisses. But
there are questions which might be raised in respect of the apprehension
of these immediate premisses: one might not only ask whether it is of the
same kind as the apprehension of the conclusions, but also whether there is
or is not scientific knowledge of both; or scientific knowledge of the latter,
and of the former a different kind of knowledge; and, further, whether the
developed states of knowledge are not innate but come to be in us, or are
innate but at first unnoticed. Now it is strange if we possess them from
birth; for it means that we possess apprehensions more accurate than
demonstration and fail to notice them. If on the other hand we acquire them and do not previously possess them, how could we apprehend and learn without a basis of pre-existent knowledge? For that is
impossible, as we used to find in the case of demonstration. So it emerges
that neither can we possess them from birth, nor can they come to be in
us if we are without knowledge of them to the extent of having no such
developed state at all. Therefore we must possess a capacity of some sort,
but not such as to rank higher in accuracy than these developed states. And
this at least is an obvious characteristic of all animals, for they possess a
congenital discriminative capacity which is called sense-perception. But
though sense-perception is innate in all animals, in some the sense-impression comes to persist, in others it does not. So animals in which this per-

* Part 1 is from Aristotle's *Posterior Analytics*, Bk. II, ch. 19, translated by G. R. G.
Mure; Part 2 from *Metaphysics*, Bk. I, ch. 1, translated by W. D. Ross. Reprinted by
permission of The Clarendon Press, Oxford. The title of this selection has been supplied
by the editors.

sistence does not come to be have either no knowledge at all outside the act of perceiving, or no knowledge of objects of which no impression persists; animals in which it does come into being have perception and can continue to retain the sense-impression in the soul: and when such persistence is frequently repeated a further distinction at once arises between those which out of the persistence of such sense-impressions develop a power of systematizing them and those which do not. So out of sense-perception comes to be what we call memory, and out of frequently repeated memories of the same thing develops experience; for a number of memories constitute a single experience. From experience again—i.e., from the universal now stabilized in its entirety within the soul, the one beside the many which is a single identity within them all—originate the skill of the craftsman and the knowledge of the man of science, skill in the sphere of coming to be and science in the sphere of being.

We conclude that these states of knowledge are neither innate in a determinate form, nor developed from other higher states of knowledge, but from sense-perception. It is like a rout in battle stopped by first one man making a stand and then another, until the original formation has been restored. The soul is so constituted as to be capable of this process.

Let us now restate the account given already, though with insufficient clearness. When one of a number of logically indiscriminable particulars has made a stand, the earliest universal is present in the soul: for though the act of sense-perception is of the particular, its content is universal—is man, for example, not the man Callias. A fresh stand is made among these rudimentary universals, and the process does not cease until the indivisible concepts, the true universals, are established: e.g., such and such a species of animal is a step towards the genus animal, which by the same process is a step towards a further generalization.

Thus it is clear that we must get to know the primary premisses by induction; for the method by which even sense-perception implants the universal is inductive. Now of the thinking states by which we grasp truth, some are unfailingly true, others admit of error—opinion, for instance, and calculation, whereas scientific knowing and intuition are always true: further, no other kind of thought except intuition is more accurate than scientific knowledge, whereas primary premisses are more knowable than demonstrations, and all scientific knowledge is discursive. From these considerations it follows that there will be no scientific knowledge of the primary premisses, and since except intuition nothing can be truer than scientific knowledge, it will be intuition that apprehends the primary premisses—a result which also follows from the fact that demonstration cannot be the originative source of demonstration, nor, consequently, scientific knowledge of scientific knowledge. If, therefore, it is the only other kind of true thinking except scientific knowing, intuition will be the originative source of scientific knowledge. And the originative source of science grasps the original basic premiss, while science as a whole is similarly related as originative source to the whole body of fact.

2. All men by nature desire to know. An indication of this is the delight we take in our senses; for even apart from their usefulness they are loved for themselves; and above all others the sense of sight. For not only with a view to action, but even when we are not going to do anything, we prefer seeing (one might say) to everything else. The reason is that this, most of all the senses, makes us know and brings to light many differences between things.

By nature animals are born with the faculty of sensation, and from sensation memory is produced in some of them, though not in others. And therefore the former are more intelligent and apt at learning than those which cannot remember; those which are incapable of hearing sounds are intelligent though they cannot be taught, e.g., the bee, and any other race of animals that may be like it; and those which besides memory have this sense of hearing can be taught.

The animals other than man live by appearances and memories, and have but little of connected experience; but the human race lives also by art and reasonings. Now from memory experience is produced in men; for the several memories of the same thing produce finally the capacity for a single experience. And experience seems pretty much like science and art, but really science and art come to men *through* experience; for 'experience made art,' as Polus says, 'but inexperience luck.' Now art arises when from many notions gained by experience one universal judgement about a class of objects is produced. For to have a judgement that when Callias was ill of this disease this did him good, and similarly in the case of Socrates and in many individual cases, is a matter of experience; but to judge that it has done good to all persons of a certain constitution, marked off in one class, when they were ill of this disease, e.g., to phlegmatic or bilious people when burning with fever—this is a matter of art.

With a view to action experience seems in no respect inferior to art, and men of experience succeed even better than those who have theory without experience. (The reason is that experience is knowledge of individuals, art of universals, and actions and productions are all concerned with the individual; for the physician does not cure *man*, except in an incidental way, but Callias or Socrates or some other called by some such individual name, who happens to be a man. If, then, a man has the theory without the experience, and recognizes the universal but does not know the individual included in this, he will often fail to cure; for it is the individual that is to be cured.) But yet we think that *knowledge* and *understanding* belong to art rather than to experience, and we suppose artists to be wiser than men of experience (which implies that Wisdom depends in all cases rather on knowledge); and this because the former know the cause, but the latter do not. For men of experience know that the thing is so, but do not know why, while the others know the 'why' and the cause. Hence we think also that the master-workers in each craft are more honourable and know in a truer sense and are wiser than the manual workers, because they know the causes of the things that are done (we think the manual workers are like certain lifeless things which act indeed, but act without knowing what they do, as fire burns—but while the lifeless things perform each of their functions by a natural tendency, the labourers perform them through habit); thus we view them as being wiser not in virtue of being able to act, but of having the theory for themselves and knowing the causes. And in general it is a sign of the man who knows and of the man who does not know, that the former can teach, and therefore we think art more truly knowledge than experience is; for artists can teach, and men of mere experience cannot.

Again, we do not regard any of the senses as Wisdom; yet surely these give the most authoritative knowledge of particulars. But they do not tell us the 'why' of anything—e.g., why fire is hot; they only say *that* it is hot. . . .

• 5 •

SCIENCE AND HUMAN NATURE *

John Stuart Mill (1806–1873)

1. It is a common notion, or at least it is implied in many common modes of speech, that the thoughts, feelings, and actions of sentient beings are not a subject of science, in the same strict sense in which this is true of the objects of outward nature. This notion seems to involve some confusion of ideas, which it is necessary to begin by clearing up.

Any facts are fitted, in themselves, to be a subject of science, which follow one another according to constant laws; although those laws may

* Bk. VI, ch. 3 of *A System of Logic* (1843). The title of this selection has been supplied by the editors. Compare with selections 23 and 24.

not have been discovered, nor even be discoverable by our existing resources. Take, for instance, the most familiar class of meteorological
phenomena, those of rain and sunshine. Scientific inquiry has not yet succeeded in ascertaining the order of antecedence and consequence among
these phenomena, so as to be able, at least in our regions of the earth, to
predict them with certainty or even with any high degree of probability.
Yet no one doubts that the phenomena depend on laws, and that these
must be derivative laws resulting from known ultimate laws, those of heat,
electricity, vaporisation, and elastic fluids. Nor can it be doubted that if we
were acquainted with all the antecedent circumstances, we could, even
from those more general laws, predict (saving difficulties of calculation)
the state of the weather at any future time. Meteorology, therefore, not
only has in itself every natural requisite for being, but actually is, a science;
though, from the difficulty of observing the facts on which the phenomena
depend (a difficulty inherent in the peculiar nature of those phenomena),
the science is extremely imperfect; and were it perfect, might probably be
of little avail in practice, since the data requisite for applying its principles
to particular instances would rarely be procurable.

A case may be conceived of an intermediate character between the perfection of science and this its extreme imperfection. It may happen that
the greater causes, those on which the principal part of the phenomena
depends, are within the reach of observation and measurement; so that if
no other causes intervened, a complete explanation could be given not
only of the phenomenon in general, but of all the variations and modifications which it admits of. But inasmuch as other, perhaps many other
causes, separately insignificant in their effects, co-operate or conflict in
many or in all cases with those greater causes, the effect, accordingly, presents more or less of aberration from what would be produced by the
greater causes alone. Now if these minor causes are not so constantly accessible, or not accessible at all to accurate observation, the principal mass
of the effect may still, as before, be accounted for, and even predicted; but
there will be variations and modifications which we shall not be competent
to explain thoroughly, and our predictions will not be fulfilled accurately,
but only approximately.

It is thus, for example, with the theory of the tides. No one doubts that
Tidology is really a science. As much of the phenomena as depends on the
attraction of the sun and moon is completely understood, and may in any,
even unknown, part of the earth's surface be foretold with certainty; and
the far greater part of the phenomena depends on those causes. But circumstances of a local or casual nature, such as the configuration of the
bottom of the ocean, the degree of confinement from shores, the direction

of the wind, etc., influence in many or in all places the height and time of the tide; and a portion of these circumstances being either not accurately knowable, not precisely measurable, or not capable of being certainly foreseen, the tide in known places commonly varies from the calculated result of general principles by some difference that we cannot explain, and in unknown ones may vary from it by a difference that we are not able to foresee or conjecture. Nevertheless, not only is it certain that these variations depend on causes, and follow their causes by laws of unerring uniformity; not only, therefore, is tidology a science, like meteorology, but it is what, hitherto at least, meteorology is not, a science largely available in practice. General laws may be laid down respecting the tides; predictions may be founded on those laws, and the result will in the main, though often not with complete accuracy, correspond to the predictions.

And this is what is or ought to be meant by those who speak of sciences which are not *exact* sciences. Astronomy was once a science, without being an exact science. It could not become exact until not only the general course of the planetary motions, but the perturbations also, were accounted for, and referred to their causes. It has become an exact science, because its phenomena have been brought under laws comprehending the whole of the causes by which the phenomena are influenced, whether in a great or only in a trifling degree, whether in all or only in some cases, and assigning to each of those causes the share of effect which really belongs to it. But in the theory of the tides, the only laws as yet accurately ascertained are those of the causes which affect the phenomenon in all cases, and in a considerable degree; while others which affect it in some cases only, or, if in all, only in a slight degree, have not been sufficiently ascertained and studied to enable us to lay down their laws, still less to deduce the completed law of the phenomenon, by compounding the effects of the greater with those of the minor causes. Tidology, therefore, is not yet an exact science; not from any inherent incapacity of being so, but from the difficulty of ascertaining with complete precision the real derivative uniformities. By combining, however, the exact laws of the greater causes, and of such of the minor ones as are sufficiently known, with such empirical laws of such approximate generalisations respecting the miscellaneous variations as can be obtained by specific observation, we can lay down general propositions which will be true in the main, and on which, with allowance for the degree of their probable inaccuracy, we may safely ground our expectations and our conduct.

2. The science of human nature is of this description. It falls far short of the standard of exactness now realised in Astronomy; but there is no reason that it should not be as much a science as Tidology is, or as Astronomy was

when its calculations had only mastered the main phenomena, but not the perturbations.

The phenomena with which this science is conversant being the thoughts, feelings, and actions of human beings, it would have attained the ideal perfection of a science if it enabled us to foretell how an individual would think, feel, or act throughout life, with the same certainty with which astronomy enables us to predict the places and the occultations of the heavenly bodies. It needs scarcely be stated that nothing approaching to this can be done. The actions of individuals could not be predicted with scientific accuracy, were it only because we cannot foresee the whole of the circumstances in which those individuals will be placed. But further, even in any given combination of (present) circumstances, no assertion, which is both precise and universally true, can be made respecting the manner in which human beings will think, feel, or act. This is not, however, because every person's modes of thinking, feeling, and acting do not depend on causes; nor can we doubt that if, in the case of any individual, our data could be complete, we even now know enough of the ultimate laws by which mental phenomena are determined to enable us in many cases to predict, with tolerable certainty, what, in the greater number of supposable combinations of circumstances, his conduct or sentiments would be. But the impressions and actions of human beings are not solely the result of their present circumstances, but the joint result of those circumstances and of the characters of the individuals; and the agencies which determine human character are so numerous and diversified (nothing which has happened to the person throughout life being without its portion of influence), that in the aggregate they are never in any two cases exactly similar. Hence, even if our science of human nature were theoretically perfect, that is, if we could calculate any character as we can calculate the orbit of any planet, *from given data*; still, as the data are never all given, nor ever precisely alike in different cases, we could neither make positive predictions, nor lay down universal propositions.

Inasmuch, however, as many of those effects which it is of most importance to render amenable to human foresight and control are determined, like the tides, in an incomparably greater degree by general causes, than by all partial causes taken together; depending in the main on those circumstances and qualities which are common to all mankind, or at least to large bodies of them, and only on a small degree on the idiosyncrasies of organisation or the peculiar history of individuals; it is evidently possible, with regard to all such effects, to make predictions which will *almost* always be verified, and general propositions which are almost always true. And whenever it is sufficient to know how the great majority of the human race, or of some nation or class of persons, will think, feel, and act, these propositions are equivalent to universal ones. For the purposes of political and social science this *is* sufficient. . . . An approximate generalisation is, in social inquiries, for most practical purposes equivalent to an exact one; that which is only probable when asserted of individual human beings indiscriminately selected, being certain when affirmed of the character and collective conduct of masses.

It is no disparagement, therefore, to the science of Human Nature that those of its general propositions which descend sufficiently into detail to serve as a foundation for predicting phenomena in the concrete are for the most part only approximately true. But in order to give a genuinely scientific character to the study, it is indispensable that these approximate generalisations, which in themselves would amount only to the lowest kind of empirical laws, should be connected deductively with the laws of nature from which they result—should be resolved into the properties of the causes on which the phenomena depend. In other words, the science of Human Nature may be said to exist in proportion as the approximate truths which compose a practical knowledge of mankind can be exhibited as corollaries from the universal laws of human nature on which they rest, whereby the proper limits of those approximate truths would be shown, and we should be enabled to deduce others for any new state of circumstances, in anticipation of specific experience. . . .

• 6 •

LOGIC AND SCIENCE*

Morris R. Cohen (1880–1947) *and Ernest Nagel* (1901–)

I. LOGIC AND THE METHOD OF SCIENCE

Formal logic . . . deals with the possible relations (in regard to truth and falsity) between propositions, no matter what their subject matter. This gives us the *necessary* conditions for valid inference and enables us to

---

* Part I is from chapter 10, and part II is section 2 of chapter 20, of *An Introduction to Logic and Scientific Method*, by Morris R. Cohen and Ernest Nagel, copyright, 1934, by Harcourt, Brace & World, Inc., and used with their permission. The title of this selection has been supplied by the editors. This selection should be compared with selection 13. See also selection 51.

eliminate false reasoning, but that is not *sufficient* to establish any material or factual truth in any particular field. Formal logic shows us that any such proposition must be true *if* certain others are so. The categorical assertion that our premises are actually true cannot be a matter of logic alone without making the latter identical with all knowledge. Logic, then, is involved in all reasoned knowledge (which is the original meaning of "science") but is not the whole of it. This enables us to regard all science as applied logic, which was expressed by the Greeks in calling the science of any subject, for example, man, or the earth, the logic of it—*anthropology*, or *geology*.

The great prestige of the natural sciences, acquired largely by their aid to modern technology and by their successful fight against the ancient mythology that was sanctified by various authorities, has led us to apply the term "science" only to these or to similarly highly developed branches of knowledge and to deny it to ordinary knowledge of affairs, no matter how well founded. Thus no one thinks of a railroad time-table or of a telephone book as science even though the knowledge in it is accurate, verifiable, and organized in a definite order. We reserve the term "science" for knowledge which is general and systematic, that is, in which specific propositions are all deduced from a few general principles. Now we need not enter here into the quarrel which arises because archeologists, historians, descriptive sociologists, and others wish to call their more empirical knowledge science. . . . All the logical methods involved in proving the existence of laws are involved in establishing the truth of any historical event. In determining the weight of evidence for any human event we must reason from general propositions in regard to human affairs, though such propositions are generally implicitly rather than explicitly assumed.

If we look at all the sciences not only as they differ among each other but also as each changes and grows in the course of time, we find that the constant and universal feature of science is its general method, which consists in the persistent search for truth, constantly asking: Is it so? To what extent is it so? Why is it so?—that is, What general conditions or considerations determine it to be so? And this can be seen on reflection to be the demand for the best available evidence, the determination of which we call logic. Scientific method is thus the persistent application of logic as the common feature of all reasoned knowledge. From this point of view scientific method is simply the way in which we test impressions, opinions, or surmises by examining the best available evidence for and against them. And thus a critical historian like Thucydides can be more scientific than the more credulous Livy, and a sound philologist like Whitney can be more scientific than the more hastily speculative Max Müller. The various features of scientific method can naturally be seen more clearly in the more developed sciences; but in essence scientific method is simply the pursuit of truth as determined by logical considerations. Before determining this in detail, it is well to distinguish between scientific method and other ways of banishing doubt and arriving at stable beliefs.

Most of our beliefs . . . rest on the tacit acceptance of current attitudes or on our own unreflective assumptions. Thus we come to believe that the sun revolves around the earth daily because we see it rise in the east and sink in the west; or we send a testimonial to the makers of a certain toothpaste to the effect that it is an excellent preserver of teeth because we have had no dental trouble since we have used that preparation; or we offer alms to some beggar because we perceive his poverty by his rags and emaciated appearance. But too often and sometimes, alas! too late, we learn that not all "seeing" is "believing." Beliefs so formed do not stand up against a more varied experience. There is too little agreement in opinions so formed and too little security in acting upon them. Most of us then find ourselves challenged to support or change our opinions. And we do so by diverse methods.

THE METHOD OF TENACITY

Habit or inertia makes it easier for us to continue to believe a proposition simply because we have always believed it. Hence, we may avoid doubting it by closing our mind to all contradictory evidence. That frequent verbal reiteration may strengthen beliefs which have been challenged is a truth acted upon by all organized sects or parties. If anyone questions the superior virtues of ourselves, our dear ones, our country, race, language, or religion, our first impulse and the one generally followed is to repeat our belief as an act of loyalty and to regard the questioning attitude as ignorant, disloyal, and unworthy of attention. We thus insulate ourselves from opinions or beliefs contrary to those which we have always held. As a defense of this attitude the believer often alleges that he would be unhappy if he were to believe otherwise than he in fact does. But while a change in opinion may require painful effort, the new beliefs may become habitual, and perhaps more satisfying than the old ones.

This method of tenacity cannot always secure the stability of one's beliefs. Not all men believe alike, in part because the climate of opinion varies with historical antecedents, and in part because the personal and social interests which men wish to guard are unlike. The pressure of opinions other than one's own cannot always be so disregarded. The man who tenaciously holds on to his own way occasionally admits that not all those who differ from him are fools. When once the incidence of other views is felt, the method of tenacity is incapable of deciding between conflicting opinions. And since a lack of uniformity in beliefs is itself a powerful source of doubt concerning them, some method other than the method of tenacity is required for achieving stable views.

THE METHOD OF AUTHORITY

Such a method is sometimes found in the appeal to authority. Instead of simply holding on doggedly to one's beliefs, appeal is made to some highly respected source to substantiate the views held. Most propositions of religion and conduct claim support from some sacred text, tradition, or tribunal whose decision on such questions is vested with finality. Political, economic, and social questions are frequently determined in similar fashion. What one should wear at a funeral, what rule of syntax one should follow in writing, what rights one has in the product of his labor, how one should behave in some social crisis like war—these are problems repeatedly resolved by the authoritative method.

We may distinguish two forms of the appeal to authority. One form is inevitable and reasonable. It is employed whenever we are unable for lack of time or training to settle some problem, such as, What diet or exercise will relieve certain distressing symptoms? or, What was the system of weights which the Egyptians used? We then leave the resolution of the problem to experts, whose authority is acknowledged. But their authority is only relatively final, and we reserve the right to others (also competent to judge), or to ourselves (finding the time to acquire competence), to modify the findings of our expert. The second form of the appeal to authority invests some sources with infallibility and finality and invokes some external force to give sanction to their decisions. On questions of politics, economics, and social conduct, as well as on religious opinions, the method of authority has been used to root out, as heretical or disloyal, divergent opinions. Men have been frightened and punished into conformity in order to prevent alternative views from unsettling our habitual beliefs.

The aim of this method, unanimity and stability of belief, cannot be achieved so long as authorities differ. Buddhists do not accept the authorities of the Christians, just as the latter reject the authority of Mahomet and the Koran. In temporal matters experts frequently disagree and are often found in error. Moreover, authoritative regulation of all beliefs is not feasible practically, and much must be left to be decided in some other way. The method of authority has thus to be supplemented, if not replaced, by some other method for resolving doubt and uncertainty.

THE METHOD OF INTUITION

A method repeatedly tried in order to guarantee stable beliefs is the appeal to "self-evident" propositions—propositions so "obviously true" that the understanding of their *meaning* will carry with it an indubitable conviction of their *truth*. Very few men in the history of philosophy and that of the sciences have been able to resist at all times the lure of intuitively revealed truths. Thus all the great astronomers, including Copernicus, believed it to be self-evident that the orbits of the planets must be circular, and no mathematician or physicist before Gauss seriously doubted the proposition that two straight lines cannot enclose an area. Other examples of propositions which have been, or still are, believed by some to be self-evident are: that the whole is greater than any one of its parts; that the right to private property is inalienable; that bigamy is a sin; that nothing can happen without an adequate cause.

Unfortunately, it is difficult to find a proposition for which at some time or other "self-evidence" has not been claimed. Propositions regarded as indubitable by many, for example, that the earth is flat, have been shown to be false. It is well known that "self-evidence" is often a function of current fashions and of early training. The fact, therefore, that we feel absolutely certain, or that a given proposition has not before been questioned, is no guarantee against its being proved false. Our intuitions must, then, be tested.

THE METHOD OF SCIENCE OR REFLECTIVE INQUIRY

None of the methods for settling doubts we have examined so far is free from human caprice and willfulness. As a consequence, the propositions which are held on the basis of those methods are uncertain in the range of their application and in their accuracy. If we wish clarity and accuracy, order and consistency, security and cogency, in our actions and intellectual allegiances we shall have to resort to some method of fixing beliefs whose efficacy in resolving problems is independent of our desires and wills. Such a method, which takes advantage of the objective connections in the world around us, should be found reasonable not because of its appeal to the idiosyncrasies of a selected few individuals, but because it can be tested repeatedly and by all men.

The other methods discussed are all inflexible, that is, none of them can admit that it will lead us into error. Hence none of them can make provision for correcting its own results. What is called *scientific method* differs radically from these by encouraging and developing the utmost possible doubt, so that what is left after such doubt is always supported by the best available evidence. As new evidence or new doubts arise it is the essence of scientific method to incorporate them—to make them an integral part of the body of knowledge so far attained. Its method, then, makes science progressive because it is never too certain about its results.

It is well to distinguish between scientific method and general skepticism. The mere resolution to doubt all things is not necessarily effective. For the propositions most in need of questioning may seem to us unquestionable. We need a technique that will enable us to discover possible alternatives to propositions which we may regard as truisms or necessarily true. In this process formal logic aids us in devising ways of formulating our propositions explicitly and accurately, so that their possible alternatives become clear. When thus faced with alternative hypotheses, logic develops their consequences, so that when these consequences are compared with observable phenomena we have a means of testing which hypothesis is to be eliminated and which is most in harmony with the facts of observation. . . .

II. THE VALUE OF SCIENTIFIC METHOD

The desire for knowledge for its own sake is more widespread than is generally recognized by anti-intellectualists. It has its roots in the animal curiosity which shows itself in the cosmological questions of children and in the gossip of adults. No ulterior utilitarian motive makes people want to know about the private lives of their neighbors, the great, or the notorious. There is also a certain zest which makes people engage in various intellectual games or exercises in which one is required to find out something. But while the desire to know is wide, it is seldom strong enough to overcome the more powerful organic desires, and few indeed have both the inclination and the ability to face the arduous difficulties of scientific method in more than one special field. The desire to know is not often strong enough to sustain critical inquiry. Men generally are interested in the results, in the story or romance of science, not in the technical methods whereby these results are obtained and their truth continually is tested and qualified. Our first impulse is to accept the plausible as true and to reject the uncongenial as false. We have not the time, inclination, or energy to investigate everything. Indeed, the call to do so is often felt as irksome and joy-killing. And when we are asked to treat our cherished beliefs as mere hypotheses, we rebel as violently as when those dear to us are insulted. This provides the ground for various movements that are hostile to rational scientific procedure (though their promoters do not often admit that it is science to which they are hostile).

Mystics, intuitionists, authoritarians, voluntarists, and fictionalists are all trying to undermine respect for the rational methods of science. These attacks have always met with wide acclaim and are bound to continue to do so, for they strike a responsive note in human nature. Unfortunately they do not offer any reliable alternative method for obtaining verifiable knowledge. The great French writer Pascal opposed to logic the spirit of subtlety or finesse (*esprit geometrique and esprit de finesse*) and urged that the heart has its reasons as well as the mind, reasons that cannot be accurately formulated but which subtle spirits apprehend none the less. Men as diverse as James Russell Lowell and George Santayana are agreed that:

"The soul is oracular still,"

and

"It is wisdom to trust the heart . . .
To trust the soul's invincible surmise."

Now it is true that in the absence of omniscience we must trust our soul's surmise; and great men are those whose surmises or intuitions are deep or penetrating. It is only by acting on our surmise that we can procure the evidence in its favor. But only havoc can result from confusing a surmise with a proposition for which there is already evidence. Are all the reasons of the heart sound? Do all oracles tell the truth? The sad history of human experience is distinctly discouraging to any such claim. Mystic intuition may give men absolute subjective certainty, but can give no proof that contrary intuitions are erroneous. It is obvious that when authorities conflict we must weigh the evidence in their favor logically if we are to make a rational choice. Certainly, when a truth is questioned it is no answer to say, "I am convinced," or, "I prefer to rely on this rather than on another authority." The view that physical science is no guide to proof, but is a mere fiction, fails to explain why it has enabled us to anticipate phenomena of nature and to control them. These attacks on scientific method receive a certain color of plausibility because of some indefensible claims made by uncritical enthusiasts. But it is of the essence of scientific method to limit its own pretension. Recognizing that we do not know everything, it does not claim the ability to solve all of our practical problems. It is an error to suppose, as is often done, that science denies the truth of all unverified propositions. For that which is unverified today may be verified tomorrow. We may get at truth by guessing or in other ways. Scientific method, however, is concerned with verification. Admittedly the wisdom of those engaged in this process has not been popularly ranked as high as that of the sage, the prophet, or the poet. Admittedly, also, we know of no way of supplying creative intelligence to those who lack it. Scientists, like all other human beings, may get into ruts and apply their techniques regardless of varying circumstances. There will always be formal procedures which are fruitless. Definitions and formal distinctions may be a sharpening of tools without the wit to use them properly, and statistical information may conform to the highest technical standards and yet be irrelevant and inconclusive. Nevertheless, scientific method is the only way to increase the general body of tested and verified truth and to eliminate arbitrary opinion. It is well to clarify our ideas by asking for the precise meaning of our words, and to try to check our favorite ideas by applying them to accurately formulated propositions.

In raising the question as to the social need for scientific method, it is well to recognize that the suspension of judgment which is essential to that method is difficult or impossible when we are pressed by the demands of immediate action. When my house is on fire, I must act quickly and promptly—I cannot stop to consider the possible causes, nor even to estimate the exact probabilities involved in the various alternative ways of reacting. For this reason, those who are bent upon some specific course of action often despise those devoted to reflection; and certain ultramodernists seem to argue as if the need for action guaranteed the truth of our decision. But the fact that I must either vote for candidate X or refrain from doing so does not of itself give me adequate knowledge. The frequency of our regrets makes this obvious. Wisely ordered society is therefore provided with means for deliberation and reflection *before* the pressure of action becomes irresistible. In order to assure the most thorough investigation, all possible views must be canvassed, and this means toleration of views that are *prima facie* most repugnant to us.

In general the chief social condition of scientific method is a widespread desire for truth that is strong enough to withstand the powerful forces which make us cling tenaciously to old views or else embrace every novelty because it is a change. Those who are engaged in scientific work need not only leisure for reflection and material for their experiments, but also a community that respects the pursuit of truth and allows freedom for the expression of intellectual doubt as to its most sacred or established institutions. Fear of offending established dogmas has been an obstacle to the growth of astronomy and geology and other physical sciences; and the fear of offending patriotic or respected sentiment is perhaps one of the strongest hindrances to scholarly history and social science. On the other hand, when a community indiscriminately acclaims every new doctrine the love of truth becomes subordinated to the desire for novel formulations.

On the whole it may be said that the safety of science depends on there being men who care more for the justice of their methods than for any results obtained by their use. For this reason it is unfortunate when scientific research in the social field is largely in the hands of those not in a favorable position to oppose established or popular opinion.

We may put it the other way by saying that the physical sciences can be more liberal because we are sure that foolish opinions will be readily eliminated by the shock of facts. In the social field, however, no one can tell what harm may come of foolish ideas before the foolishness is finally, if ever, demonstrated. None of the precautions of scientific method can prevent human life from being an adventure, and no scientific investigator knows whether he will reach his goal. But scientific method does enable large numbers to walk with surer step. By analyzing the possibilities of any step or plan, it becomes possible to anticipate the future and adjust ourselves to it in advance. Scientific method thus minimizes the shock of novelty and the uncertainty of life. It enables us to frame policies of action and of moral judgment fit for a wider outlook than those of immediate physical stimulus or organic response.

Scientific method is the only effective way of strengthening the love of truth. It develops the intellectual courage to face difficulties and to overcome illusions that are pleasant temporarily but destructive ultimately. It settles differences without any external force by appealing to our common rational nature. The way of science, even if it is up a steep mountain, is open to all. Hence, while sectarian and partisan faiths are based on personal choice or temperament and divide men, scientific procedure unites men in something nobly devoid of all pettiness. Because it requires detachment, disinterestedness, it is the finest flower and test of a liberal civilization.

• 7 •

UMBRELLAOLOGY AND PROBLEMATICS *

John Somerville (1905–   )

I. UMBRELLAOLOGY

. . . Dear Sir:

I am taking the liberty of calling upon you to be the judge in a dispute between me and an acquaintance who is no longer a friend. The question

* Part I is part of an essay entitled "Umbrellaology" that originally appeared in *Philosophy of Science*, Vol. VIII, no. 1 (January, 1941). Reprinted with the kind permission of the author and publisher, The Williams and Wilkins Co., Baltimore. Part II is from "Problematics: A Methodological Aspect of Philosophy of Science," which originally appeared in Vol. VI of the *Proceedings of the XIth International Congress of Philosophy*, 1953. Reprinted with the kind permission of the author and publisher, North-Holland Publishing Company, Amsterdam. The title of this selection has been supplied by the editors. Compare with selection 10.

at issue is this: Is my creation, umbrellaology, a science? Allow me to explain this situation. For the past eighteen years, assisted by a few faithful disciples, I have been collecting materials on a subject hitherto almost wholly neglected by scientists, the umbrella. The results of my investigations to date are embodied in the nine volumes which I am sending to you under a separate cover. Pending their receipt, let me describe to you briefly the nature of their contents and the method I pursued in compiling them. I began on the Island of Manhattan. Proceeding block by block, house by house, family by family and individual by individual I ascertained (1) the number of umbrellas possessed, (2) their size, (3) their weight, (4) their color. Having covered Manhattan after many years, I eventually extended the survey to the other boroughs of the City of New York, and at length completed the entire city. Thus I was ready to carry forward the work to the rest of the state and indeed the rest of the United States and the whole known world.

It was at this point that I approached my erstwhile friend. I am a modest man, but I felt I had the right to be recognized as the creator of a new science. He, on the other hand, claimed that umbrellaology was not a science at all. First, he said, it was silly to investigate umbrellas. Now this argument is false because science scorns not to deal with any object, however humble and lowly, even to the "hind leg of a flea." Then why not umbrellas? Next he said that umbrellaology could not be recognized as a science because it was of no use or benefit to mankind. But is not the truth the most precious thing in life? And are not my nine volumes filled with the truth about my subject? Every word is true. Every sentence contains a hard, cold fact. When he asked me what was the object of umbrellaology I was proud to say, "To seek and discover the truth is object enough for me." I am a pure scientist; I have no ulterior motives. Hence it follows that I am satisfied with truth alone. Next, he said my truths were dated and that any one of my findings might cease to be true tomorrow. But this, I pointed out, is not an argument against umbrellaology, but rather an argument for keeping it up to date, which is exactly what I propose. Let us have surveys monthly, weekly or even daily to keep our knowledge abreast of the changing facts. His next contention was that umbrellaology had entertained no hypotheses and had developed no theories or laws. This is a great error. In the course of my investigations, I employed innumerable hypotheses. Before entering each new block and each new section of the city, I entertained an hypothesis as regards the number and characteristics of the umbrellas that would be found there, which hypotheses were either verified or nullified by my subsequent observations, in accordance with proper scientific procedure, as explained in authoritative texts. (In fact, it is interesting to note that I can substantiate and document every one of my replies to these objections by numerous quotations from standard works, leading journals, public speeches of eminent scientists and the like.) As for theories and laws, my work presents an abundance of them. I will here mention only a few, by way of illustration. There is the Law of Color Variation Relative to Ownership by Sex. (Umbrellas owned by women tend to great variety of color, whereas those owned by men are almost all black.) To this law I have given exact statistical formulation. (See vol. 6, Appendix 1, Table 3, p. 582.) There are the curiously interrelated Laws of Individual Ownership of Plurality of Umbrellas, and Plurality of Owners of Individual Umbrellas. The interrelationship assumes the form, in the first law, of almost direct ratio to annual income, and in the second, of almost inverse ratio to annual income. (For an exact statement of the modifying circumstances, see vol. 8, p. 350.) There is also the Law of Tendency towards Acquisition of Umbrellas in Rainy Weather. To this law I have given experimental verification in chapter 3 of volume 3. In the same way I have performed numerous other experiments in connection with my generalizations.

Thus I feel that my creation is in all respects a genuine science, and I appeal to you for substantiation of my opinion. . . .

II. PROBLEMATICS

By the word problematics I mean to indicate a phase of scientific methodology which, for some strange reason, has never been systematically worked out. Indeed, it seems to have been scarcely noticed and never named, although it is of cardinal importance. I refer to that aspect of scientific method which has to do with the selection of problems. The study of it I propose to call problematics. . . .

The history of science shows that in many cases there was a long groping for the fruitful problems to work upon, and that once these were precisely formulated, fruitful solutions were not long in coming forth. Indeed, it is self-evident that the original selection of problems must in a sense determine the whole quality of what is subsequently done. If people are not working on significant problems, they will never arrive at significant solutions, even though they find what they are looking for. On the other hand, once the right problem has been formulated, that in itself represents an enormous step forward. For this reason the wrong solution or even no solution of the right problem is infinitely preferable to the right solution of the wrong problem.

But what is the criterion of significance as regards problems? How can we tell what are the right problems to work upon? Is there a subjective determinant operative in the situation? On what basis is the selection of problems actually made in science? . . .

Let us look at the matter from the viewpoint of what actually takes place in the procedures of the scientists. What makes one problem more significant, more worth working upon, than another? For example, it is quite likely scientists would unanimously agree that to find the cause of cancer is, scientifically speaking, a more significant problem than to find the average number of letters in the names of all living people. That is, it would probably be agreed that the solution of the first mentioned problem would mean much more to science than the solution of the second. But on what basis? Can we discover any common criterion which is being employed, consciously or unconsciously? . . .

Our thesis is that this criterion is prognosis. Scientists generally regard one problem as more significant than another if the solving of it would yield more new predictions than the solving of the other. To take the example mentioned, we know (before any work is done) that if we discover the cause of cancer we shall be able to make a multitude of predictions which we cannot make now. Under present conditions, multitudes of people get cancer, and we do not know what specific causal agent is common to these cases, in the sense that we know bacillus tuberculosis is a common causal agent in cases of consumption. If we discovered the full cause of cancer, we could then predict not only what would be found common to a multitude of cancer cases; we could also predict that wherever that specific factor or complex of factors appeared, cancer would follow; wherever it was eliminated, cancer would be eliminated; wherever it was decreased, cancer would be decreased, and so on. If we could not make correct predictions of that kind, it would show we had not really found the cause. Conversely, the only way to prove we have found the cause is to make correct predictions of that kind, among other things.

Now, what would follow if we solved the problem of the average number of letters in the names of all living persons? We need not do it first in order to realize that we would have a great deal of truth, but that truth would add little to our present ability either to explain or to predict. Perhaps we should say it would add little to our present ability to explain *because* it would add little to our ability to predict. For it would seem that *scientific* explanation always involves prognosis, although this may not be true of other forms of explanation, which are more subjective. . . .

There are certainly other factors besides prognosis entering into scientific explanation, but prognosis is an important one. However, the decisive point is seen in the converse sense: whenever newly discovered relationships, connections or other facts add greatly to predictability, it is always considered that they add greatly to explanation. There are other things that make a science grow, but one of the main ones is the continued discovery of the kind of facts which significantly increase predictability. This is true of every field of knowledge universally recognized as a science in the modern sense of that term (such fields as astronomy, physics, chemistry, biology). . . .

. . . *Insofar as the natural sciences are concerned* . . . the selection of problems has become almost automatic, although the criterion employed is rarely formulated, or perhaps even consciously apprehended. If we believed in scientific instincts, we might say that natural scientists manifest an instinct to work on problems which, if solved, would significantly promote predictability.

However, the situation is very different in the social sciences, where the most urgent need of a clearly worked out problematics is evident. In these fields there seems to be no common criterion used, either consciously or unconsciously, for the selection of problems. There seems to be no agreement, either explicit or implicit, in regard to what constitutes explanation. At least, there seems to be no general tendency to use the criterion of predictability. And this, I think, is one of the reasons why the social sciences have made little progress as compared to the natural sciences. . . .

• 8 •

PRINCIPLES OF REALLY SOUND THINKING *

Max Black (1909–   )

. . . There are two major principles of really sound thinking:

A. Think only as a last resource.
B. Trust your feelings.

THINK ONLY AS A LAST RESOURCE

The really sound thinker knows thinking to be an uncomfortable, disturbing, and anti-social occupation. Consider the attitude of Rodin's statue "The Thinker." This is not the favorite posture of a successful executive or a regular guy.

Modern life fortunately provides a number of defenses against the early onslaught of thinking. The radio is always close at hand—use it. The com-

* Reprinted from *Scientific Monthly*, March 1948, pp. 232–234, by permission of the publisher, The American Association for the Advancement of Science. Compare with selection 9.

pany of others, preferably of the opposite sex, is to be strongly recommended. If the irritation is too severe, one may retreat to bed until restored to a healthier frame of mind.

It has to be confessed, however, that complete protection against thinking still remains to be achieved:

> But men at whiles are sober
> And think by fits and starts
> And if they think, they fasten
> Their hands upon their hearts.
> —A. E. Housman

Conscientious adherence to the next principle will go far to palliate the discomforts of unavoidable and involuntary thinking.

Trust Your Feelings

The logic texts have created the fiction of Logical Man, coldly calculating the probabilities of alternative hypotheses, willfully blind to human sentiment and passion. Do you want to be this kind of philosophical monster, interminably vacillating between conflicting conclusions? Of course not. In any matter of serious concern, you will *feel* strongly that a certain conclusion *must* be right. This is the clue to success in really sound thinking. Let yourself go—think in technicolor.

Suppose you are worried about the possibility of war with Russia. You will notice in yourself a tendency to think of Stalin as a bloodthirsty ruffian, dripping with the gore of murdered innocents. Dwell upon the notion— let your blood pressure rise. In a short time you will *feel* strongly enough to be able to stop *thinking* altogether. In really sound thinking, it is the conclusion that counts, not the premises. Trusting your feelings will quickly provide you with satisfying, heart-warming conclusions.

The two principles of really sound thinking can be illustrated by the following maxims, widely accepted by successful practitioners.

1. *If you must stick to the point, be sure it's blunt.* The natural human reaction to contact with a sharp point is violent motion in reverse. Such animal wisdom is deeply significant. It's the dead butterfly that stays on the point. Cultivate judicious irrelevance.

Example: Does John Smith deserve a raise in salary?

Blunted point: Doesn't everybody deserve a raise?

Really sound reasoning: Of course they do! Who is John Smith to be favored at the expense of everybody else?

2. *What's in it for me?* Remember that a really sound thinker is practical. And what can be more practical than concern for one's own inter-

ests? The chief advantage of this maxim is the strong light it throws upon the truth of many a debatable proposition.

Example: Should educational facilities be improved in the South?

Really sound reasoning: What's in it for me? Nothing—I don't live in the South.

Conclusion: NO. (Notice the directness and incisiveness of the method.)

3. *It all depends on who says it.* Men are easier to classify than arguments—attend to the man, not the argument. (For classifying the speaker, see principle B above.)

Example: Should Congress be reorganized?

Really sound reasoning: Who says so? X? Oh—he ran for the Congress three times unsuccessfully.

Conclusion: You can't trust *him.*

4. *A million people can't be wrong.* It would clearly be undemocratic, not to say snobbish, to think otherwise. We can't all be Gallups, but we have a ready fund of popular wisdom to hand in the form of proverbs. Make frequent use of such axioms as "Human nature never changes," and "An ounce of experience is worth a peck of talk," and, especially, "It will all be the same in a thousand years." The last is particularly consoling.

Example: Can we prevent another war?

R. s. r.: I've *seen* men fighting. You'll never change human nature. After all, it will all be the same in a thousand years.

This method can be usefully supplemented by the use of identical propositions, such as "East is East, West is West," "Business is Business," "A man's a man for a' that." These are best introduced by the words "after all." Even a logician can hardly dispute the truth of such tautologies.

5. *The exception proves the rule.* Corollary: The more exceptions, the better the rule. This popular maxim hardly needs recommendation. It has the great advantage of allowing us to make simple generalizations in an intolerably complex world. (See also Maxim 8 below.)

Example: You say women are no good at physics. What about Madame Curie?

R. s. r.: The exception proves the rule! (Absolutely conclusive, as r. s. r. should be.)

6. *It's all right in theory but it won't work in practice.* We might almost say: *Because* it's right in theory, it won't work in practice. This maxim is very useful in puncturing the pretentions of experts.

Example: Should we support the United Nations?

R. s. r.: (You know what!)

7. *Consistency is the hobgoblin of little minds.* None of the great thinkers from Socrates to Korzybski have been consistent. Who are you to im-

prove upon their practice? The sciences are notoriously full of unresolved contradictions. If scientists don't care, why should you?

Example: You say that we ought to work for universal free trade, but insist on raising American tariffs.

R. s. r.: I contradict myself? Very well, I contradict myself.

8. *Truth is always pure and simple.* Notice the purity and simplicity of this maxim. Oscar Wilde denied its truth, and see what happened to him (compare Maxim 3). Anything too complicated for translation into Basic English is unworthy the attention of a really sound thinker. The truth must be incapable of shocking the Johnston (formerly Hays) Office. In any case, truth is too precious to be lightly squandered. It is better to hold it a closely guarded hostage far back in reserve.

Example: Is there anything in psychoanalysis?

R. s. r.: Of course not. Why, I can't even understand it. And it isn't fit to print.

9. *Take care of the sound and the sense will take care of itself.* This is perhaps the most important of all the maxims of really sound thinking. "There is a great advantage in names" (Mark van Doren). Be sure you get the greatest benefit out of the names you use.

If you trust your feelings as you should (principle B above), you should have little trouble in finding the right name. Thus, the *Management Review* lately recommended the use of "Income Account" instead of "Profit and Loss Account," "Earnings" instead of "Profits," "Reinvested in the Business" instead of "Added to Surplus." You get the idea?

Example: On being questioned about the implications of a legislative program no really sound thinker would say, "I don't know." This is better: "It is totally unreasonable to expect a blueprint which answers every question which can arise day after tomorrow in this distraught earth, when no man knows for twenty minutes at a time what is going to happen" (Senator Vandenberg, quoted in the New York Times, April 18, 1947).

10. *Never argue with a man who is wrong.* Corollary for married ladies: Never argue with a husband. For the purposes of this maxim, a man who is wrong is easily identified as one who (a) is an unsound thinker, (b) refuses to see that you are right, or (c) has an unwholesome look (see Maxim 3 above).

The careful reader will have noticed that the reasoning used in the above exposition of the principles of really sound thinking provides numerous further illustrations of the principles discussed.

• 9 •

TRUTH AND VALIDITY *

Irving M. Copi (1917–)

An argument . . . is any group of propositions of which one is claimed to follow from the others, which are regarded as providing evidence for the truth of that one. . . . An argument is not a mere collection of propositions, but has a structure. In describing this structure, the terms "premiss" and "conclusion" are usually employed. The *conclusion* of an argument is that proposition which is affirmed on the basis of the other propositions of the argument, and these other propositions which are affirmed as providing evidence or reasons for accepting the conclusion are the *premisses* of that argument.

It should be noted that "premiss" and "conclusion" are relative terms: one and the same proposition can be a premiss of one argument and a conclusion in another. Consider, for example, the following argument:

> No act performed involuntarily should be punished.
> Some criminal acts are performed involuntarily.
> Therefore some criminal acts should not be punished.

Here the proposition *some criminal acts should not be punished* is the conclusion, and the other two propositions are the premisses. But the first premiss in this argument, *no acts performed involuntarily should be punished,* is the conclusion in the following (different) argument:

> No act beyond the control of the agent should be punished.
> All involuntary acts are beyond the control of the agent.
> Therefore no act performed involuntarily should be punished.

No proposition, taken all by itself, in isolation, is either a premiss or a conclusion. It is a premiss only when it occurs in an argument which assumes it for the sake of showing that some other proposition is thereby justified. And it is a conclusion only when it occurs in an argument which attempts to establish or prove it on the basis of other propositions which are assumed. This notion is common enough: it is like the fact that a man, taken by himself, is neither an employer nor an employee, but may be

* From chapter 1, pp. 8–12, of *Introduction to Logic;* copyright 1953 by The Macmillan Company and used with their permission. The title of this selection has been supplied by the editors. Compare with selection 8.

either in different contexts, employer to his gardener, employee of the firm for which he works.

Arguments are traditionally divided into two different types, *deductive* and *inductive*. While every argument involves the claim that its premises provide evidence for the truth of its conclusion, only a *deductive* argument claims that its premises provide *conclusive* evidence. In the case of deductive arguments the technical terms "valid" and "invalid" are used in place of "correct" and "incorrect." A deductive argument is *valid* when its premises do provide conclusive evidence for its conclusion, that is, when premises and conclusion are so related that it is absolutely impossible for the premises to be true unless the conclusion is true also. Every deductive argument is either valid or invalid, and the task of deductive logic is to clarify the nature of the relationship which holds between premises and conclusion in a valid argument, and thus to allow us to discriminate between valid and invalid arguments. . . .

An inductive argument, on the other hand, does not claim that its premises give conclusive evidence for the truth of its conclusion, but only that they provide *some* evidence for it. Inductive arguments are neither *valid* nor *invalid* in the sense in which those terms are applied to deductive arguments. Inductive arguments may, of course, be evaluated as better or worse, according to the degree of likelihood or probability which their premises confer upon their conclusions. . . .

Truth and falsehood may be predicated of propositions, but never of arguments. And the properties of validity and invalidity can belong only to deductive arguments, never to propositions. There is a connection between the validity or invalidity of an argument and the truth or falsehood of its premises and conclusion, but this connection is by no means a simple one. Some valid arguments contain only true propositions, as, for example:

> All whales are mammals.
> All mammals have lungs.
> Therefore all whales have lungs.

But an argument may contain false propositions exclusively, and be valid nevertheless, as, for example:

> All spiders have six legs.
> All six legged creatures have wings.
> Therefore all spiders have wings.

This argument is valid because *if* its premises were true its conclusion would have to be true also, even though in fact they are all false. On the other hand, if we reflect upon the argument:

If I owned all the gold in Fort Knox, then I would be very wealthy.
I do not own all the gold in Fort Knox.
Therefore I am not very wealthy.

we see that although its premisses and conclusion are true, the argument is invalid. That the premisses *could* be true and the conclusion false, if not immediately apparent, may be made clear by considering that if I were to inherit a million dollars, the premisses would remain true while the conclusion would become false. This point is further illustrated by the following argument, which is of the same form as the preceding one:

If Rockefeller owned all the gold in Fort Knox, then Rockefeller
   would be very wealthy.
Rockefeller does not own all the gold in Fort Knox.
Therefore Rockefeller is not very wealthy.

The premisses of this argument are true, and its conclusion is false. Such an argument cannot be valid, because it is impossible for the premisses of a valid argument to be true while its conclusion is false.

The preceding examples show that there are valid arguments with false conclusions, as well as invalid arguments with true conclusions. Hence the truth or falsehood of its conclusion does not determine the validity or invalidity of an argument. Nor does the validity of an argument guarantee the truth of its conclusion. There are perfectly valid arguments which have false conclusions—but any such argument must have at least one false premiss. The term "sound" is introduced to characterize a valid argument all of whose premisses are true. Clearly the conclusion of a *sound* argument is true. A deductive argument fails to establish the truth of its conclusion if it is *unsound*, which means either that it is not *valid*, or that not all of its premisses are *true*. To test the truth or falsehood of premisses is the task of science in general, since premisses may deal with any subject matter at all. The logician is not so much interested in the truth or falsehood of propositions as in the logical relations between them, where by the "logical" relations between propositions we mean those which determine the correctness or incorrectness of arguments in which they may occur. Determining the correctness or incorrectness of arguments falls squarely within the province of logic. The logician is interested in the correctness even of arguments whose premisses might be false. . . .

• 10 •

SCIENCE AND HYPOTHESIS *

Irving M. Copi (1917–)

I. EXPLANATIONS: SCIENTIFIC AND UNSCIENTIFIC

In everyday life it is the unusual or startling for which we demand explanations. An office boy may arrive at work on time every morning for ever so long, and no curiosity will be aroused. But let him come an hour late one day, and his employer will demand an *explanation*. What is it that is wanted when an explanation for something is requested? An example will help to answer this question. The office boy might reply that he had taken the seven-thirty bus to work as usual, but the bus had been involved in a traffic accident which had entailed considerable delay. In the absence of any other transportation, the boy had had to wait for the bus to be repaired, and that had taken a full hour. This account would probably be accepted as a satisfactory explanation. It can be so regarded because from the statements which constitute the explanation the fact to be explained follows logically and no longer appears puzzling. An explanation is a group of statements . . . from which the thing to be explained can logically be inferred and whose assumption removes or diminishes its problematic or puzzling character. . . . Explanation and inference are very closely related. They are, in fact, the same process regarded from opposite points of view. Given certain premises, any conclusion which can logically be inferred from them is regarded as being explained by them. And given a fact to be explained, we say that we have found an explanation for it when we have found a set of premises from which it can logically be inferred.

Of course some proposed explanations are better than others. The chief criterion for evaluating explanations is *relevance*. If the tardy office boy had offered as explanation for his late arrival the fact that there is a war in China or a famine in India, that would properly be regarded as a very poor explanation, or rather as "no explanation at all." Such a story would have "nothing to do with the case"; it would be *irrelevant*, because from it the fact to be explained can *not* be inferred. The relevance of a proposed ex-

* From chapter 13, sections 2–4, of *Introduction to Logic*. Copyright 1953 by The Macmillan Company and used with their permission. See selection 7.

planation, then, corresponds exactly to the cogency of the argument by which the fact to be explained is inferred from the proposed explanation. Any acceptable explanation must be relevant, but not all . . . which are relevant in this sense are acceptable explanations. There are other criteria for deciding the worth or acceptability of proposed explanations.

The most obvious requirement to propose is that the explanation be *true*. In the example of the office boy's lateness, the crucial part of his explanation was a particular fact, the traffic accident, of which he was (presumably) an eye witness. But the explanations of science are for the most part *general* rather than particular. The keystone of Newtonian Mechanics is the Law of Universal Gravitation, whose statement is:

> Every particle of matter in the universe attracts every other particle with a force which is directly proportional to the product of the masses of the particles and inversely proportional to the square of the distance between them.

Newton's law is not directly verifiable in the same way that a bus accident is at the time it occurs. There is simply no way in which we can inspect *all* particles of matter in the universe and see that they do attract each other in precisely the way that Newton's law asserts. Few propositions of science are *directly* verifiable as true. In fact, none of the important ones are. For the most part they concern *unobservable* entities, such as molecules and atoms, electrons and protons, and the like. Hence the proposed requirement of truth is not *directly* applicable to most scientific explanations. Before considering more useful criteria for evaluating scientific theories, it will be helpful to compare scientific with unscientific explanations.

Science is supposed to be concerned with facts, and yet in its further reaches we find it apparently committed to highly speculative notions which are far removed from the possibility of direct experience. How then are scientific explanations to be distinguished from those which are frankly mythological or superstitious? An unscientific "explanation" of the regular motions of the planets was the doctrine that each heavenly body was the abode of an "Intelligence" or "Spirit" which controlled its movement. A certain humorous currency was achieved during World War II by the unscientific explanation of certain aircraft failures as being due to "gremlins," which were said to be invisible but mischievous little men who played pranks on aviators. The point to note here is that from the point of view of observability and direct verifiability, there is no great difference between modern scientific theories and the unscientific doctrines of mythology or theology. One can no more see or touch a Newtonian "particle," an atom, or electron, than an "Intelligence" or a "gremlin." What then are the differences between scientific and unscientific explanations?

There are two important and closely related differences between the kind of explanation sought by science and the kind provided by superstitions of various sorts. The first significant difference lies in the attitudes taken towards the explanations in question. The typical attitude of one who really *accepts* an unscientific explanation is *dogmatic*. What he accepts is regarded as being absolutely true and beyond all possibility of improvement or correction. During the Middle Ages and the early modern period the word of Aristotle was the ultimate authority to which scholars appealed for deciding questions of fact. However empirically and open-mindedly Aristotle himself may have arrived at his views, they were accepted by the non-scientific schoolmen in a completely different and unscientific spirit. One of the schoolmen to whom Galileo offered his telescope to view the newly discovered moons of Jupiter declined to look, being convinced that none could possibly be seen because no mention of them could be found in Aristotle's treatise on astronomy! Because unscientific beliefs are absolute, ultimate, and final, within the framework of any such doctrine or dogma there can be no rational method of ever considering the question of its truth. The scientist's attitude towards his explanations is altogether different. Every explanation in science is put forward tentatively and provisionally. Any proposed explanation is regarded as a mere hypothesis, more or less probable on the basis of the available facts or relevant evidence. It must be admitted that the scientist's vocabulary is a little misleading on this point. When what was first suggested as a "hypothesis" becomes well confirmed, it is frequently elevated to the position of a "theory." And when, on the basis of a great mass of evidence, it achieves well nigh universal acceptance, it is promoted to the lofty status of a "law." This terminology is not always strictly adhered to: Newton's discovery is still called the "Law of Gravitation," while Einstein's contribution, which supersedes or at least improves on Newton's, is referred to as the "Theory of Relativity." The vocabulary of "hypothesis," "theory," and "law" is unfortunate, since it obscures the important fact that *all* of the general propositions of science are regarded as hypotheses, never as dogmas.

Closely allied with the difference in the way they are regarded is the second and more fundamental difference between scientific and unscientific explanations or theories. This second difference lies in the basis for accepting or rejecting the view in question. Many unscientific views are mere prejudices, which their adherents could scarcely give any reason for holding. Since they are regarded as "certain," however, any challenge or question is likely to be regarded as an affront and met with abuse. If one who accepts an unscientific explanation *can* be persuaded to discuss the basis for its acceptance, there are only a few grounds on which he will attempt to "defend" it. It is true because "we've always believed it," or because "everyone knows it." These all too familiar phrases express appeals to tradition or popularity rather than evidence. Or a questioned dogma may be defended on the grounds of revelation or authority. The absolute truth of their religious creeds and the absolute falsehood of all others have been revealed from on high, at various times, to Moses, to Paul, to Mohammed, to Joseph Smith, and to many others. That there are rival traditions, conflicting authorities, and revelations which contradict one another does not seem disturbing to those who have embraced an absolute creed. In general, unscientific beliefs are held independently of anything we should regard as *evidence* in their favor. Because they are *absolute*, questions of evidence are regarded as having little or no importance.

The case is quite different in the realm of science. Since every scientific explanation is regarded as a hypothesis, it is regarded as worthy of acceptance only to the extent that there is *evidence* for it. As a hypothesis, the question of its truth or falsehood is *open*, and there is continual search for more and more evidence to decide that question. The term "evidence" as used here refers ultimately to experience; *sensible* evidence is the ultimate court of appeal in verifying scientific propositions. Science is *empirical* in holding that sense experience is the *test of truth* for all its pronouncements. Consequently, it is of the essence of a *scientific* proposition that it be capable of being tested by observation.

Some propositions can be tested *directly*. To decide the truth or falsehood of the proposition which asserts that it is now raining outside, we need only look out the window. To tell whether a traffic light shows green or red, all we have to do is to look at it. But the propositions which scientists usually offer as explanatory hypothesis are not of this type. Such general propositions as Newton's Laws or Einstein's Theory are not *directly testable* in this fashion. They can, however, be tested *indirectly*. The *indirect method* of testing the truth of a proposition is familiar to all of us, though we may not be familiar with this name for it. For example, if his employer had been suspicious of the office boy's explanation of his tardiness, he might have checked up on it by telephoning the bus company to find out whether an accident had really happened to the seven-thirty bus. If the bus company's report checked with the boy's story, this would serve to dispel the employer's suspicions; whereas if the bus company denied that an accident had occurred, it would probably convince the employer that his office boy's story was false. This inquiry would constitute an *indirect test* of the office boy's explanation.

The pattern of *indirect testing* or *indirect verification* consists of two parts. First one deduces from the proposition to be tested one or more other propositions which *are* capable of being tested *directly*. Then these consequences are tested and found to be either true or false. If the consequences are false, any proposition which implies them must be false also. On the other hand, if the consequences are true, they are evidence for the truth of the proposition being tested, which is thus confirmed *indirectly*.

It should be noted that indirect testing is never demonstrative or certain. To deduce directly testable conclusions from a proposition usually requires additional premisses. The conclusion that the bus company will *reply* that the seven-thirty bus had an accident this morning does not follow validly from the proposition that the seven-thirty bus *did* have an accident. Additional premisses are needed, for example, that all accidents are reported to the company's office, that the reports are not mislaid or forgotten, and the company does not make a policy of denying its accidents. So the bus company's denying that an accident occurred would not demonstrate the office boy's story to be false, for the discrepancy might be due to the falsehood of one of the other premisses mentioned. Those others, however, ordinarily have such a high degree of probability that a negative reply on the part of the bus company would render the office boy's story very doubtful indeed.

Similarly, establishing the truth of a conclusion does not demonstrate the truth of the premisses from which it was deduced. We know very well that a valid argument may have a true conclusion even though its premisses are not all true. In the present example, the bus company might affirm that an accident occurred to the seven-thirty bus because of some mistake in their records, even though no accident had occurred. So the inferred consequent *might* be true even though the *premisses* from which it was deduced were not. . . .

It must be admitted that every proposition, scientific or unscientific, which is a relevant explanation for any observable fact, has *some* evidence in its favor, namely the fact to which it is relevant. Thus the regular motions of the planets must be conceded to constitute evidence for the (unscientific) theory that the planets are inhabited by "Intelligences" which cause them to move in just the orbits which are observed. The motions themselves are as much evidence for that myth as they are for Newton's or Einstein's theories. The difference lies in the fact that that is the *only* evidence for the unscientific hypothesis. Absolutely no other *directly* testable propositions can be deduced from the myth. On the other hand, a very large number of directly testable propositions can be deduced from the scientific explanations mentioned. Here, then, is *the* difference between scientific and unscientific explanations. A scientific explanation for a given fact will have directly testable propositions deducible from it other than the one asserting the fact to be explained. But an unscientific explanation will have no other directly testable propositions deducible from it. . . .

It is clear that we have been using the term "scientific explanation" in a quite general sense. As here defined, an explanation may be scientific even though it is not a part of one of the various special sciences like physics or psychology. Thus the office boy's explanation of his tardiness would be classified as a *scientific* one, for it is testable, even if only indirectly. But had he offered as explanation the proposition that *God willed him to be late that morning, and God is omnipotent*, the explanation would have been unscientific. For although his being late that morning is deducible from the proffered explanation, no other directly testable proposition is, and so the explanation is not even indirectly testable, and hence is unscientific.

II. EVALUATING SCIENTIFIC EXPLANATIONS

The question naturally arises as to how scientific explanations are to be evaluated, that is, judged as good or bad, or at least as better or worse. This question is especially important because there is usually more than a single scientific explanation for one and the same fact. A man's abrupt behavior may be explained either by the hypothesis that he is shy or by the hypothesis that he is unfriendly. In a criminal investigation two different and incompatible hypotheses about the identity of the criminal may equally well account for the known facts. In the realm of science proper, that an object expands when heated is explained by both the caloric theory of heat and the kinetic theory. The caloric theory regarded heat as an invisible weightless fluid called "caloric," with the power of penetrating, expanding, and dissolving bodies, or dissipating them in vapor. The kinetic theory, on the other hand, regards the heat of a body as consisting of random motions of the molecules of which the body is composed. These are *alternative* scientific explanations which serve equally well to explain some of the phenomena of thermal expansion. They cannot both be true, however, and the problem is to evaluate or choose between them.

What is wanted here is a list of conditions which a good hypothesis can be expected to fulfill. It must not be thought that such a list of conditions can constitute a *recipe* by whose means anyone at all can construct good hypotheses. No one has ever pretended to lay down a set of rules for the invention or discovery of hypotheses. It is likely that none could ever be laid down, for that is the *creative* side of the scientific enterprise. Ability to create is a function of a person's imagination and talent and cannot be reduced to a mechanical process. A great scientific hypothesis, with wide explanatory powers like those of Newton's or Einstein's, is as much the product of genius as a great work of art. There is no formula for discovering new hypotheses, but there are certain rules to which acceptable hypotheses can be expected to conform. These can be regarded as the criteria for evaluating hypotheses.

There are five criteria which are used in judging the worth or acceptability of hypotheses. They may be listed as (1) relevance, (2) testability, (3) compatibility with previously well established hypotheses, (4) predictive or explanatory power, and (5) simplicity. The first two have already been discussed, but we shall review them briefly here.

1. *Relevance.* No hypothesis is ever proposed for its own sake but is always intended as an explanation of some fact or other. Therefore it must be *relevant* to the fact which it is intended to explain, that is, the fact in question must be *deducible* from the proposed hypotheses—either from the hypothesis alone or from it together with certain causal laws which may be presumed to have already been established as highly probable, or from these together with certain assumptions about particular initial conditions. A hypothesis which is not relevant to the fact it is intended to explain simply fails to explain it and can only be regarded as having failed to fulfill its intended function. . . .

2. *Testability.* The chief distinguishing characteristic of scientific hypotheses (as contrasted with unscientific ones) is that they are testable. That is, there must be the possibility of making observations which tend to confirm or disprove any scientific hypothesis. It need not be *directly* testable, of course. As has already been observed, most of the really important scientific hypotheses are formulated in terms of such unobservable entities as electrons or electromagnetic waves. . . . But there must be some way of getting from statements about such unobservables to statements about directly observable entities such as tables and chairs, or pointer readings, or lines on a photographic plate. In other words, there must be some connection between any scientific hypothesis and empirical data or facts of experience.

3. *Compatibility with Previously Well Established Hypotheses.* The requirement that an acceptable hypothesis must be compatible or consistent with other hypotheses which have already been well confirmed is an eminently reasonable one. Science, in seeking to encompass more and more facts, aims at achieving a *system* of explanatory hypotheses. Of course such a system must be self-consistent, for no self-contradictory set of propositions could possibly be true—or even intelligible. Ideally, the way in which scientists hope to make progress is by gradually expanding their hypotheses to comprehend more and more facts. For such progress to be made each new hypothesis must be consistent with those already confirmed. Thus

Leverrier's hypothesis that there was an additional but not yet charted planet beyond the orbit of Uranus was perfectly consistent with the main body of accepted astronomical theory. A new theory must *fit in* with older theories if there is to be orderly progress in scientific inquiry.

It is possible, of course, to overestimate the importance of the third criterion. Although the ideal of science may be the gradual growth of theoretical knowledge by the addition of one new hypothesis after another, the actual history of scientific progress has not always followed that pattern. Many of the most important of new hypotheses have been inconsistent with older theories and have in fact replaced them rather than fitted in with them. Einstein's Relativity Theory was of that sort, shattering many of the preconceptions of the older Newtonian theory. . . .

The foregoing is not intended to give the impression that scientific progress is a helter-skelter process in which theories are abandoned right and left in favor of newer and shinier ones. Older theories are not so much abandoned as corrected. Einstein himself has always insisted that his own work is a modification rather than a rejection of Newton's. . . . Every established theory has been established through having proved adequate to explain a considerable mass of data, of observed facts. And it cannot be dethroned or discredited by any new hypothesis unless that new hypothesis can account for the same facts as well or even better. There is nothing capricious about the development of science. Every change represents an improvement, a more comprehensive and thus more adequate explanation of the way in which the world manifests itself in experience. Where inconsistencies occur between hypotheses, the greater age of one does not automatically prove it to be correct and the newer one wrong. The *presumption* is in favor of the older one if it has already been extensively confirmed. But if the new one in conflict with it *also* receives extensive confirmation, considerations of age or priority are definitely irrelevant. Where there is a conflict between two hypotheses, we must turn to the observable facts to decide between them. Ultimately, our last court of appeal in deciding between rival hypotheses is experience. What our third criterion, compatibility with previously well established hypotheses, comes to is this: the totality of hypotheses accepted at any time should be consistent with each other, and—other things being equal—of two new hypotheses, the one which fits in better with the accepted body of scientific theory is to be preferred. The question of what is involved in "other things being equal" takes us directly to our fourth criterion.

4. Predictive or Explanatory Power. By the predictive or explanatory power of a hypothesis is meant the range of observable facts that can be deduced from it. This criterion is related to, but different from, that of testability. A hypothesis is testable if *some* observable fact is deducible from it. If one of two testable hypotheses has a greater number of observable facts deducible from it than from the other, then it is said to have greater predictive or explanatory power. For example, Newton's hypothesis of universal gravitation together with his three laws of motion had greater predictive power than either Kepler's or Galileo's hypotheses, because all observable consequences of the latter two were also consequences of the former, and the former had many more besides. An observable fact which can be deduced from a given hypothesis is said to be explained by it and also can be said to be predicted by it. The greater the predictive power of a hypothesis, the more it explains, and the better it contributes to our understanding of the phenomena with which it is concerned.

Our fourth criterion has a negative side which is of crucial importance. If a hypothesis is inconsistent with any well attested fact of observation, the hypothesis is false and must be rejected. Where two different hypotheses are both relevant to explaining some set of facts and both are testable, and both are compatible with the whole body of already established scientific theory, it may be possible to choose between them by deducing incompatible propositions from them which are directly testable. . . .

5. *Simplicity.* It sometimes happens that two rival hypotheses satisfy the first four criteria equally well. Historically the most important pair of such hypotheses were those of Ptolemy (fl. 127–151) and Copernicus (1473–1543). Both were intended to explain all of the then known data of astronomy. According to the Ptolemaic theory, the earth is the center of the universe, and the heavenly bodies move about it in orbits which require a very complicated geometry of epicycles to describe. Ptolemy's theory was relevant, testable, and compatible with previously well established hypotheses, satisfying the first three criteria perfectly. According to the Copernican theory, the sun rather than the earth is at the center, and the earth itself moves around the sun along with the other planets. Copernicus' theory too satisfied the first three criteria perfectly. And with respect to the fourth criterion, the two theories were almost exactly on a par. . . . To all intents and purposes, the Ptolemaic and Copernican theories were of equal predictive or explanatory power. There was only one significant difference between the two rival hypotheses. Although both required the clumsy method of epicycles to account for the observed positions of the various heavenly bodies, *fewer* such epicycles were required within the Copernican theory. The Copernican system was therefore *simpler*, and on this basis it was accepted by all later astronomers, despite the greater age and equal predictive power of the Ptolemaic system, and in the teeth of persecution by the Medieval Church!

The criterion of simplicity is a perfectly natural one to invoke. In ordinary life as well as in science, the simplest theory which fits all the available facts is the one we tend to accept. In court trials of criminal cases the prosecution attempts to develop a hypothesis which includes the guilt of the accused and fits in with all the available evidence. Opposing him, the defense attorney seeks to set up a hypothesis which includes the innocence of the accused and also fits all the available evidence. Often both sides succeed, and then the case is usually decided—or *ought* to be decided—in favor of that hypothesis which is simpler or more "natural." Simplicity, however, is a very difficult term to define. Not all controversies are as straight-forward as the Ptolemaic-Copernican one, in which the latter's greater simplicity consisted merely in requiring a smaller number of epicycles. And of course "naturalness" is an almost hopelessly deceptive term —for it seems much more "natural" to believe that the earth is still while the apparently moving sun really does move. The fifth and last criterion, simplicity, is an important and frequently decisive one, but it is vague and not always easy to apply.

III. THE DETECTIVE AS SCIENTIST

Now that we have formulated and explained the criteria by which hypotheses are evaluated, we are in a position to describe the general pattern of scientific research. . . . It will be instructive to examine an illustration of that method. A perennial favorite in this connection is the detective, whose problem is not quite the same as that of the pure scientist, but whose approach and technique illustrate the method of science very clearly. The classical example of the astute detective who can solve even the most baffling mystery is A. Conan Doyle's immortal creation, Sherlock Holmes. Holmes, his stature undiminished by the passage of time, will be our hero in the following account.

1. *The Problem.* Some of our most vivid pictures of Holmes are those in which he is busy with magnifying glass and tape measure, searching out and finding essential clues which had escaped the attention of those stupid bunglers, the "experts" of Scotland Yard. Or those of us who are by temperament less vigorous may think back more fondly on Holmes the thinker, ". . . who, when he had an unsolved problem upon his mind, would go for days, and even for a week, without rest, turning it over, rearranging his facts, looking at it from every point of view until he had either fathomed it or convinced himself that his data were insufficient." [1] At one such time, according to Dr. Watson:

[1] "The Man with the Twisted Lip."

He took off his coat and waistcoat, put on a large blue dressing-gown, and then wandered about the room collecting pillows from his bed and cushions from the sofa and armchairs. With these he constructed a sort of Eastern divan, upon which he perched himself cross-legged, with an ounce of shag tobacco and a box of matches laid out in front of him. In the dim light of the lamp I saw him sitting there, an old briar pipe between his lips, his eyes fixed vacantly upon the corner of the ceiling, the blue smoke curling up from him, silent, motionless, with the light shining upon his strong-set aquiline features. So he sat as I dropped off to sleep, and so he sat when a sudden ejaculation caused me to wake up, and I found the summer sun shining into the apartment. The pipe was still between his lips, the smoke still curled upward, and the room was full of a dense tobacco haze, but nothing remained of the heap of shag which I had seen upon the previous night.[2]

But such memories are incomplete. Holmes was not always searching for clues or pondering over solutions. . . . When there is no mystery to be unraveled, no man in his right mind would go out to look for clues. Clues, after all, must be *clues* for something. Nor could Holmes, or anyone else, for that matter, engage in profound thought unless he had something to think *about*. Sherlock Holmes was a genius at solving problems, but even a genius must *have* a problem before he can solve it. All reflective thinking, and this term includes criminal investigation as well as scientific research, is a problem-solving activity. . . . There must be a problem felt before either the detective or the scientist can go to work.

Of course the active mind sees problems where the dullard sees only familiar objects. One Christmas season Dr. Watson visited Holmes to find that the latter had been using a lens and forceps to examine ". . . a very seedy and disreputable hard-felt hat, much the worse for wear, and cracked in several places." [3] After they had greeted each other, Holmes said of it to Watson, "I beg that you will look upon it not as a battered billycock but as an intellectual problem." It so happened that the hat led them into one of their most interesting adventures, but it could not have done so had Holmes not seen a problem in it from the start. A problem may be characterized as a fact or group of facts for which we have no acceptable explanation, which seem unusual, or which fail to fit in with our expectations or preconceptions. It should be obvious that *some* prior beliefs are required if anything is to appear problematic. If there are no expectations, there can be no surprises.

Sometimes, of course, problems came to Holmes already labeled. The

[2] "The Man with the Twisted Lip."
[3] "The Adventure of the Blue Carbuncle."

very first adventure recounted by Dr. Watson began with the following
message from Gregson of Scotland Yard:

> My Dear Mr. Sherlock Holmes:
>   There has been a bad business during the night at 3, Lauriston
> Gardens, off the Brixton Road. Our man on the beat saw a light
> there about two in the morning, and as the house was an empty one,
> suspected that something was amiss. He found the door open, and
> in the front room, which is bare of furniture, discovered the body of
> a gentleman, well dressed, and having cards in his pocket bearing the
> name of 'Enoch J. Drebber, Cleveland, Ohio, U.S.A.' There had
> been no robbery, nor is there any evidence as to how the man met
> his death. There are marks of blood in the room, but there is no
> wound upon his person. We are at a loss as to how he came into the
> empty house; indeed, the whole affair is a puzzler. If you can come
> round to the house any time before twelve, you will find me there.
> I have left everything in statu quo until I hear from you. If you are
> unable to come, I shall give you fuller details, and would esteem it
> a great kindness if you would favour me with your opinion.
>   Yours faithfully,
>   T.G.[4]

Here was a problem indeed. A few minutes after receiving the message,
Sherlock Holmes and Dr. Watson "were both in a hansom, driving furiously for the Brixton Road."

  2. *Preliminary Hypotheses*. On their ride out Brixton way, Holmes "prat-
tled away about Cremona fiddles and the difference between a Stradi-
varius and an Amati." Dr. Watson chided Holmes for not giving much
thought to the matter at hand, and Holmes replied: "No data yet. . . . It
is a capital mistake to theorize before you have all the evidence. It biases
the judgment." This point of view was expressed by Holmes again and
again. On one occasion he admonished a younger detective that "The
temptation to form premature theories upon insufficient data is the bane
of our profession." [5] Yet for all of his confidence about the matter, on
this one issue Holmes was completely mistaken. Of course one should not
reach a *final judgment* until a great deal of evidence has been considered,
but this procedure is quite different from *not theorizing*. As a matter of
fact, it is strictly impossible to make any serious attempt to collect evidence
unless one *has* theorized beforehand. . . . There are too many particular
facts, too many data in the world, for anyone to try to become acquainted
with them all. Everyone, even the most patient and thorough investigator,
must pick and choose, deciding which facts to study and which to pass

---

[4] *A Study in Scarlet.*
[5] "The Valley of Fear."

over. He must have some working hypothesis for or against which to collect relevant data. It need not be a *complete* theory, but at least the rough outline must be there. Otherwise how could one decide what facts to select for consideration out of the totality of all facts, which is too vast even to begin to sift?

Holmes' actions were wiser than his words in this connection. After all, the words were spoken in a hansom speeding towards the scene of the crime. If Holmes really had no theory about the matter, why go to Brixton Road? If facts and data were all that he wanted, any old facts and any old data, with no hypotheses to guide him in their selection, why should he have left Baker Street at all? There were plenty of facts in the rooms at 221-B, Baker Street. Holmes might just as well have spent his time counting all the words on all the pages of all the books there, or perhaps making very accurate measurements of the distances between each separate pair of articles of furniture in the house. He could have gathered data to his heart's content and saved himself cab fare into the bargain!

It may be objected that the facts to be gathered at Baker Street have nothing to do with the case, whereas those which awaited Holmes at the scene of the crime were valuable clues for solving the problem. It was, of course, just this consideration which led Holmes to ignore the "data" at Baker Street and hurry away to collect those off Brixton Road. It must be insisted, however, that the greater relevance of the latter could not be *known* beforehand but only conjectured on the basis of previous experience with crimes and clues. It was in fact a *hypothesis* which led Holmes to look in one place rather than another for his facts, the hypothesis that there was a murder, that the crime was committed at the place where the body was found, and that the murderer had left some trace or clue which could lead to his discovery. Some such hypothesis is always required to guide the investigator in his search for relevant data, for in the absence of any preliminary hypothesis there are simply too many facts in this world to examine. The preliminary hypothesis ought to be highly tentative, and it must be based on previous knowledge. But a preliminary hypothesis is as necessary as the existence of a problem for any serious inquiry to be begun.

It must be emphasized that a preliminary hypothesis, as here conceived, need not be a *complete* solution to the problem. The hypothesis that the man was murdered by someone who had left some clues to his identity on or near the body of his victim was what led Holmes to Brixton Road. This hypothesis is clearly incomplete: it does not say *who* committed the crime, or *how* it was done, or *why*. Such a preliminary hypothesis may be *very* different from the final solution to the problem. It will never be complete:

it may be a tentative explanation of only *part* of the problem. But however partial and however tentative, a preliminary hypothesis is required for any investigation to proceed.

3. *Collecting Additional Facts.* Every serious investigation begins with some fact or group of facts which strike the detective or the scientist as problematic and which initiate the whole process of inquiry. The initial facts which constitute the problem are usually too meager to suggest a wholly satisfactory explanation for themselves, but they will suggest—to the competent investigator—some preliminary hypotheses which lead him to search out additional facts. These additional facts, it is hoped, will serve as clues to the final solution. The inexperienced or bungling investigator will overlook or ignore all but the most obvious of them; but the careful worker will aim at completeness in his examination of the additional facts to which his preliminary hypotheses lead him. Holmes, of course, was the most careful and painstaking of investigators.

Holmes insisted on dismounting from the hansom a hundred yards or so from their destination and approached the house on foot, looking carefully at its surroundings and especially at the pathway leading up to it. When Holmes and Watson entered the house, they were shown the body by the two Scotland Yard operatives, Gregson and Lestrade. ("There is no clue," said Gregson. "None at all," chimed in Lestrade.) But Holmes had already started his own search for additional facts, looking first at the body:

. . . his nimble fingers were flying here, there, and everywhere, feel-ing, pressing, unbuttoning, examining . . . So swiftly was the exami-nation made, that one would hardly have guessed the minuteness with which it was conducted. Finally, he sniffed the dead man's lips, and then glanced at the soles of his patent leather boots.

Then turning his attention to the room itself,

. . . he whipped a tape measure and a large round magnifying glass from his pocket. With these two implements he trotted noiselessly about the room, sometimes stopping, occasionally kneeling, and once lying flat upon his face. So engrossed was he with his occupation that he appeared to have forgotten our presence, for he chattered away to himself under his breath the whole time, keeping up a run-ning fire of exclamations, groans, whistles, and little cries suggestive of encouragement and of hope. As I watched him I was irresistibly reminded of a pure-blooded, well-trained foxhound as it dashes back-ward and forward through the covert, whining in its eagerness, until it comes across the lost scent. For twenty minutes or more he con-tinued his researches, measuring with the most exact care the dis-tance between marks which were entirely invisible to me, and occa-sionally applying his tape to the walls in an equally incomprehensible manner. In one place he gathered up very carefully a little pile of gray dust from the floor and packed it away in an envelope. Finally he examined with his glass the word upon the wall, going over every letter of it with the most minute exactness. This done, he appeared to be satisfied, for he replaced his tape and his glass in his pocket.

"They say that genius is an infinite capacity for taking pains," he remarked with a smile. "It's a very bad definition, but it does apply to detective work."

One matter deserves to be emphasized very strongly. Steps (2) and (3) are not completely separable but are usually very intimately connected and interdependent. True enough, we require a preliminary hypothesis to begin any intelligent examination of facts, but the additional facts may themselves suggest new hypotheses, which may lead to new facts, which suggest still other hypotheses, which lead to still other additional facts, and so on. Thus having made his careful examination of the facts available in the house off Brixton Road, Holmes was led to formulate a further hypothesis which required the taking of testimony from the constable who found the body. The man was off duty at the moment, and Lestrade gave Holmes the constable's name and address.

Holmes took a note of the address.

"Come along, Doctor," he said: "we shall go and look him up. I'll tell you one thing which may help you in the case," he continued, turning to the two detectives. "There has been murder done, and the murderer was a man. He was more than six feet high, was in the prime of life, had small feet for his height, wore coarse, square-toed boots and smoked a Trichinopoly cigar. He came here with his victim in a four-wheeled cab, which was drawn by a horse with three old shoes and one new one on his off fore-leg. In all probability the murderer had a florid face, and the fingernails of his right hand were remarkably long. These are only a few indications, but they may assist you."

Lestrade and Gregson glanced at each other with an incredulous smile.

"If this man was murdered, how was it done?" asked the former.

"Poison," said Sherlock Holmes curtly, and strode off.

4. *Formulating the Hypothesis.* At some stage or other of his investigation, any man—whether detective, scientist, or ordinary mortal—will get the feeling that he has all the facts needed for his solution. He has his "2 and 2," so to speak, but the task still remains of "putting them together." At such a time Sherlock Holmes might sit up all night, consuming pipe after pipe of tobacco, trying to think things through. The result or end product of such thinking, if it is successful, is a hypothesis which accounts for all the data, both the original set of facts which constituted the prob-

lem, and the additional facts to which the preliminary hypotheses pointed. The actual discovery of such an explanatory hypothesis is a process of creation, in which imagination as well as knowledge is involved. Logic has nothing to say about the *discovery* of hypotheses; this process is more properly to be investigated by psychologists. Holmes, who was a genius at inventing hypotheses, described the process as reasoning "backwards." As he put it,

> Most people, if you describe a train of events to them, will tell you what the result would be. They can put those events together in their minds, and argue from them that something will come to pass. There are few people, however, who, if you told them a result, would be able to evolve from their own inner consciousness what the steps were which led up to that result.

Here is Holmes' description of the process of formulating an explanatory hypothesis. When a hypothesis has been proposed, however, its evaluation must be along the lines that were sketched in Section II. Granted its relevance and testability, and its compatibility with other well attested beliefs, the ultimate criterion for evaluating a hypothesis is its predictive power.

5. *Deducing Further Consequences.* A really fruitful hypothesis will not only explain the facts which originally inspired it but will explain many others in addition. A good hypothesis will point beyond the initial facts in the direction of others whose existence might otherwise not have been suspected. And of course the verification of those further consequences will tend to confirm the hypothesis which led to them. Holmes' hypothesis that the murdered man had been poisoned was soon put to such a test. A few days later the murdered man's secretary and traveling companion was also found murdered. Holmes asked Lestrade, who had discovered the second body, whether he had found anything in the room which could furnish a clue to the murderer. Lestrade answered "Nothing," and went on to mention a few quite ordinary effects. Holmes was not satisfied and pressed him, asking "And was there nothing else?" Lestrade answered, "Nothing of any importance," and named a few more details, the last of which was "a small chip ointment box containing a couple of pills." At this information,

> Sherlock Holmes sprang from his chair with an exclamation of delight.
> "The last link," he cried, exultantly. "My case is complete."
> The two detectives stared at him in amazement.
> "I have now in my hands," my companion said, confidently, "all the threads which have formed such a tangle. . . . I will give you a proof of my knowledge. Could you lay your hands upon those pills?"
> "I have them," said Lestrade, producing a small white box . . .

On the basis of his hypothesis about the original crime, Holmes was able to predict that the pills found at the scene of the second crime must contain poison. Here deduction has an essential role in the process of any scientific or inductive inquiry. The ultimate value of any hypothesis lies in its predictive or explanatory power, which means that additional facts must be deducible from an adequate hypothesis. From his theory that the first man was poisoned and that the second victim met his death at the hands of the same murderer, Holmes inferred that the pills found by Lestrade must be poison. His theory, however sure he may have felt about it, was only a theory and needed further confirmation. He obtained that confirmation by testing the consequences deduced from the hypothesis and finding them to be true. Having used deduction to make a prediction, his next step was to test it.

6. *Testing the Consequences.* The consequences of a hypothesis, that is, the predictions made on the basis of that hypothesis, may require different means for their testing. Some require only observation. In some cases, Holmes needed only to watch and wait—for the bank robbers to break into the vault, in the "Adventure of the Red-headed League," or for Dr. Roylott to slip a venomous snake through a dummy ventilator, in the "Adventure of the Speckled Band." In the present case, however, an *experiment* had to be performed.

Holmes asked Dr. Watson to fetch the landlady's old and ailing terrier, which she had asked to have put out of its misery the day before. Holmes then cut one of the pills in two, dissolved it in a wineglass of water, added some milk, and

> . . . turned the contents of the wineglass into a saucer and placed it in front of the terrier, who speedily licked it dry. Sherlock Holmes's earnest demeanour had so far convinced us that we all sat in silence, watching the animal intently, and expecting some startling effect. None such appeared, however. The dog continued to lie stretched upon the cushion, breathing in a laboured way, but apparently neither the better nor the worse for its draught.
>
> Holmes had taken out his watch, and as minute followed minute without result, an expression of the utmost chagrin and disappointment appeared upon his features. He gnawed his lip, drummed his fingers upon the table, and showed every other symptom of acute impatience. So great was his emotion that I felt sincerely sorry for him, while the two detectives smiled derisively, by no means displeased at this check which he had met.
>
> "It can't be a coincidence," he cried, at last springing from his chair and pacing wildly up and down the room: "it is impossible that it should be a mere coincidence. The very pills which I suspected in the case of Drebber are actually found after the death of Stangerson.

And yet they are inert. What can it mean? Surely my whole chain of
reasoning cannot have been false. It is impossible! And yet this
wretched dog is none the worse. Ah, I have it! I have it!" With a
perfect shriek of delight he rushed to the box, cut the other pill in
two, dissolved it, added milk, and presented it to the terrier. The
unfortunate creature's tongue seemed hardly to have been moistened
in it before it gave a convulsive shiver in every limb, and lay as rigid
and lifeless as if it had been struck by lightning.

Sherlock Holmes drew a long breath, and wiped the perspiration
from his forehead.

By the favorable outcome of his experiment, Holmes' hypothesis had received dramatic and convincing confirmation.

7. *Application.* The detective's concern, after all, is a practical one.
Given a crime to solve, he has not merely to explain the facts but to apprehend and arrest the criminal. The latter involves making *application*
of his theory, using it to predict where the criminal can be found and how
he may be caught. He must deduce still further consequences from the
hypothesis, not for the sake of additional confirmation but for practical
purposes. From his general hypothesis Holmes was able to infer that the
murderer was acting the role of a cabman. We have already seen that
Holmes had formed a pretty clear description of the man's appearance, and
he sent out his army of "Baker Street Irregulars," street urchins of the
neighborhood, to search out and summon the cab driven by just that man.
The successful "application" of this hypothesis can be described again in
Dr. Watson's words. A few minutes after the terrier's death,

. . . there was a tap at the door, and the spokesman of the street
Arabs, young Wiggins, introduced his insignificant and unsavoury
person.

"Please, sir," he said, touching his forelock, "I have the cab down-
stairs."

"Good boy," said Holmes, blandly. "Why don't you introduce
this pattern at Scotland Yard?" he continued, taking a pair of steel
handcuffs from a drawer. "See how beautifully the spring works.
They fasten in an instant."

"The old pattern is good enough," remarked Lestrade, "if we can
only find the man to put them on."

"Very good, very good," said Holmes, smiling. "The cabman may
as well help me with my boxes. Just ask him to step up, Wiggins."

I was surprised to find my companion speaking as though he were
about to set out on a journey, since he had not said anything to me
about it. There was a small portmanteau in the room, and this he
pulled out and began to strap. He was busily engaged at it when
the cabman entered the room.

"Just give me a help with this buckle, cabman," he said, kneeling over his task, and never turning his head.

The fellow came forward with a somewhat sullen, defiant air, and put down his hands to assist. At that instant there was a sharp click, the jangling of metal, and Sherlock Holmes sprang to his feet again.

"Gentlemen," he cried, with flashing eyes, "let me introduce you to Mr. Jefferson Hope, the murderer of Enoch Drebber and of Joseph Stangerson."

Here we have a picture of the detective as scientist, reasoning from observed facts to a testable hypothesis which not only explains the facts but permits of practical application. . . .

PART III

THEORY OF KNOWLEDGE

• II •

OF DOUBT AND CERTITUDE*

René Descartes (1596–1650)

MEDITATION I

OF THE THINGS OF WHICH WE MAY DOUBT

Several years have now elapsed since I first became aware that I had accepted, even from my youth, many false opinions for true, and that consequently what I afterwards based on such principles was highly doubtful; and from that time I was convinced of the necessity of undertaking once in my life to rid myself of all the opinions I had adopted, and of commencing anew the work of building from the foundation, if I desired to establish a firm and abiding superstructure in the sciences. But as this enterprise appeared to me to be one of great magnitude, I waited until I had attained an age so mature as to leave me no hope that at any stage of life more advanced I should be better able to execute my design. On this account, I have delayed so long that I should henceforth consider I was doing wrong were I still to consume in deliberation any of the time that now remains for action. Today, then, since I have opportunely freed my mind from all cares, and am happily disturbed by no passions, and since I am in the secure possession of leisure in a peaceable retirement, I will at length apply myself earnestly and freely to the general overthrow of all my former opinions. But, to this end, it will not be necessary for me to show that the whole of these are false—a point, perhaps, which I shall never reach; but as even now my reason convinces me that I ought not the less carefully to withold belief from what is not entirely certain and indubitable, than from what is manifestly false, it will be sufficient to justify the rejection of the whole if I shall find in each some ground for doubt. Nor for this purpose will it be necessary even to deal with each belief individually, which would be truly an endless labour; but, as the removal from below of the foundation necessarily involves the downfall of the whole edifice, I will at once approach the criticism of the principles on which all my former beliefs rested.

---

* The first two of the six *Meditations on the First Philosophy* (1641); translated from the Latin by John Veitch (1853). The title of this selection has been supplied by the editors. See selections 13, 17, and 27.

All that I have, up to this moment, accepted as possessed of the highest truth and certainty, I received either from or through the senses. I observed, however, that these sometimes misled us; and it is the part of prudence not to place absolute confidence in that by which we have even once been deceived.

But it may be said, perhaps, that, although the senses occasionally mislead us respecting minute objects, and such as are so far removed from us as to be beyond the reach of close observation, there are yet many other of their informations (presentations), of the truth of which it is manifestly impossible to doubt; as for example, that I am in this place, seated by the fire, clothed in a winter dressing-gown, that I hold in my hands this piece of paper, with other intimations of the same nature. But how could I deny that I possess these hands and this body, and withal escape being classed with persons in a state of insanity, whose brains are so disordered and clouded by dark bilious vapours as to cause them pertinaciously to assert that they are monarchs when they are in the greatest poverty; or clothed in gold and purple when destitute of any covering; or that their head is made of clay, their body of glass, or that they are gourds? I should certainly be not less insane that they, were I to regulate my procedure according to examples so extravagant.

Though this be true, I must nevertheless here consider that I am a man, and that, consequently, I am in the habit of sleeping, and representing to myself in dreams those same things, or even sometimes others less probable, which the insane think are presented to them in their waking moments. How often have I dreamt that I was in these familiar circumstances,—that I was dressed, and occupied this place by the fire, when I was lying undressed in bed? At the present moment, however, I certainly look upon this paper with eyes wide awake; the head which I now move is not asleep; I extend this hand consciously and with express purpose, and I perceive it; the occurrences in sleep are not so distinct as all this. But I cannot forget that, at other times, I have been deceived in sleep by similar illusions; and, attentively considering those cases, I perceive so clearly that there exist no certain marks by which the state of waking can ever be distinguished from sleep, that I feel greatly astonished; and in amazement I almost persuade myself that I am now dreaming.

Let us suppose, then, that we are dreaming, and that all these particulars —namely, the opening of the eyes, the motion of the head, the forthputting of the hands—are merely illusions; and even that we really possess neither an entire body nor hands such as we see. Nevertheless, it must be admitted at least that the objects which appear to us in sleep are, as it were, painted representations which could not have been formed unless in the likeness of realities; and, therefore, that those general objects, at all events,—namely, eyes, a head, hands, and an entire body—are not simply imaginary, but really existent. For, in truth, painters themselves, even when they study to represent sirens and satyrs by forms the most fantastic and extraordinary, cannot bestow upon them natures absolutely new, but can only make a certain medley of the members of different animals; or if they chance to imagine something so novel that nothing at all similar has ever been seen before, and such as is, therefore, purely fictitious and absolutely false, it is at least certain that the colours of which this is composed are real.

And on the same principle, although these general objects, viz. a body, eyes, a head, hands, and the like, be imaginary, we are nevertheless absolutely necessitated to admit the reality at least of some other objects still more simple and universal than these, of which, just as of certain real colours, all those images of things, whether true and real, or false and fantastic, that are found in our consciousness, are formed.

To this class of objects seem to belong corporeal nature in general and its extension; the figure of extended things, their quantity or magnitude, and their number, as also the place in, and the time during, which they exist, and other things of the same sort. We will not, therefore, perhaps reason illegitimately if we conclude from this that Physics, Astronomy, Medicine, and all the other sciences that have for their end the consideration of composite objects, are indeed of a doubtful character; but that Arithmetic, Geometry, and the other sciences of the same class, which regard merely the simplest and most general objects, and scarcely inquire whether or not these are really existent, contain somewhat that is certain and indubitable; for whether I am awake or dreaming, it remains true that two and three makes five, and that a square has but four sides; nor does it seem possible that truths so apparent can ever fall under a suspicion of falsity or incertitude.

Nevertheless, the belief that there is a God who is all-powerful, and who created me, such as I am, has, for a long time, obtained steady possession of my mind. How, then, do I know that he has not arranged that there should be neither earth, nor sky, nor any extended thing, nor figure, nor magnitude, nor place, providing at the same time, however, for the rise in me of the perceptions of all these objects, and the persuasion that these do not exist otherwise than as I perceive them? And further, as I sometimes think that others are in error respecting matters of which they believe themselves to possess a perfect knowledge, how do I know that I am not also deceived each time I add together two and three, or number the sides of a square, or form some judgment still more simple, if more simple indeed can be imagined? But perhaps Deity has not been willing that I should be thus deceived, for He is said to be supremely good. If, however, it were repugnant to the goodness of Deity to have created me subject to constant deception, it would seem likewise to be contrary to his goodness to allow me to be occasionally deceived; and yet it is clear that this is permitted. Some, indeed, might perhaps be found who would be disposed rather to deny the existence of a Being so powerful than to believe that there is nothing certain. But let us for the present refrain from opposing this opinion, and grant that all which is here said of a Deity is fabulous; nevertheless in whatever way it be supposed that I reached the state in which I exist, whether by fate, or chance, or by an endless series of antecedents and consequents, or by any other means, it is clear (since to be deceived and to err is a certain defect) that the probability of my being so imperfect as to be the constant victim of deception, will be increased exactly in proportion as the power possessed by the cause, to which they assign my origin, is lessened. To these reasonings I have assuredly nothing to reply, but am constrained at last to avow that there is nothing of all that I formerly believed to be true of which it is impossible to doubt, and that not through thoughtlessness or levity, but from cogent and maturely considered reasons; so that henceforward, if I desire to discover anything certain, I ought not the less carefully to refrain from assenting to those same opinions than to what might be shown to be manifestly false.

But it is not sufficient to have made these observations; care must be taken likewise to keep them in remembrance. For those old and customary opinions perpetually recur—long and familiar usage giving them the right of occupying my mind, even almost against my will, and subduing my belief; nor will I lose the habit of deferring to them and confiding in them so long as I shall consider them to be what in truth they are, viz., opinions to some extent doubtful, as I have already shown, but still highly probable, and such as it is much more reasonable to believe than deny. It is for this reason I am persuaded that I shall not be doing wrong, if, taking an opposite judgment of deliberate design, I become my own deceiver, by supposing, for a time, that all those opinions are entirely false and imaginary, until at length, having thus balanced my old by my new prejudices, my judgment shall no longer be turned aside by perverted usage from the path that may conduct to the perception of truth. For I am assured that, meanwhile, there will arise neither peril nor error from this course, and that I cannot for the present yield too much to distrust, since the end I now seek is not action but knowledge.

I will suppose, then, not that Deity, who is sovereignly good and the fountain of truth, but that some malignant demon, who is at once exceedingly potent and deceitful, has employed all his artifice to deceive me; I will suppose that the sky, the air, the earth, colours, figures, sounds, and all external things, are nothing better than the illusions of dreams, by means of which this being has laid snares for my credulity; I will consider myself as without hands, eyes, flesh, blood, or any of the senses, and as falsely believing that I am possessed of these; I will continue resolutely fixed in this belief, and if indeed by this means it be not in my power to arrive at the knowledge of truth, I shall at least do what is in my power, viz., suspend my judgment, and guard with settled purpose against giving my assent to what is false, and being imposed upon by this deceiver, whatever be his power and artifice.

But this undertaking is arduous, and a certain indolence insensibly leads me back to my ordinary course of life; and just as the captive, who, perchance, was enjoying in his dreams an imaginary liberty, when he begins to suspect that it is but a vision, dreads awakening, and conspires with the agreeable illusions that the deception may be prolonged; so I, of my own accord, fall back into the train of my former beliefs, and fear to arouse myself from my slumber, lest the time of laborious wakefulness that would succeed this quiet rest, in place of bringing any light of day, should prove inadequate to dispel the darkness that will arise from the difficulties that have now been raised.

MEDITATION II

OF THE NATURE OF THE HUMAN MIND; AND THAT IT IS MORE EASILY KNOWN THAN THE BODY

The Meditation of yesterday has filled my mind with so many doubts, that it is no longer in my power to forget them. Nor do I see, meanwhile, any principle on which they can be resolved; and, just as if I had fallen all of a sudden into very deep water, I am so greatly disconcerted as to be unable either to plant my feet firmly on the bottom or sustain myself by swimming on the surface. I will, nevertheless, make an effort, and try anew the same path on which I had entered yesterday, that is, proceed by casting aside all that admits of the slightest doubt, not less than if I had discovered it to be absolutely false; and I will continue always in this track until I shall find something that is certain, or at least, if I can do nothing more, until I shall know with certainty that there is nothing certain. Archimedes, that he might transport the entire globe from the place it occupied to another, demanded only a point that was firm and immoveable; so also, I shall be entitled to entertain the highest expectations, if I am fortunate enough to discover only one thing that is certain and indubitable.

I suppose, accordingly, that all the things which I see are false (fictitious); I believe that none of those objects which my fallacious memory represents ever existed; I suppose that I possess no senses; I believe that body, figure, extension, motion, and place are merely fictions of my mind. What is there, then, that can be esteemed true? Perhaps this only, that there is absolutely nothing certain.

But how do I know that there is not something different altogether from the objects I have now enumerated, of which it is impossible to entertain the slightest doubt? Is there not a God, or some being, by whatever name I may designate him, who causes these thoughts to arise in my mind? But why suppose such a being, for it may be I myself am capable of producing them? Am I, then, at least not something? But I before denied that I possessed senses or a body; I hesitate, however, for what follows from that? Am I so dependent on the body and the senses that without these I cannot exist? But I had the persuasion that there was absolutely nothing in the world, that there was no sky and no earth, neither minds nor bodies; was I not, therefore, at the same time, persuaded that I did not exist? Far from it; I assuredly existed, since I was persuaded. But there is I know not what being, who is possessed at once of the highest power and the deepest cunning, who is constantly employing all his ingenuity in deceiving me. Doubtless, then, I exist, since I am deceived; and, let him deceive me as he may, he can never bring it about that I am nothing, so long as I shall be conscious that I am something. So that it must, in fine, be maintained, all things being maturely and carefully considered, that this proposition, I am, I exist, is necessarily true each time it is expressed by me, or conceived in my mind.

But I do not yet know with sufficient clearness what I am, though assured that I am; and hence, in the next place, I must take care, lest perchance I inconsiderately substitute some other object in room of what is properly myself, and thus wander from truth, even in that knowledge which I hold to be of all others the most certain and evident. For this reason, I will now consider anew what I formerly believed myself to be, before I entered on the present train of thought; and of my previous opinion I will retrench all that can in the least be invalidated by the grounds of doubt I have adduced, in order that there may at length remain nothing but what is certain and indubitable. What then did I formerly think I was? Undoubtedly I judged that I was a man. But what is a man? Shall I say a rational animal? Assuredly not; for it would be necessary forthwith to inquire into what is meant by animal, and what by rational, and thus, from a single question, I should insensibly glide into others, and these more difficult than the first; nor do I now possess enough of leisure to warrant me in wasting my time amid subtleties of this sort. I prefer here to attend to the thoughts that sprung up of themselves in my mind, and were inspired by my own nature alone, when I applied myself to the consideration of what I was. In the first place, then, I thought that I possessed a countenance, hands, arms, and all the fabric of members that appears in a corpse, and which I called by the name of body. It further occurred to me that I was nourished, that I walked, perceived, and thought, and all those actions I referred to the soul; but what the soul itself was I either did not stay to consider, or, if I did, I imagined that it was something extremely rare and subtle, like wind, or flame, or ether, spread through my grosser parts. As regarded the body, I did not even doubt of its nature, but thought I distinctly knew it, and if I had wished to describe it according to the notions I then entertained, I should have explained myself in this manner: By body I understand all that can be terminated by a certain figure; that can be comprised in a certain place, and so fill a certain space as therefrom to exclude every other body; that can be perceived either by touch, sight, hearing, taste, or smell; that can be moved in different ways, not indeed of itself, but by something foreign to it by which it is touched and from which it receives the impression; for the power of self-motion, as likewise that of perceiving and thinking, I held as by no means pertaining to the nature of body; on the contrary, I was somewhat astonished to find such faculties existing in some bodies.

But as to myself, what can I now say that I am, since I suppose there exists an extremely powerful, and, if I may so speak, malignant being, whose whole endeavours are directed towards deceiving me? Can I affirm that I possess any one of all those attributes of which I have lately spoken as belonging to the nature of body? After attentively considering them in my own mind, I find none of them that can properly be said to belong to myself. To recount them were idle and tedious. Let us pass, then, to the attributes of the soul. The first mentioned were the powers of nutrition and walking; but, if it be true that I have no body, it is true likewise that I am capable neither of walking nor of being nourished. Perception is another attribute of the soul; but perception too is impossible without the body: besides, I have frequently during sleep, believed that I perceived objects which I afterwards observed I did not in reality perceive. Thinking is another attribute of the soul; and here I discover what properly belongs to myself. This alone is inseparable from me. I am—I exist: this is certain; but how often? As often as I think; for perhaps it would even happen, if I should wholly cease to think, that I should at the same time altogether cease to be. I now admit nothing that is not necessarily true: I am therefore, precisely speaking, only a thinking thing, that is, a mind,

understanding, or reason,—terms whose signification was before unknown to me. I am, however, a real thing, and really existent; but what
thing? The answer was, a thinking thing. The question now arises, am I
aught besides? I will stimulate my imagination with a view to discover
whether I am not still something more than a thinking being. Now it is
plain I am not the assemblage of members called the human body;
I am not a thin and penetrating air diffused through all these members, or
wind, or flame, or vapour, or breath, or any of all the things I can imagine;
for I supposed that all these were not, and, without changing the supposition, I find that I still feel assured of my existence.

But it is true, perhaps, that those very things which I suppose to be non-
existent, because they are unknown to me, are not in truth different from
myself whom I know. This is a point I cannot determine, and do not now
enter into any dispute regarding it. I can only judge of things that are
known to me: I am conscious that I exist, and I who know that I exist
inquire into what I am. It is, however, perfectly certain that the knowledge of my existence, thus precisely taken, is not dependent on things, the
existence of which is as yet unknown to me: and consequently it is not
dependent on any of the things I can feign in imagination. Moreover, the
phrase itself, I frame an image, reminds me of my error; for I should in
truth frame one if I were to imagine myself to be anything, since to imagine
is nothing more than to contemplate the figure or image of a corporeal
thing; but I already know that I exist, and that it is possible at the same
time that all those images, and in general all that relates to the nature of
body, are merely dreams or chimeras. From this I discover that it is not
more reasonable to say, I will excite my imagination that I may know more
distinctly what I am, than to express myself as follows: I am now awake,
and perceive something real; but because my perception is not sufficiently
clear, I will of express purpose go to sleep that my dreams may represent
to me the object of my perception with more truth and clearness. And,
therefore, I know that nothing of all that I can embrace in imagination
belongs to the knowledge which I have of myself, and that there is need
to recall with the utmost care the mind from this mode of thinking, that
it may be able to know its own nature with perfect distinctness.

But what, then, am I? A thinking thing, it has been said. But what is a
thinking thing? It is a thing that doubts, understands, conceives, affirms,
denies, wills, refuses, that imagines also, and perceives. Assuredly it is
not little, if all these properties belong to my nature. But why should they
not belong to it? Am I not that very being who now doubts of almost
everything; who, for all that, understands and conceives certain things; who

affirms one alone as true, and denies the others; who desires to know more of them, and does not wish to be deceived; who imagines many things, sometimes even despite his will; and is likewise percipient of many, as if through the medium of the senses. Is there nothing of all this as true as that I am, even although I should be always dreaming, and although he who gave me being employed all his ingenuity to deceive me? Is there also any one of these attributes that can be properly distinguished from my thought, or that can be said to be separate from myself? For it is of itself so evident that it is I who doubt, I who understand, and I who desire, that it is here unnecessary to add anything by way of rendering it more clear. And I am as certainly the same being who imagines; for, although it may be (as I before supposed) that nothing I imagine is true, still the power of imagination does not cease really to exist in me and to form part of my thought. In fine, I am the same being who perceives, that is, who apprehends certain objects as by the organs of sense, since, in truth, I see light, hear a noise, and feel heat. But it will be said that these presentations are false, and that I am dreaming. Let it be so. At all events it is certain that I seem to see light, hear a noise, and feel heat; this cannot be false, and this is what in me is properly called perceiving, which is nothing else than thinking. From this I begin to know what I am with somewhat greater clearness and distinctness than heretofore.

But, nevertheless, it still seems to me, and I cannot help believing, that corporeal things, whose images are formed by thought, which fall under the senses, and are examined by the same, are known with much greater distinctness than that I know not what part of myself which is not imaginable; although, in truth, it may seem strange to say that I know and comprehend with greater distinctness things whose existence appears to me doubtful, that are unknown, and do not belong to me, than others of whose reality I am persuaded, that are known to me, and appertain to my proper nature; in a word, than myself. But I see clearly what is the state of the case. My mind is apt to wander, and will not yet submit to be restrained within the limits of truth. Let us therefore leave the mind to itself once more, and, according to it every kind of liberty, permit it to consider the objects that appear to it from without, in order that, having afterwards withdrawn it from these gently and opportunely, and fixed it on the consideration of its being and the properties it finds in itself, it may then be the more easily controlled.

Let us now accordingly consider the objects that are commonly thought to be the most easily, and likewise the most distinctly known, viz., the bodies we touch and see; not, indeed, bodies in general, for these general notions are usually somewhat more confused, but one body in particular. Take, for example, this piece of wax; it is quite fresh, having been but recently taken from the bee-hive; it has not yet lost the sweetness of the honey it contained; it still retains somewhat of the odour of the flowers from which it was gathered; its colour, figure, size, are apparent to the sight, it is hard, cold, easily handled; and sounds when struck upon with the finger. In fine, all that contributes to make a body as distinctly known as possible, is found in the one before us. But, while I am speaking, let it be placed near the fire—what remained of the taste exhales, the smell evaporates, the colour changes, its figure is destroyed, its size increases, it becomes liquid, it grows hot, it can hardly be handled, and, although struck upon, it emits no sound. Does the same wax still remain after this change? It must be admitted that it does remain; no one doubts it, or judges otherwise. What, then, was it I knew with so much distinctness in the piece of wax? Assuredly, it could be nothing of all that I observed by means of the senses, since all the things that fell under taste, smell, sight, touch, and hearing are changed, and yet the same wax remains. It was perhaps what I now think, viz., that this wax was neither the sweetness of honey, the pleasant odour of flowers, the whiteness, the figure, nor the sound, but only a body that a little before appeared to me conspicuous under these forms, and which is now perceived under others. But, to speak precisely, what is it that I imagine when I think of it in this way? Let it be attentively considered, and, retrenching all that does not belong to the wax, let us see what remains. There certainly remains nothing, except something extended, flexible, and movable. But what is meant by flexible and movable? Is it not that I imagine that the piece of wax, being round, is capable of becoming square, or of passing from a square into a triangular figure? Assuredly such is not the case, because I conceive that it admits of an infinity of similar changes; and I am, moreover, unable to compass this infinity by imagination, and consequently this conception which I have of the wax is not the product of the faculty of imagination. But what now is this extension? Is it not also unknown? For it becomes greater when the wax is melted, greater when it is boiled, and greater still when the heat increases; and I should not conceive clearly and according to truth, the wax as it is, if I did not suppose that the piece we are considering admitted even of a wider variety of extension than I ever imagined. I must, therefore, admit that I cannot even comprehend by imagination what the piece of wax is, and that it is the mind alone which perceives it. I speak of one piece in particular; for, as to wax in general, this is still more evident. But what is the piece of wax that can be perceived only by the understanding or mind? It is certainly the same which I see, touch, imagine; and, in fine, it is the same which, from the beginning, I believed it to be. But (and this it is of moment to observe) the perception of it is neither an act of sight, of touch, nor of imagination, and never was either of these, though it might formerly seem so, but is simply an intuition of the mind, which may be imperfect and confused, as it formerly was, or very clear and distinct, as it is at present, according as the attention is more or less directed to the elements which it contains, and of which it is composed.

But, meanwhile, I feel greatly astonished when I observe the weakness of my mind, and its proneness to error. For although, without at all giving expression to what I think, I consider all this in my own mind, words yet occasionally impede my progress, and I am almost led into error by the terms of ordinary language. We say, for example, that we see the same wax when it is before us, and not that we judge it to be the same from its retaining the same colour and figure: whence I should forthwith be disposed to conclude that the wax is known by the act of sight, and not by the intuition of the mind alone, were it not for the analogous instance of human beings passing on in the street below, as observed from a window. In this case I do not fail to say that I see the men themselves, just as I say that I see the wax; and yet what do I see from the window beyond hats and cloaks that might cover artificial machines, whose motions might be determined by springs? But I judge that there are human beings from these appearances, and thus I comprehend, by the faculty of judgment alone which is in the mind, what I believed I saw with my eyes.

The man who makes it his aim to rise to knowledge superior to the common, ought to be ashamed to seek occasions of doubting from the vulgar forms of speech: instead, therefore, of doing this, I shall proceed with the matter in hand, and inquire whether I had a clearer and more perfect perception of the piece of wax when I first saw it, and when I thought I knew it by means of the external sense itself, or, at all events, by the common sense, as it is called, that is, by the imaginative faculty; or whether I rather apprehend it more clearly at present, after having examined with greater care, both what it is, and in what way it can be known. It would certainly be ridiculous to entertain any doubt on this point. For what, in that first perception, was there distinct? What did I perceive which any animal might not have perceived? But when I distinguish the wax from its exterior forms, and when, as if I had stripped it of its vestments, I consider it quite naked, it is certain, although some error may still be found in my judgment, that I cannot, nevertheless, thus apprehend it without possessing a human mind.

But, finally, what shall I say of the mind itself, that is, of myself? For as yet I do not admit that I am anything but mind. What, then! I who seem to possess so distinct an apprehension of the piece of wax,—do I not know myself, both with greater truth and certitude, and also much more distinctly and clearly? For if I judge that the wax exists because I see it, it assuredly follows, much more evidently, that I myself am or exist, for the same reason: for it is possible that what I see may not in truth be wax, and that I do not even possess eyes with which to see anything; but it cannot be that when I see, or, which comes to the same thing, when I think I see, I myself who think am nothing. So likewise, if I judge that the wax exists because I touch it, it will still also follow that I am; and if I determine that my imagination, or any other cause, whatever it be, persuades me of the existence of the wax, I will still draw the same conclusion. And what is here remarked of the piece of wax, is applicable to all the other things that are external to me. And further, if the notion or perception of wax appeared to me more precise and distinct, after that not only sight and touch, but many other causes besides, rendered it manifest to my apprehension, with how much greater distinctness must I now know myself, since all the reasons that contribute to the knowledge of the nature of wax, or of any body whatever, manifest still better the nature of my mind? And there are besides so many other things in the mind itself that contribute to the illustration of its nature, that those dependent on the body, to which I have here referred, scarcely merit to be taken into account.

But, in conclusion, I find I have insensibly reverted to the point I desired; for, since it is now manifest to me that bodies themselves are not properly perceived by the senses nor by the faculty of imagination, but by the intellect alone; and since they are not perceived because they are seen and touched, but only because they are understood or rightly comprehended by thought, I readily discover that there is nothing more easily or clearly apprehended than my own mind. But because it is difficult to rid one's self so promptly of an opinion to which one has been long accustomed, it will be desirable to tarry for some time at this stage, that, by long continued meditation, I may more deeply impress upon my memory this new knowledge.

• 12 •

TWO KINDS OF KNOWLEDGE*
David Hume (1711–1776)

All the objects of human reason or enquiry may naturally be divided
into two kinds, to wit, *Relations of Ideas*, and *Matters of Fact*. Of the
first kind are the sciences of Geometry, Algebra, and Arithmetic; and in
short, every affirmation which is either intuitively or demonstratively certain. *That the square of the hypothenuse is equal to the square of the two
sides*, is a proposition which expresses a relation between these figures. *That
three times five is equal to the half of thirty*, expresses a relation between
these numbers. Propositions of this kind are discoverable by the mere
operation of thought, without dependence on what is anywhere existent
in the universe. Though there never were a circle or triangle in nature,
the truths demonstrated by Euclid would for ever retain their certainty
and evidence.

Matters of fact, which are the second objects of human reason, are not
ascertained in the same manner; nor is our evidence of their truth, however great, of a like nature with the foregoing. The contrary of every
matter of fact is still possible; because it can never imply a contradiction,
and is conceived by the mind with the same facility and distinctness, as if
ever so conformable to reality. *That the sun will not rise tomorrow* is no
less intelligible a proposition, and implies no more contradiction than the
affirmation, *that it will rise*. We should in vain, therefore, attempt to demonstrate its falsehood. Were it demonstratively false, it would imply a
contradiction, and could never be distinctly conceived by the mind.

It may, therefore, be a subject worthy of curiosity, to enquire what is
the nature of that evidence which assures us of any real existence and
matter of fact, beyond the present testimony of our senses, or the records
of our memory. This part of philosophy, it is observable, has been little
cultivated, either by the ancients or moderns; and therefore our doubts
and errors, in the prosecution of so important an enquiry, may be the more

---

* From *An Enquiry Concerning Human Understanding*, 1748, sec. IV, pt. 1. The title
of this selection has been supplied by the editors. Compare with selections 19, 22, 23,
and 54.

excusable; while we march through such difficult paths without any guide or direction. They may even prove useful, by exciting curiosity, and destroying that implicit faith and security, which is the bane of all reasoning and free enquiry. The discovery of defects in the common philosophy, if any such there be, will not, I presume, be a discouragement, but rather an incitement, as is usual, to attempt something more full and satisfactory than has yet been proposed to the public.

All reasonings concerning matter of fact seem to be founded on the relation of *Cause and Effect*. By means of that relation alone we can go beyond the evidence of our memory and senses. If you were to ask a man, why he believes any matter of fact, which is absent; for instance, that his friend is in the country, or in France; he would give you a reason; and this reason would be some other fact; as a letter received from him, or the knowledge of his former resolutions and promises. A man finding a watch or any other machine in a desert island, would conclude that there had once been men in that island. All our reasonings concerning fact are of the same nature. And here it is constantly supposed that there is a connexion between the present fact and that which is inferred from it. Were there nothing to bind them together, the inference would be entirely precarious. The hearing of an articulate voice and rational discourse in the dark assures us of the presence of some person: Why? Because these are the effects of the human make and fabric, and closely connected with it. If we anatomize all the other reasonings of this nature, we shall find that they are founded on the relation of cause and effect, and that this relation is either near or remote, direct or collateral. Heat and light are collateral effects of fire, and the one effect may justly be inferred from the other.

If we would satisfy ourselves, therefore, concerning the nature of that evidence, which assures us of matters of fact, we must enquire how we arrive at the knowledge of cause and effect.

I shall venture to affirm, as a general proposition, which admits of no exception, that the knowledge of this relation is not, in any instance, attained by reasonings *a priori*; but arises entirely from experience, when we find that any particular objects are constantly conjoined with each other. Let an object be presented to a man of ever so strong natural reason and abilities; if that object be entirely new to him, he will not be able, by the most accurate examination of its sensible qualities, to discover any of its causes or effects. Adam, though his rational faculties be supposed, at the very first, entirely perfect, could not have inferred from the fluidity and transparency of water that it would suffocate him, or from the light and warmth of fire that it would consume him. No object ever discovers, by the qualities which appear to the senses, either the causes which produced it, or the effects which will arise from it; nor can our reason, unassisted by experience, ever draw any inference concerning real existence and matter of fact.

This proposition, *that causes and effects are discoverable, not by reason but by experience,* will readily be admitted with regard to such objects, as we remember to have once been altogether unknown to us; since we must be conscious of the utter inability, which we then lay under, of foretelling what would arise from them. Present two smooth pieces of marble to a man who has no tincture of natural philosophy; he will never discover that they will adhere together in such a manner as to require great force to separate them in a direct line, while they make so small a resistance to a lateral pressure. Such events, as bear little analogy to the common course of nature, are also readily confessed to be known only by experience; nor does any man imagine that the explosion of gunpowder, or the attraction of a loadstone, could ever be discovered by arguments *a priori*. In like manner, when an effect is supposed to depend upon an intricate machinery or secret structure of parts, we make no difficulty in attributing all our knowledge of it to experience. Who will assert that he can give the ultimate reason, why milk or bread is proper nourishment for a man, not for a lion or a tiger?

But the same truth may not appear, at first sight, to have the same evidence with regard to events, which have become familiar to us from our first appearance in the world, which bear a close analogy to the whole course of nature, and which are supposed to depend on the simple qualities of objects, without any secret structure of parts. We are apt to imagine that we could discover these effects by the mere operation of our reason, without experience. We fancy, that were we brought on a sudden into this world, we could at first have inferred that one Billiard-ball would communicate motion to another upon impulse; and that we needed not to have waited for the event, in order to pronounce with certainty concerning it. Such is the influence of custom, that, where it is strongest, it not only covers our natural ignorance, but even conceals itself, and seems not to take place, merely because it is found in the highest degree.

But to convince us that all the laws of nature, and all the operations of bodies without exception, are known only by experience, the following reflections may, perhaps, suffice. Were any object presented to us, and were we required to pronounce concerning the effect, which will result from it, without consulting past observation; after what manner, I beseech you, must the mind proceed in this operation? It must invent or imagine some event, which it ascribes to the object as its effect; and it is plain that this invention must be entirely arbitrary. The mind can never possibly find the effect in the supposed cause, by the most accurate scrutiny and examination. For the effect is totally different from the cause, and consequently can never be discovered in it. Motion in the second Billiard-ball is a quite distinct event from motion in the first; nor is there anything in the one to suggest the smallest hint of the other. A stone or piece of metal raised into the air, and left without any support, immediately falls: but to consider the matter *a priori*, is there anything we discover in this situation which can beget the idea of a downward, rather than an upward, or any other motion, in the stone or metal?

And as the first imagination or invention of a particular effect, in all natural operations, is arbitrary, where we consult not experience; so must we also esteem the supposed tie or connexion between the cause and effect, which binds them together, and renders it impossible that any other effect could result from the operation of that cause. When I see, for instance, a Billiard-ball moving in a straight line towards another; even suppose motion in the second ball should by accident be suggested to me, as the result of their contact or impulse; may I not conceive, that a hundred different events might as well follow from that cause? May not both these balls remain at absolute rest? May not the first ball return in a straight line, or leap off from the second in any line or direction? All these suppositions are consistent and conceivable. Why then should we give the preference to one, which is no more consistent or conceivable than the rest? All our reasonings *a priori* will never be able to show us any foundation for this preference.

In a word, then, every effect is a distinct event from its cause. It could not, therefore, be discovered in the cause, and the first invention or conception of it, *a priori*, must be entirely arbitrary. And even after it is suggested, the conjunction of it with the cause must appear equally arbitrary; since there are always many other effects, which, to reason, must seem fully as consistent and natural. In vain, therefore, should we pretend to determine any single event, or infer any cause or effect, without the assistance of observation and experience. . . .

• 13 •

THE FIXATION OF BELIEF *

Charles Sanders Peirce (1839–1914)

. . . We generally know when we wish to ask a question and when we wish to pronounce a judgment, for there is a dissimilarity between the sensation of doubting and that of believing.

But this is not all which distinguishes doubt from belief. There is a practical difference. Our beliefs guide our desires and shape our actions. The Assassins, or followers of the Old Man of the Mountain, used to rush into death at his least command, because they believed that obedience to him would insure everlasting felicity. Had they doubted this, they would not have acted as they did. So it is with every belief, according to its degree. The feeling of believing is a more or less sure indication of there being established in our nature some habit which will determine our actions. Doubt never has such an effect.

Nor must we overlook a third point of difference. Doubt is an uneasy and dissatisfied state from which we struggle to free ourselves and pass into the state of belief; while the latter is a calm and satisfactory state which we do not wish to avoid, or to change to a belief in anything else. On the contrary, we cling tenaciously, not merely to believing, but to believing just what we do believe.

Thus, both doubt and belief have positive effects upon us, though very different ones. Belief does not make us act at once, but puts us into such a condition that we shall behave in a certain way, when the occasion arises. Doubt has not the least effect of this sort, but stimulates us to action until it is destroyed. This reminds us of the irritation of a nerve and the reflex action produced thereby; while for the analogue of belief, in the nervous system, we must look to what are called nervous associations—for example, to that habit of the nerves in consequence of which the smell of a peach will make the mouth water.

The irritation of doubt causes a struggle to attain a state of belief. I shall term this struggle *inquiry*, though it must be admitted that this is sometimes not a very apt designation.

* From "The Fixation of Belief," *Popular Science Monthly*, November, 1877; the first of a series of six papers entitled "Illustrations of the Logic of Science." Compare with selections 6, 11, 14, and 51.

The irritation of doubt is the only immediate motive for the struggle to attain belief. It is certainly best for us that our beliefs should be such as may truly guide our actions so as to satisfy our desires; and this reflection will make us reject any belief which does not seem to have been so formed as to insure this result. But it will only do so by creating a doubt in the place of that belief. With the doubt, therefore, the struggle begins, and with the cessation of doubt it ends. Hence, the sole object of inquiry is the settlement of opinion. We may fancy that this is not enough for us, and that we seek not merely an opinion, but a true opinion. But put this fancy to the test, and it proves groundless; for as soon as a firm belief is reached we are entirely satisfied, whether the belief be false or true. And it is clear that nothing out of the sphere of our knowledge can be our object, for nothing which does not affect the mind can be a motive for a mental effort. The most that can be maintained is, that we seek for a belief that we shall *think* to be true. But we think each one of our beliefs to be true, and, indeed, it is mere tautology to say so.

That the settlement of opinion is the sole end of inquiry is a very important proposition. It sweeps away, at once, various vague and erroneous conceptions of proof. A few of these may be noticed here.

1. Some philosophers have imagined that to start an inquiry it was only necessary to utter a question or set it down on paper, and have even recommended us to begin our studies with questioning everything! But the mere putting of a proposition into the interrogative form does not stimulate the mind to any struggle after belief. There must be a real and living doubt, and without this all discussion is idle.

2. It is a very common idea that a demonstration must rest on some ultimate and absolutely indubitable propositions. These, according to one school, are first principles of a general nature; according to another, are first sensations. But, in point of fact, an inquiry, to have that completely satisfactory result called demonstration, has only to start with propositions perfectly free from all actual doubt. If the premises are not in fact doubted at all, they cannot be more satisfactory than they are.

3. Some people seem to love to argue a point after all the world is fully convinced of it. But no further advance can be made. When doubt ceases, mental action on the subject comes to an end; and, if it did go on, it would be without a purpose.

If the settlement of opinion is the sole object of inquiry, and if belief is of the nature of a habit, why should we not attain the desired end, by taking any answer to a question, which we may fancy, and constantly reiterating it to ourselves, dwelling on all which may conduce to that belief, and learning to turn with contempt and hatred from anything which might disturb it? This simple and direct method is really pursued by many men. I remember once being entreated not to read a certain newspaper lest it might change my opinion upon free-trade. "Lest I might be entrapped by its fallacies and misstatements," was the form of expression. "You are not," my friend said, "a special student of political economy. You might, therefore, easily be deceived by fallacious arguments upon the subject. You might, then, if you read this paper, be led to believe in protection. But you admit that free-trade is the true doctrine; and you do not wish to believe what is not true." I have often known this system to be deliberately adopted. Still oftener, the instinctive dislike of an undecided state of mind, exaggerated into a vague dread of doubt, makes men cling spasmodically to the views they already take. The man feels that, if he only holds to his belief without wavering, it will be entirely satisfactory. Nor can it be denied that a steady and immovable faith yields great peace of mind. It may, indeed, give rise to inconveniences, as if a man should resolutely continue to believe that fire would not burn him, or that he would be eternally damned if he received his *ingesta* otherwise than through a stomach pump. But then the man who adopts this method will not allow that its inconveniences are greater than its advantages. He will say, "I hold steadfastly to the truth and the truth is always wholesome." And in many cases it may very well be that the pleasure he derives from his calm faith overbalances any inconveniences resulting from its deceptive character. Thus, if it be true that death is annihilation, then the man who believes that he will certainly go straight to heaven when he dies, provided he have fulfilled certain simple observances in this life, has a cheap pleasure which will not be followed by the least disappointment. A similar consideration seems to have weight with many persons in religious topics, for we frequently hear it said, "Oh, I could not believe so-and-so, because I should be wretched if I did." When an ostrich buries its head in the sand as danger approaches, it very likely takes the happiest course. It hides the danger, and then calmly says there is no danger; and, if it feels perfectly sure there is none, why should it raise its head to see? A man may go through life, systematically keeping out of view all that might cause a change in his opinions, and if he only succeeds—basing his method, as he does, on two fundamental psychological laws—I do not see what can be said against his doing so. It would be an egotistical impertinence to object that his procedure is irrational, for that only amounts to saying that his method of settling belief is not ours. He does not propose to himself to be rational, and indeed, will often talk with scorn of man's weak and illusive reason. So let him think as he pleases.

But this method of fixing belief, which may be called the method of tenacity, will be unable to hold its ground in practice. The social impulse is against it. The man who adopts it will find that other men think differently from him, and it will be apt to occur to him in some saner moment that their opinions are quite as good as his own, and this will shake his confidence in his belief. This conception, that another man's thought or sentiment may be equivalent to one's own, is a distinctly new step, and a highly important one. It arises from an impulse too strong in man to be suppressed, without danger of destroying the human species. Unless we make ourselves hermits, we shall necessarily influence each other's opinions; so that the problem becomes how to fix belief, not in the individual merely, but in the community.

Let the will of the state act, then, instead of that of the individual. Let an institution be created which shall have for its object to keep correct doctrines before the attention of the people, to reiterate them perpetually, and to teach them to the young; having at the same time power to prevent contrary doctrines from being taught, advocated, or expressed. Let all possible causes of a change of mind be removed from men's apprehensions. Let them be kept ignorant, lest they should learn of some reason to think otherwise than they do. Let their passions be enlisted, so that they may regard private and unusual opinions with hatred and horror. Then, let all men who reject the established belief be terrified into silence. Let the people turn out and tar-and-feather such men, or let inquisitions be made into the manner of thinking of suspected persons, and, when they are found guilty of forbidden beliefs, let them be subjected to some signal punishment. When complete agreement could not otherwise be reached, a general massacre of all who have not thought in a certain way has proved a very effective means of settling opinion in a country. If the power to do this be wanting, let a list of opinions be drawn up, to which no man of the least independence of thought can assent, and let the faithful be required to accept all these propositions, in order to segregate them as radically as possible from the influence of the rest of the world.

This method has, from the earliest times, been one of the chief means of upholding correct theological and political doctrines, and of preserving their universal or catholic character. In Rome, especially, it has been practiced from the days of Numa Pompilius to those of Pius Nonus. This is the most perfect example in history; but wherever there is a priesthood— and no religion has been without one—this method has been more or less made use of. Wherever there is aristocracy, or a guild, or any association of a class of men whose interests depend or are supposed to depend on certain propositions, there will be inevitably found some traces of this natural product of social feeling. Cruelties always accompany this system; and when it is consistently carried out, they become atrocities of the most horrible kind in the eyes of any rational man. Nor should this occasion surprise, for the officer of a society does not feel justified in surrendering the interests of that society for the sake of mercy, as he might his own private interests. It is natural, therefore, that sympathy and fellowship should thus produce a most ruthless power.

In judging this method of fixing belief, which may be called the method of authority, we must in the first place, allow its immeasurable mental and moral superiority to the method of tenacity. Its success is proportionally greater; and in fact it has over and over again worked the most majestic results. The mere structures of stone which it has caused to be put together—in Siam, for example, in Egypt, and in Europe—have many of them a sublimity hardly more than rivaled by the greatest works of Nature. And, except the geological epochs, there are no periods of time so vast as those which are measured by some of these organized faiths. If we scrutinize the matter closely, we shall find that there has not been one of their creeds which has remained always the same; yet the change is so slow as to be imperceptible during one person's life, so that individual belief remains sensibly fixed. For the mass of mankind, then, there is perhaps no better method than this. If it is their highest impulse to be intellectual slaves, then slaves they ought to remain.

But no institution can undertake to regulate opinions upon every subject. Only the most important ones can be attended to, and on the rest men's minds must be left to the action of natural causes. This imperfection will be no source of weakness so long as men are in such a state of culture that one opinion does not influence another—that is, so long as they cannot put two and two together. But in the most priest-ridden states some individuals will be found who are raised above that condition. These men possess a wider sort of social feeling; they see that men in other countries and in other ages have held to very different doctrines from those which they themselves have been brought up to believe; and they cannot help seeing that it is the mere accident of their having been taught as they have, and of their having been surrounded with the manners and associations they have, that has caused them to believe as they do and not far differently. And their candor cannot resist the reflection that there is no reason to rate their own views at a higher value than those of other nations and other centuries; and this gives rise to doubts in their minds.

They will further perceive that such doubts as these must exist in their minds with reference to every belief which seems to be determined by the caprice either of themselves or of those who originated the popular opinions. The willful adherence to a belief, and the arbitrary forcing of it upon others, must, therefore, both be given up and a new method of settling opinions must be adopted, which shall not only produce an impulse to believe, but shall also decide what proposition it is which is to be believed. Let the action of natural preferences be unimpeded, then, and under their influence let men conversing together and regarding matters in different lights, gradually develop beliefs in harmony with natural causes. This method resembles that by which conceptions of art have been brought to maturity. The most perfect example of it is to be found in the history of metaphysical philosophy. Systems of this sort have not usually rested upon observed facts, at least not in any great degree. They have been chiefly adopted because their fundamental propositions seemed "agreeable to reason." This is an apt expression; it does not mean that which agrees with experience, but that which we find ourselves inclined to believe. Plato, for example, finds it agreeable to reason that the distances of the celestial spheres from one another should be proportional to the different lengths of strings which produce harmonious chords. Many philosophers have been led to their main conclusions by considerations like this; but this is the lowest and least developed form which the method takes, for it is clear that another man might find Kepler's (earlier) theory, that the celestial spheres are proportional to the inscribed and circumscribed spheres of the different regular solids, more agreeable to *his* reason. But the shock of opinions will soon lead men to rest on preferences of a far more universal nature. Take, for example, the doctrine that man only acts selfishly—that is, from the consideration that acting in one way will afford him more pleasure than acting in another. This rests on no fact in the world, but it has had a wide acceptance as being the only reasonable theory.

This method is far more intellectual and respectable from the point of view of reason than either of the others which we have noticed. But its failure has been the most manifest. It makes of inquiry something similar to the development of taste; but taste, unfortunately, is always more or less a matter of fashion, and accordingly, metaphysicians have never come to any fixed agreement, but the pendulum has swung backward and forward between a more material and a more spiritual philosophy, from the earliest times to the latest. And so from this, which has been called the *a priori* method, we are driven, in Lord Bacon's phrase, to a true induction. We have examined into this *a priori* method as something which promised to deliver our opinions from their accidental and capricious element. But development, while it is a process which eliminates the effect of some casual circumstances, only magnifies that of others. This method, therefore, does not differ in a very essential way from that of authority. The government may not have lifted its finger to influence my convictions; I may have been left outwardly quite free to choose, we will say, between monogamy and polygamy, and appealing to my conscience only, I may have concluded that the latter practice is in itself licentious. But when I come to see that the chief obstacle to the spread of Christianity among a people of as high culture as the Hindoos has been a conviction of the immorality of our way of treating women, I cannot help seeing that, though governments do not interfere, sentiments in their development will be very greatly determined by accidental causes. Now, there are some people, among whom I must suppose that my reader is to be found, who, when they see that any belief of theirs is determined by any circumstance extraneous to the facts, will from that moment not merely admit in words that that belief is doubtful, but will experience a real doubt of it, so that it ceases to be a belief.

To satisfy our doubts, therefore, it is necessary that a method should be found by which our beliefs may be caused by nothing human, but by some external permanency—by something upon which our thinking has no effect. Some mystics imagine that they have such a method in a private inspiration from on high. But that is only a form of the method of tenacity, in which the conception of truth as something public is not yet developed. Our external permanency would not be external, in our sense, if it was restricted in its influence to one individual. It must be something which affects, or might affect, every man. And, though these affections are necessarily as various as are individual conditions, yet the method must be such that the ultimate conclusion of every man shall be the same. Such is the method of science. Its fundamental hypothesis, restated in more familiar language, is this: There are real things, whose characters are entirely independent of our opinions about them; those realities affect our senses according to regular laws, and, though our sensations are as different as our relations to the objects, yet, by taking advantage of the laws of perception, we can ascertain by reasoning how things really are, and any man, if he have sufficient experience and reason enough about it, will be led to the one true conclusion. The new conception here involved is that of reality. It may be asked how I know that there are any realities. If this hypothesis is the sole support of my method of inquiry, my method of inquiry must not be used to support my hypothesis. The reply is this: (1) If investigation cannot be regarded as proving that there are real things, it at least does not lead to a contrary conclusion; but the method and the conception on which it is based remain ever in harmony. No doubts of the method, therefore, necessarily arise from its practice, as is the case with all the others. (2) The feeling which gives rise to any method of fixing belief is a dissatisfaction at two repugnant propositions. But here already is a vague concession that there is some *one* thing to which a proposition should conform. Nobody, therefore, can really doubt that there are realities, or if he did, doubt would not be a source of dissatisfaction. The hypothesis, therefore, is one which every mind admits. So that the social impulse does not cause me to doubt it. (3) Everybody uses the scientific method about a great many things, and only ceases to use it when he does not know how to apply it. (4) Experience of the method has not led me to doubt it, but, on the contrary, scientific investigation has had the most wonderful triumphs in the way of settling opinion. These afford the explanation of my not doubting the method or the hypothesis which it supposes; and not having any doubt, nor believing that anybody else whom I could influence has, it would be the merest babble for me to say more about it. If there be anybody with a living doubt upon the subject, let him consider it.

To describe the method of scientific investigation is the object of this series of papers. At present I have only room to notice some points of contrast between it and other methods of fixing belief.

This is the only one of the four methods which presents any distinction of a right and a wrong way. If I adopt the method of tenacity and shut myself out from all influences, whatever I think necessary to doing this is necessary according to that method. So with the method of authority: the state may try to put down heresy by means which, from a scientific point of view, seems very ill-calculated to accomplish its purposes; but the only test *on that method* is what the state thinks, so that it cannot pursue the method wrongly. So with the *a priori* method. The very essence of it is to think as one is inclined to think. . . . But with the scientific method the case is different. I may start with known and observed facts to proceed to the unknown; and yet the rules which I follow in doing so may not be such as investigation would approve. The test of whether I am truly following the method is not an immediate appeal to my feelings and purposes, but, on the contrary, itself involves the application of the method. Hence it is that bad reasoning as well as good reasoning is possible; and this fact is the foundation of the practical side of logic.

It is not to be supposed that the first three methods of settling opinion present no advantage whatever over the scientific method. On the contrary, each has some peculiar convenience of its own. The *a priori* method is distinguished for its comfortable conclusions. It is the nature of the process to adopt whatever belief we are inclined to, and there are certain flatteries to one's vanities which we all believe by nature, until we are awakened from our pleasing dream by rough facts. The method of authority will always govern the mass of mankind; and those who wield the various forms of organized force in the state will never be convinced that dangerous reasoning ought not to be suppressed in some way. If liberty of speech is to be untrammeled from the grosser forms of constraint, then uniformity of opinion will be secured by a moral terrorism to which the respectability of society will give its thorough approval. Following the method of authority is the path of peace. Certain non-conformities are permitted; certain others (considered unsafe) are forbidden. These are different in different countries and in different ages; but, wherever you are let it be known that you seriously hold a tabooed belief, and you may be perfectly sure of being treated with a cruelty no less brutal but more refined than hunting you like a wolf. Thus, the greatest intellectual bene-factors of mankind have never dared, and dare not now, to utter the whole of their thought; and thus a shade of *prima facie* doubt is cast upon every proposition which is considered essential to the security of society. Sin-gularly enough, the persecution does not all come from without; but a man torments himself and is oftentimes most distressed at finding himself be-lieving propositions which he has been brought up to regard with aversion. The peaceful and sympathetic man will, therefore, find it hard to resist the temptation to submit his opinions to authority. But most of all I ad-mire the method of tenacity for its strength, simplicity, and directness. Men who pursue it are distinguished for their decision of character, which becomes very easy with such a mental rule. They do not waste time in trying to make up their minds to what they want, but, fastening like lightning upon whatever alternative comes first, they hold to it to the end, whatever happens, without an instant's irresolution. This is one of the splendid qualities which generally accompany brilliant, unlasting success. It is impossible not to envy the man who can dismiss reason, although we know how it must turn out at last.

Such are the advantages which the other methods of settling opinions have over scientific investigation. A man should consider well of them; and then he should consider that, after all, he wishes his opinions to coincide with the fact, and that there is no reason why the results of these three methods should do so. To bring about this effect is the prerogative of the method of science. Upon such considerations he has to make his choice— a choice which is far more than the adoption of any intellectual opinion, which is one of the ruling decisions of his life, to which when once made he is bound to adhere. The force of habit will sometimes cause a man to hold on to old beliefs, after he is in a condition to see that they have no sound basis. But reflection upon the state of the case will overcome these habits, and he ought to allow reflection full weight. People sometimes shrink from doing this, having an idea that beliefs are wholesome which they can-not help feeling rest on nothing. But let such persons suppose an analogous though different case from their own. Let them ask themselves what they would say to a reformed Mussulman who should hesitate to give up his old notions in regard to the relations of the sexes; or to a reformed Catholic who should still shrink from the Bible. Would they not say that these persons ought to consider the matter fully, and clearly understand the new doctrine, and then ought to embrace it in its entirety? But, above all, let it be considered that what is more wholesome than any particular belief, is integrity of belief; and that to avoid looking into the support of any belief from a fear that it may turn out rotten is quite as immoral as it is disadvantageous. The person who confesses that there is such a thing as truth, which is distinguished from falsehood simply by this, that if acted on it will carry us to the point we aim at and not astray, and then though convinced of this, dares not know the truth and seeks to avoid it, is in a sorry state of mind, indeed.

Yes, the other methods do have their merits: a clear logical conscience does cost something—just as any virtue, just as all that we cherish, costs us dear. But, we should not desire it to be otherwise. The genius of a man's logical method should be loved and reverenced as his bride, whom he has chosen from all the world. He need not condemn the others; on the contrary, he may honor them deeply, and in doing so he only honors her the more. But she is the one that he has chosen, and he knows that he was right in making that choice. And having made it, he will work and fight for her, and will not complain that there are blows to take, hoping that there may be as many and as hard to give, and will strive to be the worthy knight and champion of her from the blaze of whose splendors he draws his inspiration and his courage.

• 14 •

THE ETHICS OF BELIEF *
W. K. Clifford (1845–1879)

A shipowner was about to send to sea an emigrant-ship. He knew that she was old, and not over-well built at the first; that she had seen many seas and climes, and often had needed repairs. Doubts had been suggested to him that possibly she was not seaworthy. These doubts preyed upon

* The first part of a three part essay which appeared originally in the *Contemporary Review*, January 1877, and was reprinted in Clifford's posthumous *Lectures and Essays*, 1879. Compare with selections 33 and 34.

his mind and made him unhappy; he thought that perhaps he ought to have her thoroughly overhauled and refitted, even though this should put him to great expense. Before the ship sailed, however, he succeeded in overcoming these melancholy reflections. He said to himself that she had gone safely through so many voyages and weathered so many storms that it was idle to suppose she would not come safely home from this trip also. He would put his trust in Providence, which could hardly fail to protect all these unhappy families that were leaving their father-land to seek for better times elsewhere. He would dismiss from his mind all ungenerous suspicions about the honesty of builders and contractors. In such ways he acquired a sincere and comfortable conviction that his vessel was thoroughly safe and seaworthy; he watched her departure with a light heart, and benevolent wishes for the success of the exiles in their strange new home that was to be; and he got his insurance-money when she went down in mid-ocean and told no tales.

What shall we say of him? Surely this, that he was verily guilty of the death of those men. It is admitted that he did sincerely believe in the soundness of his ship; but the sincerity of his conviction can in no wise help him, because *he had no right to believe on such evidence as was before him*. He had acquired his belief not by honestly earning it in patient investigation, but by stifling his doubts. And although in the end he may have felt so sure about it that he could not think otherwise, yet inasmuch as he had knowingly and willingly worked himself into that frame of mind, he must be held responsible for it.

Let us alter the case a little, and suppose that the ship was not unsound after all; that she made her voyage safely, and many others after it. Will that diminish the guilt of her owner? Not one jot. When an action is once done, it is right or wrong for ever; no accidental failure of its good or evil fruits can possibly alter that. The man would not have been innocent, he would only have been not found out. The question of right or wrong has to do with the origin of his belief, not the matter of it; not what it was, but how he got it; not whether it turned out to be true or false, but whether he had a right to believe on such evidence as was before him.

There was once an island in which some of the inhabitants professed a religion teaching neither the doctrine of original sin nor that of eternal punishment. A suspicion got abroad that the professors of this religion had made use of unfair means to get their doctrines taught to children. They were accused of wresting the laws of their country in such a way as to remove children from the care of their natural and legal guardians; and even of stealing them away and keeping them concealed from their friends and relations. A certain number of men formed themselves into a society for the purpose of agitating the public about this matter. They published grave accusations against individual citizens of the highest position and character, and did all in their power to injure those citizens in the exercise of their professions. So great was the noise they made, that a Commission was appointed to investigate the facts; but after the Commission had carefully inquired into all the evidence that could be got, it appeared that the accused were innocent. Not only had they been accused on insufficient evidence, but the evidence of their innocence was such as the agitators might easily have obtained, if they had attempted a fair inquiry. After these disclosures the inhabitants of that country looked upon the members of the agitating society, not only as persons whose judgment was to be distrusted, but also as no longer to be counted honourable men. For although they had sincerely and conscientiously believed in the charges they had made, *yet they had no right to believe on such evidence as was before them.* Their sincere convictions, instead of being honestly earned by patient inquiring, were stolen by listening to the voice of prejudice and passion.

Let us vary this case also, and suppose, other things remaining as before, that a still more accurate investigation proved the accused to have been really guilty. Would this make any difference in the guilt of the accusers? Clearly not; the question is not whether their belief was true or false, but whether they entertained it on wrong grounds. They would no doubt say, "Now you see that we were right after all; next time perhaps you will believe us." And they might be believed, but they would not thereby become honourable men. They would not be innocent, they would only be not found out. Every one of them, if he chose to examine himself *in foro conscientiae,* would know that he had acquired and nourished a belief, when he had no right to believe on such evidence as was before him; and therein he would know that he had done a wrong thing.

It may be said, however, that in both of these supposed cases it is not the belief which is judged to be wrong, but the action following upon it. The shipowner might say, "I am perfectly certain that my ship is sound, but still I feel it my duty to have her examined, before trusting the lives of so many people to her." And it might be said to the agitator, "However convinced you were of the justice of your cause and the truth of your convictions, you ought not to have made a public attack upon any man's character until you had examined the evidence on both sides with the utmost patience and care."

In the first place, let us admit that, so far as it goes, this view of the case is right and necessary; right, because even when a man's belief is so fixed that he cannot think otherwise, he still has a choice in regard to the action suggested by it, and so cannot escape the duty of investigating on the ground of the strength of his convictions; and necessary, because those who are not yet capable of controlling their feelings and thoughts must have a plain rule dealing with overt acts.

But this being premised as necessary, it becomes clear that it is not sufficient, and that our previous judgment is required to supplement it. For it is not possible so to sever the belief from the action it suggests as to condemn the one without condemning the other. No man holding a strong belief on one side of a question, or even wishing to hold a belief on one side, can investigate it with such fairness and completeness as if he were really in doubt and unbiassed; so that the existence of a belief not founded on fair inquiry unfits a man for the performance of this necessary duty.

Nor is that truly a belief at all which has not some influence upon the actions of him who holds it. He who truly believes that which prompts him to an action has looked upon the action to lust after it, he has committed it already in his heart. If a belief is not realised immediately in open deeds, it is stored up for the guidance of the future. It goes to make a part of that aggregate of beliefs which is the link between sensation and action at every moment of all our lives, and which is so organised and compacted together that no part of it can be isolated from the rest, but every new addition modifies the structure of the whole. No real belief, however trifling and fragmentary it may seem, is ever truly insignificant; it prepares us to receive more of its like, confirms those which resembled it before, and weakens others; and so gradually it lays a stealthy train in our inmost thoughts, which may some day explode into overt action, and leave its stamp upon our character for ever.

And no one man's belief is in any case a private matter which concerns himself alone. Our lives are guided by that general conception of the course of things which has been created by society for social purposes. Our words, our phrases, our forms and processes and modes of thought, are common property, fashioned and perfected from age to age; an heirloom which every succeeding generation inherits as a precious deposit and a sacred trust to be handed on to the next one, not unchanged but enlarged and purified, with some clear marks of its proper handiwork. Into this, for good or ill, is woven every belief of every man who has speech of his fellows. An awful privilege, and an awful responsibility, that we should help to create the world in which posterity will live.

In the two supposed cases which have been considered, it has been judged wrong to believe on insufficient evidence, or to nourish belief by suppressing doubts and avoiding investigation. The reason of this judgment is not far to seek: it is that in both these cases the belief held by one man was of great importance to other men. But forasmuch as no belief held by one man, however seemingly trivial the belief, and however obscure the believer, is ever actually insignificant or without its effect on the fate of mankind, we have no choice but to extend our judgment to all cases of belief whatever. Belief, that sacred faculty which prompts the decisions of our will, and knits into harmonious working all the compacted energies of our being, is ours not for ourselves, but for humanity. It is rightly used on truths which have been established by long experience and waiting toil, and which have stood in the fierce light of free and fearless questioning. Then it helps to bind men together, and to strengthen and direct their common action. It is desecrated when given to unproved and unquestioned statements, for the solace and private pleasure of the believer; to add a tinsel splendour to the plain straight road of our life and display a bright mirage beyond it; or even to drown the common sorrows of our kind by a self-deception which allows them not only to cast down, but also to degrade us. Whoso would deserve well of his fellows in this matter will guard the purity of his belief with a very fanaticism of jealous care, lest at any time it should rest on an unworthy object, and catch a stain which can never be wiped away.

It is not only the leader of men, statesman, philosopher, or poet, that owes this bounden duty to mankind. Every rustic who delivers in the village alehouse his slow, infrequent sentences, may help to kill or keep alive the fatal superstitions which clog his race. Every hard-worked wife of an artisan may transmit to her children beliefs which shall knit society together, or rend it in pieces. No simplicity of mind, no obscurity of station, can escape the universal duty of questioning all that we believe.

It is true that this duty is a hard one, and the doubt which comes out of it is often a very bitter thing. It leaves us bare and powerless where we thought that we were safe and strong. To know all about anything is to know how to deal with it under all circumstances. We feel much happier and more secure when we think we know precisely what to do, no matter what happens, than when we have lost our way and do not know where to turn. And if we have supposed ourselves to know all about anything, and to be capable of doing what is fit in regard to it, we naturally do not like to find that we are really ignorant and powerless, that we have to begin again at the beginning, and try to learn what the thing is and how it is to be dealt with—if indeed anything can be learnt about it. It is the sense of power attached to a sense of knowledge that makes men desirous of believing, and afraid of doubting.

This sense of power is the highest and best of pleasures when the belief on which it is founded is a true belief, and has been fairly earned by investigation. For then we may justly feel that it is common property, and holds good for others as well as for ourselves. Then we may be glad, not that *I* have learned secrets by which I am safer and stronger, but that *we men* have got mastery over more of the world; and we shall be strong, not for ourselves, but in the name of Man and in his strength. But if the belief has been accepted on insufficient evidence, the pleasure is a stolen one. Not only does it deceive ourselves by giving us a sense of power which we do not really possess, but it is sinful, because it is stolen in defiance of our duty to mankind. That duty is to guard ourselves from such beliefs as from a pestilence, which may shortly master our own body and then spread to the rest of the town. What would be thought of one who, for the sake of a sweet fruit, should deliberately run the risk of bringing a plague upon his family and his neighbours?

And, as in other such cases, it is not the risk only which has to be considered; for a bad action is always bad at the time when it is done, no matter what happens afterwards. Every time we let ourselves believe for unworthy reasons, we weaken our powers of self-control, of doubting, of judicially and fairly weighing evidence. We all suffer severely enough from the maintenance and support of false beliefs and the fatally wrong actions which they lead to, and the evil born when one such belief is entertained is great and wide. But a greater and wider evil arises when the credulous character is maintained and supported, when a habit of believing for unworthy reasons is fostered and made permanent. If I steal money from any person, there may be no harm done by the mere transfer of possession; he may not feel the loss, or it may prevent him from using the money badly. But I cannot help doing this great wrong towards Man, that I make myself dishonest. What hurts society is not that it should lose its property, but that it should become a den of thieves; for then it must cease to be society. This is why we ought not to do evil that good may come; for at any rate this great evil has come, that we have done evil and are made wicked thereby. In like manner, if I let myself believe anything on insufficient evidence, there may be no great harm done by the mere belief; it may be true after all, or I may never have occasion to exhibit it in outward acts. But I cannot help doing this great wrong towards Man, that I make myself credulous. The danger to society is not merely that it should believe wrong things, though that is great enough; but that it should become credulous, and lose the habit of testing things and inquiring into them; for then it must sink back into savagery.

The harm which is done by credulity in a man is not confined to the fostering of a credulous character in others, and consequent support of false beliefs. Habitual want of care about what I believe leads to habitual want of care in others about the truth of what is told to me. Men speak the truth to one another when each reveres the truth in his own mind and in the other's mind; but how shall my friend revere the truth in my mind when I myself am careless about it, when I believe things because I want to believe them, and because they are comforting and pleasant? Will he not learn to cry, "Peace," to me, when there is no peace? By such a course I shall surround myself with a thick atmosphere of falsehood and fraud, and in that I must live. It may matter little to me, in my cloud-castle of sweet illusions and darling lies; but it matters much to Man that I have made my neighbours ready to deceive. The credulous man is father to the liar and the cheat; he lives in the bosom of this his family, and it is no marvel if he should become even as they are. So closely are our duties knit together, that whoso shall keep the whole law, and yet offend in one point, he is guilty of all.

To sum up: it is wrong always, everywhere, and for any one, to believe anything upon insufficient evidence.

If a man, holding a belief which he was taught in childhood or persuaded of afterwards, keeps down and pushes away any doubts which arise about it in his mind, purposely avoids the reading of books and the company of men that call in question or discuss it, and regards as impious those questions which cannot easily be asked without disturbing it—the life of that man is one long sin against mankind.

If this judgment seems harsh when applied to those simple souls who have never known better, who have been brought up from the cradle with a horror of doubt, and taught that their eternal welfare depends on what they believe, then it leads to the very serious question, Who hath made Israel to sin? . . .

Inquiry into the evidence of a doctrine is not to be made once for all, and then taken as finally settled. It is never lawful to stifle a doubt; for either it can be honestly answered by means of the inquiry already made, or else it proves that the inquiry was not complete.

"But," says one, "I am a busy man; I have no time for the long course of study which would be necessary to make me in any degree a competent judge of certain questions, or even able to understand the nature of the arguments." Then he should have no time to believe. . . .

• 15 •

IS TRUTH RELATIVE? *

William Pepperell Montague (1873–1953)

. . . There are, I believe, three . . . reasons for the growth of . . . relativism: (1) its apparent connection with the doctrine of evolution; (2) its apparent connection with the attitude of scepticism; (3) an ambiguity of the term "truth." Let us consider these reasons in turn.

The theory of evolution has made us familiar with the extent to which the universe is pervaded by change; even the things that appear to be most permanent, such as the heavenly bodies, the seas and mountains, and the species of plants and animals, are in a process of change. Human institutions and human beliefs that at one time seemed eternal are now being revised. It is natural for us to suppose that this evolutionary process to which all existing things are subject should extend to the realm of logical meaning; and consequently we tend to regard the notion of an unchangeable system of truth as a relic of the pre-Darwinian age. Yet while the extension of the notion of change from the things of physics to the things of logic may be natural, it is absolutely unjustifiable and leads only to confusion. In the first place, change itself has no meaning unless the terms of the process remain fixed. I cannot speak of a man changing from youth to age, or of a species changing from simian to human, unless the terms "youth," "age," "simian," "human," are supposed to preserve their meanings unchanged. What holds true of logical terms holds true equally of propositions which are relations between terms. If the proposition that the earth has been spherical for the ten billion years prior to the year 1900 is true at this moment, then that proposition will always be true on pain of losing its meaning as a proposition. The earth might change to-morrow from a globe to a disc without changing the truth of the above proposition. In short, the maxims: *True for one, true for all* and *once true, always true*, apply not only to all abstract or non-existential propositions, but to all other propositions in so far as they are made thoroughly unambiguous with respect to the time and space of the facts asserted. Change resides only in physical processes and in the psychological processes by which we

* From chapter 5, section 3 of *The Ways of Knowing* (1925). Reprinted with the permission of the publisher, George Allen & Unwin Ltd., London. The title of this selection has been supplied by the editors.

become aware of physical processes. But between those processes and the logical relations which they reveal there is fixed a gulf which no change can cross.

Let us turn now to the second of the three causes for the spread of the doctrine of relativism, *viz.* its connection with scepticism. And here the relativistic pragmatist can make out a somewhat better case. We may imagine him to speak to us as follows: "You talk about an absolute truth, independent of anyone's belief in it or knowledge of it. Well, supposing that there were such a thing, we could never attain it; or at least if we did attain it, we could never recognize it for what it was. All that we can know in the way of truth is something that is believed. Each man calls his own belief by the eulogistic name of *truth*, and with respect to this as an absolute standard, he describes his neighbour's opinions by such uncomplimentary names as 'apparent truths' or 'subjective beliefs.' Consequently, we pragmatists, recognizing this universal shortcoming of human nature, are frank enough to say that there is no truth with a capital T; no absolute impersonal objective reality, not even our own, and that whether we like it or not we have to put up with *the best in the way of belief.* We may still use the word truth in this semi-subjective sense, and it is in this sense that truth is relative to different persons and subject to change."

Now, the only trouble with this reply of the pragmatist is that it is a virtual confession that the relativistic feature of his doctrine, when freed from ambiguities, reduces to pure scepticism. For scepticism is the theory that truth in its objective sense is unattainable by any means within our power. The only difference between pragmatic relativism and scepticism is that the former doctrine uses the word "truth" in a purely subjective sense that is different from the sense in which it is used by the other methodological theories. The thoroughgoing sceptic believes with the relativist that we possess beliefs which we prefer to those of our neighbours, but he gives himself no false verbal comfort by calling these preferred beliefs "truth." He reserves that word for the objective reality which he thinks lies beyond the reach of our knowledge. . . .

The third of the reasons for the popularity of Epistemological relativism may be stated as follows: *All truth depends upon or is in part created by individuals. It is, therefore, inseparable from them and relative to them; and as such, it changes as they change.* Now there are two meanings involved in this statement of relativism which depend upon the two meanings that can be given to the word truth. By "truth" may be meant (1) whatever is believed, or (2) whatever is real or is a fact. If the word is taken in the first or subjective sense, then the relativistic principle that truth changes becomes a truism, for it means only that *people's beliefs change as people's minds change.* If truth is taken in the second or objective sense, the relativistic principle ceases to be a truism and becomes a paradox, for it then means that *the facts or realities of the world change as people's minds change.* We may illustrate the difference by the following example: " 'That the earth is flat' was for the ancients an obvious truth; 'that the earth is round' is for us an established truth. Their truth was not our truth. Truth, therefore, is relative and changing, and what is true for one may be false for another." These statements sound pretty well, and we should probably pass them over unchallenged, because we should take for granted that the word "truth" was being used in its subjective sense as a synonym of belief. It is a truism that people's beliefs can differ, that one can believe what another disbelieves; and it is a commonplace that a change in beliefs took place with regard to the shape of the earth. The ancients believed it to be flat, and we believe it to be round. But if we were told that the author of the statements cited meant "truth" to be taken in the objective sense, we should suppose that he had been indulging in either a geological or a logical paradox. If he meant that the flatness of the earth was a truth (fact) in ancient times and also that its roundness was a truth (fact) in modern times, we should assume that he believed that the earth's shape had undergone a marvellous geological change from a disc to a globe. If in still adhering to the objective meaning of the term "truth" he denied that he intended any such geological absurdity as the above, we should have to assume that he was committing the still greater logical absurdity of supposing that the shape of the earth could be both flat and spherical at once.

The . . . doctrine of the relativity of truth is thus seen to owe some of its plausibility to an ambiguity. Before the ambiguity is revealed, the truism and the paradox conceal one another and unite to produce the appearance of a novel and important discovery. In exactly the same way a black cardboard seen through white tissue paper appears to be a single surface of grey. When we look at the thing edgewise, however, the effect of grey disappears and we see only the black and the white. So, when once we recognize the ambiguity of the term "truth," and insist upon the relativist . . . using the word in one sense or the other, we find only an ill-looking juxtaposition of the paradox that facts depend upon people believing them, and the truism that our beliefs about facts change and vary. In case the illustration chosen fails to satisfy the reader, I would suggest that he make up for himself examples of statements which can loosely be regarded as cases of "truth changing" or of "true for one but false for another," and see for himself whether a little analysis of the meanings involved in all such statements will not disclose the above-mentioned ambiguity or duplicity of the "truth" in question. . . .

• 16 •

EPISTEMOLOGICAL SKEPTICISM *

C. E. M. Joad (1891–1953)

. . . Let us suppose that I am looking at a star, Sirius say, on a dark night. If physics is to be believed, light waves which started to travel from Sirius many years ago reach (after a specified time which astronomers calculate) the earth, impinge upon my retinae and cause me to say that I am seeing Sirius. Now the Sirius about which they convey information to me is the Sirius which existed at the time when they started. This Sirius, may, however, no longer exist; it may have disappeared in the interim. To say that one can see what no longer exists is absurd. It follows that, whatever it is that I am seeing, it is not Sirius. What, in fact, I do see is a yellow patch of a particular size, shape and intensity. I infer that this yellow patch had an origin (with which it is connected by a continuous chain of physical events) several years ago and many million miles away. But this inference may be mistaken; the origin of the yellow patch, which I call a star, may be a blow on the nose, or a lamp hanging on the mast of a ship.

Nor is this the only inference involved. It is true that I *think* I am seeing a yellow patch, but am I really justified in holding this belief? So far as physics and physiology are concerned, all that we are entitled to say is that the optic nerve is being stimulated in a certain way, as a result of which certain events are being caused in the brain. Are we really justified in saying any more than this? Possibly we are . . . but it is important to realize that once again an inference is involved, and once again the inference may be mistaken. Directly we go beyond the bare statement "the optic nerve is being stimulated in such and such a way" and conclude from this fact "therefore I am seeing an object of such and such a character," we are drawing an inference and are liable to fall into error. What, then, if the physicist and physiologist are right, we in fact know are certain events taking place in our own brains. The outside world is not itself known; its existence

---

* Excerpted from *Guide to Modern Thought* (London: Faber and Faber, Ltd., 1933), pp. 88–93. Reprinted here with the kind permission of the Executors of the late C. E. M. Joad. The title of this selection has been supplied by the editors. Compare with selections 11 and 17.

is merely an inference due to the fact that we think these events must have a cause. . . .

If we accept the teaching of physics and physiology, what we know in perception are not the movements of matter, but certain events in ourselves connected with those movements; not objects external to ourselves, but the effects of the impact of light-rays and other forms of energy proceeding from these objects upon our bodies. . . .

What, then, is left in the world outside us? We cannot tell. . . .

· 17 ·

THE WORLD WE PERCEIVE *

Arthur E. Murphy (1901–   )

The contrast between mere ideas and their relations on the one hand and substantial matter of fact on the other is central to the common sense notion of a world we find and do not make, a world to which our ideas must conform if they are to be factually true and informationally reliable. And while common sense has had some very hard things said about it by sophisticated critics, it has the advantage, when it is about its own business, of being both common (that is, publicly sharable and testable) and sensible, which is more than can be said of many of the theories that the critics seek to put in its place. We shall do well, therefore, to start our inquiry from its standpoint, and see how far we can go with it. What is the world we find ourselves living in, the world which, to adapt a famous saying of Bishop Berkeley's, we need only open our eyes to see? The full answer to this question would require all the knowledge that men, starting by opening their eyes and looking, and proceeding by using their minds to inquire, and their eyes and hands again to test their ideas, have been able to accumulate, and all they may still accumulate by the further use of their senses and their minds. Fortunately we need not here undertake so full an answer. For whatever else or more this world may prove to be, it is at least the familiar world that we see with our eyes and handle with our hands, the world in which we move about and greet our friends and live and work

* From Part I, chapter 1 of *The Uses of Reason*. Copyright 1943 by The Macmillan Company and used with their permission. Compare with selections 11 and 16.

together. It is also the world in which we do our thinking, and what we can observe of it provides the clue and the test for beliefs about its more remote and perceptually inaccessible areas. We can construct in our minds a more intellectually coherent world, and wish for a more emotionally satisfying one, but in so far as our wishes and our intellectual constructions claim informational accuracy with respect to what is actually going on, or has occurred, or is likely to happen in this world in which, for better or worse, we find ourselves, they must meet the test of truthfulness by agreement with what we find this world to be when and in so far as we are able perceptually to observe it.

It is for this reason that the appeal to *experience*, to what we find when we actually observe things at first hand, as distinct from what we might antecedently think or desire them to be, has so important and honorable a place in the history of critical thought. The empiricists have been preeminently the *fact* men, where "fact" is simply something that is found to be so in tested experience, and their function has been to insist on the informational primacy (for reasonable belief) of what is thus discovered, whether we like it or not, and on the primary importance, for such discovery, of accurate observation through the senses, of what is going on around us. So far they have been plainly right, and we shall be on their side in all that follows. Nor is their doctrine a trivial or merely obvious one. There are indeed truths that a man need only open his eyes to see. But to open one's eyes and see what is there to be seen, honestly, accurately and without the bias of preconception, prejudice or tradition, is an intellectual, and not merely a physiological, achievement. The ability to *learn* by experience, that is, to derive ideas from what we observe and to correct beliefs in terms of what is found to be the case, is the most basic factor in our intellectual progress, when such progress actually occurs. And it involves as its precondition the capacity to see and report what happens in just those cases in which what happens does not agree with antecedent ideas, but stands in contrast to them as mere stubborn matter of fact, *to be* taken account of but not, as it stands, either "rational" or pleasant. It is no wonder, then, that modern philosophers have so often stressed the value of experience and tried to make it the standard for all thinking that pretends to informational accuracy concerning the world and ourselves.

But what do we *really* experience? What is the final and ultimate "given" to which our ideas have added nothing and about which, therefore, we cannot possibly be mistaken? . . . "Experience" in epistemological controversy may mean anything or nothing, and there have been appeals to all sorts of experience—"inner" or "outer," scientific, aesthetic or religious, fallible or infallible—for all sorts of purposes. What we propose to ask instead is what we experience, or are aware of, when we are observing the world perceptually, by seeing, hearing, smelling or handling the things in our more immediate bodily environment. This is *one* of the ways, at least, in which we find out, by observation, what is going on around us, and guide and correct our ideas by what we find. If we can see how experience functions in this capacity as a source of reliable information, we shall have a solid basis on which to proceed. . . .

There are three things about the process of perceptual observation, critically considered as a source of reliable information about ourselves and our bodily environment, that deserve special attention. First, this process, considered as a source of information, not merely as a physiological event, is fallible. Second, it is corrigible, and it is in the process of correction that the difference between reliable and unreliable information is reasonably made out. Third, it is quite ultimate for us as a source of information about the world, since there is no other or better way of finding out what we learn by its means. And what we learn in this way maintains itself, under philosophical scrutiny, as trustworthy information to which belief in other fields, so far as it refers to the same matters of fact, ought reasonably to conform.

First, perceptual observation is fallible. I use my eyes and my hands in observing objects in my bodily environment, and what I observe in this process is what is going on in the world, not what is going on in my body or in my mind when I observe it. And I observe such objects as they look, or feel or smell, under the conditions in which I can observe them; that is, in the relations in which they stand to me at that time. I can see objects under a variety of conditions, with the aid of a microscope or through blue spectacles or when I am so drunk that I cannot make out what they are. But I shall never see objects when I am not seeing them, or think of them when they are not objects of my thought. It has sometimes—rather oddly —been argued that this is proof that I am not "really" seeing them, or at least not seeing them as they "really" are. On the contrary, however, to see things as they look is evidently and naturally the way to see them, no other or better having yet been devised, and if what they "really" are is at all relevant to what as observable objects they are found to be, then it is through just this process that what they really are must be disclosed. It is quite true, however, that things, as thus observed, are not always what they seem. What looks to be a man may prove on inspection to have been a shadow, and the pink rats of drunken experience and epistemological controversy have no local habitation in my bodily environment, though under some conditions they seem to some people to be there. Hence, I must learn to look carefully, and to look again, and to guide my looking by the lessons of past experience, both my own and that of others as reliably reported to me. There is, however, no mystery about this. What we observe are objects and events in our bodily environment as they appear under the conditions in which we *can* observe them, and what they really are, in this context, is what they reliably prove to be on further perceptual inspection. . . .

Hence, secondly, perceptual observation is corrigible, and it is in this process of correction through further and more careful observation that the distinction between what is reliable in it, as information about the world, and what is unreliable appearance is reasonably made out. Those who seek to find in a single instance of such observation the infallible certainty in terms of which alone they can distinguish *real* knowledge from mere opinion, will stare fixedly at the object until it becomes transparent, and all they are aware of in it is what they *can* thus be certain about: the shape or color or feel of it which would be there even if they were drunk or dreaming, and about which there is, as they keep on telling themselves, "no reasonably probable shadow of doubt, no possible doubt whatever." The trouble is that while they will then know *something* certainly—unless, as their critics allege, they have been in error even here—what they know will no longer be a material object but only an impression, or sense-datum, which is not itself an object of perceptual observation at all, or a part of the material world. How to get from such disembodied fragments of epistemologically infallible experience to the outdoor world of men and events is a further problem, but for us a quite gratuitous one. The kind of criticism and correction that perceptual observation requires presupposes no such unprofitable quest for certainty. There are other means of correcting the illusion of the drunkard than that of retreating to a world so tenuous that there is nothing left in it that even a drunkard could be mistaken about. There is the process by which the sober man, or the drunkard when he becomes sober, learns, by observation, what sort of world he lives in. No single observation here is infallible; about any one the question can meaningfully be raised as to whether what is observed is, in fact, what it appears to be. Fortunately, however, while the question can be asked, it can also, sometimes, be answered beyond all reasonable doubt. The process of answering it, reasonably, is the process by means of which ideas are used in the pursuit of truth about the nature and behavior of the world of bodies of which our own bodies are a part. The aim of the rational criticism of belief on this subject is not to halt inquiry at the point at which we claim to know so little about the world that no question of error can arise, but to carry it through to a point at which we know enough to distinguish what is permanently reliable in our observations from what is random, superficial and misleading.

And, thirdly, this process of criticism is sufficient to show that, in the rational ordering of our beliefs, perceptual observation, as a self-correcting process, has a quite ultimate and fundamental place. We know that there is a world of bodies, because we perceive it, because we open our eyes and our minds to find ourselves involved in it and capable of learning the lessons it has to teach. If we did not know it in this way, it would be quite futile to try to "construct" it from private sense data, or deduce it from the necessities of speculative reason, or postulate it as the area in which our duty is to be done. Such constructions, postulations and deductions are familiar enough, but all are shamelessly parasitic on the information which perceptual observation provides about the kind of world we actually live in, the world to which, after many wanderings, their speculations somehow bring them back. There may . . . be much more in the "reality" to which they aspire than perceptual observation can disclose, but there cannot be less. Unless this "more" can be understood along with what we find out perceptually, and interpreted in conformity with its veracious and reliable testimony on the subjects with which it is competent to deal, the doctrine that reports it must remain suspect. What can we reason, but from what we know? And *part* of what we know—or have reliable information about —is the observable nature and behavior of objects in our bodily environment. The use of reason in the acquisition of this information, and the use of this information as a criterion for the credibility and authenticity of further beliefs to which it is pertinent are not the end and sum of human wisdom by any means. But they are somewhere near the beginning of it, and no theory, however exalted its pretensions, which ignores or falsifies their findings, can stand the test of rational examination.

PART IV

METAPHYSICS

MIND AS THE CAUSE AND DISPOSER OF ALL *
Plato (427–347 B.C.)

. . . Then I will tell you, said Socrates. When I was young, Cebes, I had a prodigious desire to know that department of philosophy which is called the investigation of nature; to know the causes of things, and why a thing is and is created or destroyed appeared to me to be a lofty profession; and I was always agitating myself with the consideration of questions such as these: Is the growth of animals the result of some decay which the hot and cold principle contracts, as some have said? Is the blood the element with which we think, or the air, or the fire? or perhaps nothing of the kind —but the brain may be the originating power of the perceptions of hearing and sight and smell, and memory and opinion may come from them, and science may be based on memory and opinion when they have attained fixity. And then I went on to examine the corruption of them, and then to the things of heaven and earth, and at last I concluded myself to be utterly and absolutely incapable of these enquiries, as I will satisfactorily prove to you. For I was fascinated by them to such a degree that my eyes grew blind to things which I had seemed to myself, and also to others, to know quite well; I forgot what I had before thought self-evident truths; e.g., such a fact as that the growth of man is the result of eating and drinking; for when by the digestion of food flesh is added to flesh and bone to bone, and whenever there is an aggregation of congenial elements, the lesser bulk becomes larger and the small man great. Was not that a reasonable notion?

Yes, said Cebes, I think so.

Well; but let me tell you something more. There was a time when I thought that I understood the meaning of greater and less pretty well; and when I saw a great man standing by a little one, I fancied that one was taller than the other by a head; or one horse would appear to be greater than another horse; and still more clearly did I seem to preceive that ten

---

* From Plato's *Phaedo*, St. 96–99, translated from the Greek by Benjamin Jowett (1871), and used by permission of The Clarendon Press, Oxford. The title of this selection has been supplied by the editors. Compare with selections 20 and 27.

is two more than eight, and that two cubits are more than one, because two is the double of one.

And what is now your notion of such matters? said Cebes.

I should be far enough from imagining, he replied, that I knew the cause of any of them, by heaven I should; for I cannot satisfy myself that, when one is added to one, the one to which the addition is made becomes two, or that the two units added together make two by reason of the addition. I cannot understand how when separated from the other, each of them was one and not two, and now, when they are brought together, the mere juxtaposition or meeting of them should be the cause of their becoming two: neither can I understand how the division of one is the way to make two; for then a different cause would produce the same effect, as in the former instance the addition and juxtaposition of one to one was the cause of two, in this the separation and subtraction of one from the other would be the cause. Nor am I any longer satisfied that I understand the reason why one or anything else is either generated or destroyed or is at all, but I have in mind some confused notion of a new method, and can never admit the other.

Then I heard some one reading, as he said, from a book of Anaxagoras, that mind was the disposer and cause of all, and I was delighted at this notion, which appeared quite admirable, and I said to myself: If mind is the disposer, mind will dispose all for the best, and put each particular in the best place; and I argued that if any one desired to find out the cause of the generation or destruction or existence of anything, he must find out what state of being or doing or suffering was best for that thing, and therefore a man had only to consider the best for himself and others, and then he would also know the worse, since the same science comprehended both. And I rejoiced to think that I had found in Anaxagoras a teacher of the causes of existence such as I desired, and I imagined that he would tell me first whether the earth is flat or round; and whichever was true, he would proceed to explain the cause and the necessity of this being so, and then he would teach me the nature of the best and show that this was best; and if he said that the earth was in the centre, he would further explain that this position was the best, and I should be satisfied with the explanation given, and not want any other sort of cause. And I thought that I would then go on and ask him about the sun and moon and stars, and that he would explain to me their comparative swiftness, and their returnings and various states, active and passive, and how all of them were for the best. For I could not imagine that when he spoke of mind as the disposer of them, he would give any other account of their being as they are, except that this was best; and I thought that when he had explained to me in detail the cause of each and the cause of all, he would go on to explain to me what was best for each and what was good for all. These hopes I would not have sold for a large sum of money, and I seized the books and read them as fast as I could in my eagerness to know the better and the worse.

What expectations I had formed, and how grievously was I disappointed! As I proceeded, I found my philosopher altogether forsaking mind or any other principle of order, but having recourse to air, and ether, and water, and other eccentricities. I might compare him to a person who began by maintaining generally that mind is the cause of the actions of Socrates, but who, when he endeavoured to explain the causes of my several actions in detail, went on to show that I sit here because my body is made up of bones and muscles; and the bones, as he would say, are hard and have joints which divide them, and the muscles are elastic, and they cover the bones, which have also a covering or environment of flesh and skin which contains them; and as the bones are lifted at their joints by the contraction or relaxation of the muscles, I am able to bend my limbs, and this is why I am sitting here in curved posture—that is what he would say; and he would have a similar explanation of my talking to you, which he would attribute to sound, and air, and hearing, and he would assign ten thousand other causes of the same sort, forgetting to mention the true cause, which is, that the Athenians have thought fit to condemn me, and accordingly I have thought it better and more right to remain here and undergo my sentence; for I am inclined to think that these muscles and bones of mine would have gone off long ago to Megara or Boeotia—by the dog, they would, if they had been moved only by their own idea of what was best, and if I had not chosen the better and nobler part, instead of playing truant and running away, of enduring any punishment which the state inflicts. There is surely a strange confusion of causes and conditions in all this. It may be said, indeed, that without bones and muscles and the other parts of the body I cannot execute my purposes. But to say that I do as I do because of them and that this is the way in which mind acts, and not from the choice of the best, is a very careless and idle mode of speaking. I wonder that they cannot distinguish the cause from the condition, which the many, feeling about in the dark, are always mistaking and misnaming. And thus one man makes a vortex all round and steadies the earth by the heaven; another gives the air as a support to the earth, which is a sort of broad trough. Any power which in arranging them as they are arranges them for the best never enters into their minds; and instead of finding any superior strength in it, they rather expect to discover another Atlas of the world who is stronger and more everlasting and more containing than the good; of the obligatory and containing power of the good they think nothing; and yet this is the principle which I would fain learn if any one would teach me. . . .

• 19 •

ON CHANGE AND THE FOUR CAUSES *

Aristotle (384–322 B.C.)

[I. CHANGE]

1. . . . Everything that changes is something and is changed by something and into something. That by which it is changed is the immediate mover; that which is changed, the matter; that into which it is changed, the form. The process, then, will go on to infinity, if not only the bronze comes to be round but also the round or the bronze comes to be; therefore there must be a stop.

Note, next, that each substance comes into being out of something that shares its name. (Natural objects and other things both rank as substances.) For things come into being either by art or by nature or by luck or by spontaneity. Now art is a principle of movement in something other than the thing moved, nature is a principle in the thing itself (for man begets man), and the other causes are privations of these two.

There are three kinds of substance—the matter, which is a 'this' in appearance (for all things that are characterized by contact and not by organic unity are matter and substratum, e.g., fire, flesh, head; for these are all matter, and the last matter is the matter of that which is in the full sense substance); the nature, which is a 'this' or positive state towards which movement takes place; and again, thirdly, the particular substance which is composed of these two, e.g., Socrates or Callias. Now in some cases the 'this' does not exist apart from the composite substance,

---

* Part I is from Aristotle's *Metaphysics*, Book XII, chapters 3 and 5; translated from the Greek by W. D. Ross, and reprinted by permission of The Clarendon Press, Oxford. Part II is from Aristotle's *Physics*, Book II, parts of chapters 3, 4, 7, and 8; translated from the Greek by W. H. Hay especially for this volume. The title of this selection has been supplied by the editors. Compare with selections 20 and 22.

e.g., the form of house does not so exist, unless the art of building exists apart (nor is there generation and destruction of these forms, but it is in another way that the house apart from its matter, and health, and all ideals of art, exist and do not exist); but if the 'this' exists apart from the concrete thing, it is only in the case of natural objects. And so Plato was not far wrong when he said that there are as many Forms as there are kinds of natural object (if there *are* Forms distinct from the things of this earth). The moving causes exist as things preceding the effects, but causes in the sense of definitions are simultaneous with their effects. For when a man is healthy, then health also exists; and the shape of a bronze sphere exists at the same time as the bronze sphere. (But we must examine whether any form also survives afterwards. For in some cases there is nothing to prevent this; e.g., the soul may be of this sort—not all soul but the reason; for presumably it is impossible that *all* soul should survive.) Evidently then there is no necessity, on this ground at least, for the existence of the Ideas. For man is begotten by man, a given man by an individual father; and similarly in the arts; for the medical art is the formal cause of health. . . .

2. Some things can exist apart and some cannot, and it is the former that are substances. And therefore all things have the same causes, because, without substances, modifications and movements do not exist. Further, these causes will probably be soul and body, or reason and desire and body.

And in yet another way, analogically identical things are principles, i.e., actuality and potency; but these also are not only different for different things but also apply in different ways to them. For in some cases the same thing exists at one time actually and at another potentially, e.g., wine or flesh or man does so. (And these two fall under the above-named causes. For the form exists actually if it can exist apart, and so does the complex of form and matter, and the privation, e.g., darkness or disease; but the matter exists potentially; for this is that which can become qualified either by the form or by the privation.) But the distinction of actuality and potentiality applies in another way to cases where the matter of cause and of effect is not the same, in some of which cases the form is not the same but different; e.g., the cause of man is (1) the elements in man (viz., fire and earth as matter, and the peculiar form), and further (2) something else outside, i.e., the father, and (3) besides these the sun and its oblique course, which are neither matter nor form nor privation of man nor of the same species with him, but moving causes.

Further, one must observe that some causes can be expressed in universal terms, and some cannot. The proximate principles of all things are the 'this' which is proximate in actuality, and another which is proximate in potentiality. The universal causes, then, of which we spoke do not *exist*.

For it is the individual that is the originative principle of the individuals. For while man is the originative principle of man universally, there *is* no universal man, but Peleus is the originative principle of Achilles, and your father of you, and this particular *b* of this particular *ba*, though *b* in general is the originative principle of *ba* taken without qualification. . . .

[II. FOUR CAUSES]

. . . We do not think that we know a thing until we grasp the "why" of it, that is, the primary cause of it. It is plain that we must grasp the "why" of coming into existence, of ceasing to exist, and every natural change, so that knowing the origin of such things, we may try to refer each thing we investigate to its origin. MATERIAL CAUSE: In one case what is called a cause is *that out of which something comes into existence and which continues to exist in the result*, for example, the bronze of a statue, the silver of a bowl. . . . FORMAL CAUSE: In another case what is called a cause is *the form* and the model of a thing. This is the definition, the essence, and the genus of a thing, for example, the ratio of two to one and in general number is the cause of the octave of a tone. EFFICIENT or MOVING CAUSE: In a third case what is called a cause is *the primary source of the change or coming to rest*, for example, a man who gave advice is the cause, a father the cause of the child, and in general *the maker is the cause of what is made* and one who changes is the cause of a thing being changed. FINAL CAUSE: In still a fourth case what is called a cause is the end or *that for the sake of which*, for example, health is the end of taking a walk. For when we ask, "Why is he taking a walk?" and answer, "For his health" we think that we have pointed out the cause. . . . These are about all the things that are called causes.

Since we use the word, cause, in many ways, it follows that there are many causes of the same things, and not in the trivial sense of the causes of accidental features. For example, the sculptor and the bronze are both causes of a statue, not of accidental features of it, but of it being a statue. The bronze is the material and the sculptor is that from which the change originated. . . .

All causes may be spoken of as potential or as actual. For example, we may say either that the builder or that the builder building is the cause of a house being built. . . . The difference between the potential and the actual causes is that the actual as a cause exists and ceases to exist at the same time as that of which it is the cause. For example, a man is curing disease just while the patient is getting well, and a man is building just while the house is being built. This is not always true for potential causes, since, for example, the house does not cease to exist when the builder dies. . . .

It is plain that we have given the complete list of kinds of cause, since it is the same as the number of the kinds of questions that are asked by "Why?" For to answer "Why?" about unchanging things eventually brings us to the form, what it is (such as in mathematics, to the definition of "straight line" or "commensurable"). The question may bring us to what first changed. For example, "Why did they go to war?" is answered by "Because there had been a border raid." The question "Why?" may be asking: For the sake of what? and be answered, for example, by "so that they may maintain their rule over the district." The question "Why?" about things that have come into existence may be answered by referring to the material out of which they were made. It is plain that these are causes and that there are just four. It is the job of the scientist to know about all, and by referring to all of them he will render an account of why in a scientific manner, in terms of the matter, the form, that which changes things, and that for the sake of which. The three last are often found together in one thing, since what it is and that for the sake of which it is are the same, and that from which the change first comes is the same in form with them. For man generates man, and in general all things that are changing *are changing because* something else is changing them. . . .

. . . In things that come into existence by nature there is that for the sake of which they come into existence. Further, where there is an end-stage, what came first and what succeeded it were done for the sake of that end-stage. Now as in human action, so in nature; and as in nature so in each case of human action, unless something interferes. Things are done for the sake of something, therefore in nature things happen for the sake of something. For example, if a house should come into existence naturally, it would do so in the same way that it is now made by human skill. Also if things that come into existence naturally should also be brought into existence by human skill, it would be in the same way as it happens naturally. In general, human skill completes what nature has not been able to carry through, and imitates nature. If, then, works of human skill are done for the sake of something, it is plain that things happen in the same way in nature. For the relation of the later stages to the earlier is much alike in products of human skill and products of nature. This is plainest in the case of animals and living creatures other than men. For they make things without an acquired skill, without having investigated, and without having planned. For this reason people debate whether spiders, ants, and things of that sort work by intelligence or by something else.

So little by little it becomes clear that even in plants suitable things come into existence for the sake of an end result. For example, leaves grow for the sake of the protection of the fruit from the sun. So if it is by nature and for the sake of something that the swallow makes a nest and a spider a web, and plants grow leaves for the sake of the fruit and roots down (not up) for the sake of nourishment, it is plain that there is this kind of use in things that come into existence by nature. Nature means sometimes matter, sometimes form. Since the latter is the state of the end result and since the rest is for the sake of the end result, the form is that for the sake of which.

Mistakes happen even in things done by human skill. For example, the grammarian makes a mistake in writing and the doctor pours out the wrong dose of a drug. It is clear then that mistakes are to be met with in things done by nature. For if there are instances of skill in which it was done right for the sake of a certain end, and cases of failure where the same end result was attempted but not achieved, so it might be in natural processes. The births of abnormal monsters would be failures to achieve that for the sake of which it was all done. . . .

The purpose and the means to it may come about by chance. For example, it is by chance, we say, that a stranger comes by, pays a ransom for a captive, and goes on, when it is *as if* he had come for the purpose of doing it, though it was *not* for the purpose of doing that that he came. . . . But when some sort of thing happens always or almost always, it has not happened accidentally or by chance. In natural processes it happens always in the same way, unless something interferes.

It would be strange to think that something was not done for the sake of something else just because we do not see the man who does it deliberating. There is no deliberation either in cases of skill. If the skill of shipbuilding were in the wood itself, it would make the same thing by nature. Therefore, if purpose is present in cases of skill, it is present in nature. A clear example is that of a doctor curing himself. That is the way nature is. It is clear then that nature is a cause and the sort of cause which is that for the sake of which things are done. . . .

• 20 •

TELEOLOGY *

Aristotle (384–322 B.C.)

1. . . . . Nature belongs to the class of causes which act for the sake of something. . . .

A difficulty presents itself: why should not nature work, not for the sake of something, nor because it is better so, but just as the sky rains, not in order to make the corn grow, but of necessity? What is drawn up must cool, and what has been cooled must become water and descend, the result of this being that the corn grows. Similarly if a man's crop is spoiled on the threshing-floor, the rain did not fall for the sake of this—in order that the crop might be spoiled—but that result just followed. Why then should it not be the same with the parts in nature, e.g., that our teeth should come up *of necessity*—the front teeth sharp, fitted for tearing, the molars broad and useful for grinding down the food—since they did not arise for this end, but it was merely a coincident result; and so with all other parts in which we suppose that there is purpose? Wherever then all the parts came about just what they would have been if they had come to be for an end, such things survived, being organized spontaneously in a fitting way; whereas those which grew otherwise perished and continue to perish. . . .

Such are the arguments . . . which may cause difficulty on this point. Yet it is impossible that this should be the true view. For teeth and all other natural things either invariably or normally come about in a given way; but of not one of the results of chance or spontaneity is this true. We do not ascribe to chance or mere coincidence the frequency of rain in winter, but frequent rain in summer we do; nor heat in the dog-days, but only if we have it in winter. If then, it is agreed that things are either the

* Part 1 is from Aristotle's *Physics*, Bk. II, ch. 8; translated by R. P. Hardie and R. K. Gaye. Part 2 is from *On the Soul*, Bk. II, ch. 4; translated by J. A. Smith. Part 3 is from *On Generation and Corruption*, Bk. II, ch. 10; translated by H. H. Joachim. Reprinted by permission of The Clarendon Press, Oxford. Part 4 is from Thomas Aquinas: *Summa Contra Gentiles*, Bk. III, chs. 2 and 24, translated by Anton C. Pegis and reprinted by the kind permission of Random House, Inc., New York, publishers of *Basic Writings of St. Thomas Aquinas* (1945). The title of this selection has been supplied by the editors. Compare with selections 18, 19, and 27.

result of coincidence or for an end, and these cannot be the result of coincidence or spontaneity, it follows that they must be for an end; and that such things are all due to nature even the champions of the theory which is before us would agree. Therefore action for an end is present in things which come to be and are by nature.

Further, where a series has a completion, all the preceding steps are for the sake of that. Now surely as in intelligent action, so in nature; and as in nature, so it is in each action, if nothing interferes. Now intelligent action is for the sake of an end; therefore the nature of things also is so. Thus if a house, e.g., had been a thing made by nature, it would have been made in the same way as it is now by art; and if things made by nature were made also by art, they would come to be in the same way as by nature. Each step then in the series is for the sake of the next; and generally art partly completes what nature cannot bring to a finish, and partly imitates her. If, therefore, artificial products are for the sake of an end, so clearly also are natural products. The relation of the later to the earlier terms of the series is the same in both. . . .

. . . Those things are natural which, by a continuous movement originated from an internal principle, arrive at some completion: the same completion is not reached from every principle; nor any chance completion, but always the tendency in each is towards the same end, if there is no impediment. . . .

. . . When an event takes place always or for the most part, it is not incidental or by chance. In natural products the sequence is invariable, if there is no impediment.

It is absurd to suppose that purpose is not present because we do not observe the agent deliberating. Art does not deliberate . . .

2. . . . We must treat of nutrition and reproduction, for the nutritive soul is found along with all the others and is the most primitive and widely distributed power of soul, being indeed that one in virtue of which all are said to have life. The acts in which it manifests itself are reproduction and the use of food—reproduction, I say, because for any living thing that has reached its normal development and which is un-mutilated, and whose mode of generation is not spontaneous, the most natural act is the production of another like itself, an animal producing an animal, a plant a plant, in order that, as far as its nature allows, it may partake in the eternal and divine. That is the goal towards which all things strive, that for the sake of which they do whatsoever their nature renders possible. . . .

3. . . . Coming-to-be and passing-away will . . . always be continuous, and will never fail owing to the cause we have stated (the permanence of

matter) . . . And this continuity has a sufficient reason on our theory. For in all things, as we affirm, nature always strives after "the better." Now "being" . . . is better than "non-being": but not all things can possess "being," since they are too far removed from the "originative source." God therefore adopted the remaining alternative, and fulfilled the perfection of the universe by making coming-to-be uninterrupted: for the greatest possible coherence would thus be secured to existence, because, that "coming-to-be should itself come to be perpetually" is the closest approximation to eternal being. . . .

[4. Teleology in Aristotle: As Interpreted by Aquinas]

. . . Natural bodies devoid of knowledge are moved and act for the sake of an end. For they tend to an end as directed thereto by an intelligent substance, in the same way as an arrow, directed by the archer, tends to the mark. Because as the arrow receives its direction to a fixed end through the impulse of the archer, so, too, natural bodies receive an inclination to their natural ends from their natural movers, from whom they derive their forms, powers and movements.

Therefore it is also clear that every work of nature is the work of an intelligent substance. . . .

. . . Every agent acts either by nature or by intellect. Now there can be no doubt that those which act by intellect act for an end, since they act *with* an intellectual preconception of what they attain by their action, and they act *through* such a preconception; for this is to act by intellect. Now just as in the preconceiving intellect there exists the entire likeness of the effect that is attained by the action of the intellectual being, so in the natural agent there pre-exists the likeness of the natural effect, by virtue of which the action is determined to the appointed effect, for fire begets fire, and an olive produces an olive. Therefore, even as that which acts by intellect tends by its action to a definite end, so also does that which acts by nature. Therefore every agent acts for an end. . . .

• 21 •

MIND AND MATTER *

George Berkeley (1685–1753)

It is evident to anyone who takes a survey of the *objects of human knowledge*, that they are either *ideas* actually imprinted on the senses; or else such as are perceived by attending to the passions and operations of the mind; or lastly, *ideas* formed by help of memory and imagination—either compounding, dividing, or barely representing those originally perceived in the aforesaid ways. By sight I have the ideas of light and colours, with their several degrees and variations. By touch I perceive hard and soft, heat and cold, motion and resistance; and of all these more and less either as to quantity or degree. Smelling furnishes me with odours; the palate with tastes; and hearing conveys sounds to the mind in all their variety of tone and composition.

And as several of these are observed to accompany each other, they come to be marked by one name, and so to be reputed as one *thing*. Thus, for example, a certain colour, taste, smell, figure and consistence having been observed to go together, are accounted one distinct thing, signified by the name apple; other collections of ideas constitute a stone, a tree, a book, and the like sensible things; which as they are pleasing or disagreeable excite the passions of love, hatred, joy, grief, and so forth.

But besides all that endless variety of ideas or objects of knowledge, there is likewise Something which knows or perceives them; and exercises divers operations, as willing, imagining, remembering, about them. This perceiving, active being is what I call *mind, spirit, soul* or *myself*. By which words I do not denote any one of my ideas, but a thing entirely distinct from them, wherein they exist, or, which is the same thing, whereby they are perceived; for the existence of an idea consists in being perceived.

That neither our thoughts, nor passions, nor ideas formed by the imagination, exist without the mind is what everybody will allow. And to me it seems no less evident that the various sensations or ideas imprinted on the Sense, however blended or combined together (that is, whatever ob-

---

* From A *Treatise Concerning the Principles of Human Knowledge*, Part I, sections 1–10, 17–21. The title of this selection has been supplied by the editors. Compare with selections 11 and 27.

jects they compose), cannot exist otherwise than in a mind perceiving them. I think an intuitive knowledge may be obtained of this, by any one that shall attend to what is meant by the term *exist* when applied to sensible things. The table I write on I say exists; that is, I see and feel it: and if I were out of my study I should say it existed; meaning thereby that if I was in my study I might perceive it, or that some other spirit actually does perceive it. There was an odour, that is, it was smelt; there was a sound, that is, it was heard; a colour or figure, and it was perceived by sight or touch. This is all that I can understand by these and the like expressions. For as to what is said of the *absolute* existence of unthinking things, without any relation to their being perceived, that is to me perfectly unintelligible. Their *esse* is *percipi*; nor is it possible they should have any existence out of the minds or thinking things which perceive them.

It is indeed an opinion strangely prevailing amongst men, that houses, mountains, rivers and in a word all sensible objects, have an existence, natural or real, distinct from their being perceived by the understanding. But, with how great an assurance and acquiescence soever this Principle may be entertained in the world, yet whoever shall find in his heart to call it in question may, if I mistake not, perceive it to involve a manifest contradiction. For, what are the aforementioned objects but the things we perceive by sense? and what do we perceive besides our own ideas or sensations? and is it not plainly repugnant that any one of these, or any combination of them, should exist unperceived?

If we thoroughly examine this tenet it will, perhaps, be found at bottom to depend on the doctrine of *abstract ideas*. For can there be a nicer strain of abstraction than to distinguish the existence of sensible objects from their being perceived, so as to conceive them existing unperceived? Light and colours, heat and cold, extension and figures—in a word the things we see and feel—what are they but so many sensations, notions, ideas or impressions on the sense? and is it possible to separate, even in thought, any of these from perception? For my part, I might as easily divide a thing from itself. I may, indeed, divide in my thoughts, or conceive apart from each other, those things which perhaps I never perceived by sense so divided. Thus, I imagine the trunk of a human body without the limbs, or conceive the smell of a rose without thinking on the rose itself. So far, I will not deny, I can abstract; if that may properly be called *abstraction* which extends only to the conceiving separately such objects as it is possible may really exist or be actually perceived asunder. But my conceiving or imagining power does not extend beyond the possibility of real existence or perception. Hence, as it is impossible for me to see or feel anything without an actual sensation of that thing, so is it impossible for me to conceive in my thoughts any sensible thing or object distinct from the sensation or perception of it. . . .

Some truths there are so near and obvious to the mind that a man need only open his eyes to see them. Such I take this important one to be, *viz.* that all the choir of heaven and furniture of the earth, in a word all those bodies which compose the mighty frame of the world, have not any subsistence without a mind; that their *being* is to be perceived or known; that consequently so long as they are not actually perceived by me, or do not exist in my mind, or that of any other created spirit, they must either have no existence at all, or else subsist in the mind of some Eternal Spirit: it being perfectly unintelligible, and involving all the absurdity of abstraction, to attribute to any single part of them an existence independent of a spirit. . . .

From what has been said it is evident there is not any other Substance than *Spirit*, or that which perceives. But, for the fuller proof of this point, let it be considered the sensible qualities are colour, figure, motion, smell, taste and such like, that is, the ideas perceived by sense. Now, for an idea to exist in an unperceiving thing is a manifest contradiction; for to have an idea is all one as to perceive: that therefore wherein colour, figure, and the like qualities exist must perceive them. Hence it is clear there can be no unthinking substance or substratum of those ideas.

But, say you, though the ideas themselves do not exist without the mind, yet there may be things like them, whereof they are copies or resemblances; which things exist without the mind, in an unthinking substance. I answer, an idea can be like nothing but an idea; a colour or figure can be like nothing but another colour or figure. If we look but never so little into our thoughts, we shall find it impossible for us to conceive a likeness except only between our ideas. Again I ask whether those supposed *originals*, or external things, of which our ideas are the pictures or representations, be themselves perceivable or no? If they are, then *they* are ideas, and we have gained our point: but if you say they are not, I appeal to any one whether it be sense to assert a colour is like something which is invisible; hard or soft, is like something which is intangible; and so of the rest.

Some there are who make a distinction betwixt *primary* and *secondary* qualities. By the former they mean extension, figure, motion, rest, solidity or impenetrability, and number; by the latter they denote all other sensible qualities, as colours, sounds, tastes, and so forth. The ideas we have of these last they acknowledge not to be the resemblances of anything existing without the mind, or unperceived: but they will have our ideas of the *primary qualities* to be patterns or images of things which

exist without the mind, in an unthinking substance which they call
Matter. By Matter, therefore, we are to understand an inert, senseless
substance, in which extension, figure, and motion do actually subsist. But
it is evident, from what we have already shewn, that extension, figure and
motion are only ideas existing in the mind, and that an idea can be like
nothing but another idea; and that consequently neither they nor their
archetypes can exist in an unperceiving substance. Hence it is plain that
the very notion of what is called *Matter* or *corporeal substance* involves a
contradiction in it. . . .

They who assert that figure, motion, and the rest of the primary or
original qualities do exist without the mind, in unthinking substances, do
at the same time acknowledge that colours, sounds, heat, cold, and such-
like secondary qualities, do not; which they tell us are sensations, existing
in the mind alone, that depend on and are occasioned by the different size,
texture, and motion of the minute particles of matter. This they take for
an undoubted truth, which they can demonstrate beyond all exception.
Now, if it be certain that those *original* qualities are inseparably united with
the other sensible qualities, and not, even in thought, capable of being
abstracted from them, it plainly follows that *they* exist only in the mind.
But I desire any one to reflect and try whether he can, by any abstraction
of thought, conceive the extension and motion of a body without all other
sensible qualities. For my own part, I see evidently that it is not in my
power to frame an idea of a body extended and moving, but I must withal
give it some colour or other sensible quality, which is acknowledged to
exist only in the mind. In short, extension, figure, and motion, abstracted
from all other qualities, are inconceivable. Where therefore the other
sensible qualities are, there must these be also, to wit, in the mind and
nowhere else. . . .

If we inquire into what the most accurate philosophers declare themselves to mean by *material substance*, we shall find them acknowledge
they have no other meaning annexed to those sounds but the idea of Being
in general, together with the relative notion of its supporting accidents.
The general idea of Being appeareth to me the most abstract and incomprehensible of all other; and as for its supporting accidents, this . . . cannot be understood in the common sense of those words: it must therefore
be taken in some other sense, but what that is they do not explain. So
that when I consider the two parts or branches which make the signification of the words *material substance*, I am convinced there is no distinct
meaning annexed to them. . . .

But, though it were possible that solid, figured, moveable substances may
exist without the mind, corresponding to the ideas we have of bodies, yet

how is it possible for us to know this? Either we must know it by Sense or by Reason. As for our senses, by them we have the knowledge only of our sensations, ideas, or those things that are immediately perceived by sense, call them what you will: but they do not inform us that things exist without the mind, or unperceived, like to those which are perceived. This the materialists themselves acknowledge.—It remains therefore that if we have any knowledge at all of external things, it must be by reason inferring their existence from what is immediately perceived by sense. But, what reason can induce us to believe the existence of bodies without the mind, from what we perceive, since the very patrons of Matter themselves do not pretend there is any necessary connection betwixt them and our ideas? I say it is granted on all hands (and what happens in dreams, frensies, and the like, puts it beyond dispute) that it is possible we might be affected with all the ideas we have now, though no bodies existed without resembling them. Hence it is evident the supposition of external bodies is not necessary for the producing our ideas; since it is granted they are produced sometimes, and might possibly be produced always, in the same order we see them in at present, without their concurrence.

But though we might possibly have all our sensations without them, yet perhaps it may be thought easier to conceive and explain the manner of their production, by supposing external bodies in their likeness rather than otherwise; and so it might be at least probable there are such things as bodies that excite their ideas in our minds. But neither can this be said. For, though we give the materialists their external bodies, they by their own confession are never the nearer knowing how our ideas are produced; since they own themselves unable to comprehend in what manner body can act upon spirit, or how it is possible it should imprint any idea in the mind. Hence it is evident the production of ideas or sensations in our minds, can be no reason why we should suppose Matter or corporeal substances; since that is acknowledged to remain equally inexplicable with or without this supposition. If therefore it were possible for bodies to exist without the mind, yet to hold they do so must needs be a very precarious opinion; since it is to suppose, without any reason at all, that God has created innumerable beings that are entirely useless, and serve to no manner of purpose.

In short, if there were external bodies, it is impossible we should ever come to know it; and if there were not, we might have the very same reasons to think there were that we have now. Suppose—what no one can deny possible—an intelligence, without the help of external bodies, to be affected with the same train of sensations or ideas that you are, imprinted in the same order and with like vividness in his mind. I ask whether that intelligence hath not all the reason to believe the existence of Corporeal Substances, represented by his ideas, and exciting them in his mind, that you can possibly have for believing the same thing? Of this there can be no question. Which one consideration were enough to make any reasonable person suspect the strength of whatever arguments he may think himself to have, for the existence of bodies without the mind. . . .

· 22 ·

CAUSATION AND NECESSITY *

David Hume (1711–1776)

WHY A CAUSE IS ALWAYS NECESSARY

. . . 'Tis a general maxim in philosophy, that *whatever begins to exist, must have a cause of existence.* This is commonly taken for granted in all reasonings, without any proof given or demanded. 'Tis suppos'd to be founded on intuition, and to be one of those maxims, which tho' they may be deny'd with the lips, 'tis impossible for men in their hearts really to doubt of. But if we examine this maxim . . . we shall discover in it no mark of any such intuitive certainty; but on the contrary shall find, that 'tis of a nature quite foreign to that species of conviction. . . .

. . . Here is an argument, which proves at once, that the foregoing proposition is neither intuitively nor demonstrably certain. We can never demonstrate the necessity of a cause to every new existence, or new modification of existence, without shewing at the same time the impossibility there is, that any thing can ever begin to exist without some productive principle; and where the latter proposition cannot be prov'd, we must despair of ever being able to prove the former. Now that the latter proposition is utterly incapable of a demonstrative proof, we may satisfy ourselves by considering, that as all distinct ideas are separable from each other, and as the ideas of cause and effect are evidently distinct, 'twill be easy for us to conceive any object to be non-existent this moment, and existent the next, without conjoining to it the distinct idea of a cause or productive principle. The separation, therefore, of the idea of a cause

* Bk. I, Part III, secs. 3 and 14 (in part) of A *Treatise of Human Nature* (1739). The title of this selection has been supplied by the editors. Compare with selections 12, 19, and 54.

from that of a beginning of existence, is plainly possible for the imagination; and consequently the actual separation of these objects is so far possible, that it implies no contradiction or absurdity; and is therefore incapable of being refuted by any reasoning from mere ideas; without which 'tis impossible to demonstrate the necessity of a cause.

Accordingly we shall find upon examination, that every demonstration, which has been produc'd for the necessity of a cause, is fallacious and sophistical. All the points of time and place, say some philosophers, in which we can suppose any object to begin to exist, are in themselves equal; and unless there be some cause, which is peculiar to one time and to one place, and which by that means determines and fixes the existence, it must remain in eternal suspence; and the object can never begin to be, for want of something to fix its beginning. But I ask; Is there any more difficulty in supposing the time and place to be fix'd without a cause, than to suppose the existence to be determin'd in that manner? The first question that occurs on this subject is always, *whether* the object shall exist or not: The next, *when* and *where* it shall begin to exist. If the removal of a cause be intuitively absurd in the one case, it must be so in the other: And if that absurdity be not clear without a proof in the one case, it will equally require one in the other. The absurdity, then, of the one supposition can never be a proof of that of the other; since they are both upon the same footing, and must stand or fall by the same reasoning.

The second argument, which I find us'd on this head, labours under an equal difficulty. Every thing, 'tis said, must have a cause; for if any thing wanted a cause, *it* would produce *itself*; that is, exist before it existed; which is impossible. But this reasoning is plainly unconclusive; because it supposes, that in our denial of a cause we still grant what we expressly deny, *viz.*, that there must be a cause; which therefore is taken to be the object itself; and *that*, no doubt, is an evident contradiction. But to say that any thing is produc'd, or to express myself more properly, comes into existence, without a cause, is not to affirm, that 'tis itself its own cause; but on the contrary, in excluding all external causes, excludes *a fortiori* the thing itself which is created. An object, that exists absolutely without any cause, certainly is not its own cause; and when you assert, that the one follows from the other, you suppose the very point in question, and take it for granted, that 'tis utterly impossible any thing can ever begin to exist without a cause, but that upon the exclusion of one productive principle, we must still have recourse to another.

'Tis exactly the same case with the third argument, which has been employ'd to demonstrate the necessity of a cause. Whatever is produc'd without any cause, is produc'd by *nothing*; or in other words, has nothing for its cause. But nothing can never be a cause, no more than it can be something, or equal to two right angles. By the same intuition, that we perceive nothing not to be equal to two right angles, or not to be something, we perceive, that it can never be a cause; and consequently must perceive, that every object has a real cause of its existence.

I believe it will not be necessary to employ many words in shewing the weakness of this argument, after what I have said of the foregoing. They are all of them founded on the same fallacy, and are deriv'd from the same turn of thought. 'Tis sufficient only to observe, that when we exclude all causes we really do exclude them, and neither suppose nothing nor the object itself to be the causes of the existence; and consequently can draw no argument from the absurdity of these suppositions to prove the absurdity of that exclusion. If every thing must have a cause, it follows, that upon the exclusion of other causes we must accept of the object itself or of nothing as causes. But 'tis the very point in question, whether every thing must have a cause or not; and therefore, according to all just reasoning, it ought never to be taken for granted.

They are still more frivolous, who say, that every effect must have a cause, because 'tis imply'd in the very idea of effect. Every effect necessarily presupposes a cause; effect being a relative term, of which cause is the correlative. But this does not prove, that every being must be preceded by a cause; no more than it follows, because every husband must have a wife, that therefore every man must be marry'd. The true state of the question is, whether every object, which begins to exist, must owe its existence to a cause; and this I assert neither to be intuitively nor demonstratively certain, and hope to have prov'd it sufficiently by the foregoing arguments. . . .

Of the Idea of Necessary Connexion

. . . *What is our idea of necessity, when we say that two objects are necessarily connected together?* . . . As we have no idea, that is not deriv'd from an impression, we must find some impression, that gives rise to this idea of necessity, if we assert we have really such an idea. In order to this I consider, in what objects necessity is commonly suppos'd to lie; and finding that it is always ascrib'd to causes and effects, I turn my eye to two objects suppos'd to be plac'd in that relation; and examine them in all the situations, of which they are susceptible. I immediately perceive, that they are *contiguous* in time and place, and that the object we call cause *precedes* the other we call effect. In no one instance can I go any farther, nor is it possible for me to discover any third relation betwixt these objects. I therefore enlarge my view to comprehend several instances; where I find like objects always existing in like relations of contiguity and succession. At first sight this seems to serve but little to my purpose. The reflection on several instances only repeats the same objects; and therefore can never give rise to a new idea. But upon farther inquiry I find, that the repetition is not in every particular the same, but produces a new impression, and by that means the idea, which I at present examine. For after a frequent repetition, I find, that upon the appearance of one of the objects, the mind is *determin'd* by custom to consider its usual attendant, and to consider it in a stronger light upon account of its relation to the first object. 'Tis this impression, then, or *determination,* which affords me the idea of necessity.

I doubt not but these consequences will at first sight be receiv'd without difficulty, as being evident deductions from principles, which we have already establish'd, and which we have often employ'd in our reasonings. This evidence both in the first principles, and in the deductions, may seduce us unwarily into the conclusion, and make us imagine it contains nothing extraordinary, nor worthy of our curiosity. But tho' such an inadvertence may facilitate the reception of this reasoning, 'twill make it be the more easily forgot; for which reason I think it proper to give warning, that I have just now examin'd one of the most sublime questions in philosophy, *viz., that concerning the power and efficacy of causes;* where all the sciences seem so much interested. Such a warning will naturally rouze up the attention of the reader, and make him desire a more full account of my doctrine, as well as of the arguments, on which it is founded. This request is so reasonable, that I cannot refuse complying with it; especially as I am hopeful that these principles, the more they are examin'd, will acquire the more force and evidence.

There is no question, which on account of its importance, as well as difficulty, has caus'd more disputes both among antient and modern philosophers, than this concerning the efficacy of causes, or that quality which makes them be followed by their effects. But before they enter'd upon these disputes, methinks it wou'd not have been improper to have examin'd what idea we have of that efficacy, which is the subject of the controversy. This is what I find principally wanting in their reasonings, and what I shall here endeavour to supply.

I begin with observing that the terms of *efficacy, agency, power, force, energy, necessity, connexion,* and *productive quality,* are all nearly synonimous; and therefore 'tis an absurdity to employ any of them in defining the rest. By this observation we reject at once all the vulgar definitions, which philosophers have given of power and efficacy; and instead of searching for the idea in these definitions, must look for it in the impressions, from which it is originally deriv'd. If it be a compound idea, it must arise from compound impressions. If simple, from simple impressions.

I believe the most general and most popular explication of this matter, is to say, that finding from experience, that there are several new productions in matter, such as the motions and variations of body, and concluding that there must somewhere be a power capable of producing them, we arrive at last by this reasoning at the idea of power and efficacy. But to be convinc'd that this explication is more popular than philosophical, we need but reflect on two very obvious principles. *First*, that reason alone can never give rise to any original idea, and *secondly*, that reason, as distinguish'd from experience, can never make us conclude, that cause or productive quality is absolutely requisite to every beginning of existence. Both these considerations have been sufficiently explain'd and therefore shall not at present be any farther insisted on.

I shall only infer from them, that since reason can never give rise to the idea of efficacy, that idea must be deriv'd from experience, and from some particular instances of this efficacy, which make their passage into the mind by the common channels of sensation or reflection. Ideas always represent their objects or impressions; and *vice versa*, there are some objects necessary to give rise to every idea. If we pretend, therefore to have any just idea of this efficacy, we must produce some instance wherein the efficacy is plainly discoverable to the mind, and its operations obvious to our consciousness or sensation. By the refusal of this, we acknowledge, that the idea is impossible and imaginary; since the principle of innate ideas, which alone can save us from this dilemma, has been already refuted, and is now almost universally rejected in the learned world. Our present business, then, must be to find some natural production, where the operation and efficacy of a cause can be clearly conceiv'd and comprehended by the mind, without any danger of obscurity or mistake. . . .

. . . Upon the whole, we may conclude, that 'tis impossible in any one instance to shew the principle, in which the force and agency of a cause is plac'd; and that the most refin'd and most vulgar understandings are equally at a loss in this particular. If any one think proper to refute this assertion, he need not put himself to the trouble of inventing any long reasonings; but may at once shew us an instance of a cause, where we discover the power or operating principle. This defiance we are oblig'd frequently to make use of, as being almost the only means of proving a negative in philosophy. . . .

Suppose two objects to be presented to us, of which the one is the cause and the other the effect; 'tis plain, that from the simple consideration of one, or both these objects we never shall perceive the tie, by which they are united, or be able certainly to pronounce, that there is a connexion betwixt them. 'Tis not, therefore, from any one instance, that we arrive at the idea of cause and effect, of a necessary connexion of power, of force, of energy, and of efficacy. Did we never see any but particular conjunctions of objects, entirely different from each other, we shou'd never be able to form any such ideas.

But again; suppose we observe several instances, in which the same objects are always conjoin'd together, we immediately conceive a connexion betwixt them, and begin to draw an inference from one to another. This multiplicity of resembling instances, therefore, constitutes the very essence of power or connexion, and is the source, from which the idea of it arises. In order, then, to understand the idea of power, we must consider that multiplicity; nor do I ask more to give a solution of that difficulty, which has so long perplex'd us. For thus I reason. The repetition of perfectly similar instances can never *alone* give rise to an original idea, different from what is to be found in any particular instance, as has been observ'd, and as evidently follows from our fundamental principle, *that all ideas are copy'd from impressions.* Since therefore the idea of power is a new original idea, not to be found in any one instance, and which yet arises from the repetition of several instances, it follows, that the repetition *alone* has not that effect, but must either *discover* or *produce* something new, which is the source of that idea. Did the repetition neither discover nor produce any thing new, our ideas might be multiply'd by it, but wou'd not be enlarg'd above what they are upon the observation of one single instance. Every enlargment, therefore, (such as the idea of power or connexion) which arises from the multiplicity of similar instances, is copy'd from some effects of the multiplicity, and will be perfectly understood by understanding these effects. Wherever we find any thing new to be discover'd or produc'd by the repetition, there we must place the power, and must never look for it in any other object.

But 'tis evident, in the first place, that the repetition of like objects in like relations of succession and contiguity *discovers* nothing new in any one of them; since we can draw no inference from it, nor make it a subject either of our demonstrative or probable reasonings; as has been already prov'd. Nay suppose we cou'd draw an inference, 'twou'd be of no consequence in the present case; since no kind of reasoning can give rise to a new idea, such as this of power is; but wherever we reason, we must antecedently be possest of clear ideas, which may be the objects of our reasoning. The conception always precedes the understanding; and where the one is obscure, the other is uncertain; where the one fails, the other must fail also.

Secondly, 'tis certain that this repetition of similar objects in similar situations *produces* nothing new either in these objects, or in any external body. For 'twill readily be allow'd that the several instances we have of the conjunction of resembling causes and effects are in themselves entirely independent, and that the communication of motion, which I see result at present from the shock of two billiard-balls, is totally distinct from that which I saw result from such an impulse a twelve-month ago. These impulses have no influence on each other. They are entirely divided by time and place; and the one might have existed and communicated motion, tho' the other never had been in being.

There is, then, nothing new either discover'd or produc'd in any objects by their constant conjunction, and by the uninterrupted resemblance of their relations of succession and contiguity. But 'tis from this resemblance, that the ideas of necessity, of power, and of efficacy, are deriv'd. These ideas, therefore, represent not any thing, that does or can belong to the objects, which are constantly conjoin'd. This is an argument, which, in every view we can examine it, will be found perfectly unanswerable. Similar instances are still the first source of our idea of power or necessity; at the same time that they have no influence by their similarity either on each other, or on any external object. We must therefore, turn ourselves to some other quarter to seek the origin of that idea.

Tho' the several resembling instances, which give rise to the idea of power, have no influence on each other, and can never produce any new quality *in the object* which can be the model of that idea, yet the *observation* of this resemblance produces a new impression *in the mind*, which is its real model. For after we have observ'd the resemblance in a sufficient number of instances, we immediately feel a determination of the mind to pass from one object to its usual attendant, and to conceive it in a stronger light upon account of that relation. This determination is the only effect of the resemblance; and therefore must be the same with power or efficacy, whose idea is deriv'd from the resemblance. The several instances of resembling conjunctions lead us into the notion of power and necessity. These instances are in themselves totally distinct from each other, and have no union but in the mind, which observes them, and collects their ideas. Necessity, then, is the effect of this observation, and is nothing but an internal impression of the mind, or a determination to carry our thoughts from one object to another. Without considering it in this view, we can never arrive at the most distant notion of it, or be able to attribute it either to external or internal objects, to spirit or body, to causes or effects.

The necessary connexion betwixt causes and effects is the foundation of our inference from one to the other. The foundation of our inference is the transition arising from the accustom'd union. These are, therefore, the same.

The idea of necessity arises from some impression. There is no impression convey'd by our senses, which can give rise to that idea. It must, therefore, be deriv'd from some internal impression, or impression of reflection. There is no internal impression, which has any relation to the present business, but that propensity, which custom produces, to pass from an object to the idea of its usual attendant. This therefore is the essence of necessity. Upon the whole, necessity is something, that exists in the mind, not in objects; nor is it possible for us ever to form the most distant idea of it, consider'd as a quality in bodies. Either we have no idea of necessity, or necessity is nothing but that determination of the thought to pass from causes to effects and from effects to causes, according to their experienc'd union. . . .

I am sensible, that of all the paradoxes, which I have had, or shall hereafter have occasion to advance in the course of this treatise, the present one is the most violent, and that 'tis merely by dint of solid proof and reasoning I can ever hope it will have admission, and overcome the inveterate prejudices of mankind. Before we are reconcil'd to this doctrine, how often must we repeat to ourselves, *that* the simple view of any two objects or actions, however related can never give us any idea of power, or of a connexion betwixt them: *that* this idea arises from the repetition of their union: *that* the repetition neither discovers nor causes any thing in the objects, but has an influence only on the mind, by that customary transition it produces: *that* this customary transition is, therefore, the same with the power and necessity; which are consequently qualities of perceptions, not of objects, and are internally felt by the soul, and not perceiv'd externally in bodies? There is commonly an astonishment attending every thing extraordinary; and this astonishment changes immediately into the highest degree of esteem or contempt, according as we approve or disapprove of the subject. I am much afraid, that tho' the foregoing reasoning appears to me the shortest and most decisive imaginable; yet with the generality of readers the biass of the mind will prevail, and give them a prejudice against the present doctrine.

This contrary biass is easily accounted for. 'Tis a common observation, that the mind has a great propensity to spread itself on external objects, and to conjoin with them any internal impressions, which they occasion, and which always make their appearance at the same time that these objects discover themselves to the senses. Thus as certain sounds and smells are always found to attend certain visible objects, we naturally imagine a conjunction, even in place, betwixt the objects and qualities, tho' the qualities be of such a nature as to admit of no such conjunction, and really exist no where. But of this more fully hereafter. Mean while 'tis sufficient to observe, that the same propensity is the reason, why we suppose necessity and power to lie in the objects we consider, not in our mind, that considers them; notwithstanding it is not possible for us to form the most distant idea of that quality, when it is not taken for the determination of the mind, to pass from the idea of an object to that of its usual attendant.

But tho' this be the only reasonable account we can give of necessity, the contrary notion is so riveted in the mind from the principles above-mention'd, that I doubt not but my sentiments will be treated by many as extravagant and ridiculous. What! The efficacy of causes lie in the determination of the mind! As if causes did not operate entirely independent of the mind, and wou'd not continue their operation even tho' there was no mind existent to contemplate them, or reason concerning them. Thought may well depend on causes for its operation, but not causes on thought. This is to reverse the order of nature, and make that secondary, which is really primary. To every operation there is a power proportion'd; and this power must be plac'd on the body, that operates. If we remove the power from one cause, we must ascribe it to another: But to remove it from all causes, and bestow it on a being, that is no ways related to the cause or effect, but by perceiving them, is a gross absurdity, and contrary to the most certain principles of human reason.

I can only reply to all these arguments, that the case is here much the same, as if a blind man shou'd pretend to find a great many absurdities in the supposition that the colour of scarlet is not the same with the sound of a trumpet, nor light the same with solidity. If we have really no idea of a power or efficacy in any object, or of any real connexion betwixt causes and effects, 'twill be to little purpose to prove, that an efficacy is necessary in all operations. We do not understand our own meaning in talking so, but ignorantly confound ideas, which are entirely distinct from each other. I am, indeed, ready to allow, that there may be several qualities both in material and immaterial objects, with which we are utterly unacquainted; and if we please to call these *power* or *efficacy*, 'twill be of little consequence to the world. But when, instead of meaning these unknown qualities, we make the terms of power and efficacy signify something, of which we have a clear idea, and which is incompatible with those objects, to which we apply it, obscurity and error begin then to take place, and we are led astray by a false philosophy. This is the case, when we transfer the determination of the thought to external objects, and suppose any real intelligible connexion betwixt them; that being a quality, which can only belong to the mind that considers them.

As to what may be said, that the operations of nature are independent of our thought and reasoning, I allow it; and accordingly have observ'd that objects bear to each other the relations of contiguity and succession; that like objects may be observ'd in several instances to have like relations; and that all this is independent of, and antecedent to the operations of the understanding. But if we go any farther, and ascribe a power or necessary connexion to these objects; this is what we can never observe in them, but must draw the idea of it from what we feel internally in contemplating them. And this I carry so far, that I am ready to convert my present reasoning into an instance of it, by a subtility, which it will not be difficult to comprehend.

When any object is presented to us, it immediately conveys to the mind a lively idea of that object, which is usually found to attend it; and this determination of the mind forms the necessary connexion of the objects. But when we change the point of view, from the objects to the perceptions; in that case the impression is to be considered as the cause, and the lively idea as the effect; and their necessary connexion is that new determination, which we feel to pass from the idea of the one to that of the other. The uniting principle among our internal perceptions is as unintelligible as that among external objects, and is not known to us any other way than by experience. Now the nature and effects of experience have been already sufficiently examin'd and explain'd. It never gives us any insight into the internal structure or operating principle of objects, but only accustoms the mind to pass from one to another.

'Tis now time to collect all the different parts of this reasoning, and by joining them together form an exact definition of the relation of cause and effect, which makes the subject of the present enquiry. This order wou'd not have been excusable, of first examining our inference from the relation before we have explain'd the relation itself, had it been possible to proceed in a different method. But as the nature of the relation depends so much on that of the inference, we have been oblig'd to advance in this seemingly preposterous manner, and make use of terms before we were able exactly to define them, or fix their meaning. We shall now correct this fault by giving a precise definition of cause and effect.

There may two definitions be given of this relation, which are only different, by their presenting a different view of the same object, and making us consider it either as a *philosophical* or as a *natural* relation; either as a comparison of two ideas, or as an association betwixt them. We may define a CAUSE to be 'An object precedent and contiguous to another, and where all the objects resembling the former are plac'd in like relations of precedency and contiguity to those objects, that resemble the latter.' If this definition be esteem'd defective, because drawn from objects foreign to the cause, we may substitute this other definition in its place, viz., 'A CAUSE is an object precedent and contiguous to another, and so united with it, that the idea of the one determines the mind to form the idea of the other, and the impression of the one to form a more lively idea of the other.' Shou'd this definition also be rejected for the same reason, I know no other remedy, than that the persons, who express this delicacy, should substitute a juster definition in its place. But for my part I must own my incapacity for such an undertaking. When I examine with the utmost accuracy those objects, which are commonly denominated causes and effects, I find, in considering a single instance, that the one object is precedent and contiguous to the other; and in inlarging my view to consider several instances, I find only, that like objects are constantly plac'd in like relations of succession and contiguity. Again, when I consider the influence of this constant conjunction, I perceive, that such a relation can never be an object of reasoning, and can never operate upon the mind, but by means of custom, which determines the imagination to make a transition from the idea of one object to that of its usual attendant, and from the impression of one to a more lively idea of the other. However extraordinary these sentiments may appear, I think it fruitless to trouble myself with any further enquiry or reasoning upon the subject, but shall repose myself on them as on establish'd maxims. . . .

• 23 •

FREE WILL *

John Stuart Mill (1806–1873)

1. The question, whether the law of causality applies in the same strict sense to human actions as to other phenomena, is the celebrated controversy concerning the freedom of the will; which, from at least as far back as the time of Pelagius, has divided both the philosophical and reli-

* Part of ch. 2 of Book VI of A System of Logic (1843). The title of this selection has been supplied by the editors. Compare with selections 22, 24, 26, and 28.

gious world. The affirmative opinion is commonly called the doctrine of Necessity, as asserting human volitions and actions to be necessary and inevitable. The negative maintains that the will *is not determined*, like other phenomena, by antecedents, but determines itself; that our volitions are not, properly speaking, the effects of causes, or at least have no causes which they uniformly and implicitly obey. . . .

The former of these opinions is that which I consider the true one; but the misleading terms in which it is often expressed, and the indistinct manner in which it is usually apprehended, have both obstructed its reception, and perverted its influence when received. The metaphysical theory of free-will, as held by philosophers (for the practical feeling of it, common in a greater or less degree to all mankind, is in no way inconsistent with the contrary theory), was invented because the supposed alternative of admitting human actions to be *necessary* was deemed inconsistent with every one's instinctive consciousness, as well as humiliating to the pride and even degrading to the moral nature of man. Nor do I deny that the doctrine, as sometimes held, is open to these imputations; for the misapprehension in which I shall be able to show that they originate, unfortunately is not confined to the opponents of the doctrine, but is participated in by many, perhaps we might say by most, of its supporters.

2. Correctly conceived, the doctrine called Philosophical Necessity is simply this: that, given the motives which are present to an individual's mind, and given likewise the character and disposition of the individual, the manner in which he will act might be unerringly inferred; that if we knew the person thoroughly, and knew all the inducements which are acting upon him, we could foretell his conduct with as much certainty as we can predict any physical event. This proposition I take to be a mere interpretation of universal experience, a statement in words of what every one is internally convinced of. No one who believed that he knew thoroughly the circumstances of any case, and the characters of the different persons concerned, would hesitate to foretell how all of them would act. Whatever degree of doubt he may in fact feel, arises from the uncertainty whether he really knows the circumstances, or the character of some one or other of the persons, with the degree of accuracy required; but by no means from thinking that if he did know these things, there could be any uncertainty what the conduct would be. Nor does this full assurance conflict in the smallest degree with what is called our feeling of freedom. We do not feel ourselves the less free, because those to whom we are intimately known are well assured how we shall will to act in a particular case. We often, on the contrary, regard the doubt what our conduct will be, as a mark of ignorance of our character, and sometimes even resent it as an

imputation. The religious metaphysicians who have asserted the freedom of the will, have always maintained it to be consistent with divine fore-knowledge of our actions: and if with divine, then with any other fore-knowledge. We may be free, and yet another may have reason to be perfectly certain what use we shall make of our freedom. It is not, therefore, the doctrine that our volitions and actions are invariable consequents of our antecedent states of mind, that is either contradicted by our consciousness, or felt to be degrading.

But the doctrine of causation, when considered as obtaining between our volitions and their antecedents, is almost universally conceived as involving more than this. Many do not believe, and very few practically feel, that there is nothing in causation but invariable, certain, and unconditional sequence. There are few to whom mere constancy of succession appears a sufficiently stringent bond of union for so peculiar a relation as that of cause and effect. Even if the reason repudiates, the imagination retains, the feeling of some more intimate connection, of some peculiar tie, or mysterious constraint exercised by the antecedent over the consequent. Now this it is which, considered as applying to the human will, conflicts with our consciousness, and revolts our feelings. We are certain that, in the case of our volitions, there is not this mysterious constraint. We know that we are not compelled, as by a magical spell, to obey any particular motive. We feel, that if we wished to prove that we have the power of resisting the motive, we could do so (that wish being, it needs scarcely be observed, a *new antecedent*); and it would be humiliating to our pride, and (what is of more importance) paralyzing to our desire of excellence, if we thought otherwise. But neither is any such mysterious compulsion now supposed, by the best philosophical authorities, to be exercised by any other cause over its effect. Those who think that causes draw their effects after them by a mystical tie, are right in believing that the relation between volitions and their antecedents is of another nature. But they should go farther, and admit that this is also true of all other effects and their antecedents. If such a tie is considered to be involved in the word Necessity, the doctrine is not true of human actions; but neither is it then true of inanimate objects. It would be more correct to say that matter is not bound by necessity, than that mind is so.

That the free-will metaphysicians, being mostly of the school which rejects Hume's . . . analysis of Cause and Effect, should miss their way for want of the light which that analysis affords, can not surprise us. The wonder is, that the necessitarians, who usually admit that philosophical theory, should in practice equally lose sight of it. The very same misconception of the doctrine called Philosophical Necessity, which prevents the opposite party from recognizing its truth, I believe to exist more or less obscurely in the minds of most necessitarians, however they may in words disavow it. I am much mistaken if they habitually feel that the necessity which they recognize in actions is but uniformity of order, and capability of being predicted. They have a feeling as if there were at bottom a stronger tie between the volitions and their causes; as if, when they asserted that the will is governed by the balance of motives, they meant something more cogent than if they had only said, that whoever knew the motives, and our habitual susceptibilities to them, could predict how we should will to act. They commit, in opposition to their own scientific system, the very same mistake which their adversaries commit in obedience to theirs; and in consequence do really in some instances suffer those depressing consequences which their opponents erroneously impute to the doctrine itself.

3. I am inclined to think that this error is almost wholly an effect of the associations with a word, and that it would be prevented, by forbearing to employ, for the expression of the simple fact of causation, so extremely inappropriate a term as Necessity. That word, in its other acceptations, involves much more than mere uniformity of sequence: it implies irresistibleness. Applied to the will, it only means that the given cause will be followed by the effect, subject to all possibilities of counteraction by other causes; but in common use it stands for the operation of those causes exclusively which are supposed too powerful to be counteracted at all. When we say that all human actions take place of necessity, we only mean that they will certainly happen if nothing prevents; when we say that dying of want, to those who can not get food, is a necessity, we mean that it will certainly happen whatever may be done to prevent it. The application of the same term to the agencies on which human actions depend, as is used to express those agencies of nature which are really uncontrollable, can not fail, when habitual, to create a feeling of uncontrollableness in the former also. This, however, is a mere illusion. There are physical sequences which we call necessary, as death for want of food or air; there are others which, though as much cases of causation as the former, are not said to be necessary, as death from poison, which an antidote, or the use of the stomach-pump, will sometimes avert. It is apt to be forgotten by people's feelings, even if remembered by their understandings, that human actions are in this last predicament; they are never (except in some cases of mania) ruled by any one motive with such absolute sway that there is no room for the influence of any other. The causes, therefore, on which action depends, are never uncontrollable; and any given effect is only necessary provided that the causes tending to produce it are not controlled. That whatever happens, could not have happened otherwise, unless something had taken

place which was capable of preventing it, no one surely needs hesitate to admit. But to call this by the name Necessity is to use the term in a sense so different from its primitive and familiar meaning, from that which it bears in the common occasions of life, as to amount almost to a play upon words. The associations derived from the ordinary sense of the term will adhere to it in spite of all we can do; and though the doctrine of Necessity, as stated by most who hold it is very remote from fatalism, it is probable that most necessitarians are fatalists, more or less, in their feelings.

A fatalist believes, or half believes (for nobody is a consistent fatalist), not only that whatever is about to happen will be the infallible result of the causes which produce it (which is the true necessitarian doctrine), but moreover that there is no use in struggling against it; that it will happen, however we may strive to prevent it. Now, a necessitarian, believing that our actions follow from our characters, and that our characters follow from our organization, our education, and our circumstances, is apt to be, with more or less of consciousness on his part, a fatalist as to his own actions, and to believe that his nature is such, or that his education and circumstances have so moulded his character, that nothing can now prevent him from feeling and acting in a particular way, or at least that no effort of his own can hinder it. In the words of the sect which in our own day has most perseveringly inculcated and most perversely misunderstood this great doctrine, his character is formed *for* him, and not *by* him; therefore his wishing that it had been formed differently is of no use; he has no power to alter it. But this is a grand error. He has, to a certain extent, a power to alter his character. Its being, in the ultimate resort, formed for him, is not inconsistent with its being, in part, formed *by* him as one of the intermediate agents. His character is formed by his circumstances (including among these his particular organization); but his own desire to mould it in a particular way, is one of those circumstances, and by no means one of the least influential. We can not, indeed, directly will to be different from what we are. But neither did those who are supposed to have formed our characters directly will that we should be what we are. Their will had no direct power except over their own actions. They made us what they did make us, by willing, not the end, but the requisite means; and we, when our habits are not too inveterate, can, by similarly willing the requisite means, make ourselves different. If they could place us under the influence of certain circumstances, we, in like manner, can place ourselves under the influence of other circumstances. We are exactly as capable of making our own character, if we will, as others are of making it for us.

Yes (answers the Owenite),* but these words, *"if we will,"* surrender the

* A follower of Robert Owen (1771–1858), English reformer and author of an influential book which argued that all human actions have definite causes.

whole point: since the will to alter our own character is given us, not by any efforts of ours, but by circumstances which we can not help, it comes to us either from external causes, or not at all. Most true: if the Owenite stops here, he is in a position from which nothing can expel him. Our character is formed by us as well as for us; but the wish which induces us to attempt to form it is formed for us; and how? Not, in general, by our organization, nor wholly by our education, but by our experience; experience of the painful consequences of the character we previously had; or by some strong feeling of admiration or aspiration, accidentally aroused. But to think that we have no power of altering our character, and to think that we shall not use our power unless we desire to use it, are very different things, and have a very different effect on the mind. A person who does not wish to alter his character, can not be the person who is supposed to feel discouraged or paralyzed by thinking himself unable to do it. The depressing effect of the fatalist doctrine can only be felt where there *is* a wish to do what that doctrine represents as impossible. It is of no consequence what we think forms our character, when we have no desire of our own about forming it; but it is of great consequence that we should not be prevented from forming such a desire by thinking the attainment impracticable, and that if we have the desire, we should know that the work is not so irrevocably done as to be incapable of being altered.

And indeed, if we examine closely, we shall find that this feeling, of our being able to modify our own character *if we wish*, is itself the feeling of moral freedom which we are conscious of. A person feels morally free who feels that his habits or his temptations are not his masters, but he theirs; who, even in yielding to them, knows that he could resist; that were he desirous of altogether throwing them off, there would not be required for that purpose a stronger desire than he knows himself to be capable of feeling. It is of course necessary, to render our consciousness of freedom complete, that we should have succeeded in making our character all we have hitherto attempted to make it; for if we have wished and not attained, we have, to that extent, not power over our own character; we are not free. Or at least, we must feel that our wish, if not strong enough to alter our character, is strong enough to conquer our character when the two are brought into conflict in any particular case of conduct. And hence it is said with truth, that none but a person of confirmed virtue is completely free.

The application of so improper a term as Necessity to the doctrine of cause and effect in the matter of human character, seems to me one of the most signal instances in philosophy of the abuse of terms, and its practical consequences one of the most striking examples of the power of language over our associations. The subject will never be generally understood until that objectionable term is dropped. The free-will doctrine, by keeping in view precisely that portion of the truth which the word Necessity puts out of sight, namely the power of the mind to co-operate in the formation of its own character, has given to its adherents a practical feeling much nearer to the truth than has generally (I believe) existed in the minds of necessitarians. The latter may have had a stronger sense of the importance of what human beings can do to shape the characters of one another; but the free-will doctrine has, I believe, fostered in its supporters a much stronger spirit of self-culture. . . .

• 24 •

HISTORY AND DETERMINISM *

John Stuart Mill (1806–1873)

1. . . . . The collective series of social phenomena, in other words, the course of history, is subject to general laws, which philosophy may possibly detect. . .

Among the impediments to the general acknowledgment, by thoughtful minds, of the subjection of historical facts to scientific laws, the most fundamental continues to be that which is grounded on the doctrine of Free Will, or, in other words, on the denial that the law of invariable Causation holds true of human volitions; for if it does not, the course of history, being the result of human volitions, cannot be a subject of scientific laws, since the volitions on which it depends can neither be foreseen nor reduced to any canon of regularity even after they have occurred. I have discussed this question, as far as seemed suitable to the occasion, in a former chapter, and I only think it necessary to repeat that the doctrine of the Causation of human actions, improperly called the doctrine of Necessity, affirms no mysterious *nexus* or overruling fatality; it asserts only that men's actions are the joint result of the general laws and circumstances of human nature, and of their own particular characters, those characters again being the consequence of the natural and artificial circumstances that constituted their education, among which circumstances must be reckoned

* From Bk. VI, ch. 11 of *A System of Logic* (1843). The title of this selection has been supplied by the editors. Compare with selections 23 and 25.

their own conscious efforts. Any one who is willing to take (if the expression may be permitted) the trouble of thinking himself into the doctrine as thus stated, will find it, I believe, not only a faithful interpretation of the universal experience of human conduct, but a correct representation of the mode in which he himself, in every particular case, spontaneously interprets his own experience of that conduct.

But if this principle is true of individual man, it must be true of collective man. If it is the law of human life, the law must be realised in history. The experience of human affairs when looked at *en masse*, must be in accordance with it if true, or repugnant to it if false. . . .

The facts of statistics, since they have been made a subject of careful recordation and study, have yielded conclusions, some of which have been very startling to persons not accustomed to regard moral actions as subject to uniform laws. The very events which in their own nature appear most capricious and uncertain, and which in any individual case no attainable degree of knowledge would enable us to foresee, occur, when considerable numbers are taken into the account, with a degree of regularity approaching to mathematical. What act is there which all would consider as more completely dependent on individual character, and on the exercise of individual free will, than that of slaying a fellow-creature? Yet in any large country, the number of murders, in proportion to the population, varies (it has been found) very little from one year to another, and in its variations never deviates widely from a certain average. What is still more remarkable, there is a similar approach to constancy in the proportion of these murders annually committed with every particular kind of instrument. There is a like approximation to identity, as between one year and another, in the comparative number of legitimate and illegitimate births. The same thing is found true of suicides, accidents, and all other social phenomena of which the registration is sufficiently perfect; one of the most curiously illustrative examples being the fact, ascertained by the registers of the London and Paris post-offices, that the number of letters posted which the writers have forgotten to direct is nearly the same, in proportion to the whole number of letters posted, in one year as in another. . . .

This singular degree of regularity *en masse*, combined with the extreme of irregularity in the cases composing the mass, is a felicitous verification *a posteriori* of the law of causation in its application to human conduct. Assuming the truth of that law, every human action, every murder, for instance, is the concurrent result of two sets of causes. On the one part, the general circumstances of the country and its inhabitants; the moral, educational, economical, and other influences operating on the whole people, and constituting what we term the state of civilisation. On the other part, the great variety of influences special to the individual: his temperament, and other peculiarities of organisation, his parentage, habitual associates, temptations, and so forth. If we now take the whole of the instances which occur within a sufficiently large field to exhaust all the combinations of these special influences, or, in other words, to eliminate chance; and if all these instances have occurred within such narrow limits of time that no material change can have taken place in the general influences constituting the state of civilisation of the country, we may be certain that if human actions are governed by invariable laws, the aggregate result will be something like a constant quantity. The number of murders committed within that space and time being the effect partly of general causes which have not varied, and partly of partial causes the whole round of whose variations has been included, will be, practically speaking, invariable.

Literally and mathematically invariable it is not, and could not be expected to be; because the period of a year is too short to include *all* the possible combinations of partial causes, while it is, at the same time, sufficiently long to make it probable that in some years, at least, of every series, there will have been introduced new influences of a more or less general character; such as a more vigorous or a more relaxed police; some temporary excitement from political or religious causes; or some incident generally notorious, of a nature to act morbidly on the imagination. That in spite of these unavoidable imperfections in the data, there should be so very trifling a margin of variation in the annual results, is a brilliant confirmation of the general theory.

2. The same considerations which thus strikingly corroborate the evidence of the doctrine that historical facts are the invariable effects of causes, tend equally to clear that doctrine from various misapprehensions. . . . Some persons, for instance, seemingly imagine the doctrine to imply, not merely that the total number of murders committed in a given space and time is entirely the effect of the general circumstances of society, but that every particular murder is so too; that the individual murderer is, so to speak, a mere instrument in the hands of general causes; that he himself has no option, or, if he has, and chose to exercise it, some one else would be necessitated to take his place; that if any one of the actual murderers had abstained from the crime, some person who would otherwise have remained innocent would have committed an extra murder to make up the average. Such a corollary would certainly convict any theory which necessarily led to it of absurdity. It is obvious, however, that each particular murder depends, not on the general state of society only, but on that combined with causes special to the case, which are generally much more powerful; and if these special causes, which have greater influence than the

general ones in causing every particular murder, have no influence on the number of murders in a given period, it is because the field of observation is so extensive as to include all possible combinations of the special causes —all varieties of individual character and individual temptation compatible with the general state of society. The collective experiment, as it may be termed, exactly separates the effect of the general from that of the special causes, and shows the net result of the former; but it declares nothing at all respecting the amount of influence of the special causes, be it greater or smaller, since the scale of the experiment extends to the number of cases within which the effects of the special causes balance one another, and disappear in that of the general causes.

I will not pretend that all the defenders of the theory have always kept their language free from this same confusion, and have shown no tendency to exalt the influence of general causes at the expense of special. I am of opinion, on the contrary, that they have done so in a very great degree, and by so doing have encumbered their theory with difficulties, and laid it open to objections which do not necessarily affect it. Some, for example . . . have inferred, or allowed it to be supposed that they inferred, from the regularity in the recurrence of events which depend on moral qualities, that the moral qualities of mankind are little capable of being improved, or are of little importance in the general progress of society, compared with intellectual or economic causes. But to draw this inference is to forget that the statistical tables from which the invariable averages are deduced were compiled from facts occurring within narrow geographical limits, and in a small number of successive years; that is, from a field the whole of which was under the operation of the same general causes, and during too short a time to allow of much change therein. All moral causes but those common to the country generally have been eliminated by the great number of instances taken; and those which are common to the whole country have not varied considerably in the short space of time comprised in the observations. If we admit the supposition that they have varied; if we compare one age with another, or one country with another, or even one part of a country with another, differing in position and character as to the moral elements, the crimes committed within a year give no longer the same, but a widely different numerical aggregate. And this cannot but be the case; for inasmuch as every single crime committed by an individual mainly depends on his moral qualities, the crimes committed by the entire population of the country must depend in an equal degree on their collective moral qualities. To render this element inoperative upon the large scale it would be necessary to suppose that the general moral average of mankind does not vary from country to country, or from age to age; which is not true, and even if it were true, could not possibly be proved by any existing statistics. I do not on this account the less agree in the opinion . . . that the intellectual element in mankind, including in that expression the nature of their beliefs, the amount of their knowledge, and the development of their intelligence, is the predominant circumstance in determining their progress. But I am of this opinion, not because I regard their moral or economical condition either as less powerful or less variable agencies, but because these are in a great degree the consequences of the intellectual condition, and are, in all cases, limited by it . . . The intellectual changes are the most conspicuous agents in history, not from their superior force, considered in themselves, but because practically they work with the united power belonging to all three.

3. There is another distinction often neglected in the discussion of this subject, which it is extremely important to observe. The theory of the subjection of social progress to invariable laws is often held in conjunction with the doctrine that social progress cannot be materially influenced by the exertions of individual persons or by the acts of governments. But though these opinions are often held by the same persons, they are two very different opinions, and the confusion between them is the eternally recurring error of confounding Causation with Fatalism. Because whatever happens will be the effect of causes, human volitions among the rest, it does not follow that volitions, even those of peculiar individuals, are not of great efficacy as causes. If any one in a storm at sea, because about the same number of persons in every year perish by shipwreck, should conclude that it was useless for him to attempt to save his own life, we should call him a Fatalist, and should remind him that the efforts of shipwrecked persons to save their lives are so far from being immaterial, that the average amount of those efforts is one of the causes on which the ascertained annual number of deaths by shipwreck depend. However universal the laws of social development may be, they cannot be more universal or more rigorous than those of the physical agencies of nature; yet human will can convert these into instruments of its designs, and the extent to which it does so makes the chief difference between savages and the most highly civilised people. Human and social facts, from their more complicated nature, are not less, but more, modifiable than mechanical and chemical facts; human agency, therefore, has still greater power over them. And accordingly, those who maintain that the evolution of society depends exclusively, or almost exclusively, on general causes, always include among these the collective knowledge and intellectual development of the race. But if of the race, why not also of some powerful monarch or thinker, or of the ruling portion of some political society, acting through its government?

Though the varieties of character among ordinary individuals neutralise one another on any large scale, exceptional individuals in important positions do not in any given age neutralise one another; there was not another Themistocles, or Luther, or Julius Caesar, of equal powers and contrary dispositions, who exactly balanced the given Themistocles, Luther, and Caesar, and prevented them from having any permanent effect. Moreover, for aught that appears, the volitions of exceptional persons, or the opinions and purposes of the individuals who at some particular time compose a government, may be indispensable links in the chain of causation by which even the general causes produce their effects; and I believe this to be the only tenable form of the theory.

Lord Macaulay, in a celebrated passage of one of his early essays (let me add that it was one which he did not himself choose to reprint), gives expression to the doctrine of the absolute inoperativeness of great men, more unqualified, I should think, than has been given to it by any writer of equal abilities. He compares them to persons who merely stand on a loftier height, and thence receive the sun's rays a little earlier than the rest of the human race. "The sun illuminates the hills while it is still below the horizon, and truth is discovered by the highest minds a little before it becomes manifest to the multitude. This is the extent of their superiority. They are the first to catch and reflect a light which, without their assistance, must in a short time be visible to those who lie far beneath them." If this metaphor is to be carried out, it follows that if there had been no Newton the world would not only have had the Newtonian system, but would have had it equally soon, as the sun would have risen just as early to spectators in the plain if there had been no mountain at hand to catch still earlier rays. And so it would be if truths, like the sun, rose by their own proper motion, without human effort, but not otherwise. I believe that if Newton had not lived, the world must have waited for the Newtonian philosophy until there had been another Newton or his equivalent. No ordinary man, and no succession of ordinary men, could have achieved it. I will not go the length of saying that what Newton did in a single life might not have been done in successive steps by some of those who followed him, each singly inferior to him in genius. But even the least of those steps required a man of great intellectual superiority. Eminent men do not merely see the coming light from the hill-top; they mount on the hill-top and evoke it; and if no one had ever ascended thither, the light, in many cases, might never have risen upon the plain at all. Philosophy and religion are abundantly amenable to general causes; yet few will doubt that had there been no Socrates, no Plato, and no Aristotle, there would have been no philosophy for the next two thousand years, nor in all probability then; and that if there had been no Christ and no St. Paul, there would have been no Christianity.

The point in which, above all, the influence of remarkable individuals is decisive, is in determining the celerity of the movement. In most states of society it is the existence of great men which decides even whether there shall be any progress. It is conceivable that Greece, or that Christian Europe, might have been progressive in certain periods of their history through general causes only; but if there had been no Mahomet, would Arabia have produced Avicenna or Averroes, or Caliphs of Bagdad or of Cordova? In determining, however, in what manner and order the progress of mankind shall take place, if it take place at all, much less depends on the character of individuals. There is a sort of necessity established in this respect by the general laws of human nature, by the constitution of the human mind. Certain truths cannot be discovered or inventions made unless certain others have been made first; certain social improvements, from the nature of the case, can only follow, and not precede, others. The order of human progress, therefore, may to a certain extent have definite laws assigned to it; while as to its celerity, or even as to its taking place at all, no generalisation, extending to the human species generally, can possibly be made, but only some very precarious approximate generalisations, confined to the small portion of mankind in whom there has been anything like consecutive progress within the historical period, and deduced from their special position, or collected from their particular history. Even looking to the *manner* of progress, the order of succession of social states, there is need of great flexibility in our generalisations. The limits of variation in the possible development of social, as of animal life, are a subject of which little is yet understood, and are one of the great problems in social science. It is, at all events, a fact that different portions of mankind, under the influence of different circumstances, have developed themselves in a more or less different manner and into different forms; and among these determining circumstances, the individual character of their great speculative thinkers or practical organisers may well have been one. Who can tell how profoundly the whole subsequent history of China may have been influenced by the individuality of Confucius? and of Sparta (and hence of Greece and the world) by that of Lycurgus?

Concerning the nature and extent of what a great man under favourable circumstances can do for mankind, as well as of what a government can do for a nation, many different opinions are possible; and every shade of opinion on these points is consistent with the fullest recognition that there are invariable laws of historical phenomena. Of course the degree of influence which has to be assigned to these more special agencies makes a great difference in the precision which can be given to the general laws, and in the confidence with which predictions can be grounded on them. Whatever depends on the peculiarities of individuals, combined with the accident of the positions they hold, is necessarily incapable of being foreseen. Undoubtedly, these casual combinations might be eliminated like any others by taking a sufficiently large cycle: the peculiarities of a great historical character make their influence felt in history sometimes for several thousand years, but it is highly probable that they will make no difference at all at the end of fifty millions. Since, however, we cannot obtain an average of the vast length of time necessary to exhaust all the possible combinations of great men and circumstances, as much of the law of evolution of human affairs as depends upon this average is and remains inaccessible to us; and within the next thousand years, which are of considerably more importance to us than the whole remainder of the fifty millions, the favourable and unfavourable combinations which will occur will be to us purely accidental. We cannot foresee the advent of great men. Those who introduce new speculative thoughts or great practical conceptions into the world cannot have their epoch fixed beforehand. What science can do is this. It can trace through past history the general causes which had brought mankind into that preliminary state, which, when the right sort of great man appeared, rendered them accessible to his influence. If this state continues, experience renders it tolerably certain that in a longer or shorter period the great man will be produced, provided that the general circumstances of the country and people are (which very often they are not) compatible with his existence; of which point also science can in some measure judge. It is in this manner that the results of progress, except as to the celerity of their production, can be, to a certain extent, reduced to regularity and law. And the belief that they can be so is equally consistent with assigning very great, or very little efficacy, to the influence of exceptional men, or of the acts of governments. And the same may be said of all other accidents and disturbing causes.

4. It would nevertheless be a great error to assign only a trifling importance to the agency of eminent individuals, or of governments. It must not be concluded that the influence of either is small because they cannot bestow what the general circumstances of society, and the course of its previous history, have not prepared it to receive. Neither thinkers nor governments effect all that they intend, but in compensation they often produce important results which they did not in the least foresee. Great men and great actions are seldom wasted: they send forth a thousand unseen influences, more effective than those which are seen; and though nine out of every ten things done, with a good purpose, by those who are in

advance of their age, produce no material effect, the tenth thing produces effects twenty times as great as any one would have dreamed of predicting from it. Even the men who for want of sufficiently favourable circumstances left no impress at all upon their own age have often been of the greatest value to posterity. Who could appear to have lived more entirely in vain than some of the early heretics? They were burnt or massacred, their writings extirpated, their memory anathematised, and their very names and existence left for seven or eight centuries in the obscurity of musty manuscripts—their history to be gathered, perhaps, only from the sentences by which they were condemned. Yet the memory of these men —men who resisted certain pretensions or certain dogmas of the Church in the very age in which the unanimous assent of Christendom was afterwards claimed as having been given to them, and asserted as the ground of their authority—broke the chain of tradition, established a series of precedents for resistance, inspired later Reformers with the courage, and armed them with the weapons, which they needed when mankind were better prepared to follow their impulse. . . .

If a government can do much, even when it seems to have done little, in causing positive improvement, still greater are the issues dependent on it in the way of warding off evils, both internal and external, which else would stop improvement altogether. A good or a bad counsellor, in a single city at a particular crisis, has affected the whole subsequent fate of the world. It is as certain as any contingent judgment respecting historical events can be, that if there had been no Themistocles there would have been no victory of Salamis; and had there not, where would have been all our civilisation? . . . Historical science authorises not absolute, but only conditional predictions. General causes count for much, but individuals also "produce great changes in history, and colour its whole complexion long after their death. . . ."

. . . The whole stream of Grecian history . . . is one series of examples how often events on which the whole destiny of subsequent civilisation turned were dependent on the personal character for good or evil of some one individual. It must be said, however, that Greece furnishes the most extreme example of this nature to be found in history, and is a very exaggerated specimen of the general tendency. It has happened only that once, and will probably never happen again, that the fortunes of mankind depended upon keeping a certain order of things in existence in a single town, or a country scarcely larger than Yorkshire; capable of being ruined or saved by a hundred causes, of very slight magnitude in comparison with the general tendencies of human affairs. Neither ordinary accidents nor the characters of individuals can ever again be so vitally important as they then were. The longer our species lasts and the more civilised it becomes, the more . . . does the influence of past generations over the present, and of mankind *en masse* over every individual in it, predominate over other forces: and though the course of affairs never ceases to be susceptible of alteration both by accidents and by personal qualities, the increasing preponderance of the collective agency of the species over all minor causes is constantly bringing the general evolution of the race into something which deviates less from a certain and preappointed track. Historical science, therefore, is always becoming more possible; not solely because it is better studied, but because, in every generation, it becomes better adapted for study.

• 25 •

ECONOMIC DETERMINISM AND
HISTORICAL DEVELOPMENT *

Friedrich Engels (1820–1895)

1. What we understand by the economic conditions which we regard as the determining basis of the history of society are the methods by which human beings in a given society produce their means of subsistence and exchange the products among themselves (in so far as division of labor exists). Thus the *entire technique* of production and transport is here included. According to our conception this technique also determines the method of exchange and, further, the division of products and with it, after the dissolution of tribal society, the division into classes also and hence the relations of lordship and servitude and with them the state, politics, law, etc. Under economic conditions are further included the geographical basis in which they operate and those remnants of earlier stages of economic development which have actually been transmitted and have survived—often only through tradition or the force of inertia; also of course the external milieu which surrounds this form of society.

If, as you say, technique largely depends on the state of science, science

---

* From a letter to Heinz Starkenburg, January 25, 1894. Reprinted from pp. 516–519 of *The Selected Correspondence of Karl Marx and Friedrich Engels, 1846–1895* (1942), with the kind permission of the International Publishers Co., New York. The title of this selection has been supplied by the editors. Compare with selection 24.

depends far more still on the *state* and the *requirements* of technique. If society has a technical need, that helps science forward more than ten universities. The whole of hydrostatics (Torricelli, etc.,) was called forth by the necessity for regulating the mountain streams of Italy in the sixteenth and seventeenth centuries. We have only known anything reasonable about electricity since its technical applicability was discovered. But unfortunately it has become the custom in German to write the history of the sciences as if they had fallen from the skies.

2. We regard economic conditions as the factor which ultimately determines historical development. But race is itself an economic factor. Here, however, two points must not be overlooked:

(a) Political, juridical, philosophical, religious, literary, artistic, etc., development is based on economic development. But all these react upon one another and also upon the economic base. It is not that the economic position is the *cause and alone active,* while everything else only has a passive effect. There is, rather, interaction on the basis of the economic necessity, which *ultimately* always asserts itself. The state, for instance, exercises an influence by tariffs, free trade, good or bad fiscal system; and even the deadly inanition and impotence of the German petty bourgeois, arising from the miserable economic position of Germany from 1648 to 1830 and expressing itself at first in pietism, then in sentimentality and cringing servility to princes and nobles, was not without economic effect. It was one of the greatest hindrances to recovery and was not shaken until the revolutionary and Napoleonic wars made the chronic misery an acute one. So it is not, as people try here and there conveniently to imagine, that the economic position produces an automatic effect. Men make their history themselves, only in given surroundings which condition it and on the basis of actual relations already existing, among which the economic relations, however much they may be influenced by the other political and ideological ones, are still ultimately the decisive ones, forming the red thread which runs through them and alone leads to understanding.

(b) Men make their history themselves, but not as yet with a collective will or according to a collective plan or even in a definitely defined, given society. Their efforts clash, and for that very reason all such societies are governed by *necessity*, which is supplemented by and appears under the forms of *accident*. The necessity which here asserts itself amidst all accident is again ultimately economic necessity. This is where the so-called great men come in for treatment. That such and such a man and precisely that man arises at that particular time in that given country is of course pure accident. But cut him out and there will be a demand for a substitute, and this substitute will be found, good or bad, but in the long run he will be found. That Napoleon, just that particular Corsican, should have been the military dictator whom the French Republic, exhausted by its own war, had rendered necessary, was an accident; but that, if a Napoleon had been lacking, another would have filled the place, is proved by the fact that the man has always been found as soon as he became necessary: Caesar, Augustus, Cromwell, etc. While Marx discovered the materialist conception of history, Thierry, Mignet, Guizot, and all the English historians up to 1850 are the proof that it was being striven for, and the discovery of the same conception by Morgan proved that the time was ripe for it and that indeed it *had* to be discovered.

So with all the other accidents, and apparent accidents, of history. The further the particular sphere which we are investigating is removed from the economic sphere and approaches that of pure abstract ideology, the more shall we find it exhibiting accidents in its development, the more will its curve run in a zig-zag. But if you plot the average axis of the curve, you will find that the axis of this curve will approach more and more nearly parallel to the axis of the curve of economic development the longer the period considered and the wider the field dealt with. . . .

• 26 •

CRIME AND FREE WILL *

Clarence Darrow (1857–1938)

. . . That man is the product of heredity and environment and that he acts as his machine responds to outside stimuli and nothing else, seem amply proven by the evolution and history of man. But, quite aside from this, logic and philosophy must lead to the same conclusions. This is not a universe where acts result from chance. Law is everywhere supreme. Every process of nature and life is a continuous sequence of cause and effect. . . .

All the teaching of the world is based on the theory that there is no free will. Why else should children be trained with so much care? Why should they be taught what is right and what is wrong? Why should so much pains be taken in forming habits? To what effect is the storing of knowledge in

* From *Crime: Its Cause and Treatment* by Clarence Darrow, pp. 34–36. Copyright 1922, 1950 by the publishers, Thomas Y. Crowell Company, New York, and used with their permission. The title of this selection has been supplied by the editors. Compare with selections 23, 28, and section IV of 47.

the brain of the child, except that it may be taught to avoid the wrong and to do the right? Man's every action is caused by motive. Whether his action is wise or unwise, the motive was at least strong enough to move him. If two or more motives pulled in opposite directions, he could not have acted from the weakest but must have obeyed the strongest. The same motives applied to some other machine might have produced an opposite result, but to his particular structure it was all-controlling. How any special motive will affect any special machine must depend upon the relative strength of the motive and make of the machine. It is for this reason that intelligent people have always taken so much pains to fortify the machine, so that it would respond to what they believed was right. To say that one could ever act from the weakest motive would bring chaos and chance into a world of method and order. Even punishment could have no possible effect to deter the criminal after release, or to influence others by the example of the punishment. As well might the kernel of corn refuse to grow upward to the sunlight, and grow downward instead.

Before any progress can be made in dealing with crime the world must fully realize that crime is only a part of conduct; that each act, criminal or otherwise, follows a cause; that given the same conditions the same result will follow forever and ever; that all punishment for the purpose of causing suffering, or growing out of hatred, is cruel and anti-social; that however much society may feel the need of confining the criminal, it must first of all understand that the act had an all-sufficient cause for which the individual was in no way responsible, and must find the cause of his conduct, and, so far as possible, remove the cause.

• 27 •

MODERN MATERIALISM *
Hugh Elliot (1881–1930)

. . . The main purpose of the present work is to defend the doctrine of materialism. . . . The outlines of this system are not new; the main features of it, indeed, have been admittedly associated with scientific progress for centuries past. An age of science is necessarily an age of materialism;

* Parts of chapters 5 and 6 of Modern Science and Materialism (1927). Reprinted by permission of the publishers, Longmans, Green & Co. Ltd., London. The title of this selection has been supplied by the editors. Compare with selections 11 and 21.

ours is a scientific age, and it may be said with truth that we are all materialists now. The main principles which I shall endeavour to emphasize
are three.

1. The uniformity of law. In early times events appeared to be entirely
hazardous and unaccountable, and they still seem so, if we confine attention purely to the passing moment. But as science advances, there is disclosed a uniformity in the procedure of Nature. When the conditions at
any one moment are precisely identical with those which prevailed at some
previous moment, the results flowing from them will also be identical. It is
found, for instance, that a body of given mass attracts some other body of
given mass at a given distance with a force of a certain strength. It is
found that when the masses, distances, and other conditions are precisely
repeated, the attraction between the bodies is always exactly the same. It
is found, further, that when the distance between the bodies is increased
the force of their attraction is diminished in a fixed proportion, and this
again is found to hold true at all distances at which they may be placed.
The force of their attraction again varies in a different but still constant
proportion to their masses. And hence results the law of gravitation, by
which the force of attraction can be precisely estimated from a knowledge
of the masses and distances between any two bodies whatever. A uniformity
is established which remains absolute within the experience of Man, and to
an equivalent extent the haphazard appearance of events is found to be
only an appearance. Innumerable other laws of a similar character are
gradually discovered, establishing a sort of nexus between every kind of
event. If oxygen and hydrogen in the proportion by weight of eight to one
are mixed together, and an electric spark is passed through them, water
is formed; and on every occasion where precisely the same conditions are
realized precisely the same result ensues. . . .

2. The denial of teleology. Scientific materialism warmly denies that
there exists any such thing as purpose in the Universe, or that events have
any ulterior motive or goal to which they are striving. It asserts that all
events are due to the interaction of matter and motion acting by blind
necessity in accordance with those invariable sequences to which we have
given the name of laws. This is an important bond of connection between
the materialism of the ancient Greeks and that of modern science. Among
all peoples not highly cultivated there reigns a passionate conviction, not
only that the Universe as a whole is working out some pre-determined purpose, but that every individual part of it subserves some special need in the
fulfilment of this purpose. Needless to say, the purpose has always been
regarded as associated with human welfare. The Universe, down to its
smallest parts, is regarded by primitive superstition as existing for the spe-

cial benefit of man. To such extreme lengths has this view been carried that even Bernardin de Saint-Pierre, who only died last century, argued that the reason why melons are ribbed is that they may be eaten more easily by families.

The reason for this early teleology is obvious. We all of us survey the Universe from the standpoint of our own centrality. Subjectively we all do stand actually at the centre of the Universe. Our entire experience of the Universe is an experience of it as it affects ourselves; for if it does not affect ourselves, we know of it only indirectly, and in primitive stages we do not know of it at all. As our education endows us with a wider outlook and a wider knowledge, we come to see that the objective Universe is very different from our own private subjective Universe. At first we discover that we as individuals are not the centre of the Universe, as appears to uncorrected experience, but that we are merely one individual among many others of equal status constituting a nation or society. We then perhaps regard our own society as the centre of the Universe, as many primitive peoples do, such, for instance, as the ancient Romans and the modern Chinese. Or we may regard our own sex as the purposed product of the Universe, as in many Mohammedan peoples, who hold that women have not souls like men, and that they exist purely for the benefit or use of men, in the same way that cattle exist in order to be eaten, or that melons are ribbed to indicate the proper amount of one portion.

With still further cultivation, the entire human species becomes regarded as the centre and object of all events in the Universe. This is the stage now reached by the masses in modern civilizations. Just as the existence of one particular individual has not the world-wide or cosmic importance that that individual is apt to suppose; just as the existence of a particular tribe or society is not of the profound historic import that that tribe or society very commonly imagines; so too the human species as a whole is far from being, as it too often believes, the sole object for which the Universe was created, with all things in it, great and small. The human species is, indeed, a mere incident in the universal redistribution of matter and motion; its existence has not the smallest cosmic significance. Our species is biologically very modern. Neither in numbers nor in antiquity can it compare with infinitely numerous species of other animals inhabiting the Earth. The Earth itself is one of the smaller planets, revolving round a minor star. The entire solar system of which the Earth is so insignificant a portion, is itself a system of contemptible minuteness, set among other luminaries and other systems which surpass it many times in magnitude, in brightness, and in every other ascertainable quality that we are accustomed to admire.

When it is alleged that the Universe is purposive, it is assumed that humanity is intimately connected with the purpose. Without that assumption, none but the most transcendental of philosophers would have any interest in maintaining teleology. As the anthropocentric doctrine falls, therefore, the doctrine of teleology must fall with it. This, at all events, is the position taken up by scientific, as indeed by all materialism; it is the position that I hope I shall have little difficulty in defending in the following pages. Nevertheless, however obvious its truth, we must recognize that it involves a profound alteration in the existing mental point of view of the majority of mankind; for most men have as yet not shaken off the habit, which all men necessarily start from, that they themselves, or their family, nation or kind, are in fact, as in appearance, the very centre of the cosmos.

3. The denial of any form of existence other than those envisaged by physics and chemistry, that is to say, other than existences that have some kind of palpable material characteristics and qualities. It is here that modern materialism begins to part company with ancient materialism, and it is here that I expect the main criticisms of opponents to be directed. The modern doctrine stands in direct opposition to a belief in any of those existences that are vaguely classed as "spiritual." To this category belong not only ghosts, gods, souls, *et hoc genus omne,** for these have long been rejected from the beliefs of most advanced thinkers. The time has now come to include also in the condemned list that further imaginary entity which we call "mind," "consciousness," etc., together with its various sub-species of intellect, will, feeling, etc., in so far as they are supposed to be independent or different from material existences or processes. . . .

It seems to the ordinary observer that nothing can be more remotely and widely separated than some so-called "act of consciousness" and a material object. An act of consciousness or mental process is a thing of which we are immediately and indubitably aware: so much I admit. But that it differs in any sort of way from a material process, that is to say, from the ordinary transformations of matter and energy, is a belief which I very strenuously deny, and which I propose to discuss and elucidate at length. . . . The proposition which I here desire to advance is that every event occurring in the Universe, including those events known as mental processes, and all kinds of human action or conduct, are expressible purely in terms of matter and motion. If we assume in the primeval nebula of the solar system no other elementary factors beyond those of matter and energy or motion, we can theoretically, as above remarked, deduce the existing Universe, including mind, consciousness, etc., without the introduction of any new

* and all things of this kind.

factor whatsoever. The existing Universe and all things and events therein may be theoretically expressed in terms of matter and energy, undergoing continuous redistribution in accordance with the ordinary laws of physics and chemistry. If all manifestations within our experience can be thus expressed, as has for long been believed by men of science, what need is there for the introduction of any new entity of spiritual character, called mind? It has no part to play; it is impotent in causation. According to Huxley's theory it accompanies certain physical processes as a shadow, without any power, or any reason, or any use. The world, as Huxley and the great majority of physiologists affirm, would be just the same without it. Now there is an ancient logical precept which retains a large validity: *entia non sunt multiplicanda praeter necessitatem.** It is sometimes referred to as William of Occam's razor, which cuts off and rejects from our theories all factors or entities which are superfluous in guiding us to an explanation. "Mind" as a separate entity is just such a superfluity. I will not deny—indeed I cordially affirm—that it is a direct datum of experience; but there is no direct datum of experience to the effect that it is anything different from certain cerebral processes . . .

The materialism which I shall advocate, therefore, is centred round three salient points: the uniformity of law, the exclusion of purpose, and the assertion of monism; that is to say, that there exists no kind of spiritual substance or entity of a different nature from that of which matter is composed.

The first of these propositions, otherwise called the Law of Universal Causation, affirms that nothing happens without a cause, and that the same causes under the same conditions always produce the same effects. In order to gain a true comprehension of this law, we have to define what we mean by "cause" and "effect," and what is the nature of the nexus between them. The conception of the Universe from which we start is that of a great system of matter and motion undergoing redistribution according to fixed sequences, which in the terminology of science are called laws. The matter is constantly undergoing transformation from one of its forms into another, and the energy is redistributed and transformed in a corresponding manner. From this primary conception alone, we are able to derive a precise definition of what is meant by cause, a problem which is almost insuperable from any other standpoint. . . . If we regard an event as a momentary phase in the redistribution of matter and motion, then the cause of the event is found in the immediately preceding state of distribution of that same matter and motion. Let us ask, for instance, what is the cause of the sudden appearance of a new fixed star in the heavens. Sup-

* entities are not to be multiplied beyond necessity.

posing that there were previously two extinct suns moving rapidly towards each other and coming into collision, we should be making a statement of events which would be recognized as a possibly true "cause." The second event, or "effect," is represented exclusively in terms of matter and motion by the idea of two coalesced and volatilized bodies giving rise to vast quantities of heat and light. And the cause is given merely by stating the previous distribution of that matter and energy which is concerned in the production of the event. The *matter* concerned in the event consisted of two solid bodies at a rapidly diminishing distance from one another. The *energy* consisted of half the product of their momentum and velocity. By the collision the matter contained in the solid bodies underwent that redistribution involved in passing into a gaseous state, with the decomposition of many of its molecules, that is to say, with a rearrangement or redistribution of its atoms. The energy of motion previously contained in the solid bodies underwent at the same time a transformation into heat and light. The sudden light, therefore, is explained, or derives its cause, merely by furnishing a statement of the previous distribution of the matter and energy concerned in its production. . . .

This leads me to the second problem which I have here to deal with, the problem of teleology. I have hitherto endeavoured to represent the notion of cause and effect in purely materialistic terms, to the exclusion of all metaphysical transcendentalism; to state the relation of cause and effect in terms of the redistribution of matter and motion. I now have to perform the same task for the conception of purpose, and more particularly of human purpose, in order to show how purposiveness may be translated into purely materialistic and mechanical terms; that is to say, how it, too, may be expressed as a phase of the normal process of redistribution of matter and motion under fixed and invariable laws.

At the outset of this inquiry, we have to notice that the word purpose is involved in the same vagueness of significance that attends almost all words used in popular speech. In general a word in popular use has to be defined and limited to some precise meaning before it is fit for employment in a philosophical discussion. In the present case the word is commonly employed in at least two meanings, which differ greatly from each other; and this duality of meaning leads to a duality in the derivative conceptions of "teleology," "finalism," "end," etc., which has not infrequently given rise to confusion and error. The two significations may be roughly grouped as intelligent purposiveness and unintelligent purposiveness, and the reduction of each of these to mechanistic terms involves two different lines of analysis. I shall deal first with unintelligent purposiveness.

In this case, the word is usually applied to a certain kind of organic reactions that bear an obvious relation to the requirements of the reacting organism. An *Amoeba* in the water throws out pseudopodia at random in all directions. When one of these pseudopodia comes into contact with some substance suitable for food, the protoplasm streams round and encloses the particle, which is thus incorporated in the body of the *Amoeba* and there digested. The reaction is purposive in the sense that a somewhat complicated series of movements is carried out, which leads to the preservation of the active organism.

In just the same way, when we ascend the animal scale, the sea-anemone spreads its tentacles at large under the surface of the water. On contact with any substance suitable for food the tentacles contract around the substance and draw it into the interior of the sea-anemone. This action is similarly purposive in that it procures the continued existence of the animal. In all animals the common movements and reactions are predominantly of this purposive type. If an object suddenly appears close to our eyes, we involuntarily close them for an instant, and this reaction is obviously purposive, as directed towards the protection of the eyes.

All these instinctive actions are purposive in character, yet equally, without doubt, they are all of the nature of reflex action, working blindly and inevitably to their conclusion. On contact with the tentacle of a sea-anemone, the stimulus thus applied to that tentacle sets up by entirely mechanical procedure organic processes which necessarily result in the observed contractions. Similarly, in the case of the human being, the sudden appearance of a near object causes an impulse to be conveyed down the optic nerve, which immediately and mechanically propagates its effect to the efferent nerves which lead to the muscles that close the eyelids. The same kind of reaction is characteristic of the functions in plants. The turning of flowers towards the light, and all the processes of absorption, transpiration, etc., are, on the one hand, subservient to the life and prosperity of the plant, while, on the other hand, they are blind mechanical reactions to stimuli.

Seeing that a single action may thus be at the same time both purposive and mechanical, it is plain that there can be no antithesis between the two; but that the difference between purpose and blind mechanism arises simply from our point of view, and not from any difference of objective character. Purposive reactions are not different from mechanical reactions, but they *are* mechanical reactions of a certain kind. Not all mechanical reactions are purposive, but all purposive reactions are mechanical; and it remains to determine *what* mechanical actions may be correctly described as purposive, and what are simply blind and meaningless. . . .

I now come to the second class of activities to which the name of purpose is applied, that is to say, cases of activity which bear reference to an end consciously and intelligently foreseen, such as the acts inspired by the conscious will in human beings. These activities are commonly regarded as being in a higher degree teleological than the unintelligent reactions hitherto considered; and in many uses of the word "purpose," reference is intended exclusively to these intelligent anticipations of future events, and to the activities carried out in consequence of such anticipations. In this sense purpose is allied to will, and purposive actions are more or less synonymous with voluntary actions. . . .

We are now in a position to appreciate the true meaning of those acts which are described as intelligently purposive. Being deliberate and reasoned activities, they are as far as possible removed from the simple type of reflex action in which response follows immediately on external stimulus. They belong to the category in which the immediate stimulus is in the brain itself, and is to be regarded as consisting of rearrangements of the matter and energy contained in the nervous substance of the brain. The brain during consciousness can never be still, and its unceasing activities supply the stimulus, not only for purposive, but for all actions of an intellectual character. . . . Among these cerebral processes is that which is known psychologically as a desire for some external object or event, a visualization of some external phenomenon as an end or purpose to be attained. This desire may then act upon efferent nerves and give rise to the activities which we know as purposive. The essence of a purposive action, and the standard by which it is distinguished from other kinds of actions, is that the "end" to which the action leads was previously represented in the brain of the agent, and composes the stimulus of action. The compound stimulus arises, as I have said, from the composition of large numbers of elementary stimuli previously received. It consists psychologically of a faint representation of the sensation which would be vividly presented by the realization of some outward occurrence. And when this faint representation actually functions as a stimulus which innervates the muscles whose contraction brings about the external occurrence represented, we have what is called an action of intelligent purpose. . . .

Intelligent purpose, like unintelligent purpose, is then only a name given to a particular kind of incident in the midst of the eternal redistribution of matter and motion under blind mechanical laws. It is in perfect harmony with that materialistic scheme; it can be stated in terms of the purest mechanism. As the matter and motion undergo their invariable and unalterable redistribution, we naturally find ourselves more interested in some phases of it than in others; and in one class of evolving events we are so interested and we have such frequent occasion to refer to them, that we denominate them by a special name—the name of purposive. By this name we designate the majority of those redistributions which issue from the little whirlpools of matter and energy called organisms, and those factors in particular by which the immediate continuance of such whirlpools is ensured.

I have now dealt with the law of universal causation, and with the doctrines of teleology. It remains only to say a few preliminary words about the third main pillar of materialism—the assertion of monism, that is, that there are not two kinds of fundamental existences, material and spiritual, but one kind only. . . . Mental manifestations and bodily manifestations are not two different things, as generally supposed, but one and the same thing appearing under different aspects. I shall not attempt to deal with any of the so-called "non-material" existences with the exception of mind; for if mind can be identified with matter, all other kinds of non-material entities must lapse, even those described by religious systems. . . .

We reached the conclusion in a previous chapter that the bodily organism is a complex machine. We found that all its processes and activities are attributable to physico-chemical forces, identical with those which are organized in the inorganic realm. We learnt that there is no "vital force" or other spiritual interference with the normal physical sequences. If, then, there be a mind, it is reduced to the function of inertly and uselessly accompanying the activities of certain neural elements. This is the doctrine of epiphenomenalism, and it is the last word possible to one who accepts the duality of mind and matter. It is a theory which on the face of it is devoid of verisimilitude. What can be the use of such a shadowy and inefficient entity? What parallel can be found in Nature for the existence of so gratuitous a superfluity? Moreover, what mechanism, conceivable or inconceivable, could cause it thus to shadow neural processes, which *ex hypothesi* do not produce it? If one such mental state is the cause of the next, how does it happen that it causes the one which is necessary to accompany the actual neural process at the moment? Epiphenomenalism involves us in a pre-established harmony that is profoundly opposed to the scientific spirit of the twentieth century. The problem, however, is not one that need be discussed on the grounds of *a priori* probability. It is a theory that may be rigidly refuted, and to that task I now turn.

It is a part of the doctrine of epiphenomenalism that a man would to all external appearance be precisely the same whether he was possessed of his epiphenomenal mind or not. Conduct, action, expression, would not in the slightest extent be affected were he completely devoid of mind and consciousness; for all these things depend upon material sequences alone. Men are puppets or automata, and we have no further grounds for supposing them to have minds than the fact that we know we have a mind ourselves, and the argument by analogy from ourselves to them. But arguments from analogy are notoriously insecure, and it seems, therefore, to be quite within the bounds of possibility to the epiphenomenalist that some or all other men may be mindless syntheses of matter. Descartes did, indeed, affirm this very thing of lower animals.

Now let us assume that such a man actually exists, or, if you prefer, let us assume that physical chemistry has advanced to such a pitch that a man may be synthetized in the laboratory, starting from the elements, carbon, nitrogen, etc., of which protoplasm is composed. Let us assume in any case a "synthetic man" without a mind, yet indistinguishable by the epiphenomenalist hypothesis from another man identically constituted materially but having a mind. Ask the synthetic man whether he has a mind. What will he say? Inevitably he will say yes. For he must say the same thing as the man, identically made, who *has* a mind. Otherwise the same question would set up different responses in the nervous systems of the two, and that is by hypothesis impossible. The sound of the words "have you a mind?" entering the ears of the synthetic man sets up highly complex cerebral associations (which we call grasping their meaning); these associations will, after a short time, culminate in nervous currents to the tongue, lips and larynx, which will be moved in such a way as to produce an audible and intelligent answer. Now this answer must be the same in the case of the man who has a mind as in the case of the mindless man, since their nervous systems are the same. If there was a different vocal response to an identical aural stimulus, then there must in one of them have been some external interference with the physico-chemical sequences. Mind must have broken through the chain of physical causality, and that is contrary to hypothesis.

What can the epiphenomenalist say? That the mindless man is a liar, to say he has a mind? That will not do, for if the two men are objectively identical one cannot be a liar, and the other not; one engaged in deceit, while the other speaks the truth. The epiphenomenalist is thrown back, therefore, on the assumption that the mindless man has made a mistake; that he thinks he has a mind, but really has not one; that his nervous constitution is such as to impel him to the conviction that he has a mind when he really has not, to lead him to talk upon psychical phenomena and their differences from matter, and in general to behave exactly as if he knew all about mind and matter, had considered the subject of their relationship, etc.

The example shows, furthermore, that the condition of "knowing one has a mind" is a condition which can be stated and accounted for in rigidly materialistic terms. When the epiphenomenalist himself asserts that he has a mind, the movements of his vocal cords by which he makes that pronouncement are by his own theory led up to by a chain of purely material sequences. He would make just the same pronouncement if he had no mind at all. His claim to possess a mind, therefore, is wholly irrelevant to the real question whether he actually has a mind or not. The events that make him say he has a mind are not the actual possession of a mind, but those cerebral processes which, in epiphenomenalist language, are said to underlie states of consciousness. It is the cerebral processes alone which make him speak, and his utterance, his belief in a mind, furnish testimony alone to the existence of those cerebral processes. Were the mind truly able to compel a belief and an announcement of its own existence, it could only be by breaking through the chain of material bodily sequences, and this is a vitalistic supposition that is ruled out by physiology. The belief in the possession of a mind is a cerebral condition, due, not to the actual possession of a mind, but to definite pre-existing cerebral conditions on the same material plane.

I do not see how epiphenomenalism could be much more effectively refuted. Yet it is the only respectable dualistic theory that is compatible with physiological mechanism. Let me recapitulate for a moment the facts, now before us, upon which we have to establish a theory of the relationship of mind and body.

Physiology has shown that bodily activity of every kind is a product of purely material sequences, into the course of which there is no irruption of any spiritualistic factor. On the dualistic theory, that doctrine is excessively difficult to understand. You move your arm by an act of will, or what seems to be a non-material cause, and yet it is conclusively established that the movement of the arm is due to definite material changes occurring in the brain, and caused by the fixed laws of physics and chemistry in the most determinist fashion. Now, anchoring ourselves firmly to that fact, we are confronted with the problem of where to put the mind. For every mental state there is some corresponding cerebral state; the one appears to be the exact counterpart of the other down to the smallest discoverable particular. Now on the dualistic assumption, there is only one possible hypothesis, namely, that of epiphenomenalism. Or, rather, it is incorrect to call it an hypothesis; for *if* there are two things, mind and body, epiphenomenalism is no more than a statement of the facts established by physiology and psychology. Dualistic physiologists, therefore, are practically forced to accept it. Yet, as I have shown, it is utterly untenable when properly thought out.

We are faced, therefore, by two possible alternatives: (1) to abandon mechanism, (2) to abandon dualism. Now mechanism is a physiological theory which is proved. We must hold fast to it therefore at any expense to our metaphysical preconceptions. The only remaining alternative, then, is the abandonment of dualism. We must affirm that there is no thin shadow accompanying cerebral processes as alleged; that there are *not* two things, mind and body, fundamentally distinct. We must, in short, affirm that the mind *is* the cerebral processes themselves, not an imaginary accompaniment of them. . . . When we recollect that matter is but one form of experience, while mental manifestations are another similar form; when we recollect that elementary experiences may be associated into larger groups, we shall scarcely have greater difficulty in understanding how a sensation can be identified with a cerebral process than we have in understanding how, for instance, redness and hardness can be identified as properties of one material object.

I have said that mind is not an independent existence, but that it is a name for the sum-total of certain kinds of nervous or cerebral processes, and that it is therefore to be identified with phenomena of a material order. The difficulty of grasping this proposition will be very largely mitigated by the fact that there exists a phenomenon from the inorganic world which furnishes a remarkably true and precise analogy to this strange product of the organic world. The phenomenon to which I refer is the phenomenon of fire. In very early Greek philosophy, the Universe was believed to consist of earth, air, fire, and water. Fire was held to be a distinct entity on a par with the other three. We now know that it is not itself an entity of any kind, but is a manifestation of a certain chemical process, as for instance, the oxidation of carbon, in the course of which the carbon particles give forth light and heat. There is nothing whatever present in a flame except these molecules undergoing chemical change; yet, to an uneducated eye, the flame seems to be a distinct entity, differing altogether from a mere collection of chemically active material particles.

We may interpret the existence of mind in a precisely analogous manner. All that really exists is the material particles of the substance of the nervous system. When these particles enter upon a certain kind of chemical activity, the effect is to suggest the existence of some new kind of elusive non-material entity called mind. But this entity has no more real existence than has fire. In each case we have to do exclusively with molecules undergoing disintegration or combination. This chemical activity suffices in itself to account for the whole of the phenomena flowing from the centre of activity, and the belief in any additional independent entity is a fallacy which itself can be expressed and explained in physico-chemical terms. The flames of a fire flash out swiftly in a closely similar form. So, too, the ideation or emotion of the individual may open up new avenues of mind for a brief moment, as they travel on to a new position. In each case the fluctuations of form are due to the constantly changing area of chemical activity; and just as the fire maintains for short periods a relative constancy of size and shape, so the mental content of an individual is apt to remain for a time at about the same value of intensity, and fastened to the same subjects of attention. At times the fire burns low; at other times it bursts forth into exuberant activity. The accuracy of the analogy is due to the fact that both phenomena are based upon the same foundation; the one is a manifestation from inorganic matter, while the other is a manifestation from organic matter, and therefore immeasurably more complex as to its chemistry.

When once we have got over the shock which monism carries to those accustomed to think in dualistic terms, we find that the great majority of the difficulties of metaphysics fall away. By an act of will I raise my arm. The plain man insists that his will did it; the physiologist knows that it was physico-chemical processes in the brain. The dilemma is at once overcome when the philosopher points out that the will *is* the physico-chemical processes, and that they both mean the same thing. The whole controversy of free-will and determinism is resolved by the discovery that each side means exactly the same thing, the only difference being in the terms used. The difficulty of the epiphenomenalist is also solved. He says he has a mind. What makes him say so is not a transcendental "knowledge of having mind," but a certain cerebral state. When we have affirmed the absolute identity of that knowledge with that cerebral state, all difficulties vanish. The mind is the sum-total of cerebral conditions. He says he has a mind; it is the existence of the cerebral conditions which cause him to say so. He says he has a mind because he has cerebral conditions, and his remark is true and intelligible only on the one hypothesis that the mind *is* the cerebral conditions.

A further difficulty that is abolished by monism is that of the unity and personality of mind. We feel that our consciousness is not made up merely of a succession of discrete elements, but that these are bound together as properties of a single entity, mind or soul. This unity of consciousness finds its exact parallel in the unity of the nervous system. I have already pointed out that neural activity tends at any moment to be focussed at some particular part of the nervous system. The focus of activity may travel from one part to another of the nervous system, but activity does not normally extend over any large portion of the nervous system at any one moment. The region of the nervous system momentarily illuminated by functional activity corresponds to the state of consciousness momentarily experienced.

And just as the focus of activity can travel freely from one part of the nervous system to another, but can never travel *outside* the nervous system, so states of consciousness can follow one another within the limits of the mind, and no state of consciousness can be experienced which is not a part of the personal and individual mind.

Monism again resolves the great biological difficulty as to the origin of consciousness. The biological conclusions as to the origin of life are to the effect that living and organic matter was developed by evolution from non-living and inorganic matter. The evolution of Man from unicellular parentage is a fact. There is little or no reason to doubt that his unicellular ancestor was evolved just as gradually from inorganic matter. Now, says the dualist, we know that the man has a mind. It follows, therefore, either that inorganic matter has a psychical accompaniment, or else that, in the course of evolution, there was a sudden leap: mind was suddenly intruded at some period of Man's past history. Neither of these hypotheses is easy to entertain, or perhaps even practicable to conceive. The doctrine of monism, with its assertion that there are not two ultimate things, but one, causes the difficulty to vanish; for there is then no necessity to introduce a new entity at any period of an organism's evolution. According to our theory, a conscious state is a specific neural functioning. If there is no discontinuity in the evolution of nervous elements from inorganic matter, there is then no discontinuity in the evolution of consciousness. . . .

• 28 •

A DEFENCE OF FREE WILL *

C. Arthur Campbell (1897–   )

. . . The problem of free will gets its urgency for the ordinary educated man by reason of its close connection with the conception of moral responsibility. When we regard a man as morally responsible for an act, we regard him as a legitimate object of moral praise or blame in respect of it. But it seems plain that a man cannot be a legitimate object of moral praise

* Part of "In Defence of Free Will," an Inaugural Address delivered in the University of Glasgow on April 26th, 1938. Reprinted with the kind permission of the author and the publishers, Jackson, Son & Company, publishers to the University of Glasgow. The title of this selection has been supplied by the editors. Compare with selections 23 and 26.

or blame for an act unless in willing the act he is in some important sense a "free" agent. Evidently free will in some sense, therefore, is a precondition of moral responsibility. Without doubt it is the realisation that any threat to freedom is thus a threat to moral responsibility—with all that that implies—combined with the knowledge that there are a variety of considerations, philosophic, scientific, and theological, tending to place freedom in jeopardy, that gives to the problem of free will its perennial and universal appeal. And it is therefore in close connection with the question of the conditions of moral responsibility that any discussion of the problem must proceed, if it is not to be academic in the worst sense of the term.

We raise the question at once, therefore, what are the conditions, in respect of freedom, which must attach to an act in order to make it a morally responsible act? It seems to me that the fundamental conditions are two. . . .

The first condition is the universally recognised one that the act must be *self*-caused, *self*-determined. But it is important to accept this condition in its full rigour. The agent must be not merely *a* cause but the *sole* cause of that for which he is deemed morally responsible. If entities other than the self have also a causal influence upon an act, then that act is not one for which we can say without qualification that the *self* is morally responsible. If in respect of it we hold the self responsible at all, it can only be for some feature of the act—assuming the possibility of disengaging such a feature —of which the self *is* the sole cause. I do not see how this conclusion can be evaded. But it has awkward implications which have led not a few people to abandon the notion of individual moral responsibility altogether.

This first condition, however, is quite clearly not sufficient. It is possible to conceive an act of which the agent is the sole cause, but which is at the same time an act *necessitated* by the agent's nature. . . . In the case of such an act, where the agent could not do otherwise than he did, we must all agree, I think, that it would be inept to say that he *ought* to have done otherwise and is thus morally blameworthy, or *ought not* to have done otherwise and is thus morally praiseworthy. It is perfectly true that we do sometimes hold a person morally responsible for an act, even when we believe that he, being what he now is, virtually could not do otherwise. But underlying that judgement is always the assumption that the person has *come* to be what he now is in virtue of past acts of will in which he *was* confronted by real alternatives, by genuinely open possibilities: and, strictly speaking, it is in respect of these *past* acts of his that we praise or blame the agent *now*. For ultimate analysis, the agent's power of alternative action would seem to be an inexpugnable condition of his liability to moral praise or blame, i.e. of his moral responsibility.

We may lay down, therefore, that an act is a "free" act in the sense required for moral responsibility only if the agent (a) is the sole cause of the act; and (b) could exert his causality in alternative ways. . . . The doctrine which demands, and asserts, the fulfilment of both conditions is the doctrine we call "Libertarianism." . . .

And now, the conditions of free will being defined in these general terms, we have to ask whether human beings are in fact capable of performing free acts; and if so, where precisely such acts are to be found. In order to prepare the way for an answer, it is desirable, I think, that we should get clear at once about the significance of a certain very familiar, but none the less formidable, criticism of free will which . . . the Libertarian has to meet. This is the criticism which bases itself upon the facts of heredity on the one hand and of environment on the other. I may briefly summarise the criticism as follows.

Every historic self has an hereditary nature consisting of a group of in-born propensities, in range more or less common to the race, but specific to the individual in their respective strengths. With this equipment the self just *happens* to be born. Strictly speaking, it antedates the existence of the self proper, i.e. the existence of the self-conscious subject, and it is it-self the effect of a series of causes leading back to indefinitely remote antiquity. It follows, therefore, that any of the self's choices that manifests the influence of his hereditary nature is not a choice of which *he*, the actual historic self, is the sole cause. The choice is determined, at least in part, by factors external to the self. The same thing holds good of "environment." Every self is born and bred in a particular physical and social environment, not of his own choosing, which plays upon him in innumerable ways, encouraging this propensity, discouraging that, and so on. Clearly any of the self's choices that manifests the influence of environmental factors is likewise a choice which is determined, at least in part, by factors external to the self. But if we thus grant, as seems inevitable, that heredity and environment are external influences, where shall we find a choice in the whole history of a self that is not subject to external influence? Surely we must admit that every particular act of choice bears the marks of the agent's hereditary nature and environmental nurture; in which case a free act, in the sense of an act determined solely by the self, must be dismissed as a mere chimaera. . . .

The externality of these influences is taken for granted in our reflective practical judgements upon persons. On those occasions when we are in real earnest about giving a critical and considered estimate of a man's moral

calibre—as, e.g. in any serious biographical study—we impose upon ourselves as a matter of course the duty of enquiring with scrupulous care into
his hereditary propensities and environmental circumstances, with a view
to discovering how far his conduct is influenced by these factors. And
having traced these influences, we certainly do not regard the result as
having no bearing on the question of the man's moral responsibility for
his conduct. On the contrary, the very purpose of the enquiry is to enable
us, by due appreciation of the *external* influences that affect his conduct,
to gain as accurate a view as possible of that which can justly be attributed
to the man's own *self*-determination. The allowances that we all of us do
in practice make for hereditary and environmental influences in passing
judgement on our fellows would be meaningless if we did not suppose
these influences to be in a real sense "external" to the self. . . .

We know now that condition (a) is not fulfilled by any act in respect
of which inheritance or environment exerts a causal influence. For that
type of influence has been shown to be in a real sense external to the self.
The free act of which we are in search has therefore got to be one into
which influences of this kind do not enter at all. . . .

. . . Our reflective practical judgements on persons, while fully recog-
nising the externality of the influence of heredity and environment, do
nevertheless presuppose throughout that there *is something* in conduct
which is genuinely self-determined; something which the agent contributes
solely on his own initiative, unaffected by external influences; something
for which, accordingly, he may justly be held morally responsible. That
conviction may, of course, be a false one. But the fact of its wide-spread
existence can hardly be without significance for our problem.

Let us proceed, then, by following up this clue. Let us ask, why do human beings so obstinately persist in believing that there is an indissoluble
core of purely *self*-originated activity which even heredity and environment are powerless to affect? There can be little doubt, I think, of the
answer in general terms. They do so, at bottom, because they feel certain
of the existence of such activity from their immediate practical experience
of themselves. Nor can there be in the end much doubt, I think, in what
function of the self that activity is to be located. There seems to me to be
one, and only one, function of the self with respect to which the agent can
even pretend to have an assurance of that absolute self-origination which
is here at issue. But to render precise the nature of that function is obviously
of quite paramount importance: and we can do so, I think, only by way
of a somewhat thorough analysis—which I now propose to attempt—of
the experiential situation in which it occurs, *viz.* the situation of "moral
temptation."

It is characteristic of that situation that in it I am aware of an end A which I believe to be morally right, and also of an end B, incompatible with A, towards which, in virtue of that system of conative dispositions which constitutes my "character" as so far formed, I entertain a strong desire. There may be, and perhaps must be, desiring elements in my nature which are directed to A also. But what gives to the situation its specific character as one of moral temptation is that the urge of our desiring nature towards the right end, A, is felt to be *relatively* weak. We are sure that if our desiring nature is permitted to issue directly in action, it is end B that we shall choose. That is what is meant by saying, as William James does, that end B is "in the line of least resistance" relatively to our conative dispositions. The expression is, of course, a metaphorical one, but it serves to describe, graphically enough, a situation of which we all have frequent experience, *viz.* where we recognise a specific end as that towards which the "set" of our desiring nature most strongly inclines us, and which we shall indubitably choose if no inhibiting factor intervenes.

But inhibiting factors, we should most of us say, *may* intervene: and that in two totally different ways which it is vital to distinguish clearly. The inhibiting factor may be of the nature of another desire (or aversion), which operates by changing the balance of the desiring situation. Though at one stage I desire B, which I believe to be wrong, more strongly than I desire A, which I believe to be right, it may happen that before action is taken I become aware of certain hitherto undiscerned consequences of A which I strongly desire, and the result may be that now not B but A presents itself to me as the end in the line of least resistance. Moral temptation is here overcome by the simple process of ceasing to be a moral temptation.

That is one way, and probably by far the commoner way, in which an inhibiting factor intervenes. But it is certainly not regarded by the self who is confronted by moral temptation as the *only* way. In such situations we all believe, rightly or wrongly, that even although B *continues* to be in the line of least resistance, even although, in other words, the situation remains one with the characteristic marks of moral temptation, we *can* nevertheless align ourselves with A. We can do so, we believe, because we have the power to introduce a new energy, to make what we call an "effort of will," whereby we are able to act contrary to the felt balance of mere desire, and to achieve the higher end despite the fact that it continues to be in the line of greater resistance relatively to our desiring nature. The self in practice believes that it has this power; and believes, moreover, that the decision rests solely with its self, here and now, whether this power be exerted or not.

Now the objective validity or otherwise of this belief is not at the moment in question. I am here merely pointing to its existence as a psychological fact. No amount of introspective analysis, so far as I can see, even tends to disprove that we do as a matter of fact believe, in situations of moral temptation, that it rests with our self absolutely to decide whether we exert the effort of will which will enable us to rise to duty, or whether we shall allow our desiring nature to take its course.

I have now to point out, further, how this act of moral decision, at least in the significance which it has for the agent himself, fulfils in full the two conditions which we found it necessary to lay down at the beginning for the kind of "free" act which moral responsibility presupposes.

For obviously it is, in the first place, an act which the agent believes he could perform in alternative ways. He believes that it is genuinely open to him to put forth effort—in varying degrees, if the situation admits of that —or withhold it altogether. And when he *has* decided—in whatever way —he remains convinced that these alternative courses were really open to him.

It is perhaps a little less obvious, but, I think, equally certain, that the agent believes the second condition to be fulfilled likewise, i.e. that the act of decision is determined *solely* by his self. It appears less obvious, because we all realise that formed character has a great deal to do with the choices that we make; and formed character is, without a doubt, partly dependent on the external factors of heredity and environment. But it is crucial here that we should not misunderstand the precise nature of the influence which formed character brings to bear upon the choices that constitute conduct. No one denies that it determines, at least largely, what things we desire, and again how greatly we desire them. It may thus fairly be said to determine the felt balance of desires in the situation of moral temptation. But all that that amounts to is that formed character prescribes the nature of the situation *within* which the act of moral decision takes place. It does not in the least follow that it has any influence whatsoever in determining the act of decision itself—the decision as to whether we shall exert effort or take the easy course of following the bent of our desiring nature: take, that is to say, the course which, in virtue of the determining influence of our character as so far formed, we feel to be in the line of least resistance.

When one appreciates this, one is perhaps better prepared to recognise the fact that the agent himself in the situation of moral temptation does not, and indeed could not, regard his formed character as having any influence whatever upon his act of decision as such. For the very nature of that decision, as it presents itself to him, is as to whether he will or will not permit his formed character to dictate his action. In other words, the agent distinguishes sharply between the self which makes the decision, and the self which, as formed character, determines not the decision but the situation within which the decision takes place. Rightly or wrongly, the agent believes that through his act of decision he can oppose and transcend his own formed character in the interest of duty. We are therefore obliged to say, I think, that the agent *cannot* regard his formed character as in any sense a determinant of the act of decision as such. The act is felt to be a genuinely creative act, originated by the self *ad hoc*, and by the self alone. . . .

Now in considering the claim to truth of this belief of our practical consciousness, we should begin by noting that the onus of proof rests upon the critic who rejects this belief. Until cogent evidence to the contrary is adduced, we are entitled to put our trust in a belief which is so deeply embedded in our experience as practical beings as to be, I venture to say, ineradicable from it. Anyone who doubts whether it is ineradicable may be invited to think himself imaginatively into a situation of moral temptation as we have above described it, and then to ask himself whether in that situation he finds it possible to *disbelieve* that his act of decision has the characteristics in question. I have no misgivings about the answer. It is possible to disbelieve only when we are thinking abstractly about the situation; not when we are living through it, either actually or in imagination. This fact certainly establishes a strong *prima facie* presumption in favour of the Libertarian position. Nevertheless I agree that we shall have to weigh carefully several criticisms of high authority before we can feel justified in asserting free will as an ultimate and unqualified truth. . . .

I shall begin with one which, though it is a simple matter to show its irrelevance to the Libertarian doctrine as I have stated it, is so extremely popular that it cannot safely be ignored.

The charge made is that the Libertarian view is incompatible with the *predictability* of human conduct. For we do make rough predictions of people's conduct, on the basis of what we know of their character, every day of our lives, and there can be no doubt that the practice, within certain limits, is amply justified by results. Indeed if it were not so, social life would be reduced to sheer chaos. The close relationship between character and conduct which prediction postulates really seems to be about as certain as anything can be. But the Libertarian view, it is urged, by ascribing to the self a mysterious power of decision uncontrolled by character, and capable of issuing in acts inconsistent with character, denies that continuity between character and conduct upon which prediction depends. If Libertarianism is true, prediction is impossible. But prediction *is* possible, therefore Libertarianism is untrue.

My answer is that the Libertarian view is perfectly compatible with prediction within certain limits, and that there is no empirical evidence at all that prediction is in fact possible beyond these limits. The following considerations will, I think, make the point abundantly clear.

(1) There is no question, on our view, of a free will that can will just anything at all. The range of possible choices is limited by the agent's character in every case; for nothing can be an object of possible choice which is not suggested by either the agent's desires or his moral ideals, and these depend on "character" for us just as much as for our opponents. We have, indeed explicitly recognised at an earlier stage that character determines the situation within which the act of moral decision takes place, although not the act of moral decision itself. This consideration obviously furnishes a broad basis for at least approximate predictions.

(2) There is *one* experiential situation, and *one only*, on our view, in which there is any possibility of the act of will not being in accordance with character; *viz.* the situation in which the course which formed character prescribes is a course in conflict with the agent's moral ideal: in other words, the situation of moral temptation. Now this is a situation of comparative rarity. Yet with respect to all other situations in life we are in full agreement with those who hold that conduct is the response of the agent's formed character to the given situation. Why should it not be so? There could be no reason, on our view any more than on another, for the agent even to consider deviating from the course which his formed character prescribes and he most strongly desires, *unless* that course is believed by him to be incompatible with what is right.

(3) Even within that one situation which is relevant to free will, our view can still recognise a certain basis for prediction. In that situation our character as so far formed prescribes a course opposed to duty, and an effort of will is required if we are to deviate from that course. But of course we are all aware that a greater effort of will is required in proportion to the degree in which we have to transcend our formed character in order to will the right. Such action is, as we say, "harder." But if action is "harder" in proportion as it involves deviation from formed character, it seems reasonable to suppose that, on the whole, action will be of rarer occurrence in that same proportion: though perhaps we may not say that at any level of deviation it becomes flatly impossible. It follows that even with respect to situations of moral temptation we may usefully employ our knowledge of the agent's character as a clue to prediction. It will be a clue of limited, but of by no means negligible, value. It will warrant us in predicting, e.g., of a person who has become enslaved to alcohol, that he is unlikely, even if fully aware of the moral evil of such slavery, to be success

ful immediately and completely in throwing off its shackles. Predictions
of this kind we all make often enough in practice. And there seems no
reason at all why a Libertarian doctrine should wish to question their
validity.

Now when these three considerations are borne in mind, it becomes
quite clear that the doctrine we are defending is compatible with a very
substantial measure of predictability indeed. And I submit that there is
not a jot of empirical evidence that any larger measure than this obtains in
fact.

Let us pass on then to consider a much more interesting and, I think,
more plausible criticism. It is constantly objected against the Libertarian
doctrine that it is fundamentally *unintelligible*. Libertarianism holds that
the act of moral decision is the *self's* act, and yet insists at the same time
that it is not influenced by any of those determinate features in the self's
nature which go to constitute its "character." But, it is asked, do not these
two propositions contradict one another? Surely a *self*-determination which
is determination by something other than the self's *character* is a contradiction in terms? What meaning is there in the conception of a "self"
in abstraction from its "character"? If you really wish to maintain, it is
urged, that the act of decision is not determined by the self's character, you
ought to admit frankly that it is not determined by the *self* at all. But in
that case, of course, you will not be advocating a freedom which lends any
kind of support to moral responsibility; indeed very much the reverse.

Now this criticism, and all of its kind, seem to me to be the product of a
simple, but extraordinarily pervasive, error: the error of confining one's self
to the categories of the external observer in dealing with the actions of
human agents. Let me explain.

It is perfectly true that the stand-point of the external observer, which
we are obliged to adopt in dealing with physical processes, does not furnish
us with even a glimmering of a notion of what can be meant by an entity
which acts causally and yet not through any of the determinate features
of its character. So far as we confine ourselves to external observation, I
agree that this notion must seem to us pure nonsense. But then we are *not*
obliged to confine ourselves to external observation in dealing with the
human agent. Here, though here alone, we have the inestimable advantage
of being able to apprehend operations from the *inside*, from the standpoint of *living* experience. But if we do adopt this internal stand-point—
surely a proper stand-point, and one which we should be only too glad to
adopt if we could in the case of other entities—the situation is entirely
changed. We find that we not merely can, but constantly do, attach meaning to a causation which is the self's causation but is yet not exercised by

the self's character. We have seen as much already in our analysis of the situation of moral temptation. When confronted by such a situation, we saw, we are certain that it lies with our *self* to decide whether we shall let our character as so far formed dictate our action or whether we shall by effort oppose its dictates and rise to duty. We are certain, in other words, that the act is *not* determined by our *character*, while we remain equally certain that the act *is* determined by our *self*.

Or look, for a further illustration . . . to the experience of effortful willing itself, where the act of decision has found expression in the will to rise to duty. In such an experience we are certain that it is our self which makes the effort. But we are equally certain that the effort does not flow from that system of conative dispositions which we call our formed character; for the very function that the effort has for us is to enable us to act against the "line of least resistance," i.e. to act in a way *contrary* to that to which our formed character inclines us.

I conclude, therefore, that those who find the Libertarian doctrine of the self's causality in moral decision inherently unintelligible find it so simply because they restrict themselves, quite arbitrarily, to an inadequate stand-point: a stand-point from which, indeed, a genuinely creative activity, if it existed, never *could* be apprehended. . . .

PART V

PHILOSOPHY OF RELIGION

• 29 •

THE NECESSARY EXISTENCE OF GOD *
St. Anselm (1033–1109)

. . . Lord, I acknowledge and I thank thee that thou hast created me in this thine image, in order that I may be mindful of thee, may conceive of thee, and love thee; but that image has been so consumed and wasted away by vices, and obscured by the smoke of wrong-doing, that it cannot achieve that for which it was made, except thou renew it, and create it anew. I do not endeavor, O Lord, to penetrate thy sublimity, for in no wise do I compare my understanding with that; but I long to understand in some degree thy truth, which my heart believes and loves. For I do not seek to understand that I may believe, but I believe in order to understand. For this also I believe,—that unless I believed, I should not understand. . . .

And so, Lord, do thou, who dost give understanding to faith, give me, so far as thou knowest it to be profitable, to understand that thou art as we believe; and that thou art that which we believe. And, indeed, we believe that thou art a being than which nothing greater can be conceived. Or is there no such nature, since the fool hath said in his heart, there is no God? . . . But, at any rate, this very fool, when he hears of this being of which I speak—a being than which nothing greater can be conceived—understands what he hears, and what he understands is in his understanding; although he does not understand it to exist.

For, it is one thing for an object to be in the understanding, and another to understand that the object exists. When a painter first conceives of what he will afterwards perform, he has it in his understanding, but he does not yet understand it to be, because he has not yet performed it. But after he has made the painting, he both has it in his understanding, and he understands that it exists, because he has made it.

Hence, even the fool is convinced that something exists in the understanding, at least, than which nothing greater can be conceived. For, when he hears of this, he understands it. And whatever is understood, exists in

---

* Part of Ch. 1, and Chs. 2 through 4 of the *Proslogium*, translated from the Latin by Sidney Norton Deane, Open Court Publishing Co., 1903; reprinted with the kind permission of the publisher. The title of this selection has been supplied by the editors. See also selections 30 and 31.

183

the understanding. And assuredly that, than which nothing greater can be conceived, cannot exist in the understanding alone. For, suppose it exists in the understanding alone: then it can be conceived to exist in reality; which is greater.

Therefore, if that, than which nothing greater can be conceived, exists in the understanding alone, the very being, than which nothing greater can be conceived, is one, than which a greater can be conceived. But obviously this is impossible. Hence, there is no doubt that there exists a being, than which nothing greater can be conceived, and it exists both in the understanding and in reality. . . .

And it assuredly exists so truly, that it cannot be conceived not to exist. For, it is possible to conceive of a being which cannot be conceived not to exist; and this is greater than one which can be conceived not to exist. Hence, if that, than which nothing greater can be conceived, can be conceived not to exist, it is not that, than which nothing greater can be conceived. But this is an irreconcilable contradiction. There is, then, so truly a being than which nothing greater can be conceived to exist, that it cannot even be conceived not to exist; and this being thou art, O Lord, our God.

So truly, therefore, dost thou exist, O Lord, my God, that thou canst not be conceived not to exist; and rightly. For, if a mind could conceive of a being better than thee, the creature would rise above the Creator; and this is most absurd. And, indeed, whatever else there is, except thee alone, can be conceived not to exist. To thee alone, therefore, it belongs to exist more truly than all other beings, and hence in a higher degree than all others. For, whatever else exists does not exist so truly, and hence in a less degree it belongs to it to exist. Why, then, has the fool said in his heart, there is no God . . . since it is so evident, to a rational mind, that thou dost exist in the highest degree of all? Why, except that he is dull and a fool? . . .

But how has the fool said in his heart what he could not conceive; or how is it that he could not conceive what he said in his heart? Since it is the same to say in the heart, and to conceive.

But, if really, nay, since really, he both conceived, because he said in his heart; and did not say in his heart, because he could not conceive; there is more than one way in which a thing is said in the heart or conceived. For, in one sense, an object is conceived, when the word signifying it is conceived; and in another, when the very entity, which the object is, is understood.

In the former sense, then, God can be conceived not to exist; but in the latter, not at all. For no one who understands what fire and water are can conceive fire to be water, in accordance with the nature of the facts themselves, although this is possible according to the words. So, then, no one who understands what God is can conceive that God does not exist; although he says these words in his heart, either without any, or with some foreign, signification. For, God is that than which a greater cannot be conceived. And he who thoroughly understands this, assuredly understands that this being so truly exists, that not even in concept can it be nonexistent. Therefore, he who understands that God so exists, cannot conceive that he does not exist.

I thank thee, gracious Lord, I thank thee; because what I formerly believed by thy bounty, I now so understand by thine illumination, that if I were unwilling to believe that thou dost exist, I should not be able not to understand this to be true.

· 30 ·

REASON, FAITH, AND
GOD'S EXISTENCE *

St. Thomas Aquinas (1225–1274)

I. ON THE WAY IN WHICH DIVINE TRUTH
IS TO BE MADE KNOWN

. . . There is a twofold mode of truth in what we profess about God. Some truths about God exceed all the ability of the human reason. Such is the truth that God is triune. But there are some truths which the natural reason also is able to reach. Such are that God exists, that He is one, and the like. In fact, such truths about God have been proved demonstratively by the philosophers, guided by the light of the natural reason.

That there are certain truths about God that totally surpass man's ability appears with the greatest evidence. Since, indeed, the principle of all knowledge that the reason perceives about some thing is the understanding of the very substance of that being . . . it is necessary that the way in

* Part I is from On the Truth of the Catholic Faith: Summa Contra Gentiles, Book 1, chapters 3, 7, 10, and 11; translated from the Latin by Anton C. Pegis. Copyright 1955 by Doubleday and Co., Inc. Reprinted by permission of the publisher. Part II is from Summa Theologica, Part 1, Question 2, Article 3; translated by Julius R. Weinberg especially for this volume. The title of this selection has been supplied by the editors. Compare with selections 29, 31, and 34.

which we understand the substance of a thing determines the way in which we know what belongs to it. Hence, if the human intellect comprehends the substance of some thing, for example, that of a stone or of a triangle, no intelligible characteristic belonging to that thing surpasses the grasp of the human reason. But this does not happen to us in the case of God. For the human intellect is not able to reach a comprehension of the divine substance through its natural power. For, according to its manner of knowing in the present life, the intellect depends on the sense for the origin of knowledge; and so those things that do not fall under the senses cannot be grasped by the human intellect except in so far as the knowledge of them is gathered from sensible things. Now, sensible things cannot lead the human intellect to the point of seeing in them the nature of the divine substance; for sensible things are effects that fall short of the power of their cause. Yet, beginning with sensible things, our intellect is led to the point of knowing about God that He exists, and other such characteristics that must be attributed to the First Principle. There are, consequently, some intelligible truths about God that are open to the human reason; but there are others that absolutely surpass its power. . . .

That the Truth of Reason Is Not Opposed to the Truth of the Christian Faith

Now, although the truth of the Christian faith . . . surpasses the capacity of the reason, nevertheless that truth that the human reason is naturally endowed to know cannot be opposed to the truth of the Christian faith. For that with which the human reason is naturally endowed is clearly most true; so much so, that it is impossible for us to think of such truths as false. Nor is it permissible to believe as false that which we hold by faith, since this is confirmed in a way that is so clearly divine. Since, therefore, only the false is opposed to the true, as is clearly evident from an examination of their definitions, it is impossible that the truth of faith should be opposed to those principles that the human reason knows naturally.

Furthermore, that which is introduced into the soul of the student by the teacher is contained in the knowledge of the teacher—unless his teaching is fictitious, which it is improper to say of God. Now, the knowledge of the principles that are known to us naturally has been implanted in us by God; for God is the Author of our nature. These principles, therefore, are also contained by the divine Wisdom. Hence, whatever is opposed to them is opposed to the divine Wisdom, and, therefore, cannot come from God. That which we hold by faith as divinely revealed, therefore, cannot be contrary to our natural knowledge. . . .

From this we evidently gather the following conclusion: whatever arguments are brought forward against the doctrines of faith are conclusions incorrectly derived from the first and self-evident principles imbedded in nature. Such conclusions do not have the force of demonstration; they are arguments that are either probable or sophistical. And so, there exists the possibility to answer them. . . .

The Opinion of Those Who Say That the Existence of God, Being Self-Evident, Cannot be Demonstrated

There are some persons to whom the inquiry seeking to demonstrate that God exists may perhaps appear superfluous. These are the persons who assert that the existence of God is self-evident, in such wise that its contrary cannot be entertained in the mind. It thus appears that the existence of God cannot be demonstrated, as may be seen from the following arguments.

Those propositions are said to be self-evident that are known immediately upon the knowledge of their terms. Thus, as soon as you know the nature of a *whole* and the nature of a *part*, you know immediately that every whole is greater than its part. The proposition *God exists* is of this sort. For by the name *God* we understand something than which a greater cannot be thought. This notion is formed in the intellect by one who hears and understands the name *God*. As a result, God must exist already at least in the intellect. But He cannot exist solely in the intellect, since that which exists both in the intellect and in reality is greater than that which exists in the intellect alone. Now, as the very definition of the name points out, nothing can be greater than God. Consequently, the proposition that God exists is self-evident, as being evident from the very meaning of the name God.

Again, it is possible to think that something exists whose non-existence cannot be thought. Clearly, such a being is greater than the being whose non-existence can be thought. Consequently, if God Himself could be thought not to be, then something greater than God could be thought. This, however, is contrary to the definition of the name God. Hence, the proposition that God exists is self-evident.

Furthermore, those propositions ought to be the most evident in which the same thing is predicated of itself, for example, *man is man*, or whose predicates are included in the definition of their subjects, for example, *man is an animal*. Now, in God . . . it is pre-eminently the case that His being is His essence, so that to the question *what is He?* and to the question *is He?* the answer is one and the same. Thus, in the proposition *God exists*, the predicate is consequently either identical with the subject or at least included in the definition of the subject. Hence, that God exists is self-evident. . . .

These, then, and others like them are the arguments by which some think that the proposition *God exists* is so self-evident that its contrary cannot be entertained by the mind. . . .

A Refutation of the Abovementioned Opinion and a Solution of the Arguments

In part, the above opinion arises from the custom by which from their earliest days people are brought up to hear and to call upon the name of God. Custom, and especially custom in a child, comes to have the force of nature. As a result, what the mind is steeped in from childhood it clings to very firmly, as something known naturally and self-evidently.

In part, however, the above opinion comes about because of a failure to distinguish between that which is self-evident in an absolute sense and that which is self-evident in relation to us. For assuredly that God exists is, absolutely speaking, self-evident, since what God is is His own being. Yet, because we are not able to conceive in our minds that which God is, that God exists remains unknown in relation to us. So, too, that every whole is greater than its part is, absolutely speaking, self-evident; but it would perforce be unknown to one who could not conceive the nature of a whole. . . .

And, contrary to the point made by the *first* argument, it does not follow immediately that, as soon as we know the meaning of the name *God*, the existence of God is known. It does not follow first because it is not known to all, even including those who admit that God exists, that God is that than which a greater cannot be thought. After all, many ancients said that this world itself was God. . . . What is more, granted that everyone should understand by the name *God* something than which a greater cannot be thought, it will still not be necessary that there exist in reality something than which a greater cannot be thought. For a thing and the definition of a name are posited in the same way. Now, from the fact that that which is indicated by the name *God* is conceived by the mind, it does not follow that God exists save only in the intellect. Hence, that than which a greater cannot be thought will likewise not have to exist save only in the intellect. From this it does not follow that there exists in reality something than which a greater cannot be thought. No difficulty, consequently, befalls anyone who posits that God does not exist. For that something greater can be thought than anything given in reality or in the intellect is a difficulty only to him who admits that there is something than which a greater cannot be thought in reality.

Nor, again, is it necessary, as the *second* argument advanced, that something greater than God can be thought if God can be thought not to be. For that He can be thought not to be does not arise either from the imperfection or the uncertainty of His own being, since this is in itself most manifest. It arises, rather, from the weakness of our intellect, which cannot behold God Himself except through His effects and which is thus led to know His existence through reasoning.

This enables us to solve the *third* argument as well. For just as it is evident to us that a whole is greater than a part of itself, so to those seeing the divine essence in itself it is supremely self-evident that God exists because His essence is His being. But, because we are not able to see His essence, we arrive at the knowledge of His being, not through God Himself, but through His effects. . . .

II. [FIVE ARGUMENTS FOR GOD'S EXISTENCE]

. . . The existence of God can be demonstrated in five ways.

The first and more obvious way is taken from the consideration of motion. Now it is certain and evident to sense that something is in motion in this world. But everything which is in motion is moved by another thing. For nothing is in motion save as it is in potency to that to which it is moved. This is because to move is to lead something from potency into act, and a thing can be led from potency to act only by something in act. For example, that which is actually hot such as fire makes wood which is potentially hot to be actually hot. Thus, by so doing, it moves and alters the wood. Now it is impossible that the same thing be simultaneously in act and potency in the same respect. For this is possible only according to diverse respect. For that which is actually hot can not simultaneously be potentially hot; at that time it is potentially cold. Hence, it is impossible that something be both mover and moved in the same respect. That is, it is impossible that something move itself. Therefore, everything which is in motion is moved by something else. Hence, if that by which something is moved is also moved, it is necessary that it be moved by another and the last mentioned by still another. But this can not go on to infinity, because if it did there would be no first moving thing and hence no other moving thing. This is because secondary movers only move because they have been moved by a first mover, just as a stick only moves something because it has been moved by the hand. Therefore, it is necessary to arrive at some first moving thing which is moved by nothing. Everyone understands this to be God.

The second way is taken from the nature of an efficient cause. For we discover in these sensible things that there is an order of efficient causes.

Now, it is neither observed nor is it even possible that something be its own efficient cause. For if anything were its own efficient cause, it would exist prior to itself which is impossible. However, it is not possible that in efficient causes we proceed to infinity, because in all ordered efficient causes the first is the cause of the intermediary and the intermediary is the cause of the last, regardless of whether there is only one or there are many intermediaries. Now, if the cause has been taken away, the effect is removed. Hence, if there had not been a first among efficient causes, there will be neither intermediary causes nor an ultimate effect. But if there is an infinite process among efficient causes, there will be no first efficient cause. Hence there will be neither an ultimate effect nor intermediary efficient causes. Now this is obviously false. Hence it is necessary to posit some first efficient cause which everyone calls God.

The third way is taken from the possible and the necessary which is as follows: We discover among things some which are able to exist and not exist. For some things are found to be generated and corrupted and thus they are able to exist and not exist. Now, it is impossible that all such things always exist because what is able not to exist will at some time not exist. Hence, if all things are capable of not existing, at some time nothing will exist. And if this were so, nothing would now exist because what does not exist only begins to exist through something which does exist. If, therefore, nothing existed it would be impossible for anything to begin to exist. Thus nothing would exist. Now this is obviously false. Hence, not all beings are merely possible, but something necessary must exist among things. However, every necessary being either has some cause of its necessity or it does not. Now it is not possible to proceed to infinity among necessary things which have a cause of their necessity (just as has been proved in the case of efficient causes). Hence it is necessary to posit something which is necessary through itself and which does not have the cause of its necessity elsewhere, but which is the cause of the necessity in other things. Everyone calls this something God.

The fourth way is taken from the degrees which are found among things. For among things some are found to be more or less good, or true, or noble, etc. But greater and less are asserted of divers things according as they approximate in diverse ways something which is greatest, as the greater heat is that which more closely approaches the greatest in heat. Hence there is something which is truest and best and noblest, and hence the greatest being. For those things which are most true are to the greatest extent beings, as [Aristotle says] in the 2nd book of the *Metaphysics*. Now that which is said to be greatest in any genus is the cause of all things which are in that genus, as fire which is most hot, is the cause of all hot things, as is said in the same text of the *Metaphysics*. Hence there is something which is the cause of being and goodness and any other perfection in all beings. This we call God.

The fifth way is taken from the governance of things. For we see that some things which lack intelligence (namely natural bodies) act because of some purpose. The evidence for this is that they always, or for the most part, act in the same way so that they attain that which is best. Hence it is not by chance but rather by intention that these things proceed toward an end. However, those things which do not have intelligence only tend to an end by being directed by something which knows and understands (as in the case of the arrow and the archer). Hence there is some intelligent being by which all natural things are ordered to an end. This we call God. . . .

• 31 •

ON EVIL AND THE ARGUMENT
FROM DESIGN *

David Hume (1711–1776)

[I. THE ARGUMENT FROM DESIGN]

. . . Not to lose any time in circumlocutions, said Cleanthes, addressing himself to Demea, much less in replying to the pious declamations of Philo; I shall briefly explain how I conceive this matter. Look round the world; contemplate the whole and every part of it: you will find it to be nothing but one great machine, subdivided into an infinite number of lesser machines, which again admit of subdivisions, to a degree beyond what human senses and faculties can trace and explain. All these various machines, and even their most minute parts, are adjusted to each other with an accuracy, which ravishes into admiration all men, who have ever contemplated them. The curious adapting of means to ends, throughout all nature, resembles exactly, though it much exceeds, the productions of

* From Hume's *Dialogues Concerning Natural Religion* (1779), Parts II and X. This work consists of a discussion among three philosophers, named Cleanthes, Demea, and Philo, concerning the foundations of religious belief. The title of this selection has been supplied by the editors. Compare Part I with selections 29 and 30; compare Part II with selection 32.

human contrivance; of human design, thought, wisdom, and intelligence. Since therefore the effects resemble each other, we are led to infer, by all the rules of analogy, that the causes also resemble; and that the Author of Nature is somewhat similar to the mind of men; though possessed of much larger faculties, proportioned to the grandeur of the work, which he has executed. By this argument *a posteriori*, and by this argument alone, do we prove at once the existence of a Deity, and this similarity to human mind and intelligence.

I shall be so free, Cleanthes, said Demea, as to tell you, that from the beginning, I could not approve of your conclusion concerning the similarity of the Deity to men; still less can I approve of the mediums, by which you endeavor to establish it. What! No demonstration of the being of a God! No abstract arguments! No proofs *a priori!* Are these, which have hitherto been so much insisted on by philosophers, all fallacy, all sophism? Can we reach no farther in this subject than experience and probability? I will not say, that this is betraying the cause of a deity: but surely, by this affected candor, you give advantage to atheists, which they never could obtain, by the mere dint of argument and reasoning.

What I chiefly scruple in this subject, said Philo, is not so much, that all religious arguments are by Cleanthes reduced to experience, as that they appear not to be even the most certain and irrefragable of that inferior kind. That a stone will fall, that fire will burn, that the earth has solidity, we have observed a thousand and a thousand times; and when any new instance of this nature is presented, we draw without hesitation the accustomed inference. The exact similarity of the cases gives us a perfect assurance of a similar event; and a stronger evidence is never desired nor sought after. But wherever you depart, in the least, from the similarity of the cases, you diminish proportionably the evidence; and may at last bring it to a very weak *analogy*, which is confessedly liable to error and uncertainty. After having experienced the circulation of the blood in human creatures, we make no doubt that it takes place in Titius and Maevius: but from its circulation in frogs and fishes, it is only a presumption, though a strong one, from analogy, that it takes place in men and other animals. The analogical reasoning is much weaker, when we infer the circulation of sap in vegetables from our experience that the blood circulates in animals; and those, who hastily followed that imperfect analogy, are found, by more accurate experiments, to have been mistaken.

If we see a house, Cleanthes, we conclude, with the greatest certainty, that it had an architect or builder; because this is precisely that species of effect, which we have experienced to proceed from that species of cause. But surely you will not affirm, that the universe bears such a resemblance to a house, that we can with the same certainty infer a similar cause, or that the analogy is here entire and perfect. The dissimilitude is so striking, that the utmost you can here pretend to is a guess, a conjecture, a presumption concerning a similar cause; and how that pretension will be received in the world, I leave you to consider.

It would surely be very ill received, replied Cleanthes; and I should be deservedly blamed and detested, did I allow, that the proofs of a Deity amounted to no more than a guess or conjecture. But is the whole adjustment of means to ends in a house and in the universe so slight a resemblance? The economy of final causes? The order, proportion, and arrangement of every part? Steps of a stair are plainly contrived, that human legs may use them in mounting; and this inference is certain and infallible. Human legs are also contrived for walking and mounting; and this inference, I allow, is not altogether so certain, because of the dissimilarity which you remark; but does it, therefore, deserve the name only of presumption or conjecture?

Good God! cried Demea, interrupting him, where are we? Zealous defenders of religion allow, that the proofs of a Deity fall short of perfect evidence! And you, Philo, on whose assistance I depended, in proving the adorable mysteriousness of the Divine Nature, do you assent to all these extravagant opinions of Cleanthes? For what other name can I give them? . . .

You seem not to apprehend, replied Philo, that I argue with Cleanthes in his own way; and by showing him the dangerous consequences of his tenets, hope at last to reduce him to our opinion. . . . Now, according to this method of reasoning, Demea, it follows (and is, indeed, tacitly allowed by Cleanthes himself) that order, arrangement, or the adjustment of final causes is not, of itself, any proof of design, but only so far as it has been experienced to proceed from that principle. For aught we can know *a priori*, matter may contain the source or spring of order originally, within itself, as well as mind does; and there is no more difficulty in conceiving, that the several elements, from an internal unknown cause, may fall into the most exquisite arrangement, than to conceive that their ideas, in the great, universal mind, from a like internal, unknown cause, fall into that arrangement. The equal possibility of both these suppositions is allowed. But by experience we find (according to Cleanthes), that there is a difference between them. Throw several pieces of steel together, without shape or form; they will never arrange themselves so as to compose a watch: stone, and mortar, and wood, without an architect, never erect a house. But the ideas in a human mind, we see, by an unknown, inexplicable economy, arrange themselves so as to form the plan of a watch or house.

Experience, therefore, proves, that there is an original principle of order in mind, not in matter. From similar effects we infer similar causes. The adjustment of means to ends is alike in the universe, as in a machine of human contrivance. The causes, therefore, must be resembling. . . .

That all inferences, Cleanthes, concerning fact, are founded on experience, and that all experimental reasonings are founded on the supposition, that similar causes prove similar effects, and similar effects similar causes; I shall not, at present, much dispute with you. But observe, I entreat you, with what extreme caution all just reasoners proceed in the transferring of experiments to similar cases. Unless the cases be exactly similar, they repose no perfect confidence in applying their past observation to any particular phenomenon. Every alteration of circumstances occasions a doubt concerning the event; and it requires new experiments to prove certainly, that the new circumstances are of no moment or importance. A change in bulk, situation, arrangement, age, disposition of the air, or surrounding bodies; any of these particulars may be attended with the most unexpected consequences: and unless the objects be quite familiar to us, it is the highest temerity to expect with assurance, after any of these changes, an event similar to that which before fell under our observation. The slow and deliberate steps of philosophers, here, if anywhere, are distinguished from the precipitate march of the vulgar, who, hurried on by the smallest similitudes, are incapable of all discernment or consideration.

But can you think, Cleanthes, that your usual phlegm and philosophy have been preserved in so wide a step as you have taken, when you compared to the universe, houses, ships, furniture, machines; and from their similarity in some circumstances inferred a similarity in their causes? Thought, design, intelligence, such as we discover in men and other animals, is no more than one of the springs and principles of the universe, as well as heat or cold, attraction or repulsion, and a hundred others, which fall under daily observation. It is an active cause, by which some particular parts of nature, we find, produce alterations on other parts. But can a conclusion, with any propriety, be transferred from parts to the whole? Does not the great disproportion bar all comparison and inference? From observing the growth of a hair, can we learn anything concerning the generation of a man? Would the manner of a leaf's blowing, even though perfectly known, afford us any instruction concerning the vegetation of a tree?

But allowing that we were to take the *operations* of one part of nature upon another for the foundation of our judgment concerning the *origin* of the whole (which never can be admitted), yet why select so minute, so weak, so bounded a principle as the reason and design of animals is found to be upon this planet? What peculiar privilege has this little agitation of the brain which we call *thought*, that we must thus make it the model of the whole universe? Our partiality in our own favor does indeed present it on all occasions; but sound philosophy ought carefully to guard against so natural an illusion. . . .

[II. EVIL]

. . . The whole earth, believe me, Philo, is cursed and polluted [said Demea]. A perpetual war is kindled amongst all living creatures. Necessity, hunger, want, stimulate the strong and courageous: fear, anxiety, terror, agitate the weak and infirm. The first entrance into life gives anguish to the new-born infant and to its wretched parent: weakness, impotence, distress, attend each stage of that life: and 'tis at last finished in agony and horror.

Observe too, says Philo, the curious artifices of nature, in order to embitter the life of every living being. The stronger prey upon the weaker, and keep them in perpetual terror and anxiety. The weaker too, in their turn, often prey upon the stronger, and vex and molest them without relaxation. Consider that innumerable race of insects, which either are bred on the body of each animal, or flying about infix their stings in him. These insects have others still less than themselves, which torment them. And thus on each hand, before and behind, above and below, every animal is surrounded with enemies, which incessantly seek his misery and destruction.

Man alone, said Demea, seems to be, in part, an exception to this rule. For by combination in society, he can easily master lions, tigers, and bears, whose greater strength and agility naturally enable them to prey upon him.

On the contrary, it is here chiefly, cried Philo, that the uniform and equal maxims of nature are most apparent. Man, it is true, can, by combination, surmount all his *real* enemies, and become master of the whole animal creation: but does he not immediately raise up to himself *imaginary* enemies, the demons of his fancy, who haunt him with superstitious terrors, and blast every enjoyment of life? His pleasure, as he imagines, becomes, in their eyes, a crime: his food and repose give them umbrage and offense: his very sleep and dreams furnish new materials to anxious fear: and even death, his refuge from every other ill, presents only the dread of endless and innumerable woes. Nor does the wolf molest more the timid flock, than superstition does the anxious breast of wretched mortals.

Besides, consider, Demea; this very society, by which we surmount those wild beasts, our natural enemies; what new enemies does it not raise to us? What woe and misery does it not occasion? Man is the greatest enemy of man. Oppression, injustice, contempt, contumely, violence, sedition, war, calumny, treachery, fraud; by these they mutually torment each other: and they would soon dissolve that society which they had formed, were it not for the dread of still greater ills, which must attend their separation.

But though these external insults, said Demea, from animals, from men, from all the elements, which assault us, form a frightful catalogue of woes, they are nothing in comparison of those, which arise within ourselves, from the distempered condition of our mind and body. How many lie under the lingering torment of diseases? . . . The disorders of the mind . . . though more secret, are not perhaps less dismal and vexatious. Remorse, shame, anguish, rage, disappointment, anxiety, fear, dejection, despair; who has ever passed through life without cruel inroads from these tormentors? How many have scarcely ever felt any better sensations? Labor and poverty, so abhorred by everyone, are the certain lot of the far greater number; and those few privileged persons, who enjoy ease and opulence, never reach contentment or true felicity. All the goods of life united would not make a very happy man: but all the ills united would make a wretch indeed; and anyone of them almost (and who can be free from everyone), nay often the absence of one good (and who can possess all), is sufficient to render life ineligible.

Were a stranger to drop, on a sudden, into this world, I would show him, as a specimen of its ills, an hospital full of diseases, a prison crowded with malefactors and debtors, a field of battle strewed with carcasses, a fleet floundering in the ocean, a nation languishing under tyranny, famine, or pestilence. To turn the gay side of life to him, and give him a notion of its pleasures; whither should I conduct him? to a ball, to an opera, to court? He might justly think, that I was only showing him a diversity of distress and sorrow. . . .

. . . Ask yourself, ask any of your acquaintance, whether they would live over again the last ten or twenty years of their lives. No! but the next twenty, they say, will be better:

> And from the dregs of life, hope to receive
> What the first sprightly running could not give.

Thus at last they find (such is the greatest of human misery; it reconciles even contradictions) that they complain, at once, of the shortness of life, and of its vanity and sorrow.

And is it possible, Cleanthes, said Philo, that after all these reflections, and infinitely more, which might be suggested, you can still persevere in your anthropomorphism, and assert the moral attributes of the Deity, his justice, benevolence, mercy, and rectitude, to be of the same nature with these virtues in human creatures? His power we allow infinite: whatever he wills is executed: but neither man nor any other animal is happy: therefore he does not will their happiness. His wisdom is infinite: he is never mistaken in choosing the means to any end: but the course of nature tends not to human or animal felicity: therefore it is not established for that purpose. Through the whole compass of human knowledge, there are no inferences more certain and infallible than these. In what respect, then, do his benevolence and mercy resemble the benevolence and mercy of men?

Epicurus's old questions are yet unanswered.

Is he willing to prevent evil, but not able? then is he impotent. Is he able, but not willing, then he is malevolent. Is he both able and willing? whence then is evil? . . .

• 32 •

MORALITY AND THE BELIEF
IN GOD *

Paul Henri d'Holbach (1723–1789)

[I. INTRODUCTION]

When we coolly examine the opinions of men, we are surprised to find, that even in those opinions, which they regard as the most essential, nothing is more uncommon, than common sense; or, in other words, nothing is more uncommon, than a degree of judgment sufficient to discover the most simple truths, or reject the most striking absurdities, and to be shocked with palpable contradictions. We have an example of it in Theology; a science revered in all times and countries, by the greatest number of men; an object regarded by them the most important, the most useful, and the most indispensable to the happiness of society. An examination, however slight, of the principles upon which this pretended science is founded, forces us to acknowledge, that these principles, formerly judged incontestable, are only hazardous suppositions, imagined by ignorance, propagated by enthusiasm or knavery, adopted by timid credulity, pre-

---

* From *Le Bon Sens*, first published in 1772 under a pseudonym; translated by H. D. Robinson and published at Boston as *Good Sense* by J. P. Mendum in 1856. The title of this selection has been supplied by the editors. Compare Part II with selection 31, and Part III with selection 43.

served by custom which never reasons, and revered solely because not understood. . . .

To discover the true principles of morality, men have no need of theology, of revelation, or of gods. They have need only of common sense. They have only to commune with themselves, to reflect upon their own nature, to consult their visible interests, to consider the objects of society, and of the individuals who compose it; and they will easily perceive, that virtue is advantageous, and vice disadvantageous to such beings as themselves. Let us persuade men to be just, beneficent, moderate, sociable; not because such conduct is demanded by the gods, but, because it is pleasure to men. Let us advise them to abstain from vice and crime; not because they will be punished in the other world, but because they will suffer for it in this. . . .

[II. OUR BELIEF IN GOD]

[*Fable of the Monarch.*] There is a vast empire, governed by a monarch, whose strange conduct is very proper to confound the minds of his subjects. He wishes to be known, loved, respected, obeyed; but never shows himself to his subjects, and everything conspires to render uncertain the ideas formed of his character.

The people, subjected to his power, have, of the character and laws of their invisible sovereign, such ideas only, as his ministers give them. They however confess that they have no idea of their master; that his ways are impenetrable; his views and nature totally incomprehensible. These ministers, likewise, disagree upon the commands which they pretend have been issued by the sovereign, whose instruments they call themselves. They announce them differently to each province of the empire. They defame one another, and mutually treat each other as imposters and false teachers. The decrees and ordinances, they take upon themselves to promulgate, are obscure; they are enigmas, little calculated to be understood, or even divined, by the subjects, for whose instruction they were intended. The laws of the concealed monarch require interpreters; but the interpreters are always disputing upon the true manner of understanding them. Besides they are not consistent with themselves; all they relate of their concealed prince is only a thread of contradiction. They utter concerning him not a single word that does not immediately confute itself. They call him supremely good; yet there is no one who does not complain of his decrees. They suppose him infinitely wise; and under his administration everything appears to contradict reason and good sense. They extol his justice; and the best of his subjects are generally the least favored. They assert, he sees everything; yet his presence avails nothing. He is, they say, the friend of order; yet throughout his dominions, all is in confusion and disorder. He makes all for himself; and the events seldom answer his designs. He foresees everything; but cannot prevent anything. He impatiently suffers offence, yet gives every one the power of offending him. Men admire the wisdom and perfection of his works; yet his works, full of imperfection, are short of duration. He is continually doing and undoing: repairing what he has made; but is never pleased with his work. In all his undertakings, he proposes only his own glory; yet is never glorified. His only end is the happiness of his subjects; and his subjects, for the most part, want necessaries. Those, whom he seems to favor, are generally least satisfied with their fate; almost all appear in perpetual revolt against a master, whose greatness they never cease to admire, whose wisdom to extol, whose goodness to adore, whose justice to fear, and whose laws to reverence, though never obeyed!

This empire is the world; this monarch God; his ministers are the priests; his subjects mankind.

[*The Idea of God.*] The principles of every religion are founded upon the idea of a God. Now, it is impossible to have true ideas of a being, who acts upon none of our senses. All our ideas are representations of sensible objects. What then can represent to us the idea of God, which is evidently an idea without an object? Is not such an idea as impossible, as an effect without a cause? Can an idea without an archetype be any thing, but a chimera? There are however, divines, who assure us that the idea of God is innate; or that we have this in our mother's womb. Every principle is the result of reason; all reason is the result of experience; experience is acquired only by the exercise of our senses: therefore religious principles are not founded upon reason, and are not innate.

Every system of religion can be founded only upon the nature of God and man; and upon the relations which subsist between them. But to judge of the reality of those relations, we must have some idea of the divine nature. Now, the world exclaims, the divine nature is incomprehensible to man; yet ceases not to assign attributes to this incomprehensible God, and to assure us, that it is our indispensable duty to find out that God, whom it is impossible to comprehend.

The most important concern of man is what he can least comprehend. If God is incomprehensible to man, it would seem reasonable never to think of him; but religion maintains, man cannot with impunity cease a moment to think (or rather dream) of his God.

We are told, that divine qualities are not of a nature to be comprehended by finite minds. The natural consequence must be, that divine qualities are not made to occupy finite minds. But religion tells us, that the poor finite mind of man ought never to lose sight of an inconceivable being, whose qualities he can never comprehend. Thus we see, religion is the art of turning the attention of mankind upon subjects they can never comprehend. . . .

[*God's Existence.*] The existence of God is the basis of all religion. Few appear to doubt his existence; yet this fundamental article utterly embarrasses every mind that reasons. The first question of every catechism, has been, and ever will be, the most difficult to resolve.

Can we imagine ourselves sincerely convinced of the existence of a being, whose nature we know not: who is inaccessible to all our senses; whose attributes, we are assured every moment, are incomprehensible to us? To persuade me that a being exists or can exist, I must be first told what that being is. To induce me to believe the existence or the possibility of such a being, it is necessary to tell me things concerning him that are not contradictory, and do not destroy one another. In short, fully to convince me of the existence of that being, it is necessary to tell me things that I can understand, and to prove to me that it is impossible that such a being should not exist.

A thing is impossible, when it includes two ideas that mutually destroy one another, and which can neither be conceived nor united in thought. Conviction can be founded only upon the constant testimony of our senses, which alone give birth to our ideas, and enable us to judge of their agreement or disagreement. That, which exists necessarily, is that, whose non-existence implies a contradiction. These principles, universally acknowledged, become erroneous, when applied to the existence of a God. Whatever has been hitherto said upon the subject, is either unintelligible, or perfect contradiction, and must therefore appear absurd to every rational man.

All human knowledge is more or less clear and perfect. By what strange fatality have we never been able to elucidate the science of God? The most civilized nations, and among them the most profound thinkers, are in this respect no more enlightened than the most savage tribes and ignorant peasants; and, examining the subject closely, we shall find, that, by the idle speculations and subtle refinements of men, the divine science has been only more and more obscured. Every religion has hitherto been founded only upon what is called, in logic, *begging the question*; it takes things for granted, and then proves, by suppositions, instead of principles. . . .

Metaphysics teach us, that God is a *pure spirit*. But, herein is modern theology superior to that of the savages? The savages acknowledge a *great spirit*, for the master of the world. The savages, like all ignorant people, attribute to *spirits* all the effects, of which their experience cannot discover the true causes. Ask a savage, what moves your watch? He will answer you, *it is a spirit*. Ask our divines, what moves the universe? They answer, *it is a spirit*.

The savage, when he speaks of a spirit, affixes, at least, some idea to the word; he means thereby an agent, like the air, the breeze, the breath, that invisibly produces discernible effects. By subtilizing everything, the modern theologian becomes as unintelligible to himself as to others. Ask him what he understands by a spirit? He will answer you, that it is an unknown substance, perfectly simple, that has no extension, that has nothing common with matter. Indeed, is there any one, who can form the least idea of such a substance? What then is a spirit, to speak in the language of modern theology, but the absence of an idea? The idea of *spirituality* is yet an idea without model.

Is it not more natural and intelligible to draw universal existence from the bosom of matter, whose existence is demonstrated by all the senses, and whose effects we experience every moment, which we see act, move, communicate motion, and incessantly generate, than to attribute the formation of things to an unknown power, to a spiritual being, who cannot derive from his nature what he has not himself, and who, by his spiritual essence, can create neither matter nor motion? Nothing is more evident, than that the idea they endeavor to give us, of the action of mind upon matter, represents no object, or is an idea without model. . . .

[*God and Man.*] Whence comes man? What is his origin? Is he . . . the effect of a fortuitous concourse of atoms? Did the first man spring, ready formed, from the dust of the earth? I know not. Man appears to me, like all other beings, a production of nature. I should be equally embarrassed to tell whence came the stones, the first trees, the first lions, the first elephants, the first ants, the first acorns, etc., as to explain the origin of man. We are incessantly told to acknowledge and revere the hand of God, of an infinitely wise, intelligent and powerful maker, in so wonderful a work as the human machine. I readily confess, that the human machine appears to me surprising. But as man exists in nature, I am not authorised to say that his formation is above the power of nature. But I can much less conceive of this formation, when to explain it, I am told that a pure spirit, who has neither eyes, feet, hands, head, lungs, mouth, nor breath, made man by taking a little clay, and breathing upon it.

We laugh at the savage inhabitants of Paraguay, for calling themselves the descendants of the moon. The divines of Europe call themselves the descendants, or the creation of a pure spirit. Is this pretension much more rational? Man is intelligent; thence it is inferred, that he can be the work only of an intelligent being, and not of nature, which is void of intelligence. Although nothing is more rare, than to see man make use of this intelligence, of which he seems so proud, I will grant that he is intelligent, that his wants develop this faculty, that society especially contributes to cultivate it. But I see nothing in the human machine, and in the intelligence with which it is endued, that announces very precisely the infinite intelligence of the maker, to whom it is ascribed. I see that this admirable machine is liable to be deranged; I see, that his wonderful intelligence is then disordered, and sometimes totally disappeared; I infer, that human intelligence depends upon a certain disposition of the material organs of the body, and that we cannot infer the intelligence of God any more from the intelligence of man, than from his materiality. All that we can infer from it, is, that God is material. The intelligence of man no more proves the intelligence of God, than the malice of man proves the malice of that God who is the pretended maker of man. In spite of all the arguments of divines, God will always be a cause contradicted by its effects, or of which it is impossible to judge by its works. We shall always see evil, imperfection, and folly result from such a cause, that is said to be full of goodness, perfection and wisdom. . . .

[*The Order of Nature.*] The worshippers of a God find, above all, in the order of the universe, an invincible proof of the existence of an intelligent and wise being, who governs it. But this order is nothing but a series of movements necessarily produced by causes or circumstances, which are sometimes favorable, and sometimes hurtful to us: we approve of some, and complain of others.

Nature uniformly follows the same round; that is, the same causes produce the same effects, as long as their action is not disturbed by other causes, which force them to produce different effects. When the operation of causes, whose effects we experience, is interrupted by causes, which, though unknown, are not the less natural and necessary, we are confounded; we cry out, *a miracle!* and attribute it to a cause much more unknown than any of those acting before our eyes.

The universe is always in order. It cannot be in disorder. It is our machine alone that suffers, when we complain of disorder. The bodies, causes and beings which this world contains, necessarily act in the manner in which we see them act, whether we approve or disapprove of the effects. Earthquakes, volcanos, inundations, pestilences, and famines are effects as necessary, or as much in the order of nature, as the fall of heavy bodies, the courses of rivers, the periodical motions of the seas, the blowing of the winds, the fruitful rains, and the favorable effects for which men praise God, and thank him for his goodness.

To be astonished that a certain order reigns in the world, is to be surprised that the same causes constantly produce the same effects. To be shocked at disorder, is to forget that when things change or are interrupted in their actions, the effects can no longer be the same. To wonder at the order of nature is to wonder that anything can exist; it is to be surprised at one's own existence. What is order to one being, is disorder to another. All wicked beings find that everything is in order, when they can with impunity put everything in disorder. They find, on the contrary, that everything is in disorder, when they are disturbed in the exercise of their wickedness.

Upon supposition that God is the author and mover of nature, there could be no disorder with respect to him. Would not all the causes that he should have made, necessarily act according to the properties, essences and impulses given them? If God should change the ordinary course of nature, he would not be immutable. If the order of the universe, in which man thinks he sees the most convincing proof of the existence, intelligence, power and goodness of God, should happen to contradict itself, one might suspect his existence, or at least accuse him of inconstancy, impotence, want of foresight and wisdom in the arrangement of things; one would have a right to accuse him of an oversight in the choice of the agents and instruments which he makes, prepares, and puts in action. In short, if the order of nature proves the power and intelligence of the Deity, disorder must prove his weakness, instability, and irrationality.

You say that God is omnipresent, that he fills the universe with his immensity, that nothing is done without him, that matter could not act without his agency. But in this case, you admit that your God is the author of disorder, that it is he who deranges nature, that he is the father of confusion, that he is in man, and moves him at the moment he sins. If God is everywhere, he is in me, he acts with me, he is deceived with me, he offends God with me, and combats with me the existence of God. O theologians! you never understand yourselves, when you speak of God. . . .

The logic of common sense teaches, that we cannot and ought not, to judge of a cause, but by its effects. A cause can be reputed constantly good, only when it constantly produces good, useful, and agreeable effects. A cause which produces both good and evil is sometimes good, and sometimes evil. But the logic of theology destroys all this. According to that, the phenomena of nature, or the effects we behold in this world, prove to us the existence of a cause infinitely good; and this cause is God; although this world is full of evils; although disorder often reigns in it; although men incessantly repine at their hard fate; we must be convinced that these effects are owing to a beneficent and immutable cause; and many people believe it, or feign to believe it.

Everything that passes in the world, proves to us, in the clearest manner, that it is not governed by an intelligent being. We can judge of the intelligence of a being only by the conformity of the means, which he employs to attain his proposed object. The object of God, is, it is said, the happiness of man. Yet, a like necessity governs the fate of all sensible beings, who are born only to suffer much, enjoy little, and die. The cup of man is filled with joy and bitterness; good is everywhere attended with evil; order gives place to disorder; generation is followed by destruction. If you tell me that the designs of God are mysterious and that his ways are impenetrable, I answer, that, in this case, it is impossible for me to judge whether God be intelligent.

You pretend, that God is immutable! What then produces a continual instability in this world, which you make his empire? Is there a state subject to more frequent and cruel revolutions, than that of this unknown monarch? How can we attribute to an immutable God, sufficiently powerful to give solidity to his works, the government of a nature, in which everything is a continual vicissitude? If I imagine I see a God of uniform character in all the effects favorable to my species, what kind of a God can I see in their continual misfortunes? You tell me, it is our sins, which compel him to punish. I answer, that God, according to yourselves, is then not immutable, since the sins of men force him to change his conduct towards them. Can a being, who is sometimes provoked, and sometimes appeased, be constantly the same? . . .

[*Religion and Superstition.*] Many people make a subtle distinction between true religion and superstition. They say, that the latter is only a base subordinate fear of the Deity; but that the truly religious man has confidence in his God, and loves him sincerely; whereas, the superstitious man sees in him only an enemy, has no confidence in him, and represents him to himself as a distrustful, cruel tyrant, sparing of his benefits, lavish of his chastisements. But, in reality, does not all religion give us the same ideas of God? At the same time that we are told that God is infinitely good, are we not also told that he is very easily provoked, that he grants his favors to a few people only, and that he furiously chastises those, to whom he has not been pleased to grant them?

If we take our ideas of God from the nature of things, where we find a mixture of good and evil, this God, just like the good and evil which we experience, must naturally appear capricious, inconstant, sometimes good, and sometimes malevolent; and therefore, instead of exciting our love, must generate distrust, fear, and uncertainty. There is then no real difference between natural religion, and the most gloomy and servile superstition. If the theist sees God only in a favorable light, the bigot views him in the most hideous light. The folly of the one is cheerful, that of the other is melancholy; but both are equally delirious. . . .

[*The Source of Evil.*] Nothing is more extravagant, than the part theology makes the Divinity to act in every country. Did he really exist, we should see in him the most capricious and senseless being. We should be compelled to believe, that God made the world only to be the theatre of his disgraceful wars with his creatures; that he created angels, men, demons, and evil spirits only to make himself adversaries, against whom he might exercise his power. He renders men free to offend him, malicious enough to defeat his projects, too obstinate to submit; and all this merely for the pleasure of being angry, appeased, reconciled, and of repairing the disorder they have made. Had the Deity at once formed his creatures such as he would have them, what pains would he not have spared himself, or, at least, from what embarrassments would he not have relieved his theologians!

Every religion represents God as busy only in doing himself evil. He resembles those empirics who inflict upon themselves wounds, to have an opportunity of exhibiting to the public the efficacy of their ointment. But we see not, that the Deity has hitherto been able radically to cure himself of the evil which he suffers from man.

God is the author of all; and yet, we are assured that evil does not come from God. Whence then does it come? From man. But, who made man? God. Evil then comes from God. If he had not made man as he is, moral evil or sin would not have existed in the world. The perversity of man is therefore chargeable to God. If man has power to do evil, or to offend God, we are forced to infer, that God chooses to be offended; that God, who made man, has resolved that man shall be evil; otherwise man would be an effect contrary to the cause, from which he derives his being.

Man ascribes to God the faculty of foreseeing, or knowing beforehand whatever will happen; but this prescience seldom turns to his glory, nor protects him from the lawful reproaches of man. If God foreknows the future, must he not have foreseen the fall of his creatures, whom he had destined to happiness? If he resolved in his decrees to permit this fall, it is undoubtedly because it was his will that this fall should take place, otherwise it could not have happened. If God's foreknowledge of the sins of his creatures had been necessary or forced, one might suppose, that he has been constrained by his justice to punish the guilty; but enjoying the faculty of foreseeing, and the power of predetermining everything, did it not depend upon God not to impose upon himself cruel laws; or, at least, could he not dispense with creating beings, whom he might be under the necessity of punishing, and rendering unhappy by a subsequent decree?

Of what consequence is it, whether God has destined men to happiness or misery by an anterior decree, an effect of his prescience, or by a posterior decree, an effect of his justice. Does the arrangement of his decrees alter the fate of the unhappy? Would they not have the same right to complain of a God, who, being able to omit their creation, has notwithstanding created them, although he plainly foresaw that his justice would oblige him, sooner or later, to punish them?

"Man, you say, when he came from the hands of God, was pure, innocent, and good; but his nature has been corrupted, as a punishment for sin." If man, when just out of the hands of his God, could sin, his nature was imperfect. Why did God suffer him to sin, and his nature to be corrupted? Why did God permit him to be seduced, well knowing that he was too feeble to resist temptation? Why did God create a *Satan*, an evil spirit, a tempter? Why did not God, who wishes so much good to the human race, annihilate once for all so many evil genii, who are naturally enemies of our happiness, or rather, why did God create evil spirits, whose victories and fatal influence over mankind, he must have foreseen? In fine, by what strange fatality in all religions of the world, has the evil principle such a decided advantage over the good principle, or the divinity? . . .

[*The Spirit of Man.*] Are not theologians strange reasoners? Whenever they cannot divine the *natural* causes of things, they invent those which they call *supernatural*; such as spirits, occult causes, inexplicable agents, or rather *words*, much more obscure than the *things* they endeavor to explain. Let us remain in nature, when we wish to account for the phenomena of nature; let us be content to remain ignorant of causes too delicate for our organs: and let us be persuaded, that, by going beyond nature, we shall never solve the problems which nature presents.

Even upon the hypothesis of theology (that is, supposing an all-powerful mover of matter), by what right would theologians deny, that their God has power to give this matter the faculty of thought? Was it then more difficult for him to create combinations of matter, from which thought might result, than spirits who could think? At least, by supposing a matter which thinks, we should have some notions of the subject of thought, or of what thinks in us; whereas, by attributing thought to an immaterial being, it is impossible to form the least idea of it.

It is objected against us, that materialism makes man a mere machine, which is thought very dishonorable to the whole human species. But, will it be much more honorable for man, if we should say, that he acts by the secret impulses of a spirit, or by a certain *I know not what*, that animates him in a manner totally inexplicable?

It is easy to perceive, that the supposed superiority of *spirit* over matter, or of the soul over the body, has no other foundation than men's ignorance of the nature of this soul, while they are more familiarized with *matter*, with which they imagine they are acquainted, and of which they think they can discern the springs. But the most simple movements of our bodies are to every man, who studies them, enigmas as inexplicable as thought.

The high value which so many people set upon spiritual substance, has no other motive than their absolute inability to define it intelligibly. The contempt shown for *matter* by our metaphysicians, arises only from the circumstance, that familiarity begets contempt. When they tell us, that *the soul is more excellent and noble than the body*, they only say that, what they know not at all, must be far more beautiful, than what they have some feeble ideas of. . . .

The dogma of another life is incessantly extolled as useful. It is maintained, that even though it should be only a fiction, it is advantageous, because it deceives men, and conducts them to virtue. But is it true, that this dogma makes men wiser and more virtuous? Are the nations who believe this fiction, remarkable for purity of morals? Has not the visible world ever the advantage over the invisible? If those who are intrusted with the instruction and government of men, had knowledge and virtue themselves, they would govern them much better by realities, than by fictions. But legislators, crafty, ambitious and corrupt, have everywhere found it shorter to amuse nations with fables, than to teach them truths, to unfold their reason, to excite them to virtue by sensible and real motives, in fine, to govern them in a rational manner. Priests undoubtedly had reasons for making the soul immaterial; they wanted souls and chimeras to people the imaginary regions, which they have discovered in the other life. Material souls would, like all bodies, have been subject to dissolution. Now, if men should believe that all must perish with the body, the geographers of the other world would evidently lose the right of guiding men's souls towards that unknown abode; they would reap no profits from the hope with which they feed them, and the terrors with which they oppress them. If futurity is of no real utility to mankind, it is, at least, of the greatest utility to those, who have assumed the office of conducting them thither.

"But," it will be said, "is not the dogma of the immortality of the soul comforting to beings, who are often very unhappy here below? Though it should be an error, is it not pleasing? Is it not a blessing to man to believe, that he shall be able to survive himself, and enjoy hereafter a happiness, which is denied him upon earth?" Thus, poor mortals! you make your wishes the measure of truth; because you desire to live forever, and to be happier, you at once conclude, that you shall live forever, and that you shall be more fortunate in an unknown world, than in this known world, where you often find nothing but affliction! Consent therefore to leave, without regret, this world which gives the greater part of you much more torment than pleasure. Submit to the order of nature, which demands that you, as well as all other beings, should not endure forever. But what will become of me? asketh thou, O mortal! Thou wilt be what thou wast, millions of years ago. Thou wast then, I know not what; resolve then to become instantaneously, *I know not what*, which thou wast millions of years ago; return peaceably to the universal mass, from which without thy knowledge, thou camest in thy present form, and pass away without murmuring, like all the beings who surround thee. . . .

[III. MORALITY]

Religion, especially with the moderns, has tried to identify itself with morality, the principles of which it has thereby totally obscured. It has rendered men unsociable by duty, and forced them to be inhuman to every one who thought differently from themselves. Theological disputes, equally unintelligible to each of the enraged parties, have shaken empires, caused revolutions, been fatal to sovereigns and desolated all Europe. These contemptible quarrels have not been extinguished even in rivers of blood. Since the extinction of Paganism, the people have made it a religious principle to become outrageous, whenever any opinion is advanced which their priests think contrary to *sound doctrine*. The sectaries of a religion, which preaches, in appearance, nothing but charity, concord, and peace, have proved themselves more ferocious than cannibals or savages, whenever their divines excited them to destroy their brethren. There is no crime which men have not committed under the idea of pleasing the Divinity or appeasing his wrath. . . .

A morality, which contradicts the nature of man, is not made for man. "But," say you, "the nature of man is depraved." In what consists this pretended depravity? In having passions? But, are not passions essential to man? Is he not obliged to seek, desire, and love what is, or what he thinks is conducive to his happiness? Is he not forced to fear and avoid what he judges disagreeable or fatal? Kindle his passions for useful objects; connect his welfare with those objects; divert him, by sensible and known motives, from what may injure either him or others, and you will make him a reasonable and virtuous being. A man without passions would be equally indifferent to vice and to virtue. . . .

What is virtue according to theology? *It is*, we are told, *the conformity of the actions of men to the will of God*. But what is God? A being of whom nobody has the least conception, and whom every one consequently modifies in his own way. What is the will of God? It is what men, who have seen God, or whom God has inspired, have declared to be the will of God. Who are those who have seen God? They are either fanatics or rogues, or ambitious men, whom we cannot readily believe upon their word.

To found morality upon a God, whom every one paints to himself differently, composes in his way, and arranges according to his own temperament and interest, is evidently to found morality upon the caprice and imagination of men; it is to found it upon the whims of a sect, a faction, a party, who will believe they have the advantage to adore a true God to the exclusion of all others.

To establish morality of the duties of man upon the divine will, is to found it upon the will, the reveries and the interests of those who make God speak without ever fearing that he will contradict them. In every religion, priests alone have a right to decide what is pleasing or displeasing to their God; we are certain they will always decide that it is what pleases or displeases themselves. . . .

A morality, connected with religion, is necessarily subordinate to it. In the mind of a devout man, God must be regarded more than his creatures; it is better to obey him than men. The interests of the celestial monarch must prevail over those of weak mortals. But the interests of heaven are obviously those of its ministers; whence it evidently follows, that in every religion, priests, under pretext of the interests of heaven or the glory of God, can dispense with the duties of human morality, when they clash with the duties which God has a right to impose. Besides, must not he, who has power to pardon crimes, have a right to command the commission of crimes?

We are perpetually told, that, without a God there would be no *moral obligation*; that the people and even the sovereigns require a legislator powerful enough to constrain them. Moral constraint supposes a law; but this law arises from eternal and necessary relations of things with one another; relations, which have nothing common with the existence of a God. The rules of man's conduct are derived from his own nature which he is capable of knowing, and not from the divine nature of which he has no idea. These rules constrain or oblige us; that is, we render ourselves estimable or contemptible, amiable or detestable, worthy of reward or of punishment, happy or unhappy, according as we conform to, or deviate from these rules. The law, which obliges man not to hurt himself, is founded upon the nature of a sensible being, who, in whatever way he came into the world, or whatever may be his fate in a future one, is forced by his actual essence to seek good and shun evil, to love pleasure and fear pain. The law, which obliges man not to injure, and even to do good to others, is founded upon the nature of sensible beings, living in society, whose essence compels them to despise those who are useless, and to detest those who oppose their felicity.

Whether there exists a God or not, whether this God has spoken or not, the moral duties of men will be always the same, so long as they retain their peculiar nature, that is, as long as they are sensible beings. Have men then need of a God whom they know not, of an invisible legislator, of a mysterious religion and of chimerical fears, in order to learn that every excess evidently tends to destroy them, that to preserve health they must be temperate; that to gain the love of others it is necessary to do them good, that, to do them evil is the sure means to incur their vengeance and hatred?

"Before the law there was no sin." Nothing is more false than this maxim. It suffices that man is what he is, or that he is a sensible being, in order to distinguish what gives him pleasure or displeasure. It suffices that one man knows that another man is a sensible being like himself, to perceive what is useful or hurtful to him. It suffices that man needs his fellow creature, in order to know that he must fear to excite in him sentiments unfavorable to himself. Thus the feeling and thinking being has only to feel and think, in order to discover what he must do for himself and others. I feel, and another feels like me; this is the foundation of all morals. . . .

We can judge of the goodness of a system of morals, only by its conformity to the nature of man. By this comparison, we have a right to reject it, if contrary to the welfare of our species. Whoever has seriously meditated upon religion and its supernatural morality; whoever has carefully weighed their advantages and disadvantages, will be fully convinced, that both are injurious to the interests of man, or directly opposite to his nature. . . .

It is asserted, that the dogma of another life is of the utmost importance to the peace and happiness of societies; that without it, men would be destitute of motives to do good. What need is there of terrors and fables to make every rational man sensible how he ought to conduct himself upon earth? Does not every one see, that he has the greatest interest in meriting the approbation, esteem, and benevolence of the beings who surround him, and in abstaining from everything, by which he may incur the censure, contempt, and resentment of society? However short an entertainment, a conversation, or visit, does not each desire to act his part decently, and agreeably to himself and others? If life is but a passage, let us strive to make it easy; which we cannot effect, if we fail in regard for those who travel with us.

Religion, occupied with its gloomy reveries, considers man merely as a pilgrim upon earth; and therefore supposes that, in order to travel the more securely, he must forsake company and deprive himself of the pleasures and amusements, which might console him for the tediousness and fatigue of the road. A stoical and morose philosopher sometimes gives us advice as irrational as that of religion. But a more rational philosophy invites us to spread flowers in the way of life, to dispel melancholy and panic terrors, to connect our interest with that of our fellow-travellers, and by gaiety and lawful pleasures, to divert our attention from the difficulties and cross accidents, to which we are often exposed; it teaches us, that, to travel agreeably, we should abstain from what might be injurious to ourselves, and carefully shun what might render us odious to our associates. . . .

It is asked, what motives an Atheist can have to do good? The motive to please himself and his fellow-creatures; to live happily and peaceably; to gain the affection and esteem of men, whose existence and dispositions are much more sure and known, than those of a being impossible to be known. "Can he who fears not the gods, fear anything?" He can fear men; he can fear contempt, dishonor, the punishment and vengeance of the laws; in short, he can fear himself, and the remorse felt by all those who are conscious of having incurred or merited the hatred of their fellow-creatures.

Conscience is the internal testimony, which we bear to ourselves, of having acted so as to merit the esteem or blame of the beings, with whom we live; and it is founded upon the clear knowledge we have of men, and of the sentiments which our actions must produce in them. The conscience of the religious man consists in imagining that he has pleased or displeased his God, of whom he has no idea, and whose obscure and doubtful intentions are explained to him only by men of doubtful veracity, who, like him, are utterly unacquainted with the essence of the Deity, and are little agreed upon what can please or displease him. In a word, the conscience of the credulous is directed by men, who have themselves an erroneous conscience, or whose interest stifles knowledge.

"Can an Atheist have a conscience? What are his motives to abstain from hidden vices and secret crimes, of which other men are ignorant, and which are beyond the reach of laws?" He may be assured by constant experience, that there is no vice, which by the nature of things, does not punish itself. Would he preserve this life? He will avoid every excess that may impair his health: he will not wish to lead a languishing life, which would render him a burden to himself and others. As for secret crimes, he will abstain from them, for fear he shall be forced to blush at himself, from whom he cannot fly. If he has any reason, he will know the value of the esteem which an honest man ought to have for himself. He will see that unforeseen circumstances may unveil the conduct which he feels interested in concealing from others. The other world furnishes the motives for doing good, to him who finds none here below. . . .

A man of reflection cannot be incapable of his duties, of discovering the relations subsisting between men, of mediating his own nature, of discerning his own wants, propensities, and desires, and of perceiving what he owes to beings, who are necessary to his happiness. These reflections naturally lead him to a knowledge of the morality most essential to social beings. Dangerous passions seldom fall to the lot of man who loves to commune with himself, to study, and to investigate the principles of things. The strongest passion of such a man will be to know truth, and his ambition to teach it to others. Philosophy is proper to cultivate both the mind and the heart. On the score of morals and honesty, has not he who reflects and reasons, evidently an advantage over him, who makes it a principle never to reason?

If ignorance is useful to priests, and to the oppressors of mankind, it is fatal to society. Man, void of knowledge, does not enjoy his reason; without reason and knowledge, he is a savage, every instant liable to be hurried into crimes. Morality, or the science of duties, is acquired only by the study of man, and of what is relative to man. He who does not reflect, is unacquainted with true morality, and walks with precarious steps in the path of virtue. The less men reason, the more wicked they are. Savages, princes, nobles, and the dregs of the people, are commonly the worst of men, because they reason the least. . . .

• 33 •

THE WILL TO BELIEVE *

William James (1842–1910)

1. . . . Let us give the name of *hypothesis* to anything that may be proposed to our belief; and just as the electricians speak of live and dead wires, let us speak of any hypothesis as either *live* or *dead*. A live hypothesis is one which appeals as a real possibility to him to whom it is proposed. If I ask you to believe in the Mahdi, the notion makes no electric connection with your nature—it refuses to scintillate with any credibility

* From *The Will to Believe and Other Essays* (1897). Compare with selections 14, 34, and 37.

at all. As an hypothesis it is completely dead. To an Arab, however (even if he be not one of the Mahdi's followers), the hypothesis is among the mind's possibilities: it is alive. This shows that deadness and liveness in an hypothesis are not intrinsic properties, but relations to the individual thinker. They are measured by his willingness to act. The maximum of liveness in an hypothesis means willingness to act irrevocably. Practically, that means belief; but there is some believing tendency wherever there is willingness to act at all.

Next, let us call the decision between two hypotheses an *option*. Options may be of several kinds. They may be—first, *living* or *dead*; secondly, *forced* or *avoidable*; thirdly, *momentous* or *trivial*; and for our purposes we may call an option a *genuine* option when it is of the forced, living, and momentous kind.

(1) A living option is one in which both hypotheses are live ones. If I say to you: "Be a theosophist or be a Mohammedan," it is probably a dead option, because for you neither hypothesis is likely to be alive. But if I say: "Be an agnostic or be a Christian," it is otherwise: trained as you are, each hypothesis makes some appeal, however small, to your belief.

(2) Next, if I say to you: "Choose between going out with your umbrella or without it," I do not offer you a genuine option, for it is not forced. You can easily avoid it by not going out at all. Similarly, if I say, "Either love me or hate me," "Either call my theory true or call it false," your option is avoidable. You may remain indifferent to me, neither loving nor hating, and you may decline to offer any judgment as to my theory. But if I say, "Either accept this truth or go without it," I put on you a forced option, for there is no standing place outside of the alternative. Every dilemma based on a complete logical disjunction, with no possibility of not choosing, is an option of this forced kind.

(3) Finally, if I were Dr. Nansen and proposed to you to join my North Pole expedition, your option would be momentous; for this would probably be your only similar opportunity, and your choice now would either exclude you from the North Pole sort of immortality altogether or put at least the chance of it into your hands. He who refuses to embrace a unique opportunity loses the prize as surely as if he tried and failed. *Per contra*, the option is trivial when the opportunity is not unique, when the stake is insignificant, or when the decision is reversible if it later prove unwise. Such trivial options abound in the scientific life. A chemist finds an hypothesis live enough to spend a year in its verification: he believes in it to that extent. But if his experiments prove inconclusive either way, he is quit for his loss of time, no vital harm being done. It will facilitate our discussion if we keep all these distinctions in mind. . . .

2. . . . The thesis I defend is . . . this: *Our passional nature not only lawfully may, but must, decide an option between propositions, whenever it is a genuine option that cannot by its nature be decided on intellectual grounds; for to say, under such circumstances, "Do not decide, but leave the question open," is itself a passional decision—just like deciding yes or no—and is attended with the same risk of losing the truth.* . . .

3. . . . Wherever the option between losing truth and gaining it is not momentous, we can throw the chance of *gaining truth* away, and at any rate save ourselves from any chance of *believing falsehood*, by not making up our minds at all till objective evidence has come. In scientific questions, this is almost always the case; and even in human affairs in general, the need of acting is seldom so urgent that a false belief to act on is better than no belief at all. Law courts, indeed, have to decide on the best evidence attainable for the moment, because a judge's duty is to make law as well as to ascertain it, and (as a learned judge once said to me) few cases are worth spending much time over: the great thing is to have them decided on *any* acceptable principle, and got out of the way. But in our dealings with objective nature we obviously are recorders, not makers, of the truth; and decisions for the mere sake of deciding promptly and getting on to the next business would be wholly out of place. Throughout the breadth of physical nature facts are what they are quite independently of us, and seldom is there any such hurry about them that the risks of being duped by believing a premature theory need be faced. The questions here are always trivial options, the hypotheses are hardly living (at any rate not living for us spectators), the choice between believing truth or falsehood is seldom forced. The attitude of sceptical balance is therefore the absolutely wise one if we would escape mistakes. What difference, indeed, does it make to most of us whether we have or have not a theory of the Röntgen rays, whether we believe or not in mind-stuff, or have a conviction about the causality of conscious states? It makes no difference. Such options are not forced on us. On every account it is better not to make them, but still keep weighing reasons *pro et contra* with an indifferent hand.

I speak, of course, here of the purely judging mind. For purposes of discovery such indifference is to be less highly recommended, and science would be far less advanced than she is if the passionate desires of individuals to get their own faiths confirmed had been kept out of the game. . . . If you want an absolute duffer in an investigation, you must, after all, take the man who has no interest whatever in its results: he is the warranted incapable, the positive fool. The most useful investigator, because the most sensitive observer, is always he whose eager interest in one side of the question is balanced by an equally keen nervousness lest he become deceived. Science has organized this nervousness into a regular *technique,* her so-called method of verification; and she has fallen so deeply in love with the method that one may even say she has ceased to care for truth by itself at all. It is only truth as technically verified that interests her. The truth of truths might come in merely affirmative form, and she would decline to touch it. Such truth as that, she might repeat with Clifford, would be stolen in defiance of her duty to mankind. Human passions, however, are stronger than technical rules. "*Le coeur a ses raisons,*" as Pascal says, "*que la raison ne connait pas*" *; and however indifferent to all but the bare rules of the game the umpire, the abstract intellect, may be, the concrete players who furnish him the materials to judge of are usually, each one of them, in love with some pet "live hypothesis" of his own. Let us agree, however, that wherever there is no forced option, the dispassionately judicial intellect with no pet hypothesis, saving us, as it does, from dupery at any rate, ought to be our ideal.

The question next arises: Are there not somewhere forced options in our speculative questions, and can we (as men who may be interested at least as much in positively gaining truth as in merely escaping dupery) always wait with impunity till the coercive evidence shall have arrived? It seems *a priori* improbable that the truth should be so nicely adjusted to our needs and powers as that. In the great boarding-house of nature, the cakes and the butter and the syrup seldom come out so even and leave the plates so clean. Indeed, we should view them with scientific suspicion if they did.

4. *Moral questions* immediately present themselves as questions whose solution cannot wait for sensible proof. A moral question is a question not of what sensibly exists, but of what is good, or would be good if it did exist. Science can tell us what exists; but to compare the worths, both of what exists and of what does not exist, we must consult not science, but what Pascal calls our heart. Science herself consults her heart when she lays it down that the infinite ascertainment of fact and correction of false belief are the supreme goods for man. Challenge the statement, and science can only repeat it oracularly, or else prove it by showing that such ascertainment and correction bring men all sorts of other goods which man's heart in turn declares. The question of having moral beliefs at all or not having them is decided by our will. Are our moral preferences true or false, or are they only odd biological phenomena, making things good or bad for *us,* but in themselves indifferent? How can your pure intellect decide? If your heart does not *want* a world of moral reality, your head will assuredly never make you believe in one. Mephistophelian scepticism, indeed, will satisfy the head's play-instincts much better than any rigorous idealism

* The heart has its reasons, that reason does not know.

can. Some men (even at the student age) are so naturally cool-hearted that the moralistic hypothesis never has for them any pungent life, and in their supercilious presence the hot young moralist always feels strangely ill at ease. The appearance of knowingness is on their side, of *naivete* and gullibility on his. Yet, in the articulate heart of him, he clings to it that he is not a dupe, and that there is a realm in which (as Emerson says) all their wit and intellectual superiority is no better than the cunning of a fox. Moral scepticism can no more be refuted or proved by logic than intellectual scepticism can. When we stick to it that there *is* truth (be it of either kind), we do so with our whole nature, and resolve to stand or fall by the results. The sceptic with his whole nature adopts the doubting attitude; but which of us is the wiser, Omniscience only knows.

Turn now from these wide questions of good to a certain class of questions of fact, questions concerning personal relations, states of mind between one man and another. *Do you like me or not?*—for example. Whether you do or not depends, in countless instances, on whether I meet you half-way, am willing to assume that you must like me, and show you trust and expectation. The previous faith on my part in your liking's existence is in such cases what makes your liking come. But if I stand aloof, and refuse to budge an inch until I have objective evidence . . . ten to one your liking never comes. How many women's hearts are vanquished by the mere sanguine insistence of some man that they *must* love him! He will not consent to the hypothesis that they cannot. The desire for a certain kind of truth here brings about that special truth's existence; and so it is in innumerable cases of other sorts. Who gains promotions, boons, appointments, but the man in whose life they are seen to play the part of live hypotheses, who discounts them, sacrifices other things for their sake before they have come, and takes risks for them in advance? His faith acts on the powers above him as a claim, and creates its own verification.

A social organism of any sort whatever, large or small, is what it is because each member proceeds to his own duty with a trust that the other members will simultaneously do theirs. Wherever a desired result is achieved by the co-operation of many independent persons, its existence as a fact is a pure consequence of the precursive faith in one another of those immediately concerned. A government, an army, a commercial system, a ship, a college, an athletic team, all exist on this condition, without which not only is nothing achieved, but nothing is even attempted. A whole train of passengers (individually brave enough) will be looted by a few highwaymen, simply because the latter can count on one another, while each passenger fears that if he makes a movement of resistance, he will be shot before any one else backs him up. If we believed that the whole carfull would rise at once with us, we should each severally rise, and train-robbing would never even be attempted. There are, then, cases where a fact cannot come at all unless a preliminary faith exists in its coming. *And where faith in a fact can help create the fact,* that would be an insane logic which should say that faith running ahead of scientific evidence is the "lowest kind of immorality" into which a thinking being can fall. Yet such is the logic by which our scientific absolutists pretend to regulate our lives!

5. In truths dependent on our personal action, then, faith based on desire is certainly a lawful and possibly an indispensable thing.

But now, it will be said, these are all childish human cases, and have nothing to do with great cosmical matters, like the question of religious faith. Let us then pass on to that. Religions differ so much in their accidents that in discussing the religious question we must make it very generic and broad. What then do we now mean by the religious hypothesis? Science says things are; morality says some things are better than other things; and religion says essentially two things.

First, she says that the best things are the more eternal things, the overlapping things, the things in the universe that throw the last stone, so to speak, and say the final word. "Perfection is eternal"—this phrase of Charles Secretan seems a good way of putting this first affirmation of religion, an affirmation which obviously cannot yet be verified scientifically at all.

The second affirmation of religion is that we are better off even now if we believe her first affirmation to be true.

Now, let us consider what the logical elements of this situation are *in case the religious hypothesis in both its branches be really true.* (Of course, we must admit that possibility at the outset. If we are to discuss the question at all, it must involve a living option. If for any of you religion be a hypothesis that cannot, by any living possibility, be true, then you need go no farther. I speak to the "saving remnant" alone.) So proceeding, we see, first, that religion offers itself as a *momentous* option. We are supposed to gain, even now, by our belief, and to lose by our non-belief, a certain vital good. Secondly, religion is a *forced* option, so far as that good goes. We cannot escape the issue by remaining sceptical and waiting for more light, because, although we do avoid error in that way *if religion be untrue,* we lose the good, *if it be true,* just as certainly as if we positively chose to disbelieve. It is as if a man should hesitate indefinitely to ask a certain woman to marry him because he was not perfectly sure that she would prove an angel after he brought her home. Would he not cut himself off from that particular angel-possibility as decisively as if he went and married some one else? Scepticism, then, is not avoidance of option; it is option of a certain particular kind of risk. *Better risk loss of truth than chance of error*—that is your faith-vetoer's exact position. He is actively playing his stake as much as the believer is; he is backing the field against the religious hypothesis, just as the believer is backing the religious hypothesis against the field. To preach scepticism to us as a duty until "sufficient evidence" for religion be found, is tantamount therefore to telling us, when in presence of the religious hypothesis, that to yield to our fear of its being error is wiser and better than to yield to our hope that it may be true. It is not intellect against all passions, then; it is only intellect with one passion laying down its law. And by what, forsooth, is the supreme wisdom of this passion warranted? Dupery for dupery, what proof is there that dupery through hope is so much worse than dupery through fear? I, for one, can see no proof; and I simply refuse obedience to the scientist's command to imitate his kind of option, in a case where my own stake is important enough to give me the right to choose my own form of risk. If religion be true and the evidence for it be still insufficient, I do not wish, by putting your extinguisher upon my nature (which feels to me as if it had after all some business in this matter), to forfeit my sole chance in life of getting upon the winning side—that chance depending, of course, on my willingness to run the risk of acting as if my passional need of taking the world religiously might be prophetic and right.

All this is on the supposition that it really may be prophetic and right, and that, even to us who are discussing the matter, religion is a live hypothesis which may be true. Now, to most of us religion comes in a still further way that makes a veto on our active faith even more illogical. The more perfect and more eternal aspect of the universe is represented in our religions as having personal form. The universe is no longer a mere *It* to us, but a *Thou*, if we are religious; and any relation that may be possible from person to person might be possible here. For instance, although in one sense we are passive portions of the universe, in another we show a curious autonomy, as if we were small active centres on our own account. We feel, too, as if the appeal of religion to us were made to our own active good-will, as if evidence might be forever witheld from us unless we met the hypothesis half-way. To take a trivial illustration: just as a man who in a company of gentlemen made no advances, asked a warrant for every concession, and believed no one's word without proof, would cut himself off by such churlishness from all the social rewards that a more trusting spirit would earn—so here, one who should shut himself up in snarling logicality and try to make the gods extort his recognition willy-nilly, or not get it at all, might cut himself off forever from his only opportunity of making the gods' acquaintance. This feeling, forced on us we know not whence, that by obstinately believing that there are gods (although not to do so would be so easy both for our logic and our life) we are doing the universe the deepest service we can, seems part of the living essence of the religious hypothesis. If the hypothesis *were* true in all its parts, including this one, then pure intellectualism, with its veto on our making willing advances, would be an absurdity; and some participation of our sympathetic nature would be logically required. I, therefore, for one, cannot see my way to accepting the agnostic rules for truth-seeking, or wilfully agree to keep my willing nature out of the game. I cannot do so for this plain reason, that *a rule of thinking which would absolutely prevent me from acknowledging certain kinds of truth if those kinds of truth were really there, would be an irrational rule.* That for me is the long and short of the formal logic of the situation, no matter what the kinds of truth might materially be.

I confess I do not see how this logic can be escaped. But sad experience makes me fear that some of you may still shrink from radically saying with me, *in abstracto,* that we have the right to believe at our own risk any hypothesis that is live enough to tempt our will. I suspect, however, that if this is so, it is because you have got away from the abstract logical point of view altogether, and are thinking (perhaps without realizing it) of some particular religious hypothesis which for you is dead. The freedom to "believe what we will" you apply to the case of some patent superstition; and the faith you think of is the faith defined by the schoolboy when he said, "Faith is when you believe something that you know ain't true." I can only repeat that this is misapprehension. *In concreto,* the freedom to believe can only cover living options which the intellect of the individual cannot by itself resolve; and living options never seem absurdities to him who has them to consider. When I look at the religious question as it really puts itself to concrete men, and when I think of all the possibilities which both practically and theoretically it involves, then this command that we shall put a stopper on our heart, instincts, and courage, and *wait*—acting of course meanwhile more or less as if religion were *not* true—till doomsday, or till such time as our intellect and senses working together may have raked in evidence enough—this command, I say, seems to me the queerest idol ever manufactured in the philosophic cave. Were we scholastic absolutists, there might be more excuse. If we had an infallible intellect with its objective certitudes, we might feel ourselves disloyal to such a perfect organ of knowledge in not trusting to it exclusively, in not waiting for its releasing word. But if we are empiricists, if we believe that no bell in us tolls to let us know for certain when truth is in our grasp, then it seems a piece of idle fantasticality to preach so solemnly our duty of waiting for the bell.

Indeed we *may* wait if we will—I hope you do not think that I am denying that—but if we do so, we do so at our peril as much as if we believed. In either case we *act*, taking our life in our hands. No one of us ought to issue vetoes to the other, nor should we bandy words of abuse. We ought, on the contrary, delicately and profoundly to respect one another's mental freedom: then only shall we bring about the intellectual republic; then only shall we have that spirit of inner tolerance without which all our outer tolerance is soulless, and which is empiricism's glory; then only shall we live and let live, in speculative as well as in practical things. . . .

• 34 •

FAITH, BELIEF, AND ACTION *

William James (1842–1910)

. . . There is one element of our active nature which . . . philosophers as a rule have with great insincerity tried to huddle out of sight in their pretension to found systems of absolute certainty. I mean the element of faith. Faith means belief in something concerning which doubt is still theoretically possible; and as the test of belief is willingness to act, one may say that faith is the readiness to act in a cause the prosperous issue of which is not certified to us in advance. It is in fact the same moral quality which we call courage in practical affairs. . . .

The necessity of faith as an ingredient in our mental attitude is strongly insisted on by the scientific philosophers of the present day; but by a singularly arbitrary caprice they say that it is only legitimate when used in the interests of one particular proposition—the proposition, namely that the course of nature is uniform. That nature will follow tomorrow the same laws that she follows today is, they all admit, a truth which no man can *know*; but in the interests of cognition as well as of action we must postulate or assume it. . . .

With regard to all other possible truths, however, a number of our most influential contemporaries think that an attitude of faith is not only illogical but shameful. Faith in a religious dogma for which there is no outward proof, but which we are tempted to postulate for our emotional

* Excerpted from "The Sentiment of Rationality," in *The Will to Believe* (1897). The title of this selection has been supplied by the editors. Compare with selection 33.

interests, just as we postulate the uniformity of nature for our intellectual interests, is branded by Professor Huxley as "the lowest depth of immorality." Citations of this kind from leaders of the modern *Aufklärung* * might be multiplied almost indefinitely. Take Professor Clifford's article on the "Ethics of Belief." He calls it "guilt" and "sin" to believe even the truth without "scientific evidence." But what is the use of being a genius, unless *with the same scientific evidence* as other men, one can reach more truth than they? Why does Clifford fearlessly proclaim his belief in the conscious-automaton theory, although the "proofs" before him are the same which make Mr. Lewes reject it? . . . Simply because, like every human being of the slightest mental originality, he is peculiarly sensitive to evidence that bears in some one direction. It is utterly hopeless to try to exorcise such sensitiveness by calling it the disturbing subjective factor, and branding it as the root of all evil. . . . Pretend what we may, the whole man within us is at work when we form our philosophical opinions. Intellect, will, taste, and passion co-operate just as they do in practical affairs; and lucky it is if the passion be not something as petty as a love of personal conquest over the philosopher across the way. The absurd abstraction of an intellect verbally formulating all its evidence and carefully estimating the probability thereof by a vulgar fraction by the size of whose denominator and numerator alone it is swayed, is ideally as inept as it is actually impossible. It is almost incredible that men who are themselves working philosophers should pretend that any philosophy can be, or ever has been, constructed without the help of personal preference, belief, or divination. . . .

If I am born with such a superior general reaction to evidence that I can guess right and act accordingly, and gain all that comes of right action, while my less gifted neighbor (paralyzed by his scruples and waiting for more evidence which he dares not anticipate, much as he longs to) still stands shivering on the brink, by what law shall I be forbidden to reap the advantages of my superior native sensitiveness? Of course I yield to my belief in such a case as this or distrust it, alike at my peril, just as I do in any of the great practical decisions of life. If my inborn faculties are good, I am a prophet; if poor, I am a failure: nature spews me out of her mouth, and there is an end to me. In the total game of life we stake our persons all the while; and if in its theoretic part our persons will help us to a conclusion, surely we should also stake them here, however inarticulate they may be.

But in being myself so very articulate in proving what to all readers with a sense for reality will seem a platitude, am I not wasting words? We can-

* Enlightenment.

not live or think at all without some degree of faith. Faith is synonymous with working hypothesis. The only difference is that while some hypotheses can be refuted in five minutes, others may defy ages. A chemist who conjectures that a certain wall-paper contains arsenic, and has faith enough to lead him to take the trouble to put some of it into a hydrogen bottle, finds out by the results of his action whether he was right or wrong. But theories like that of Darwin, or that of the kinetic constitution of matter, may exhaust the labors of generations in their corroboration, each tester of their truth proceeding in this simple way—that he acts as if it were true, and expects the result to disappoint him if his assumption is false. The longer disappointment is delayed, the stronger grows his faith in his theory. . . .

Now, I wish to show what to my knowledge has never been clearly pointed out, that belief (as measured by action) not only does and must continually outstrip scientific evidence, but that there is a certain class of truths of whose reality belief is a factor as well as a confessor; and that as regards this class of truths faith is not only licit and pertinent, but essential and indispensable. The truths cannot become true till our faith has made them so.

Suppose, for example, that I am climbing in the Alps, and have had the ill-luck to work myself into a position from which the only escape is by a terrible leap. Being without similar experience, I have no evidence of my ability to perform it successfully; but hope and confidence in myself make me sure I shall not miss my aim, and nerve my feet to execute what without those subjective emotions would perhaps have been impossible. But suppose that, on the contrary, the emotions of fear and mistrust preponderate; or suppose that, having just read the *Ethics of Belief*, I feel it would be sinful to act upon an assumption unverified by previous experience—why, then I shall hesitate so long that at last, exhausted and trembling, and launching myself in a moment of despair, I miss my foothold and roll into the abyss. In this case (and it is one of an immense class) the part of wisdom clearly is to believe what one desires; for the belief is one of the indispensable preliminary conditions of the realization of its object. *There are then cases where faith creates its own verification.* Believe, and you shall be right, for you shall save yourself; doubt, and you shall again be right, for you shall perish. The only difference is that to believe is greatly to your advantage.

The future movements of the stars or the facts of past history are determined now once for all, whether I like them or not. They are given irrespective of my wishes, and in all that concerns truths like these subjective preference should have no part; it can only obscure the judgment. But in every fact into which there enters an element of personal contribution on my part, as soon as this personal contribution demands a certain degree of subjective energy which, in its turn, calls for a certain amount of faith in the result—so that, after all, the future fact is conditioned by my present faith in it—how trebly asinine would it be for me to deny myself the use of the subjective method, the method of belief based on desire! . . .

The highest good can be achieved only by our getting our proper life; and that can come about only by help of a moral energy born of the faith that in some way or other we shall succeed in getting it if we try pertinaciously enough. This world *is* good, we must say, since it is what we make it—and we shall make it good. How can we exclude from the cognition of a truth a faith which is involved in the creation of the truth? . . . All depends on the character of the personal contribution. . . . Wherever the facts to be formulated contain such a contribution, we may logically, legitimately, and inexpugnably believe what we desire. The belief creates its verification. The thought becomes literally father to the fact, as the wish was father to the thought. . . .

The essential thing to notice is that our active preference is a legitimate part of the game—that it is our plain business as men to try one of the keys, and the one in which we most confide. If then the proof exist not till I have acted, and I must needs in acting run the risk of being wrong, how can the popular science professors be right in objurgating in me as infamous a "credulity" which the strict logic of the situation requires? If this really be a moral universe; if by my acts I be a factor of its destinies; if to believe where I may doubt be itself a moral act analogous to voting for a side not yet sure to win—by what right shall they close in upon me and steadily negate the deepest conceivable function of my being by their preposterous command that I shall stir neither hand nor foot, but remain balancing myself in eternal and insoluble doubt? Why, doubt itself is a decision of the widest practical reach, if only because we may miss by doubting what goods we might be gaining by espousing the winning side. But more than that! It is often practically impossible to distinguish doubt from dogmatic negation. If I refuse to stop a murder because I am in doubt whether it be not justifiable homicide, I am virtually abetting the crime. If I refuse to bale out a boat because I am in doubt whether my efforts will keep her afloat, I am really helping to sink her. If in the mountain precipice I doubt my right to risk a leap, I actively connive at my destruction. He who commands himself not to be credulous of God, of duty, of freedom, of immortality, may again and again be indistinguishable from him who dogmatically denies them. Scepticism in moral matters is an active ally of immorality. Who is not for is against. The universe will have no neutrals in these questions. In theory as in practice, dodge or hedge, or talk as we like about a wise scepticism, we are really doing volunteer military service for one side or the other. . . .

• 35 •

RELIGION *

George Santayana (1863–1952)

Experience has repeatedly confirmed that well-known maxim of Bacon's, that "a little philosophy inclineth man's mind to atheism, but depth in philosophy bringeth men's minds about to religion." In every age the most comprehensive thinkers have found in the religion of their time and country something they could accept, interpreting and illustrating that religion so as to give it depth and universal application. Even the heretics and atheists, if they have had profundity, turn out after a while to be fore-runners of some new orthodoxy. What they rebel against is a religion alien to their nature; they are atheists only by accident, and relatively to a con-vention which inwardly offends them, but they yearn mightily in their own souls after the religious acceptance of a world interpreted in their own fashion. So it appears in the end that their atheism and loud protestation were in fact the hastier part of their thought, since what emboldened them to deny the poor world's faith was that they were too impatient to under-stand it. Indeed, the enlightenment common to young wits and worm-eaten old satirists, who plume themselves on detecting the scientific ineptitude of religion—something which the blindest half see—is not nearly enlightened enough: it points to notorious facts incompatible with religious tenets literally taken, but it leaves unexplored the habits of thought from which those tenets sprang, their original meaning, and their true function. Such studies would bring the sceptic face to face with the mystery and pathos of mortal existence. They would make him understand why religion is so

* Reprinted with the permission of Charles Scribner's Sons from *Reason in Religion*, pages 3–6, by George Santayana (volume III of *The Life of Reason*). Copyright 1905 Charles Scribner's Sons; renewal copyright 1933. Permission to reprint also granted by Constable and Company Ltd., London. The title of this selection has been supplied by the editors. Compare with selection 33.

profoundly moving and in a sense so profoundly just. There must needs be something humane and necessary in an influence that has become the most general sanction of virtue, the chief occasion for art and philosophy, and the source, perhaps, of the best human happiness. If nothing, as Hooker said, is "so malapert as a splenetic religion," a sour irreligion is almost as perverse.

At the same time, when Bacon penned the sage epigram we have quoted he forgot to add that the God to whom depth in philosophy brings back men's minds is far from being the same from whom a little philosophy estranges them. It would be pitiful indeed if mature reflection bred no better conceptions than those which have drifted down the muddy stream of time, where tradition and passion have jumbled everything together. Traditional conceptions, when they are felicitous, may be adopted by the poet, but they must be purified by the moralist and disintegrated by the philosopher. Each religion, so dear to those whose life it sanctifies, and fulfilling so necessary a function in the society that has adopted it, necessarily contradicts every other religion, and probably contradicts itself. What religion a man shall have is a historical accident, quite as much as what language he shall speak. In the rare circumstances where a choice is possible, he may, with some difficulty, make an exchange; but even then he is only adopting a new convention which may be more agreeable to his personal temper but which is essentially as arbitrary as the old.

The attempt to speak without speaking any particular language is not more hopeless than the attempt to have a religion that shall be no religion in particular. A courier's or a dragoman's speech may indeed be often unusual and drawn from disparate sources, not without some mixture of personal originality; but that private jargon will have a meaning only because of its analogy to one or more conventional languages and its obvious derivation from them. So travellers from one religion to another, people who have lost their spiritual nationality, may often retain a neutral and confused residuum of belief, which they may egregiously regard as the essence of all religion, so little may they remember the graciousness and naturalness of that ancestral accent which a perfect religion should have. Yet a moment's probing of the conceptions surviving in such minds will show them to be nothing but vestiges of old beliefs, creases which thought, even if emptied of all dogmatic tenets, has not been able to smooth away at its first unfolding. Later generations, if they have any religion at all, will be found either to revert to ancient authority, or to attach themselves spontaneously to something wholly novel and immensely positive, to some faith promulgated by a fresh genius and passionately embraced by a converted people. Thus every living and healthy religion has a marked idiosyncrasy.

Its power consists in its special and surprising message and in the bias
which that revelation gives to life. The vistas it opens and the mysteries it
propounds are another world to live in; and another world to live in—
whether we expect ever to pass wholly into it or no—is what we mean by
having a religion. . . .

• 36 •

SCIENTIFIC HUMANISM *

Max C. Otto (1876–   )

All humanisms have one thing in common. It is the ideal of realizing
mankind's completest development. From here on they diverge. The most
far-reaching disagreement turns on the question whether man is or is not
absolutely distinct from everything else in the hierarchy of earthly existences. It is at this point that the designation of one humanism as scientific
takes on significance.

What does scientific mean in this connection? It means that human
beings are viewed naturalistically. They are placed in the natural world
along with the lower animals, plants, rocks, minerals, and star clusters.
Their intellectual, moral, and aesthetic powers, their ideas of decency, their
feelings of good will, all they are and aspire to be is looked upon as the
consummation of a long evolution from the animal status. Scientific humanism is a form of naturalism.

This is part of the answer. The rest of it is that the scientific humanist
is wholeheartedly committed to the use of scientific method. He favors its
extension to moral and social problems of every kind, and he believes that
a correct understanding of scientific procedure permits this to be done.
As a rule this procedure is so narrowly defined that it cannot be applied to
human beings in their actuality, to human interests as they are experienced,
or even to the world of which human beings are aware. Take Sir Arthur
Eddington's example of the elephant sliding down a grassy hillside.
From the viewpoint of physics the elephant fades out and is replaced by
the reading of the pointer indicating a certain mass. The hillside disappears

* Part of an essay that originally appeared in The Antioch Review, vol. III, no. 4;
copyright 1943 by The Antioch Review. Reprinted by permission of the author and the
editor.

and its place is taken by the reading of a plumb line against the divisions of a protractor. In the same way the descent becomes a pointer-reading on the seconds' dial of a watch. The result is, says this professor of astronomical physics, that what really slides is a bundle of pointer-readings, and the sliding is a function of space and time measures. There is simply no elephant to slide down a hill and no hill for an elephant to slide down. "The whole subject matter of exact science," as thus conceived, "consists of pointer readings and similar indications."

Ordinarily, when we think of science, it is this kind of science we think of. Our notion of scientific method is our notion of what goes on in physical or chemical laboratories, including what we believe to be the special kind of subject matter dealt with in them. Consequently, we conclude that if man is to be studied scientifically he must be reduced to a mindless, indeed lifeless, concourse of material entities, to atoms, electrons, or even to more abstract elements. And a purely material assemblage or a pattern of abstract entities is certainly anything but human.

Suppose, however, that we broaden our idea of science, as in the end I think we must, to take in every field of knowledge where a sufficiently painstaking effort is made to establish conclusions on a thorough-going examination of relevant fact. In that case the word "scientific" takes on a meaning to correspond. We may then say that a method of investigation is scientific to the extent that it exemplifies the idea of objective verification. . . .

Summarizing this phase of our study we may say that the scientific humanist sees no valid ground for believing men and women to be isolated or insulated creatures in nature. On the contrary, he regards them as strictly integrant to the great complexity of things, living and non-living, which is commonly spoken of as the world. In conformity with this naturalistic interpretation the scientific humanist rejects both pure Reason and Revelation as sources of light for the understanding of human nature or the art of life. For his part he tries to emulate as best he can in his own field of interest the temper of mind and the workmanship of scientists.

We turn now to the other word in the title—humanism. I was just saying that the scientific humanist looks upon man as belonging altogether to the order of nature. I did not say that he thinks man identical with the lower animals, not to speak of lifeless matter. The fact is that no other humanist so consistently exalts man, or looks with equal generosity upon his *humanitas*, upon those attributes which differentiate man from all other living creatures. In a word, the scientific humanist does not lose any of his interest in the human aspect of human nature because he aspires to be scientific in his thinking. . . .

What of man's religious interest? Does this humanism unite the religious and the scientific outlooks? The answer depends, as answers often do, on how the terms are defined. We have adopted a meaning for *scientific* and shall have to do likewise for *religious*.

No simple description can do justice to religion even as this has been formulated and practiced in the Occident. But a central feature of our whole religious tradition is its positive relation to the supernatural. To be religious has meant to seek companionship with a friendly being believed to abide behind or within the drift and waste of temporal events. Possibly there is actually a continuity between the "Friend behind phenomena" that men seek, to borrow Gilbert Murray's idea, and "the pack which a dog tries to smell his way back to all the time he is out walking." "It is a strange and touching thing," says Mr. Murray, "this eternal hunger of the gregarious animal for the herd of friends who are not there." "And it may be," he continues, "it may very possibly be," that our religious searchings are at bottom "the groping of a lonely-souled gregarious animal to find its herd or its herd leader in the great spaces between the stars."

Well, if this reliance upon a Cosmic Friend is what religion must be, because that is what religion in our region of the world has been, then scientific humanism can touch religion as a line can touch a circle, but the two cannot interpenetrate to form a blended philosophy. There are, however, other definitions of religion. One of these is readily seen to have close affinities with the humanism discussed in this paper. The world as described by science is accepted as such and this very description is made the ground for the highest human aspiration. It is surely an invitation to religion which W. Macneil Dixon extends to the reader in these words from his book, *Thoughts for the Times*:

> When I am told that throughout the realm of nature there is "no tendency that makes for righteousness," that justice is nowhere to be found there, that in her soil the tree of justice refuses to take root . . . I do not find nature ennobled and man humiliated. . . . Quite the reverse. To me it seems to exalt him to a plane immeasurably far above hers, and moreover to provide him with an aim, a purpose, a cause, an inspiration that fires the blood and hardens resolution. If justice be no concern either of nature or of the gods, it is the more preeminently ours. . . . If this world be without justice it is man's unique privilege to place it there—a superb design, an enterprise the immortals might envy, yet have left to mortal hands.

A similar view of religion has been defended with eloquence and learning by A. E. Haydon for a quarter of a century. Essential religion, in his view, is and has always been the shared quest of a good life in a good world, made ever more possible by advancing knowledge and now especially by science. Says Mr. Haydon in his book, *The Quest of the Ages:*

> In contrast with the great believers who imposed their noblest dreams by faith upon the universe, there have been men in all cultures who clipped the wings of their hopes and built a more modest ideal in the everyday world of fact. Though life might not be altogether lovely, they made the best of life. With no hope of help from gods, and no faith in life immortal, the beauty of human comradeship became more precious.
>
> It is encouraging, therefore, and of deep significance to religion, that a common refrain runs through the writings of modern thinkers. The notes of the melody are freedom, democratic opportunity, co-operative individualism, meliorism, internationalism. The march of religions moves toward the Great Society in which all individuals will have a fair chance for the joy of living, and personal satisfactions will blend with social responsibility and creative power.

An inspired statement of this nontheistic, socially oriented religious attitude is condensed into a paragraph at the end of John Dewey's *Human Nature and Conduct.* These four sentences bring the paragraph and the book to end:

> Within the flickering inconsequential acts of separate selves dwells a sense of the whole which claims and dignifies them. In its presence we put off mortality and live in the universal. The life of the community in which we live and have our being is the fit symbol of this relationship. The acts in which we express our perception of the ties which bind us to others are its only rites and ceremonies.

Personally, I have never been willing to stop at this point in defining religion, not because of its naturalistic, nontheistic, socially dedicated aspect, but because something seems to me left out which is more profoundly characteristic of the religious mood than any kind of special knowledge, devotion, or service. This is a response to the awesome and mysterious in life and the world. A positive response to the awesome and mysterious has had a central place in the most various religions throughout religious history. Without it religion seems to me to lose its differentiating quality and to become identical with morality, differing from it, if at all, in emotional tone. In theistic religions and in religious mysticism the response is not so much to the awesome mystery itself as to the Being behind the mystery, even though what this Being is may only be statable in symbols or not at all. In the nontheistic religion with which we are concerned the response is to the mystery as mystery. The difference between these attitudes is deeply significant, but there is at the same time a relationship between them which justifies the application of the term religious to both. At any rate I believe it necessary to add another quotation to those preceding:

> I have not said and I have no intention of saying, that the nontheist must limit his interests to what can be weighed and measured, intellectually delineated, or presented in some embodied form with clear outlines; that he must never allow himself to stray into the land described by Virginia Woolf, where words "fold their wings and sit huddled like rooks on the tops of the trees in winter." . . . We need to keep a window open toward the uncharted.
>
> A conscious awareness of this mystery does healing work on the inward man. It is the healing work of acknowledged ignorance in the revered presence of that which eludes comprehension—the incomprehensible in each other, in the life we are called upon to live, in the great cosmic setting that reaches from our feet to the infinities.

At all events, whether this sense of mystery is a religious indispensable or not, humanists of the scientific persuasion reject the dualism which assigns to religion final authority in the realm of value and to science final authority in the realm of fact. They refuse to divide the experienced world into two realms, one of which is the locus of fact and the other the locus of value; and if they recognize any authority as final, which in a manner of speaking they may be said to do, it is not any religious or scientific interpretation of the cosmos; it is man's unremitting search for a livable life and the stubborn conditioning facts of human nature and the natural and social environment. Scientific humanists share in the "quest of a good life in a good world," and hold steadily to the conviction that progress toward this authorative end is contingent upon the best kind of objective thinking whether the question is one of fact or of value. Which is another way of saying that in their philosophy the scientific and the religious spirit are united in a common enterprise. Matter and spirit may be enemies, but they may also be allies. . . .

RELIGION AND THE WILL TO BELIEVE *

Morris R. Cohen (1880–1947)

. . . I have spoken of the dark side of religion and have thus implied that there is another side. But if this implication puts me out of the class of those who are unqualified opponents of all that has been called religion, I do not wish to suggest that I am merely an advocate, or that I have any doubts as to the justice of the arguments that I have advanced. Doubtless some of my arguments may turn out to be erroneous, but at present I hold them all in good faith. I believe that this dark side of religion is a reality, and it is my duty on this occasion to let those who follow me do justice to the other side. But if what I have said has any merit, those who wish to state the bright side of religion must take account of and not ignore the realities which I have tried to indicate. This means that the defense of religion must be stated in a spirit of sober regard for truth, and not as a more or less complacent apology for beliefs which we are determined not to abandon. Anyone can, by assuming his faith to be the truth, argue from it more or less plausibly and entirely to his own satisfaction. But that is seldom illuminating or strengthening. The real case for religion must show compelling reasons why, despite the truths that I have sought to display, men who do not believe in religion should change their views. If this be so, we must reject such apologies for religion as Balfour's *Foundations of Belief*. One who accepts the Anglican Church may regard such a book as a sufficient defense. But in all essentials it is a subtle and urbane, but none the less complacent, begging of all the serious questions in the case. For similar reasons also I think we must reject the apology for religion advanced by my revered and beloved teacher William James.

Let us take up his famous essay on "The Will to Believe." Consider in the first place his argument that science (which is organized reason) is inapplicable in the realm of religion, because to compare values or worths "we must consult not science but what Pascal calls our heart" . . . But if

* From the essay "The Dark Side of Religion," in *The Faith of a Liberal* (New York: Henry Holt and Company, 1946), pp. 357–361. Reprinted by the kind permission of Harry N. Rosenfield, Administrator of the estate of Morris R. Cohen. The title of this selection has been supplied by the editors. Compare with selection 33.

it were true that science and reason have no force in matters of religion, why argue at all? Why all these elaborate reasons in defense of religion? Is it not because the arguments of men like Voltaire and Huxley did have influence that men like DeMaistre and James tried to answer them? Who, the latter ask, ever heard of anyone's changing his religion because of an argument? It is not necessary for me to give a list of instances from my own knowledge. Let us admit that few men confess themselves defeated or change their views in the course of any one argument. Does this prove that arguments have no effect? Do not men frequently use against others the very arguments which at first they professed to find unconvincing? The fact is that men do argue about religion, and it is fatuous for those who argue on one side to try also to discredit *all* rational arguments. It seems more like childish weakness to kick against a game or its rules when you are losing in it. And it is to the great credit of the Catholic Church that it has categorically condemned fideism or the effort to eliminate reason from religion. Skepticism against reason is not a real or enduring protection to religion. Its poison, like that of the Nessus shirt, finally destroys the faith that puts it on. Genuine faith in the truth is confident that it can prove itself to universal reason.

Let us look at the matter a little closer.

James argues that questions of belief are decided by our will. Now it is true that one can say: "I do not wish to argue. I want to continue in the belief that I have." But is not the one who says this already conscious of a certain weakness in his faith which might well be the beginning of its disintegration? The man who has a robust faith in his friend does not say, "I want to believe that he is honest," but "I know that he is honest, and any doubt about it is demonstrably false or unreasonable." To be willing to put your case and its evidence before the court of reason is to show real confidence in it.

But James argues that certain things are beloved not on the basis of rational or scientific weighing of evidence, but on the compulsion of our passional nature. This is true. But reflection may ease the passional compulsion. And why not encourage such reflection?

The history of the last few generations has shown that many have lost their faith in Christianity because of reflection induced by Darwinism. Reflection on the inconsistencies of the Mosaic chronology and cosmology has shown that these do not differ from other mythologies; and this has destroyed the belief of many in the plenary inspiration of the Bible. It is therefore always possible to ask: Shall I believe a given religious proposition as the absolute truth, or shall I suspend final decision until I have further evidence? I must go to church or stay out. But I may do the latter at least without hiding from myself the inadequacy of my knowledge or of the evidence. In politics I vote for X or Y without necessarily getting myself into the belief that my act is anything more than a choice of probabilities. I say: Better vote for X than for Y; although if I knew more (for which there is no time) I might vote the other way. In science I choose on the basis of all the available evidence but expressly reserve the possibility that future evidence may make me change my view. It is difficult to make such reservations within any religious system. But it is possible to remain permanently skeptical or agnostic with regard to religion itself and its absolute claims.

The momentous character of the choice in regard to religion may be dissolved by reflection which develops detachment or what James calls lightheartedness. What is the difference between believing in one religion or in another or in none? A realization of the endless variety of religious creeds, of the great diversity of beliefs that different people hold to be essential to our salvation, readily liberates us from the compulsion to believe in every Mullah that comes along or else fear eternal damnation. James draws a sharp distinction between a living and a nonliving issue. To him, I suppose, the question of whether to accept Judaism, Islam, or Buddhism was not a living one. But the question whether to investigate so-called psychical phenomena as proofs of immortality was a living one. But surely reflection may change the situation, and a student of religion may come to feel that James' choice was arbitrary and untenable.

The intensification of the feeling that religious issues are important comes about through the assumption that my eternal salvation depends upon my present choice, or—at most—on what I do during the few moments of my earthly career. There is remarkably little evidence for this assumption. If our life is eternal, we may have had more chances before and we may have more later. Why assume that the whole of an endless life is determined by an infinitesimal part of it? From this point of view, men like Jonathan Edwards, to whom eternal Hell is always present and who makes an intense religious issue out of every bite of food, appear to be just unbalanced, and in need of more play in the sunshine and fresh air and perhaps a little more sleep. I mention Jonathan Edwards because his life and teachings enable us to turn the tables on religion by what James regards as the great pragmatic argument in its favor. Accept it, James says, and you will be better off at once. . . . As most religions condemn forever those who do not follow them, it is as risky to accept any one as none at all. And it is possible to take the view that they are all a little bit ungracious, too intense, and too sure of what in our uncertain life cannot be proved. Let us better leave them all alone and console ourselves with the hypothesis—a not altogether impossible one—that the starry universe and whatever gods there be do not worry about us at all, and will not resent our enjoying whatever humane and enlightened comfort and whatever vision of truth and beauty our world offers us. Let us cultivate our little garden. The pretended certainties of religion do not really offer much more. This is of course not a refutation of religion, or of the necessity which reflective minds find to grapple with it. But it indicates that there may be more wisdom and courage as well as more faith in honest doubt than in most of the creeds.

PART VI

ETHICS AND VALUES

• 38 •

ON THE GOOD *

Plato (427–347 B.C.)

. . . Let me remind you of the distinction we drew earlier and have often drawn on other occasions, between the multiplicity of things that we call good or beautiful or whatever it may be and, on the other hand, Goodness itself or Beauty itself and so on. Corresponding to each of these sets of many things, we postulate a single Form or real essence, as we call it. . . . Further, the many things, we say, can be seen, but are not objects of rational thought; whereas the Forms are objects of thought but invisible.

Yes, certainly.

And we see things with our eyesight, just as we hear sounds with our ears and, to speak generally, perceive any sensible thing with our sense-faculties.

Of course.

Have you noticed, then, that the artificer who designed the senses has been exceptionally lavish of his materials in making the eyes able to see and their objects visible?

That never occured to me.

Well, look at it in this way. Hearing and sound do not stand in need of any third thing, without which the ear will not hear nor sound be heard; and I think the same is true of most, not to say all, of the other senses. Can you think of one that does require anything of the sort?

No, I cannot.

But there is this need in the case of sight and its objects. You may have the power of vision in your eyes and try to use it, and colour may be there in the objects; but sight will see nothing and the colours will remain invisible in the absence of a third thing peculiarly constituted to serve this very purpose.

By which you mean—?

Naturally I mean what you call light; and if light is a thing of value, the

* From Plato's *Republic*, Bk. VI, St. 507–509, translated from the Greek by F. M. Cornford (1941). Reprinted by permission of The Clarendon Press, Oxford. The title of this selection has been supplied by the editors. Compare with selections 39 and 40.

sense of sight and the power of being visible are linked together by a very precious bond, such as unites no other sense with its object.

No one could say that light is not a precious thing.

And of all the divinities in the skies is there one whose light, above all the rest, is responsible for making our eyes see perfectly and making objects perfectly visible?

There can be no two opinions: of course you mean the Sun.

And how is sight related to this deity? Neither sight nor the eye which contains it is the Sun, but of all the sense-organs it is the most sun-like; and further, the power it possesses is dispensed by the Sun, like a stream flooding the eye. And again, the Sun is not vision, but it is the cause of vision and also is seen by the vision it causes. . . . It was the Sun, then, that I meant when I spoke of that offspring which the Good has created in the visible world, to stand there in the same relation to vision and visible things as that which the Good itself bears in the intelligible world to intelligence and to intelligible objects.

How is that? You must explain further.

You know what happens when the colours of things are no longer irradiated by the daylight, but only by the fainter luminaries of the night: when you look at them, the eyes are dim and seem almost blind, as if there were no unclouded vision in them. But when you look at things on which the Sun is shining, the same eyes see distinctly and it becomes evident that they do contain the power of vision.

Certainly.

Apply this comparison, then, to the soul. When its gaze is fixed upon an object irradiated by truth and reality, the soul gains understanding and knowledge and is manifestly in possession of intelligence. But when it looks towards that twilight world of things that come into existence and pass away, its sight is dim and it has only opinions and beliefs which shift to and fro, and now it seems like a thing that has no intelligence.

That is true.

This, then, which gives to the objects of knowledge their truth and to him who knows them his power of knowing, is the Form or essential nature of Goodness. It is the cause of knowledge and truth; and so, while you may think of it as an object of knowledge, you will do well to regard it as something beyond truth and knowledge and, precious as these both are, of still higher worth. And, just as in our analogy light and vision were to be thought of as like the Sun, but not identical with it, so here both knowledge and truth are to be regarded as like the Good, but to identify either with the Good is wrong. The Good must hold a yet higher place of honour.

You are giving it a position of extraordinary splendour, if it is the source of knowledge and truth and itself surpasses them in worth. You surely cannot mean that it is pleasure.

Heaven forbid, I exclaimed. But I want to follow up our analogy still further. You will agree that the Sun not only makes the things we see visible, but also brings them into existence and gives them growth and nourishment; yet he is not the same thing as existence. And so with the objects of knowledge: these derive from the Good not only their power of being known, but their very being and reality; and Goodness is not the same thing as being, but even beyond being, surpassing it in dignity and power. . . .

• 39 •

ON THE GOOD *

Aristotle (384–322 B.C.)

Every art and every kind of inquiry, and likewise every act and purpose, seems to aim at some good; and so it has been well said that the good is that at which everything aims. . . . If then in what we do there be some end which we wish for on its own account, choosing all the others as means to this, but not every end without exception as a means to something else (for so we should go on *ad infinitum*, and desire would be left void and objectless), this evidently will be the good or the best of all things. And surely from a practical point of view it much concerns us to know this good; for then, like archers shooting at a definite mark, we shall be more likely to attain what we want. . . .

We see that there are many ends. But some of these are chosen only as means, as wealth, flutes, and the whole class of instruments. And it is plain that not all ends are final. But the best of all things must, we conceive, be something final. If then there be only one final end, this will be what we are seeking—or if there be more than one, then the most final of them.

Now that which is pursued as an end in itself is more final than that which is pursued as means to something else, and that which is never

* From Aristotle's *Nicomachean Ethics*, Bk. I, chs. 1, 2, 7, and 8, translated from the Greek by F. H. Peters (1906). Reprinted by permission of the publishers, Routledge & Kegan Paul Ltd., London. The title of this selection has been supplied by the editors. Compare with selections 38 and 40.

chosen as means than that which is chosen both as an end in itself and as means, and that is strictly final which is always chosen as an end in itself and never as means. Happiness seems more than anything else to answer to this description; for we always choose it for itself, and never for the sake of something else; while honor and pleasure and reason, and all virtue or excellence, we choose partly indeed for themselves (for, apart from any result, we should choose each of them), but partly also for the sake of happiness, supposing that they will help to make us happy. But no one chooses happiness for the sake of these things, or as a means to anything else at all.

We seem to be led to the same conclusion when we start from the notion of self-sufficiency. The final good is thought to be self-sufficing (or all-sufficing). In applying this term we do not regard a man as an individual leading a solitary life, but we also take account of parents, children, wife, and, in short, friends and fellow-citizens generally, since man is naturally a social being. Some limit must indeed be set to this; for if you go on to parents and descendants and friends of friends, you will never come to a stop. But this we will consider further on: for the present we will take self-sufficing to mean what by itself makes life desirable and in want of nothing. And happiness is believed to answer to this description.

And further, happiness is believed to be the most desirable thing in the world, and that not merely as one among other good things; if it were merely one among other good things (so that other things could be added to it), it is plain that the addition of the least of other goods must make it more desirable: for the addition becomes a surplus of good, and of two goods the greater is always more desirable. Thus it seems that happiness is something final and self-sufficing, and is the end of all that man does.

But perhaps . . . though no one will dispute the statement that happiness is the best thing in the world, yet a still more precise definition of it is needed.

This will best be gained, I think, by asking, What is the function of man? For as the goodness and the excellence of a piper or a sculptor, or the practiser of any art, and generally of those who have any function or business to do, lies in that function, so man's good would seem to lie in his function, if he has one. But can we suppose that, while a carpenter, or a cobbler has a function and a business of his own, man has no business of his own, man has no business and no function assigned to him by nature? Nay, surely as his several members, eye and hand and foot, plainly have each its own function, so we must suppose that man also has some function over and above all these. What then is it?

Life evidently he has in common even with the plants, but we want that which is peculiar to him. We must exclude, therefore, the life of mere nutrition and growth. Next to this comes the life of sense; but this too he plainly shares with horses and cattle and all kinds of animals. There remains then the life whereby he acts—the life of his rational nature, with its two sides or divisions, one rational as obeying reason, the other rational as having and exercising reason. But as this expression is ambiguous, we must be understood to mean thereby the life that consists in the exercise of the faculties; for this seems to be more properly entitled to the name. The function of man, then, is exercise of his vital faculties (or soul) on one side in obedience to reason, and on the other side with reason.

But what is called the function of a man of any profession and the function of a man who is good in that profession are generically the same, e.g., of a harper and of a good harper; and this holds in all cases without exception, only that in the case of the latter his superior excellence at his work is added; for we say a harper's function is to harp, and a good harper's to harp well. Man's function then being, as we say, a kind of life—that is to say, exercise of his faculties and action of various kinds with reason—the good man's function is to do this well and beautifully (or nobly). But the function of anything is done well when it is done in accordance with the proper excellence of that thing. Putting all this together, then, we find that the good of man is exercise of his faculties in accordance with excellence or virtue, or, if there be more than one, in accordance with the best and most complete virtue.

But there must also be a full term of years for this exercise; for one swallow or one fine day does not make a spring, nor does one day or any small space of time make a blessed or happy man. . . .

But I think we may say that it makes no small difference whether the good be conceived as the mere possession of something, or as its use—as a mere habit or trained faculty, or as the exercise of that faculty. For the habit or faculty may be present, and yet issue in no good result, as when a man is asleep, or in any other way hindered from his function; but with its exercise this is not possible, for it must show itself in acts and in good acts. And as in the Olympic games it is not the fairest and strongest who receive the crown, but those who contend (for among these are the victors), so in life, too, the winners are those who not only have all the excellences, but manifest these in deed.

And, further, the life of these men is in itself pleasant. For pleasure is an affection of the soul, and each man takes pleasure in that which he is said to love—he who loves horses in horses, he who loves sight-seeing in sight-seeing, and in the same way he who loves justice in acts of justice, and generally the lover of excellence or virtue in virtuous acts or the manifestation of excellence. And while with most men there is a perpetual conflict between the several things in which they find pleasure, since these are not naturally pleasant, those who love what is noble take pleasure in that which is naturally pleasant. For the manifestations of excellence are naturally pleasant, so that they are both pleasant to them and pleasant in themselves. Their life, then, does not need pleasure to be added to it as an appendage, but contains pleasure in itself. . . .

• 40 •

REASON, PASSION, AND MORALS *
David Hume (1711–1776)

[I.] OF THE INFLUENCING MOTIVES OF THE WILL

Nothing is more usual in philosophy, and even in common life, than to talk of the combat of passion and reason, to give the preference to reason, and to assert that men are only so far virtuous as they conform themselves to its dictates. Every rational creature, 'tis said, is oblig'd to regulate his actions by reason; and if any other motive or principle challenge the direction of his conduct, he ought to oppose it, 'till it be entirely subdu'd, or at least brought to a conformity with that superior principle. On this method of thinking the greatest part of moral philosophy, ancient and modern, seems to be founded; nor is there an ampler field, as well for metaphysical arguments, as popular declamations, than this suppos'd pre-eminence of reason above passion. The eternity, invariableness, and divine origin of the former have been display'd to the best advantage: The blindness, unconstancy and deceitfulness of the latter have been as strongly insisted on. In order to shew the fallacy of all this philosophy, I shall endeavour to prove *first*, that reason alone can never be a motive to any action of the will; and *secondly*, that it can never oppose passion in the direction of the will.

The understanding exerts itself after two different ways, as it judges from demonstration or probability; as it regards the abstract relations of our ideas, or those relations of objects, of which experience only gives us information. I believe it scarce will be asserted, that the first species of

* From A *Treatise of Human Nature* (1739–1740), Bk. II, Part III, Section 3, and Book III, Part I, Section 1. The title of this selection has been supplied by the editors. Compare with selections 12, 41, 44, and 47.

reasoning alone is ever the cause of any action. As its proper province is the world of ideas, and as the will always places us in that of realities, demonstration and volition seem, upon that account, to be totally remov'd, from each other. Mathematics, indeed, are useful in all mechanical operations, and arithmetic in almost every art and profession: But 'tis not of themselves they have any influence. Mechanics are the art of regulating the motions of bodies *to some design'd end or purpose*; and the reason why we employ arithmetic in fixing the proportions of numbers, is only that we may discover the proportions of their influence and operation. A merchant is desirous of knowing the sum total of his accounts with any person: Why? but that he may learn what sum will have the same *effects* in paying his debt, and going to market, as all the particular articles taken together. Abstract or demonstrative reasoning, therefore, never influences any of our actions, but only as it directs our judgment concerning causes and effects; which leads us to the second operation of the understanding.

'Tis obvious, that when we have the prospect of pain or pleasure from any object, we feel a consequent emotion of aversion or propensity, and are carry'd to avoid or embrace what will give us this uneasiness or satisfaction. 'Tis also obvious, that this emotion rests not here, but making us cast our view on every side, comprehends whatever objects are connected with its original one by the relation of cause and effect. Here then reasoning takes place to discover this relation; and according as our reasoning varies, our actions receive a subsequent variation. But 'tis evident in this case, that the impulse arises not from reason, but is only directed by it. 'Tis from the prospect of pain or pleasure that the aversion or propensity arises towards any object: And these emotions extend themselves to the causes and effects of that object, as they are pointed out to us by reason and experience. It can never in the least concern us to know, that such objects are causes, and such others effects, if both the causes and effects be indifferent to us. Where the objects themselves do not affect us, their connexion can never give them any influence; and 'tis plain, that as reason is nothing but the discovery of this connexion, it cannot be by its means that the objects are able to affect us.

Since reason alone can never produce any action, or give rise to volition, I infer, that the same faculty is as incapable of preventing volition, or of disputing the preference with any passion or emotion. This consequence is necessary. 'Tis impossible reason cou'd have the latter effect of preventing volition, but by giving an impulse in a contrary direction to our passion; and that impulse, had it operated alone, wou'd have been able to produce volition. Nothing can oppose or retard the impulse of passion, but a contrary impulse; and if this contrary impulse ever arises from reason, that

latter faculty must have an original influence on the will, and must be able
to cause, as well as hinder any act of volition. But if reason has no original
influence, 'tis impossible it can withstand any principle, which has such an
efficacy, or ever keep the mind in suspense a moment. Thus it appears,
that the principle, which opposes our passion, cannot be the same with
reason, and is only call'd so in an improper sense. We speak not strictly
and philosophically when we talk of the combat of passion and of reason.
Reason is, and ought only to be the slave of the passions, and can never
pretend to any other office than to serve and obey them. As this opinion
may appear somewhat extraordinary, it may not be improper to confirm
it by some other considerations.

A passion is an original existence, or, if you will, modification of existence, and contains not any representative quality, which renders it a copy
of any other existence or modification. When I am angry, I am actually
possest with the passion, and in that emotion have no more a reference to
any other object, than when I am thirsty, or sick, or more than five foot
high. 'Tis impossible, therefore, that this passion can be oppos'd by, or be
contradictory to truth and reason; since this contradiction consists in the
disagreement of ideas, consider'd as copies, with those objects, which they
represent.

What may at first occur on this head, is, that as nothing can be contrary to truth or reason, except what has a reference to it, and as the judgments of our understanding only have this reference, it must follow, that
passions can be contrary to reason only so far as they are *accompany'd*
with some judgment or opinion. According to this principle, which is so
obvious and natural, 'tis only in two senses, that any affection can be
call'd unreasonable. First, when a passion, such as hope or fear, grief or joy,
despair or security, is founded on the supposition of the existence of objects, which really do not exist. Secondly, when in exerting any passion in
action, we chuse means insufficient for the design'd end, and deceive ourselves in our judgment of causes and effects. Where a passion is neither
founded on false suppositions, nor chuses means insufficient for the end,
the understanding can neither justify nor condemn it. 'Tis not contrary to
reason to prefer the destruction of the whole world to the scratching of
my finger. 'Tis not contrary to reason for me to chuse my total ruin, to
prevent the least uneasiness of an *Indian* or person wholly unknown to me.
'Tis as little contrary to reason to prefer even my own acknowledg'd lesser
good to my greater, and have a more ardent affection for the former than
the latter. A trivial good may, from certain circumstances, produce a desire
superior to what arises from the greatest and most valuable enjoyment; nor
is there any thing more extraordinary in this, than in mechanics to see one

pound weight raise up a hundred by the advantage of its situation. In short, a passion must be accompany'd with some false judgment, in order to its being unreasonable; and even then 'tis not the passion, properly speaking, which is unreasonable, but the judgment.

The consequences are evident. Since a passion can never, in any sense, be call'd unreasonable, but when founded on a false supposition, or when it chuses means insufficient for the design'd end, 'tis impossible, that reason and passion can ever oppose each other, or dispute for the government of the will and actions. The moment we perceive the falshood of any supposition, or the insufficiency of any means our passions yield to our reason without any opposition. I may desire any fruit as of an excellent relish; but whenever you convince me of my mistake, my longing ceases. I may will the performance of certain actions as means of obtaining any desir'd good; but as my willing of these actions is only secondary, and founded on the supposition, that they are causes of the propos'd effect; as soon as I discover the falshood of that supposition, they must become indifferent to me.

'Tis natural for one, that does not examine objects with a strict philosophic eye, to imagine, that those actions of the mind are entirely the same, which produce not a different sensation, and are not immediately distinguishable to the feeling and perception. Reason, for instance, exerts itself without producing any sensible emotion; and except in the more sublime disquisitions of philosophy, or in the frivolous subtilties of the schools, scarce ever conveys any pleasure or uneasiness. Hence it proceeds, that every action of the mind, which operates with the same calmness and tranquillity, is confounded with reason by all those, who judge of things from the first view and appearance. Now 'tis certain, there are certain calm desires and tendencies, which, tho' they be real passions, produce little emotion in the mind, and are more known by their effects than by the immediate feeling or sensation. These desires are of two kinds; either certain instincts originally implanted in our natures, such as benevolence and resentment, the love of life, and kindness to children; or the general appetite to good, and aversion to evil, consider'd merely as such. When any of these passions are calm, and cause no disorder in the soul, they are very readily taken for the determinations of reason, and are suppos'd to proceed from the same faculty, with that, which judges of truth and falshood. Their nature and principles have been suppos'd the same, because their sensations are not evidently different.

Beside these calm passions, which often determine the will, there are certain violent emotions of the same kind, which have likewise a great influence on that faculty. When I receive any injury from another, I often feel a violent passion of resentment, which makes me desire his evil and punishment, independent of all considerations of pleasure and advantage to myself. When I am immediately threaten'd with any grievous ill, my fears, apprehensions, and aversions rise to a great height, and produce a sensible emotion.

The common error of metaphysicians has lain in ascribing the direction of the will entirely to one of these principles, and supposing the other to have no influence. Men often act knowingly against their interest: For which reason the view of the greatest possible good does not always influence them. Men often counter-act a violent passion in prosecution of their interests and designs: 'Tis not therefore the present uneasiness alone, which determines them. In general we may observe, that both these principles operate on the will; and where they are contrary, that either of them prevails, according to the *general* character or *present* disposition of the person. What we call strength of mind, implies the prevalence of the calm passions above the violent; tho' we may easily observe, there is no man so constantly possess'd of this virtue, as never on any occasion to yield to the sollicitations of passion and desire. From these variations of temper proceeds the great difficulty of deciding concerning the actions and resolutions of men, where there is any contrariety of motives and passions.

[II.] OF VIRTUE AND VICE IN GENERAL

. . . Those who affirm that virtue is nothing but a conformity to reason; that there are eternal fitnesses and unfitnesses of things, which are the same to every rational being that considers them; that the immutable measures of right and wrong impose an obligation, not only on human creatures, but also on the Deity himself: All these systems concur in the opinion, that morality, like truth, is discern'd merely by ideas, and by their juxta-position and comparison. In order, therefore, to judge of these systems, we need only consider, whether it be possible, from reason alone, to distinguish betwixt moral good and evil, or whether there must concur some other principles to enable us to make that distinction.

If morality had naturally no influence on human passions and actions, 'twere in vain to take such pains to inculcate it; and nothing wou'd be more fruitless than that multitude of rules and precepts, with which all moralists abound. Philosophy is commonly divided into *speculative* and *practical*; and as morality is always comprehended under the latter division, 'tis supposed to influence our passions and actions, and to go beyond the calm and indolent judgments of the understanding. And this is confirm'd by common experience, which informs us, that men are often govern'd by their duties, and are deter'd from some actions by the opinion of injustice, and impell'd to others by that of obligation.

Since morals, therefore, have an influence on the actions and affections, it follows, that they cannot be deriv'd from reason; and that because reason alone, as we have already prov'd, can never have any such influence. Morals excite passions, and produce or prevent actions. Reason of itself is utterly impotent in this particular. The rules of morality, therefore, are not conclusions of our reason.

No one, I believe, will deny the justness of this inference; nor is there any other means of evading it, than by denying that principle, on which it is founded. As long as it is allow'd, that reason has no influence on our passions and actions, 'tis in vain to pretend, that morality is discover'd only by a deduction of reason. An active principle can never be founded on an inactive; and if reason be inactive in itself, it must remain so in all its shapes and appearances, whether it exerts itself in natural or moral subjects, whether it considers the powers of external bodies, or the actions of rational beings.

It would be tedious to repeat all the arguments, by which I have prov'd that reason is perfectly inert, and can never either prevent or produce any action or affection. 'Twill be easy to recollect what has been said upon that subject. I shall only recall on this occasion one of these arguments, which I shall endeavour to render still more conclusive, and more applicable to the present subject.

Reason is the discovery of truth or falshood. Truth or falshood consists in an agreement or disagreement either to the *real* relations of ideas, or to *real* existence and matter of fact. Whatever, therefore, is not susceptible of this agreement or disagreement, is incapable of being true or false, and can never be an object of our reason. Now 'tis evident our passions, volitions, and actions, are not susceptible of any such agreement or disagreement; being original facts and realities, compleat in themselves, and implying no reference to other passions, volitions, and actions. 'Tis impossible, therefore, they can be pronounced either true or false, and be either contrary or conformable to reason.

This argument is of double advantage to our present purpose. For it proves *directly*, that actions do not derive their merit from a conformity to reason, nor their blame from a contrariety to it; and it proves the same truth more *indirectly*, by shewing us, that as reason can never immediately prevent or produce any action by contradicting or approving of it, it cannot be the source of moral good and evil, which are found to have that influence. Actions may be laudable or blameable; but they cannot be reasonable or unreasonable: Laudable or blameable, therefore, are not the same with reasonable or unreasonable. The merit and demerit of actions frequently contradict, and sometimes controul our natural propensities. But reason has no such influence. Moral distinctions, therefore, are not the offspring of reason. Reason is wholly inactive, and can never be the source of so active a principle as conscience, or a sense of morals. . . .

Nor does this reasoning only prove, that morality consists not in any relations, that are the objects of science; but if examin'd, will prove with equal certainty, that it consists not in any *matter of fact*, which can be discover'd by the understanding. This is the *second* part of our argument; and if it can be made evident, we may conclude, that morality is not an object of reason. But can there be any difficulty in proving, that vice and virtue are not matters of fact, whose existence we can infer by reason? Take any action allow'd to be vicious: Wilful murder, for instance. Examine it in all lights, and see if you can find that matter of fact, or real existence, which you call *vice*. In which-ever way you take it, you find only certain passions, motives, volitions and thoughts. There is no other matter of fact in the case. The vice entirely escapes you, as long as you consider the object. You never can find it, till you turn your reflexion into your own breast, and find a sentiment of disapprobation, which arises in you, towards this action. Here is a matter of fact; but 'tis the object of feeling, not of reason. It lies in yourself, not in the object. So that when you pronounce any action or character to be vicious, you mean nothing, but that from the constitution of your nature you have a feeling or sentiment of blame from the contemplation of it. Vice and virtue, therefore, may be compar'd to sounds, colours, heat and cold, which, according to modern philosophy, are not qualities in objects, but perceptions in the mind: And this discovery in morals, like that other in physics, is to be regarded as a considerable advancement of the speculative sciences; tho', like that too, it has little or no influence on practice. Nothing can be more real, or concern us more, than our own sentiments of pleasure and uneasiness; and if these be favourable to virtue, and unfavourable to vice, no more can be requisite to the regulation of our conduct and behaviour.

I cannot forbear adding to these reasonings an observation, which may, perhaps, be found of some importance. In every system of morality, which I have hitherto met with, I have always remark'd, that the author proceeds for some time in the ordinary way of reasoning, and establishes the being of a God, or makes observations concerning human affairs; when of a sudden I am surpriz'd to find, that instead of the usual copulations of propositions, *is*, and *is not*, I meet with no proposition that is not connected with an *ought*, or an *ought not*. This change is imperceptible; but is.

however, of the last consequence. For as this *ought*, or *ought not*, expresses some new relation or affirmation, 'tis necessary that it shou'd be observ'd and explain'd; and at the same time that a reason should be given, for what seems altogether inconceivable, how this new relation can be a deduction from others, which are entirely different from it. But as authors do not commonly use this precaution, I shall presume to recommend it to the readers; and am persuaded, that this small attention wou'd subvert all the vulgar systems or morality, and let us see, that the distinction of vice and virtue is not founded merely on the relations of objects, nor is perceiv'd by reason.

• 41 •

THE CATEGORICAL IMPERATIVE *
Immanuel Kant (1724–1804)

Nothing can possibly be conceived in the world, or even out of it, which can be called good without qualification, except a *good will*. Intelligence, wit, judgment, and the other *talents* of the mind, however they may be named, or courage, resolution, perseverance, as qualities of temperament, are undoubtedly good and desirable in many respects; but these gifts of nature may also become extremely bad and mischievous if the will which is to make use of them, and which, therefore, constitutes what is called *character*, is not good. It is the same with the *gifts of fortune*. Power, riches, honor, even health, and the general well-being and contentment with one's condition which is called *happiness*, inspire pride, and often presumption, if there is not a good will to correct the influence of these on the mind, and with this also to rectify the whole principle of acting, and adapt it to its end. The sight of a being who is not adorned with a single feature of a pure and good will, enjoying unbroken prosperity, can never give pleasure to an impartial rational spectator. Thus a good will appears to constitute the indispensable condition even of being worthy of happiness.

There are even some qualities which are of service to this good will it-

---

* From the first section of the *Fundamental Principles of the Metaphysics of Morals*, 1785, translated from the German by T. K. Abbott (1873). Reprinted by permission of Longmans, Green & Co. Limited, London. The title of this selection has been supplied by the editors. Compare with selections 40 and 49.

self, and may facilitate its action, yet which have no intrinsic unconditional value, but always presuppose a good will, and this qualifies the esteem that we justly have for them, and does not permit us to regard them as absolutely good. Moderation in the affections and passions, self-control, and calm deliberation are not only good in many respects, but even seem to constitute part of the intrinsic worth of the person; but they are far from deserving to be called good without qualification, although they have been so unconditionally praised by the ancients. For without the principles of a good will, they may become extremely bad; and the coolness of a villain not only makes him far more dangerous, but also directly makes him more abominable in our eyes than he would have been without it.

A good will is good not because of what it performs or effects, not by its aptness for the attainment of some proposed end, but simply by virtue of the volition—that is, it is good in itself, and considered by itself is to be esteemed much higher than all that can be brought about by it in favor of any inclination, nay, even of the sum-total of all inclinations. Even if it should happen that, owing to special disfavor of fortune, or the niggardly provision of a step-motherly nature, this will should wholly lack power to accomplish its purpose, if with its greatest efforts it should yet achieve nothing, and there should remain only the good will (not, to be sure, a mere wish, but the summoning of all means in our power), then, like a jewel, it would still shine by its own light, as a thing which has its whole value in itself. Its usefulness or fruitlessness can neither add to nor take away anything from this value. It would be, as it were, only the setting to enable us to handle it the more conveniently in common commerce, or to attract to it the attention of those who are not yet connoisseurs, but not to recommend it to true connoisseurs, or to determine its value. . . .

We have then to develop the notion of a will which deserves to be highly esteemed for itself, and is good without a view to anything further, a notion which exists already in the sound natural understanding, requiring rather to be cleared up than to be taught, and which in estimating the value of our actions always takes the first place and constitutes the condition of all the rest. In order to do this, we will take the notion of duty, which includes that of a good will, although implying certain subjective restrictions and hindrances. These, however, far from concealing it or rendering it unrecognizable, rather bring it out by contrast and make it shine forth so much the brighter.

I omit here all actions which are already recognized as inconsistent with duty, although they may be useful for this or that purpose, for with these the question whether they are done *from duty* cannot arise at all, since they even conflict with it. I also set aside those actions which really conform to duty, but to which men have *no* direct *inclination*, performing them because they are impelled thereto by some other inclination. For in this case we can readily distinguish whether the action which agrees with duty is done *from duty* or from a selfish view. It is much harder to make this distinction when the action accords with duty, and the subject has besides a *direct* inclination to it. For example, it is always a matter of duty that a dealer should not overcharge an inexperienced purchaser; and wherever there is much commerce the prudent tradesman does not overcharge, but keeps a fixed price for everyone, so that a child buys of him as well as any other. Men are thus *honestly* served; but this is not enough to make us believe that the tradesman has so acted from duty and from principles of honesty; his own advantage required it; it is out of the question in this case to suppose that he might besides have a direct inclination in favor of the buyers, so that, as it were, from love he should give no advantage to one over another. Accordingly the action was done neither from duty nor from direct inclination, but merely with a selfish view.

On the other hand, it is a duty to maintain one's life; and, in addition, everyone has also a direct inclination to do so. But on this account the often anxious care which most men take for it has no intrinsic worth, and their maxim has no moral import. They preserve their life *as duty requires*, no doubt, but not *because duty requires*. On the other hand, if adversity and hopeless sorrow have completely taken away the relish for life, if the unfortunate one, strong in mind, indignant at his fate rather than desponding or dejected, wishes for death, and yet preserves his life without loving it—not from inclination or fear, but from duty—then his maxim has a moral worth.

To be beneficent when we can is a duty; and besides this, there are many minds so sympathetically constituted that, without any other motive of vanity or self-interest, they find a pleasure in spreading joy around them, and can take delight in the satisfaction of others so far as it is their own work. But I maintain that in such a case an action of this kind, however proper, however amiable it may be, has nevertheless no true moral worth, but is on a level with other inclinations, for example, the inclination to honor, which, if it is happily directed to that which is in fact of public utility and accordant with duty, and consequently honorable, deserves praise and encouragement, but not esteem. For the maxim lacks the moral import, namely, that such actions be done *from duty*, not from inclination. Put the case that the mind of that philanthropist was clouded by sorrow of his own, extinguishing all sympathy with the lot of others, and that while he still has the power to benefit others in distress, he is not touched by their trouble because he is absorbed with his own; and now suppose that he tears himself out of this dead insensibility and performs the action without any inclination to it, but simply from duty, then first has his action its genuine moral worth. Further still, if nature has put little sympathy in the heart of this or that man, if he, supposed to be an upright man, is by temperament cold and indifferent to the sufferings of others, perhaps because in respect of his own he is provided with the special gift of patience and fortitude, and supposes, or even requires, that others should have the same—and such a man would certainly not be the meanest product of nature—but if nature had not specially framed him for a philanthropist, would he not still find in himself a source from whence to give himself a far higher worth than that of a good-natured temperament could be? Unquestionably. It is just in this that the moral worth of the character is brought out which is incomparably the highest of all, namely, that he is beneficent, not from inclination, but from duty. . . .

An action done from duty derives its moral worth, *not from the purpose* which is to be attained by it, but from the maxim by which it is determined, and therefore does not depend on the realization of the object of the action, but merely on the *principle of volition* by which the action has taken place, without regard to any object of desire. It is clear from what precedes that the purpose which we may have in view in our actions, or their effects regarded as ends and springs of the will, cannot give to actions any unconditional or moral worth. In what, then, can their worth lie if it is not to consist in the will and in reference to its expected effect? It cannot lie anywhere but in the *principle of the will* without regard to the ends which can be attained by the action. . . .

Thus the moral worth of an action does not lie in the effect expected from it, nor in any principle of action which requires to borrow its motive from this expected effect. For all these effects—agreeableness of one's condition, and even the promotion of the happiness of others—could have been also brought about by other causes, so that for this there would have been no need of the will of a rational being; whereas it is in this alone that the supreme and unconditional good can be found. The pre-eminent good which we call moral can therefore consist in nothing else than *the conception of law* in itself, *which certainly is only possible in a rational being,* in so far as this conception, and not the expected effect, determines the will. This is a good which is already present in the person who acts accordingly, and we have not to wait for it to appear first in the result.

But what sort of law can that be the conception of which must determine the will, even without paying any regard to the effect expected from it, in order that this will may be called good absolutely and without qualification? As I have deprived the will of every impulse which could arise to it from obedience to any law, there remains nothing but the universal conformity of its actions to law in general, which alone is to serve the will as a principle, that is, I am never to act otherwise than so *that I could also will that my maxim should become a universal law*. Here, now, it is the simple conformity to law in general, without assuming any particular law applicable to certain actions, that serves the will as its principle, and must so serve it if duty is not to be a vain delusion and a chimerical notion. The common reason of men in its practical judgments perfectly coincides with this, and always has in view the principle here suggested. Let the question be, for example: May I when in distress make a promise with the intention not to keep it? I readily distinguish here between the two significations which the question may have: whether it is prudent or whether it is right to make a false promise? The former may undoubtedly often be the case. I see clearly indeed that it is not enough to extricate myself from a present difficulty by means of this subterfuge, but it must be well considered whether there may not hereafter spring from this lie much greater inconvenience than that from which I now free myself, and as, with all my supposed *cunning*, the consequences cannot be so easily foreseen but that credit once lost may be much more injurious to me than any mischief which I seek to avoid at present, it should be considered whether it would not be more *prudent* to act herein according to a universal maxim, and to make it a habit to promise nothing except with the intention of keeping it. But it is soon clear to me that such a maxim will still only be based on the fear of consequences. Now it is a wholly different thing to be truthful from duty, and to be so from apprehension of injurious consequences. . . . For to deviate from the principle of duty is beyond all doubt wicked; but to be unfaithful to my maxim of prudence may often be very advantageous to me, although to abide by it is certainly safer. The shortest way, however, and an unerring one, to discover the answer to this question whether a lying promise is consistent with duty, is to ask myself, Should I be content that my maxim (to extricate myself from difficulty by a false promise) should hold good as a universal law, for myself as well as for others; and should I be able to say to myself, "Every one may make a deceitful promise when he finds himself in a difficulty from which he cannot otherwise extricate himself"? Then I presently become aware that, while I can will the lie, I can by no means will that lying should be a universal law. For with such a law there would be no promises at all, since it would be in vain to allege my intention in regard to my future actions to those who would not believe this allegation, or if they over-hastily did so, would pay me back in my own coin. Hence my maxim, as soon as it should be made a universal law, would necessarily destroy itself.

I do not, therefore, need any far-reaching penetration to discern what I have to do in order that my will may be morally good. Inexperienced in the course of the world, incapable of being prepared for all its contingencies, I only ask myself: Canst thou also will that thy maxim should be a universal law? If not, then it must be rejected, and that not because of a disadvantage accruing from it to myself or even to others, but because it cannot enter as a principle into a possible universal legislation, and reason extorts from me immediate respect for such legislation. I do not indeed as yet *discern* on what this respect is based . . . but at least I understand this . . . that the necessity of acting from *pure* respect for the practical law is what constitutes duty, to which every other motive must give place because it is the condition of a will being good *in itself*, and the worth of such a will is above everything. . . .

• 42 •

HEDONISTIC UTILITARIANISM *

Jeremy Bentham (1748–1832)

[I.] OF THE PRINCIPLE OF UTILITY

1. Nature has placed mankind under the governance of two sovereign masters, *pain* and *pleasure*. It is for them alone to point out what we ought to do, as well as to determine what we shall do. On the one hand the standard of right and wrong, on the other the chain of causes and effects, are fastened to their throne. They govern us in all we do, in all we say, in all we think: every effect we can make to throw off our subjection, will serve but to demonstrate and confirm it. In words a man may pretend to abjure their empire: but in reality he will remain subject to it all the while. The *principle of utility* recognises this subjection, and assumes it for the foundation of that system, the object of which is to rear the fabric of felicity by the hands of reason and of law. Systems which attempt to question it, deal in sounds instead of sense, in caprice instead of reason, in darkness instead of light.

---

* From chapters 1, 2, and 4 of An *Introduction to the Principles of Morals and Legislation*, 1789, 2nd edition, 1823. The title of this selection has been supplied by the editors. Compare with selections 41 and 43.

But enough of metaphor and declamation: it is not by such means that moral science is to be improved.

2. The principle of utility is the foundation of the present work: it will be proper therefore at the outset to give an explicit and determinate account of what is meant by it. By the principle of utility is meant that principle which approves or disapproves of every action whatsoever, according to the tendency which it appears to have to augment or diminish the happiness of the party whose interest is in question: or, what is the same thing in other words, to promote or to oppose that happiness. I say of every action whatsoever; and therefore not only of every action of a private individual, but of every measure of government.

3. By utility is meant that property in any object, whereby it tends to produce benefit, advantage, pleasure, good, or happiness, (all this in the present case comes to the same thing) or (what comes again to the same thing) to prevent the happening of mischief, pain, evil, or happiness to the party whose interest is considered: if that party be the community in general, then the happiness of the community: if a particular individual, then the happiness of that individual.

4. The interest of the community is one of the most general expressions that can occur in the phraseology of morals: no wonder that the meaning of it is often lost. When it has a meaning, it is this. The community is a fictitious *body*, composed of the individual persons who are considered as constituting as it were its *members*. The interest of the community then is, what?—the sum of the interests of the several members who compose it.

5. It is in vain to talk of the interest of the community, without understanding what is the interest of the individual. A thing is said to promote the interest, or to be *for* the interest, of an individual, when it tends to add to the sum total of his pleasures: or, what comes to the same thing, to diminish the sum total of his pains.

6. An action then may be said to be conformable to the principle of utility, or, for shortness sake, to utility, (meaning with respect to the community at large) when the tendency it has to augment the happiness of the community is greater than any it has to diminish it. . . .

10. Of an action that is conformable to the principle of utility, one may always say either that it is one that ought to be done, or at least that it is not one that ought not to be done. One may say also, that it is right it should be done; at least that it is not wrong it should be done: that it is a right action; at least that it is not a wrong action. When thus interpreted, the words *ought*, and *right* and *wrong*, and others of that stamp, have a meaning: when otherwise, they have none.

11. Has the rectitude of this principle been ever formally contested? It

should seem that it had, by those who have not known what they have been meaning. Is it susceptible of any direct proof? It should seem not: for that which is used to prove every thing else, cannot itself be proved: a chain of proofs must have their commencement somewhere. To give such proof is as impossible as it is needless.

12. Not that there is or ever has been that human creature breathing, however stupid or perverse, who has not on many, perhaps on most occasions of his life, deferred to it. By the natural constitution of the human frame, on most occasions of their lives men in general embrace this principle, without thinking of it: if not for the ordering of their own actions, yet for the trying of their own actions, as well as of those of other men. There have been, at the same time, not many, perhaps, even of the most intelligent, who have been disposed to embrace it purely and without reserve. There are even few who have not taken some occasion or other to quarrel with it, either on account of their not understanding always how to apply it, or on account of some prejudice or other which they were afraid to examine into, or could not bear to part with. For such is the stuff that man is made of: in principle and in practice, in a right track and in a wrong one, the rarest of all human qualities is consistency.

13. When a man attempts to combat the principle of utility, it is with reasons drawn, without his being aware of it, from that very principle itself. His arguments, if they prove any thing, prove not that the principle is *wrong*, but that, according to the applications he supposes to be made of it, it is *misapplied*. Is it possible for a man to move the earth? Yes; but he must first find out another earth to stand upon. . . .

[II.] OF PRINCIPLES ADVERSE TO THAT OF UTILITY

1. If the principle of utility be a right principle to be governed by, and that in all cases, it follows from what has been just observed, that whatever principle differs from it in any case must necessarily be a wrong one. To prove any other principle, therefore, to be a wrong one, there needs no more than just to show it to be what it is, a principle of which the dictates are in some point or other different from those of the principle of utility: to state it is to confute it.

2. A principle may be different from that of utility in two ways: (1) By being constantly opposed to it: this is the case with a principle which may be termed the principle of *asceticism*. (2) By being sometimes opposed to it, and sometimes not, as it may happen: this is the case with another, which may be termed the principle of *sympathy* and *antipathy*.

3. By the principle of asceticism I mean that principle, which, like the principle of utility, approves or disapproves of any action, according to

the tendency which it appears to have to augment or diminish the happiness of the party whose interest is in question; but in an inverse manner: approving of actions in as far as they tend to diminish his happiness; disapproving of them in as far as they tend to augment it.

4. It is evident that any one who reprobates any the least particle of pleasure, as such, from whatever source derived, is *pro tanto* a partizan of the principle of asceticism. It is only upon that principle, and not from the principle of utility, that the most abominable pleasure which the vilest of malefactors ever reaped from his crime would be to be reprobated, if it stood alone. The case is, that it never does stand alone; but is necessarily followed by such a quantity of pain (or, what comes to the same thing, such a chance for a certain quantity of pain) that the pleasure in comparison of it, is as nothing: and this is the true and sole, but perfectly sufficient, reason for making it a ground for punishment. . . .

10. The principle of utility is capable of being consistently pursued; and it is but tautology to say, that the more consistently it is pursued, the better it must ever be for human-kind. The principle of asceticism never was, nor ever can be, consistently pursued by any living creature. Let but one tenth part of the inhabitants of this earth pursue it consistently, and in a day's time they will have turned it into a hell.

11. Among principles adverse to that of utility, that which at this day seems to have most influence in matters of government, is what may be called the principle of sympathy and antipathy. By the principle of sympathy and antipathy, I mean that principle which approves or disapproves of certain actions, not on account of their tending to augment the happiness, nor yet on account of their tending to diminish the happiness of the party whose interest is in question, but merely because a man finds himself disposed to approve or disapprove of them: holding up that approbation or disapprobation as a sufficient reason for itself, and disclaiming the necessity of looking out for any extrinsic ground. Thus far in the general department of morals: and in the particular department of politics, measuring out the quantum (as well as determining the ground) of punishment, by the degree of the disapprobation.

12. It is manifest, that this is rather a principle in name than in reality: it is not a positive principle of itself, so much as a term employed to signify the negation of all principle. What one expects to find in a principle is something that points out some external consideration, as a means of warranting and guiding the internal sentiments of approbation and disapprobation: this expectation is but ill fulfilled by a proposition, which does neither more nor less than hold up each of those sentiments as a ground and standard for itself.

13. In looking over the catalogue of human actions (says a partizan of this principle) in order to determine which of them are to be marked with the seal of disapprobation, you need but to take counsel of your own feelings: whatever you find in yourself a propensity to condemn, is wrong for that very reason. For the same reason it is also meet for punishment: in what proportion it is adverse to utility, or whether it be adverse to utility at all, is a matter that makes no difference. In that same *proportion* also is it meet for punishment: if you hate much, punish much: if you hate little, punish little: punish as you hate. If you hate not at all, punish not at all: the fine feelings of the soul are not to be overborne and tyrannized by the harsh and rugged dictates of political utility. . . .

15. It is manifest, that the dictates of this principle will frequently coincide with those of utility, though perhaps without intending any such thing. Probably more frequently than not: and hence it is that the business of penal justice is carried on upon that tolerable sort of footing upon which we see it carried on in common at this day. For what more natural or more general ground of hatred to a practice can there be, than the mischievousness of such practice? What all men are exposed to suffer by, all men will be disposed to hate. It is far yet, however, from being a constant ground: for when a man suffers, it is not always that he knows what it is he suffers by. A man may suffer grievously, for instance, by a new tax, without being able to trace up the cause of his sufferings to the injustice of some neighbour, who has eluded the payment of an old one.

16. The principle of sympathy and antipathy is most apt to err on the side of severity. It is for applying punishment in many cases which deserve none: in many cases which deserve some, it is for applying more than they deserve. There is no incident imaginable, be it ever so trivial, and so remote from mischief, from which this principle may not extract a ground of punishment. Any difference in taste: any difference in opinion: upon one subject as well as upon another. No disagreement so trifling which perseverance and altercation will not render serious. Each becomes in the other's eyes an enemy, and, if laws permit, a criminal. This is one of the circumstances by which the human race is distinguished (not much indeed to its advantage) from the brute creation. . . .

19. There are two things which are very apt to be confounded, but which it imports us carefully to distinguish:—the motive or cause, which, by operating on the mind of an individual, is productive of any act: and the ground or reason which warrants a legislator, or other by-stander, in regarding that act with an eye of approbation. When the act happens, in the particular instance in question, to be productive of effects which we approve of, much more if we happen to observe that the same motive may fre-

quently be productive, in other instances, of the like effects, we are apt to transfer our approbation to the motive itself, and to assume, as the just ground for the approbation we bestow on the act, the circumstance of its originating from that motive. It is in this way that the sentiment of antipathy has often been considered as a just ground of action. Antipathy, for instance, in such or such a case, is the cause of an action which is attended with good effects: but this does not make it a right ground of action in that case, any more than in any other. Still farther. Not only the effects are good, but the agent sees beforehand that they will be so. This may make the action indeed a perfectly right action: but it does not make antipathy a right ground of action. For the same sentiment of antipathy, if implicitly deferred to, may be, and very frequently is, productive of the very worst effects. Antipathy, therefore, can never be a right ground of action. No more, therefore, can resentment, which, as will be seen more particularly hereafter, is but a modification of antipathy. The only right ground of action, that can possibly subsist, is, after all, the consideration of utility, which, if it is a right principle of action, and of approbation, in any one case, is so in every other. Other principles in abundance, that is, other motives, may be the reasons why such and such an act *has* been done: that is, the reasons or causes of its being done: but it is this alone that can be the reason why it might or ought to have been done. Antipathy or resentment requires always to be regulated, to prevent its doing mischief: to be regulated by what? always by the principle of utility. The principle of utility neither requires nor admits of any other regulator than itself. . . .

[III.] VALUE OF A LOT OF PLEASURE OR PAIN, HOW TO BE MEASURED

1. Pleasures then, and the avoidance of pains, are the *ends* which the legislator has in view: it behooves him therefore to understand their *value*. Pleasures and pains are the *instruments* he has to work with: it behooves him therefore to understand their force, which is again, in other words, their value.

2. To a person considered *by himself*, the value of a pleasure or pain considered *by itself*, will be greater or less, according to the four following circumstances:

    (1) Its *intensity*.
    (2) Its *duration*.
    (3) Its *certainty* or *uncertainty*.
    (4) Its *propinquity* or *remoteness*.

3. These are the circumstances which are to be considered in estimating a pleasure or a pain considered each of them by itself. But when the value

of any pleasure or pain is considered for the purpose of estimating the tendency of any *act* by which it is produced, there are two other circumstances to be taken into the account; these are,

(5) Its *fecundity*, or the chance it has of being followed by sensations of the *same* kind: that is, pleasures, if it be a pleasure: pains, if it be a pain.

(6) Its *purity*, or the chance it has of *not* being followed by sensations of the *opposite* kind: that is, pains, if it be a pleasure: pleasures, if it be a pain.

These two last, however, are in strictness scarcely to be deemed properties of the pleasure or the pain itself; they are not, therefore, in strictness to be taken into the account of the value of that pleasure or that pain. They are in strictness to be deemed properties only of the act, or other event, by which such pleasure or pain has been produced; and accordingly are only to be taken into the account of the tendency of such act or such event.

4. To a *number* of persons, with reference to each of whom the value of a pleasure or a pain is considered, it will be greater or less, according to seven circumstances: to wit, the six preceding ones; *viz.*

(1) Its *intensity*.

(2) Its *duration*.

(3) Its *certainty* or *uncertainty*.

(4) Its *propinquity* or *remoteness*.

(5) Its *fecundity*.

(6) Its *purity*.

And one other; to wit:

(7) Its *extent*; that is, the number of persons to whom it *extends*; or (in other words) who are affected by it.

5. To take an exact account then of the general tendency of any act, by which the interests of a community are affected, proceed as follows. Begin with any one person of those whose interests seem most immediately to be affected by it: and take an account,

(1) Of the value of each distinguishable *pleasure* which appears to be produced by it in the *first* instance.

(2) Of the value of each *pain* which appears to be produced by it in the *first* instance.

(3) Of the value of each pleasure which appears to be produced by it *after* the first. This constitutes the *fecundity* of the first *pleasure* and the *impurity* of the first *pain*.

(4) Of the value of each *pain* which appears to be produced by it

after the first. This constitutes the *fecundity* of the first *pain,* and the *impurity* of the first pleasure.

(5) Sum up all the values of all the *pleasures* on the one side, and those of all the pains on the other. The balance, if it be on the side of pleasure, will give the *good* tendency of the act upon the whole, with respect to the interests of that *individual* person; if on the side of pain, the *bad* tendency of it upon the whole.

(6) Take an account of the *number* of persons whose interests appear to be concerned; and repeat the above process with respect to each. *Sum up* the numbers expressive of the degrees of *good* tendency, which the act has, with respect to each individual, in regard to whom the tendency of it is *good* upon the whole . . . do this again with respect to each individual, in regard to whom the tendency of it is *bad* upon the whole. Take the *balance;* which, if on the side of *pleasure,* will give the general *good tendency* of the act, with respect to the total number or community of individuals concerned; if on the side of pain, the general *evil tendency,* with respect to the same community.

6. It is not to be expected that this process should be strictly pursued previously to every moral judgment, or to every legislative or judicial operation. It may, however, be always kept in view: and as near as the process actually pursued on these occasions approaches to it, so near will such process approach to the character of an exact one. . . .

8. . . . In all this there is nothing but what the practice of mankind, wheresoever they have a clear view of their own interest, is perfectly conformable to. An article of property, an estate in land, for instance, is valuable, on what account? On account of the pleasures of all kinds which it enables a man to produce, and what comes to the same thing the pains of all kinds which it enables him to avert. But the value of such an article of property is universally understood to rise or fall according to the length or shortness of the time which a man has in it: the certainty or uncertainty of its coming into possession: and the nearness or remoteness of the time at which, if at all, it is to come into possession. . . .

• 43 •

NATURE AND MORALITY*
John Stuart Mill (1806–1873)

Nature, natural, and the group of words derived from them, or allied to them in etymology, have at all times filled a great place in the thoughts and taken a strong hold on the feelings of mankind. That they should have done so is not surprising, when we consider what the words, in their primitive and most obvious signification, represent; but it is unfortunate that a set of terms which play so great a part in moral and metaphysical speculation, should have acquired many meanings different from the primary one, yet sufficiently allied to it to admit of confusion. The words have thus become entangled in so many foreign associations, mostly of a very powerful and tenacious character, that they have come to excite, and to be the symbols of, feelings which their original meaning will by no means justify. . . .

According to the Platonic method which is still the best type of such investigations, the first thing to be done with so vague a term is to ascertain precisely what it means. It is also a rule of the same method, that the meaning of an abstraction is best sought for in the concrete—of an universal in the particular. Adopting this course with the word Nature, the first question must be, what is meant by the "nature" of a particular object? as of fire, of water, or of some individual plant or animal? Evidently the *ensemble* or aggregate of its powers or properties: the modes in which it acts on other things (counting among those things the senses of the observer) and the modes in which other things act upon it; to which, in the case of a sentient being, must be added, its own capacities of feeling, or being conscious. The Nature of the thing means all this; means its entire capacity of exhibiting phenomena. And since the phenomena which a thing exhibits, however much they vary in different circumstances, are always the same in the same circumstances, they admit of being described in general forms of words, which are called the *laws* of the thing's nature.

---

* Although written approximately 20 years earlier, the essay, entitled "Nature," from which this selection has been taken was published, posthumously, as the first of *Three Essays on Religion* (1874). The title of this selection has been supplied by the editors. Compare with Part III of selection 32.

Thus it is a law of the nature of water that under the mean pressure of the atmosphere at the level of the sea, it boils at 212° Fahrenheit.

As the nature of any given thing is the aggregate of its powers and properties, so Nature in the abstract is the aggregate of the powers and properties of all things. Nature means the sum of all phenomena, together with the causes which produce them; including not only all that happens, but all that is capable of happening; the unused capabilities of causes being as much a part of the idea of Nature, as those which take effect. Since all phenomena which have been sufficiently examined are found to take place with regularity, each having certain fixed conditions, positive and negative, on the occurrence of which it invariably happens; mankind have been able to ascertain, either by direct observation or by reasoning processes grounded on it, the conditions of the occurrence of many phenomena; and the progress of science mainly consists in ascertaining those conditions. When discovered they can be expressed in general propositions, which are called laws of the particular phenomenon, and also, more generally, Laws of Nature. Thus, the truth that all material objects tend towards one another with a force directly as their masses and inversely as the square of their distance, is a law of Nature. The proposition that air and food are necessary to animal life, if it be as we have good reason to believe, true without exception, is also a law of nature, though the phenomenon of which it is the law is special, and not, like gravitation, universal.

Nature, then, in this its simplest acceptation, is a collective name for all facts, actual and possible: or (to speak more accurately) a name for the mode, partly known to us and partly unknown, in which all things take place. For the word suggests, not so much the multitudinous detail of the phenomena, as the conception which might be formed of their manner of existence as a mental whole, by a mind possessing a complete knowledge of them: to which conception it is the aim of science to raise itself, by successive steps of generalization from experience.

Such, then, is a correct definition of the word Nature. But this definition corresponds only to one of the senses of that ambiguous term. It is evidently inapplicable to some of the modes in which the word is familiarly employed. For example, it entirely conflicts with the common form of speech by which Nature is opposed to Art, and natural to artificial. For in the sense of the word Nature which has just been defined, and which is the true scientific sense, Art is as much Nature as anything else; and everything which is artificial is natural—Art has no independent powers of its own: Art is but the employment of the powers of Nature for an end. Phenomena produced by human agency, no less than those which as far as we are concerned are spontaneous, depend on the properties of the elementary forces, or of the elementary substances and their compounds. The united powers of the whole human race could not create a new property of matter in general, or of any one of its species. We can only take advantage for our purposes of the properties which we find. A ship floats by the same laws of specific gravity and equilibrium, as a tree uprooted by the wind and blown into the water. The corn which men raise for food, grows and produces its grain by the same laws of vegetation by which the wild rose and the mountain strawberry bring forth their flowers and fruit. A house stands and holds together by the natural properties, the weight and cohesion of the materials which compose it: a steam engine works by the natural expansive force of steam, exerting a pressure upon one part of a system of arrangements, which pressure, by the mechanical properties of the lever, is transferred from that to another part where it raises the weight or removes the obstacle brought into connexion with it. In these and all other artificial operations the office of man is, as has often been remarked, a very limited one; it consists in moving things into certain places. We move objects, and by doing this, bring some things into contact which were separate, or separate others which were in contact: and by this simple change of place, natural forces previously dormant are called into action, and produce the desired effect. Even the volition which designs, the intelligence which contrives, and the muscular force which executes these movements, are themselves powers of Nature.

It thus appears that we must recognize at least two principal meanings in the word Nature. In one sense, it means all the powers existing in either the outer or the inner world and everything which takes place by means of those powers. In another sense, it means, not everything which happens, but only what takes place without the agency, or without the voluntary and intentional agency, of man. This distinction is far from exhausting the ambiguities of the word; but it is the key to most of those on which important consequences depend.

Such, then, being the two principal senses of the word Nature; in which of these is it taken, or is it taken in either, when the word and its derivatives are used to convey ideas of commendation, approval, and even moral obligation?

It has conveyed such ideas in all ages. *Naturam sequi* * was the fundamental principle of morals in many of the most admired schools of philosophy. Among the ancients, especially in the declining period of ancient intellect and thought, it was the test to which all ethical doctrines were

* To follow nature.

brought. The Stoics and the Epicureans, however irreconcilable in the rest of their systems, agreed in holding themselves bound to prove that their respective maxims of conduct were the dictates of nature. Under their influence the Roman jurists, when attempting to systematize jurisprudence, placed in the front of their exposition a certain *Jus Naturale*, "quod natura," as Justinian declares in the Institutes, "omnia animalia docuit": * and as the modern systematic writers not only on law but on moral philosophy, have generally taken the Roman jurists for their models, treatises on the so-called Law of Nature have abounded; and references to this Law as a supreme rule and ultimate standard have pervaded literature. The writers on International Law have done more than any others to give currency to this style of ethical speculation; inasmuch as having no positive law to write about, and yet being anxious to invest the most approved opinions respecting international morality with as much as they could of the authority of law, they endeavoured to find such an authority in Nature's imaginary code. . . . At the present time it cannot be said that Nature, or any other standard, is applied as it was wont to be, to deduce rules of action with juridical precision, and with an attempt to make its application co-extensive with all human agency. The people of this generation do not commonly apply principles with any such studious exactness, nor own such binding allegiance to any standard, but live in a kind of confusion of many standards; a condition not propitious to the formation of steady moral convictions, but convenient enough to those whose moral opinions sit lightly on them, since it gives them a much wider range of arguments for defending the doctrine of the moment. But though perhaps no one could now be found who like the institutional writers of former times, adopts the so-called Law of Nature as the foundation of ethics, and endeavours consistently to reason from it, the word and its cognates must still be counted among those which carry great weight in moral argumentation. That any mode of thinking, feeling, or acting, is "according to nature" is usually accepted as a strong argument for its goodness. If it can be said with any plausibility that "nature enjoys" anything, the propriety of obeying the injunction is by most people considered to be made out: and conversely, the imputation of being contrary to nature, is thought to bar the door against any pretension on the part of the thing so designated, to be tolerated or excused; and the word unnatural has not ceased to be one of the most vituperative epithets in the language. Those who deal in these expressions, may avoid making themselves responsible for any fundamental theorem respecting the standard of moral obligation, but they do not the less imply

* what nature has taught all animals.

such a theorem, and one which must be the same in substance with that on which the more logical thinkers of a more laborious age grounded their systematic treatises on Natural Law.

Is it necessary to recognize in these forms of speech, another distinct meaning of the word Nature? Or can they be connected, by any rational bond of union, with either of the two meanings already treated of? At first it may seem that we have no option but to admit another ambiguity in the term. All inquiries are either into what is, or into what ought to be: science and history belonging to the first division, art, morals and politics to the second. But the two senses of the word Nature first pointed out, agree in referring only to what is. In the first meaning, Nature is a collective name for everything which is. In the second, it is a name for everything which is of itself, without voluntary human intervention. But the employment of the word Nature as a term of ethics seems to disclose a third meaning, in which Nature does not stand for what is, but for what ought to be; or for the rule or standard of what ought to be. A little consideration, however, will show that this is not a case of ambiguity; there is not here a third sense of the word. Those who set up Nature as a standard of action do not intend a merely verbal proposition; they do not mean that the standard, whatever it be, should be *called* Nature; they think they are giving some information as to what the standard of action really is. Those who say that we ought to act according to Nature do not mean the mere identical proposition that we ought to do what we ought to do. They think that the word Nature affords some external criterion of what we should do; and if they lay down as a rule for what ought to be, a word which in its proper signification denotes what is, they do so because they have a notion, either clearly or confusedly, that what is, constitutes the rule and standard of what ought to be. . . .

No word is more commonly associated with the word Nature, than Law; and this last word has distinctly two meanings, in one of which it denotes some definite portion of what is, in the other, of what ought to be. We speak of the law of gravitation, the three laws of motion, the law of definite proportions in chemical combination, the vital laws of organized beings. All these are portions of what is. We also speak of the criminal law, the civil law, the law of honour, the law of veracity, the law of justice; all of which are portions of what ought to be, or of somebody's suppositions, feelings, or commands respecting what ought to be. The first kind of laws, such as the laws of motion, and of gravitation, are neither more or less than the observed uniformities in the occurrence of phenomena; partly uniformities of antecedence and sequence, partly of concomitance. These are what, in science, and even in ordinary parlance, are meant by laws of nature. Laws in the other sense are the laws of the land, the law of nations, or moral laws; among which, as already noticed, is dragged in, by jurists and publicists, something which they think proper to call the Law of Nature. Of the liability of these two meanings of the word to be confounded there can be no better example than the first chapter of Montesquieu; where he remarks, that the material world has its laws, the inferior animals have their laws, and man has his laws; and calls attention to the much greater strictness with which the first two sets of laws are observed, than the last; as if it were an inconsistency, and a paradox, that things always are what they are, but men not always what they ought to be. . . .

When it is asserted, or implied, that Nature, or the laws of Nature, should be conformed to, is the Nature which is meant, Nature in the first sense of the term, meaning all which is—the powers and properties of all things? But in this signification, there is no need of a recommendation to act according to nature, since it is what nobody can possibly help doing, and equally whether he acts well or ill. There is no mode of acting which is not conformable to Nature in this sense of the term, and all modes of acting are so in exactly the same degree. Every action is the exertion of some natural power, and its effects of all sorts are so many phenomena of nature, produced by the powers and properties of some of the objects of nature, in exact obedience to some law or laws of nature. When I voluntarily use my organs to take in food, the act, and its consequences, take place according to laws of nature: if instead of food I swallow poison, the case is exactly the same. To bid people conform to the laws of nature when they have no power but what the laws of nature give them—when it is a physical impossibility for them to do the smallest thing otherwise than through some law of nature, is an absurdity. The thing they need to be told is, what particular law of nature they should make use of in a particular case. When, for example, a person is crossing a river by a narrow bridge to which there is no parapet, he will do well to regulate his proceedings by the laws of equilibrium in moving bodies, instead of conforming only to the law of gravitation, and falling into the river.

Yet, idle as it is to exhort people to do what they cannot avoid doing, and absurd as it is to prescribe as a rule of right conduct what agrees exactly as well with wrong; nevertheless a rational rule of conduct *may* be constructed out of the relation which it ought to bear to the laws of nature in this widest acceptation of the term. Man necessarily obeys the laws of nature, or in other words the properties of things, but he does not necessarily *guide* himself by them. Though all conduct is in conformity to laws of nature, all conduct is not grounded on knowledge of them, and intelligently directed to the attainment of purposes by means of them. Though we cannot emancipate ourselves from the laws of nature as a whole, we can escape from any particular law of nature, if we are able to withdraw ourselves from the circumstances in which it acts. Though we can do nothing except through laws of nature, we can use one law to counteract another. According to Bacon's maxim, we can obey nature in such a manner as to command it. Every alteration of circumstances alters more or less the laws of nature under which we act; and by every choice which we make either of ends or of means, we place ourselves to a greater or less extent under one set of laws of nature instead of another. If, therefore, the useless precept to follow nature were changed into a precept to study nature; to know and take heed of the properties of the things we have to deal with, so far as these properties are capable of forwarding or obstructing any given purpose; we should have arrived at the first principle of all intelligent action, or rather at the definition of intelligent action itself. And a confused notion of this true principle, is, I doubt not, in the minds of many of those who set up the unmeaning doctrine which superficially resembles it. They perceive that the essential difference between wise and foolish conduct consists in attending, or not attending, to the particular laws of nature on which some important result depends. And they think, that a person who attends to a law of nature in order to shape his conduct by it, may be said to obey it, while a person who practically disregards it, and acts as if no such law existed, may be said to disobey it: the circumstance being overlooked, that what is thus called disobedience to a law of nature is obedience to some other or perhaps to the very law itself. For example, a person who goes into a powder magazine either not knowing, or carelessly omitting to think of, the explosive force of gunpower, is likely to do some act which will cause him to be blown to atoms in obedience to the very law which he has disregarded.

. . . To acquire knowledge of the properties of things, and make use of the knowledge for guidance, is a rule of prudence, for the adaptation of means to ends; for giving effect to our wishes and intentions whatever they may be. But the maxim of obedience to Nature, or conformity to Nature, is held up not as a simply prudential but as an ethical maxim; and by those who talk of *jus naturae,** even as a law, fit to be administered by tribunals and enforced by sanctions. Right action, must mean something more and other than merely intelligent action: yet no precept beyond this last, can be connected with the word Nature in the wider and more philosophical of its acceptations. We must try it therefore in the other sense, that in which Nature stands distinguished from Art, and denotes,

* natural law.

not the whole course of the phenomena which come under our observation, but only their spontaneous course.

Let us then consider whether we can attach any meaning to the supposed practical maxim of following Nature, in this second sense of the word, in which Nature stands for that which takes place without human intervention. In Nature as thus understood, is the spontaneous course of things when left to themselves, the rule to be followed in endeavouring to adapt things to our use? But it is evident at once that the maxim, taken in this sense, is not merely, as it is in the other sense, superfluous and unmeaning, but palpably absurd and self-contradictory. For while human action cannot help conforming to Nature in the one meaning of the term, the very aim and object of action is to alter and improve Nature in the other meaning. If the natural course of things were perfectly right and satisfactory, to act at all would be a gratuitous meddling, which as it could not make things better, must make them worse. Or if action at all could be justified, it would only be when in direct obedience to instincts, since these might perhaps be accounted part of the spontaneous order of Nature; but to do anything with forethought and purpose, would be a violation of that perfect order. If the artificial is not better than the natural, to what end are all the arts of life? To dig, to plough, to build, to wear clothes, are direct infringements of the injunction to follow nature.

Accordingly it would be said by every one, even of those most under the influence of the feelings which prompt the injunction, that to apply it to such cases as those just spoken of, would be to push it too far. Everybody professes to approve and admire many great triumphs of Art over Nature: the junction by bridges of shores which Nature had made separate, the draining of Nature's marshes, the excavation of her wells, the dragging to light of what she has buried at immense depths in the earth; the turning away of her thunderbolts by lightning rods, of her inundations by embankments, of her ocean by breakwaters. But to commend these and similar feats, is to acknowledge that the ways of Nature are to be conquered, not obeyed: that her powers are often towards man in the position of enemies, from whom he must wrest, by force and ingenuity, what little he can for his own use, and deserves to be applauded when that little is rather more than might be expected from his physical weakness in comparison to those gigantic powers. All praise of Civilization, or Art, or Contrivance, is so much dispraise of Nature; an admission of imperfection, which it is man's business, and merit, to be always endeavouring to correct or mitigate.

The consciousness that whatever man does to improve his condition is in so much a censure and a thwarting of the spontaneous order of Nature,

has in all ages caused new and unprecedented attempts at improvement to
be generally at first under a shade of religious suspicion; as being in any
case uncomplimentary, and very probably offensive to the powerful beings
(or, when polytheism gave place to monotheism, to the all-powerful Being)
supposed to govern the various phenomena of the universe, and of whose
will the course of nature was conceived to be the expression. Any attempt
to mould natural phenomena to the convenience of mankind might easily
appear an interference with the government of those superior beings: and
though life could not have been maintained, much less made pleasant,
without perpetual interferences of the kind, each new one was doubtless
made with fear and trembling, until experience had shown that it could be
ventured on without drawing down the vengeance of the Gods. The
sagacity of priests showed them a way to reconcile the impunity of particular infringements with the maintenance of the general dread of en-
croaching on the divine administration. This was effected by representing
each of the principal human inventions as the gift and favour of some
God. . . . No one, indeed, asserts it to be the intention of the Creator
that the spontaneous order of the creation should not be altered, or even
that it should not be altered in any new way. But there still exists a vague
notion that though it is very proper to control this or the other natural
phenomenon, the general scheme of nature is a model for us to imitate:
that with more or less liberty in details, we should on the whole be guided
by the spirit and general conception of nature's own ways: that they are
God's work, and as such perfect; that man cannot rival their unapproach-
able excellence, and can best show his skill and piety by attempting, in
however imperfect a way, to reproduce their likeness; and that if not the
whole, yet some particular parts of the spontaneous order of nature, selected according to the speaker's predilections, are in a peculiar sense,
manifestations of the Creator's will. . . .

If this notion of imitating the ways of Providence as manifested in Nature, is seldom expressed plainly and downrightly as a maxim of general
application, it also is seldom directly contradicted. Those who find it on
their path, prefer to turn the obstacle rather than to attack it, being often
themselves not free from the feeling, and in any case afraid of incurring
the charge of impiety by saying anything which might be held to disparage
the works of the Creator's power. They therefore, for the most part, rather
endeavour to show, that they have as much right to the religious argument as their opponents, and that if the course they recommend seems to
conflict with some part of the ways of Providence, there is some other part
with which it agrees better than what is contended for on the other
side. . . .

A hurricane; a mountain precipice; the desert; the ocean, either agitated or at rest; the solar system, the great cosmic forces which hold it together; the boundless firmament, and to an educated mind any single star; excite feelings which make all human enterprises and powers appear so insignificant, that to a mind thus occupied it seems insufferable presumption in so puny a creature as man to look critically on things so far above him, or dare to measure himself against the grandeur of the universe. But a little interrogation of our own consciousness will suffice to convince us that what makes these phenomena so impressive is simply their vastness. The enormous extension in space and time, or the enormous power they exemplify, constitutes their sublimity; a feeling in all cases, more allied to terror than to any moral emotion. And though the vast scale of these phenomena may well excite wonder, and sets at defiance all idea of rivalry, the feeling it inspires is of a totally different character from admiration of excellence. Those in whom awe produces admiration may be aesthetically developed, but they are morally uncultivated. It is one of the endowments of the imaginative part of our mental nature that conceptions of greatness and power, vividly realized, produce a feeling which though in its higher degrees closely bordering on pain, we prefer to most of what are accounted pleasures. But we are quite equally capable of experiencing this feeling towards maleficent power; and we never experience it so strongly towards most of the powers of the universe, as when we have most present to our consciousness a vivid sense of their capacity of inflicting evil. Because these natural powers have what we cannot imitate, enormous might, and overawe us by that one attribute, it would be a great error to infer that their other attributes are such as we ought to emulate, or that we should be justified in using our small powers after the example which Nature sets us with her vast forces. . . .

In sober truth, nearly all the things which men are hanged or imprisoned for doing to one another, are nature's every day performances. Killing, the most criminal act recognized by human laws, Nature does once to every being that lives; and in a large proportion of cases, after protracted tortures such as only the greatest monsters whom we read of ever purposely inflicted on their living fellow-creatures. If, by an arbitrary reservation, we refuse to account anything murder but what abridges a certain term supposed to be allotted to human life, nature also does this to all but a small percentage of lives, and does it in all the modes, violent or insidious, in which the worst human beings take the lives of one another. Nature impales men, breaks them as if on the wheel, casts them to be devoured by wild beasts, burns them to death, crushes them with stones like the first christian martyr, starves them with hunger, freezes them with cold, poisons them by the quick or slow venom of her exhalations, and has hundreds of other hideous deaths in reserve, such as the ingenious cruelty of a Nabis or a Domitian never surpassed. All this, Nature does with the most supercilious disregard both of mercy and of justice, emptying her shafts upon the best and noblest indifferently with the meanest and worst; upon those who are engaged in the highest and worthiest enterprises, and often as the direct consequence of the noblest acts; and it might almost be imagined as a punishment for them. She mows down those on whose existence hangs the well-being of a whole people, perhaps the prospects of the human race for generations to come, with as little compunction as those whose death is a relief to themselves, or a blessing to those under their noxious influence. Such are Nature's dealings with life. . . .

But, it is said, all these things are for wise and good ends. On this I must first remark that whether they are so or not, is altogether beside the point. Supposing it true that contrary to appearances these horrors when perpetrated by Nature, promote good ends, still as no one believes that good ends would be promoted by our following the example, the course of Nature cannot be a proper model for us to imitate. Either it is right that we should kill because nature kills; torture because nature tortures; ruin and devastate because nature does the like; or we ought not to consider at all what nature does, but what it is good to do. If there is such a thing as a *reductio ad absurdum*, this surely amounts to one. If it is a sufficient reason for doing one thing, that nature does it, why not another thing? If not all things, why anything? The physical government of the world being full of the things which when done by men are deemed the greatest enormities, it cannot be religious or moral in us to guide our actions by the analogy of the course of nature. This proposition remains true, whatever occult quality of producing good may reside in those facts of nature which to our perceptions are most noxious, and which no one considers it other than a crime to produce artificially. . . .

It is undoubtedly a very common fact that good comes out of evil, and when it does occur, it is far too agreeable not to find people eager to dilate on it. But in the first place, it is quite as often true of human crimes, as of natural calamities. The fire of London, which is believed to have had so salutary an effect on the healthiness of the city, would have produced that effect just as much if it had been really the work of the "furor papisticus" * so long commemorated on the Monument. The deaths of those whom tyrants or persecutors have made martyrs in any noble cause, have done a service to mankind which would not have been obtained if they had died by accident or disease. Yet whatever incidental and

---

* destructive rage of the papists.

unexpected benefits may result from crimes, they are crimes nevertheless. In the second place, if good frequently comes out of evil, the converse fact, evil coming out of good, is equally common. Every event public or private, which, regretted on its occurrence, was declared providential at a later period on account of some unforeseen good consequence, might be matched by some other event, deemed fortunate at the time, but which proved calamitous or fatal to those whom it appeared to benefit. Such conflicts between the beginning and the end, or between the event and the expectation, are not only as frequent, but as often held up to notice, in the painful cases as in the agreeable; but there is not the same inclination to generalize on them; or at all events they are not regarded by the moderns (though they were by the ancients) as similarly an indication of the divine purposes: men satisfy themselves with moralizing on the imperfect nature of our foresight, the uncertainty of events, and the vanity of human expectations. The simple fact is, human interests are so complicated, and the effects of any incident whatever so multitudinous, that if it touches mankind at all, its influence on them is, in the great majority of cases, both good and bad. If the greater number of personal misfortunes have their good side, hardly any good fortune ever befell any one which did not give either to the same or to some other person, something to regret: and unhappily there are many misfortunes so overwhelming that their favourable side, if it exist, is entirely overshadowed and made insignificant; while the corresponding statement can seldom be made concerning blessings. . . .

But even though unable to believe that Nature, as a whole, is a realization of the designs of perfect wisdom and benevolence, men do not willingly renounce the idea that some part of Nature, at least, must be intended as an exemplar, or type; that on some portion or other of the Creator's works, the image of the moral qualities which they are accustomed to ascribe to him, must be impressed; that if not all which is, yet something which is, must not only be a faultless model of what ought to be, but must be intended to be our guide and standard in rectifying the rest. . . .

It has never been settled by any accredited doctrine, what particular departments of the order of nature shall be reputed to be designed for our moral instruction and guidance; and accordingly each person's individual predilections, or momentary convenience, have decided to what parts of the divine government the practical conclusions that he was desirous of establishing, should be recommended to approval as being analogous. One such recommendation must be as fallacious as another, for it is impossible to decide that certain of the Creator's works are more truly expressions of his character than the rest; and the only selection which does

not lead to immoral results, is the selection of those which most conduce
to the general good, in other words, of those which point to an end which
if the entire scheme is the expression of a single omnipotent and consistent
will, is evidently not the end intended by it.

There is however one particular element in the construction of the world,
which to minds on the look-out for special indications of the Creator's will,
has appeared, not without plausibility, peculiarly fitted to afford them;
viz. the active impulses of human and other animated beings. One can
imagine such persons arguing that when the Author of Nature only made
circumstances, he may not have meant to indicate the manner in which his
rational creatures were to adjust themselves to those circumstances; but
that when he implanted positive stimuli in the creatures themselves, stir-
ring them up to a particular kind of action, it is impossible to doubt that
he intended that sort of action to be practised by them. This reasoning,
followed out consistently, would lead to the conclusion that the Deity intended, and approves, whatever human beings do; since all that they do
being the consequence of some of the impulses with which their Creator
must have endowed them, all must equally be considered as done in
obedience to his will. As this practical conclusion was shrunk from, it was
necessary to draw a distinction, and to pronounce that not the whole, but
only parts of the active nature of mankind point to a special intention of
the Creator in respect to their conduct. These parts, it seemed natural to
suppose, must be those in which the Creator's hand is manifested rather
than the man's own: and hence the frequent antithesis between man as
God made him, and man as he has made himself. Since what is done with
deliberation seems more the man's own act, and he is held more completely responsible for it than for what he does from sudden impulse, the
considerate part of human conduct is apt to be set down as man's share in
the business, and the inconsiderate as God's. The result is the vein of
sentiment so common in the modern world (though unknown to the
philosophic ancients) which exalts instinct at the expense of reason; an
aberration rendered still more mischievous by the opinion commonly held
in conjunction with it, that every, or almost every, feeling or impulse
which acts promptly without waiting to ask questions, is an instinct. Thus
almost every variety of unreflecting and uncalculating impulse receives a
kind of consecration, except those which, though unreflecting at the moment, owe their origin to previous habits of reflection: these, being evidently not instinctive, do not meet with the favour accorded to the rest;
so that all unreflecting impulses are invested with authority over reason,
except the only ones which are most probably right. . . .

It is only in a highly artificialized condition of human nature that the notion grew up, or, I believe, ever could have grown up, that goodness was natural: because only after a long course of artificial education did good sentiments become so habitual, and so predominant over bad, as to arise unprompted when occasion called for them. In the times when mankind were nearer to their natural state, cultivated observers regarded the natural man as a sort of wild animal, distinguished chiefly by being craftier than the other beasts of the field; and all worth of character was deemed the result of a sort of taming; a phrase often applied by the ancient philosophers to the appropriate discipline of human beings. The truth is that there is hardly a single point of excellence belonging to human character, which is not decidedly repugnant to the untutored feelings of human nature.

If there be a virtue which more than any other we expect to find, and really do find, in an uncivilized state, it is the virtue of courage. Yet this is from first to last a victory achieved over one of the most powerful emotions of human nature. If there is any one feeling or attribute more natural than all others to human beings, it is fear; and no greater proof can be given of the power of artificial discipline than the conquest which it has at all times and places shown itself capable of achieving over so mighty and so universal a sentiment. The widest difference no doubt exists between one human being and another in the facility or difficulty with which they acquire this virtue. There is hardly any department of human excellence in which difference of original temperament goes so far. But it may fairly be questioned if any human being is naturally courageous. Many are naturally pugnacious, or irascible, or enthusiastic, and these passions when strongly excited may render them insensible to fear. But take away the conflicting emotion, and fear reasserts its dominion: consistent courage is always the effect of cultivation. . . .

Let us next consider a quality which forms the most visible, and one of the most radical of the moral distinctions between human beings and most of the lower animals; that of which the absence, more than of anything else, renders men bestial; the quality of cleanliness. Can anything be more entirely artificial? Children, and the lower classes of most countries, seem to be actually fond of dirt: the vast majority of the human race are indifferent to it: whole nations of otherwise civilized and cultivated human beings tolerate it in some of its worst forms, and only a very small minority are consistently offended by it. Indeed the universal law of the subject appears to be, that uncleanliness offends only those to whom it is unfamiliar, so that those who have lived in so artificial a state as to be unused to it in any form, are the sole persons whom it disgusts in all forms. Of all virtues this is the most evidently not instinctive, but a triumph over instinct. Assuredly neither cleanliness nor the love of cleanliness is natural to man, but only the capacity of acquiring a love of cleanliness. . . .

With regard to this particular hypothesis, that all natural impulses, all propensities sufficiently universal and sufficiently spontaneous to be capable of passing for instincts, must exist for good ends, and ought to be only regulated, not repressed; this is of course true of the majority of them, for the species could not have continued to exist unless most of its inclinations had been directed to things needful or useful for its preservation. But unless the instincts can be reduced to a very small number indeed, it must be allowed that we have also bad instincts which it should be the aim of education not simply to regulate but to extirpate, or rather (what can be done even to an instinct) to starve them by disuse. Those who are inclined to multiply the number of instincts, usually include among them one which they call destructiveness: an instinct to destroy for destruction's sake. I can conceive no good reason for preserving this, no more than another propensity which if not an instinct is very like one, what has been called the instinct of domination; a delight in exercising despotism, holding other beings in subjection to our will. The man who takes pleasure in the mere exertion of authority, apart from the purpose for which it is to be employed, is the last person in whose hands one would willingly entrust it. Again, there are persons who are cruel by character, or, as the phrase is, naturally cruel; who have a real pleasure in inflicting, or seeing the infliction of pain. This kind of cruelty is not mere hardheartedness, absence of pity or remorse; it is a positive thing; a particular kind of voluptuous excitement. The East, and Southern Europe, have afforded, and probably still afford, abundant examples of this hateful propensity. I suppose it will be granted that this is not one of the natural inclinations which it would be wrong to suppress. The only question would be whether it is not a duty to suppress the man himself along with it. . . .

The preceding observations are far from having exhausted the almost infinite variety of modes and occasions in which the idea of conformity to nature is introduced as an element into the ethical appreciation of actions and dispositions. The same favourable prejudgment follows the word nature through the numerous acceptations, in which it is employed as a distinctive term for certain parts of the constitution of humanity as contrasted with other parts. We have hitherto confined ourselves to one of these acceptations, in which it stands as a general designation for those parts of our mental and moral constitution which are supposed to be innate, in contradistinction to those which are acquired; as when nature is contrasted with education; or when a savage state, without laws, arts, or knowledge, is called a state of nature; or when the question is asked whether benevolence, or the moral sentiment, is natural or acquired; or whether some persons are poets or orators by nature and others not. But in another and a more lax sense, any manifestations by human beings are often termed natural, when it is merely intended to say that they are not studied or designedly assumed in the particular case; as when a person is said to move or speak with natural grace; or when it is said that a person's natural manner or character is so and so; meaning that it is so when he does not attempt to control or disguise it. In a still looser acceptation, a person is said to be naturally, that which he was until some special cause had acted upon him, or which it is supposed he would be if some such cause were withdrawn. Thus a person is said to be naturally dull, but to have made himself intelligent by study and perseverance; to be naturally cheerful, but soured by misfortune; naturally ambitious, but kept down by want of opportunity. Finally, the word natural, applied to feelings or conduct, often seems to mean no more than that they are such as are ordinarily found in human beings; as when it is said that a person acted, on some particular occasion, as it was natural to do; or that to be affected in a particular way by some sight, or sound, or thought, or incident in life, is perfectly natural.

In all these senses of the term, the quality called natural is very often confessedly a worse quality than the one contrasted with it; but whenever its being so is not too obvious to be questioned, the idea seems to be entertained that by describing it as natural, something has been said amounting to a considerable presumption in its favour. For my part I can perceive only one sense in which nature, or naturalness, in a human being, are really terms of praise; and then the praise is only negative: namely when used to denote the absence of affectation. Affectation may be defined, the effort to appear what one is not, when the motive or the occasion is not such as either to excuse the attempt, or to stamp it with the more odious name of hypocrisy. It must be added that the deception is often attempted to be practised on the deceiver himself as well as on others; he imitates the external signs of qualities which he would like to have, in hopes to persuade himself that he has them. Whether in the form of deception or of self-deception, or of something hovering between the two, affectation is very rightly accounted a reproach, and naturalness, understood as the reverse of affectation, a merit. But a more proper term by which to express this estimable quality would be sincerity; a term which has fallen from its original elevated meaning, and popularly denotes only a subordinate branch of the cardinal virtue it once designated as a whole. . . .

Conformity to nature, has no connection whatever with right and wrong. The idea can never be fitly introduced into ethical discussions at all, except, occasionally and partially, into the question of degrees of culpability. To illustrate this point, let us consider the phrase by which the greatest intensity of condemnatory feeling is conveyed in connection with the idea of nature—the word unnatural. That a thing is unnatural, in any precise meaning which can be attached to the word, is no argument for its being blamable; since the most criminal actions are to a being like man, not more unnatural than most of the virtues. The acquisition of virtue has in all ages been accounted a work of labour and difficulty, while the *descensus Averni* * on the contrary is of proverbial facility: and it assuredly requires in most persons a greater conquest over a greater number of natural inclinations to become eminently virtuous than transcendently vicious. But if an action, or an inclination, has been decided on other grounds to be blamable, it may be a circumstance in aggravation that it is unnatural, that is, repugnant to some strong feeling usually found in human beings; since the bad propensity, whatever it be, has afforded evidence of being both strong and deeply rooted, by having overcome that repugnance. This presumption of course fails if the individual never had the repugnance: and the argument, therefore, is not fit to be urged unless the feeling which is violated by the act, is not only justifiable and reasonable, but is one which it is blamable to be without.

The corresponding plea in extenuation of a culpable act because it was natural, or because it was prompted by a natural feeling, never, I think, ought to be admitted. There is hardly a bad action ever perpetrated which is not perfectly natural, and the motives to which are not perfectly natural feelings. In the eye of reason, therefore, this is no excuse, but it is quite "natural" that it should be so in the eyes of the multitude; because the meaning of the expression is, that they have a fellow feeling with the offender. When they say that something which they cannot help admitting to be blamable, is nevertheless natural, they mean that they can imagine the possibility of their being themselves tempted to commit it. Most people have a considerable amount of indulgence towards all acts of which they feel a possible source within themselves, reserving their rigour for those which, though perhaps really less bad, they cannot in any way understand how it is possible to commit. If an action convinces them (which it often does on very inadequate grounds) that the person who does it must be a

* descent into Hell.

being totally unlike themselves, they are seldom particular in examining the precise degree of blame due to it, or even if blame is properly due to it at all. They measure the degree of guilt by the strength of their antipathy; and hence differences of opinion, and even differences of taste, have been objects of as intense moral abhorrence as the most atrocious crimes.

It will be useful to sum up in a few words the leading conclusions of this Essay.

The word Nature has two principal meanings: it either denotes the entire system of things, with the aggregate of all their properties, or it denotes things as they would be, apart from human intervention.

In the first of these senses, the doctrine that man ought to follow nature is unmeaning; since man has no power to do anything else than follow nature; all his actions are done through, and in obedience to, some one or many of nature's physical or mental laws.

In the other sense of the term, the doctrine that man ought to follow nature, or in other words, ought to make the spontaneous course of things the model of his voluntary actions, is equally irrational and immoral.

Irrational, because all human action whatever, consists in altering, and all useful action in improving, the spontaneous course of nature:

Immoral, because the course of natural phenomena being replete with everything which when committed by human beings is most worthy of abhorrence, any one who endeavoured in his actions to imitate the natural course of things would be universally seen and acknowledged to be the wickedest of men.

The scheme of Nature regarded in its whole extent, cannot have had, for its sole or even principal object, the good of human or other sentient beings. What good it brings to them, is mostly the result of their own exertions. Whatsoever, in nature, gives indication of beneficent design, proves this beneficence to be armed only with limited power; and the duty of man is to co-operate with the beneficent powers, not by imitating but by perpetually striving to amend the course of nature—and bringing that part of it over which we can exercise control, more nearly into conformity with a high standard of justice and goodness.

· 44 ·

THE CONTINUUM OF ENDS-MEANS *
John Dewey (1859–1952)

Those who have read and enjoyed Charles Lamb's essay on the origin of roast pork have probably not been conscious that their enjoyment of its absurdity was due to perception of the absurdity of any "end" which is set up apart from the means by which it is to be attained and apart from its own further function as means. Nor is it probable that Lamb himself wrote the story as a deliberate travesty of the theories that make such a separation. Nonetheless, that is the whole point of the tale. The story, it will be remembered, is that roast pork was first enjoyed when a house in which pigs were confined was accidentally burned down. While searching in the ruins, the owners touched the pigs that had been roasted in the fire and scorched their fingers. Impulsively bringing their fingers to their mouths to cool them, they experienced a new taste. Enjoying the taste, they henceforth set themselves to building houses, inclosing pigs in them, and then burning the houses down. Now, if ends-in-view are what they are entirely apart from means, and have their value independently of valuation of means, there is nothing absurd, nothing ridiculous, in this procedure, for the end attained, the *de facto* termination, *was* eating and enjoying roast pork, and that was just the end desired. Only when the end attained is estimated in terms of the means employed—the building and burning-down of houses in comparison with other available means by which the desired result in view might be attained—is there anything absurd or unreasonable about the method employed.

The story has a direct bearing upon another point, the meaning of "intrinsic." *Enjoyment* of the taste of roast pork may be said to be immediate, although even so the enjoyment would be a somewhat troubled one, for those who have memory, by the thought of the needless cost at which it was obtained. But to pass from immediacy of enjoyment to something called "intrinsic value" is a leap for which there is no ground. The

* Reprinted from chapter 6 of *Theory of Valuation* by John Dewey, Volume II, no. 4 of the *International Encyclopedia of Unified Science*, by permission of The University of Chicago Press. Copyright 1939 by the University of Chicago. Compare with selections 40 and 47.

value of enjoyment of an object *as* an attained end is a value of something which in being an end, an outcome, stands in relation to the means of which it is the consequence. Hence if the object in question is prized *as* an end or "final" value, it is valued *in this relation* or as mediated. The first time roast pork was enjoyed, it was *not* an end-value, since by description it was not the result of desire, foresight, and intent. Upon subsequent occasions it was, by description, the outcome of prior foresight, desire, and effort, and hence occupied the position of an end-in-view. There are occasions in which previous effort enhances enjoyment of what is attained. But there are also many occasions in which persons find that, when they have attained something as an end, they have paid too high a price in effort and in sacrifice of other ends. In such situations *enjoyment* of the end attained is itself *valued*, for it is not taken in its immediacy but in terms of its cost—a fact fatal to its being regarded as "an end-in-itself," a self-contradictory term in any case.

The story throws a flood of light upon what is usually meant by the maxim "the end justifies the means" and also upon the popular objection to it. Applied in this case, it would mean that the value of the attained end, the eating of roast pork, was such as to warrant the price paid in the means by which it was attained—destruction of dwelling-houses and sacrifice of the value to which they contribute. The conception involved in the maxim that "the end justifies the means" is basically the same as that in the notion of ends-in-themselves; indeed, from a historical point of view, it is the fruit of the latter, for only the conception that certain things are ends-in-themselves can warrant the belief that the relation of ends-means is unilateral, proceeding exclusively from end to means. When the maxim is compared with empirically ascertained facts, it is equivalent to holding one of two views, both of which are incompatible with the facts. One of the views is that only the specially selected "end" held in view will actually be brought into existence by the means used, something miraculously intervening to prevent the means employed from having their other usual effects; the other (and more probable) view is that, as compared with the importance of the selected and uniquely prized end, other consequences may be completely ignored and brushed aside no matter how intrinsically obnoxious they are. This arbitrary selection of some one part of the attained consequences as *the* end and hence as the warrant of means used (no matter how objectionable are their *other* consequences) is the fruit of holding that *it*, as *the* end, is an end-in-itself, and hence possessed of "value" irrespective of all its existential relations. And this notion is inherent in *every* view that assumes that "ends" can be valued apart from appraisal of the things used as means in attaining them. The sole alternative to the view that *the* end is an arbitrarily selected part of actual consequences which *as* "the end" then justifies the use of means irrespective of the other consequences they produce, is that desires, ends-in-view, and consequences achieved be valued in turn as means of further consequences. The maxim referred to, under the guise of saying that ends, in the sense of actual consequences, provide the warrant for means employed—a correct position—actually says that some fragment of these actual consequences—a fragment arbitrarily selected because the heart has been set upon it—authorizes the use of means to obtain *it*, without the need of foreseeing and weighing other ends as consequences of the means used. It thus discloses in a striking manner the fallacy involved in the position that ends have value independent of appraisal of means involved and independent of their own further causal efficacy.

. . . In all the physical sciences (using 'physical' here as a synonym for *nonhuman*) it is now taken for granted that all "effects" are also "causes," or, stated more accurately, that nothing happens which is *final* in the sense that it is not part of an ongoing stream of events. If this principle, with the accompanying discrediting of belief in objects that are ends but not means, is employed in dealing with distinctive human phenomena, it necessarily follows that the distinction between ends and means is temporal and relational. Every condition that has to be brought into existence in order to serve as means is, *in that connection,* an object of desire and an end-in-view, while the end actually reached is a means to future ends as well as a test of valuations previously made. Since the end attained is a condition of further existential occurrences, it must be appraised as a potential obstacle and potential resource. If the notion of some objects as ends-in-themselves were abandoned, not merely in words but in all practical implications, human beings would for the first time in history be in a position to frame ends-in-view and form desires on the basis of empirically grounded propositions of the temporal relations of events to one another.

At any given time an adult person in a social group has certain ends which are so standardized by custom that they are taken for granted without examination, so that the only problems arising concern the best means for attaining them. In one group money-making would be such an end; in another group, possession of political power; in another group, advancement of scientific knowledge; in still another group, military prowess, etc. But such ends in any case are (i) more or less blank frameworks where the nominal "end" sets limits within which definite ends will fall, the latter being determined by appraisal of things as means; while (ii) as far as they simply express habits that have become established without critical examination of the relation of means and ends, they do not provide a model for a theory of valuation to follow. If a person moved by an experience of intense cold, which is highly objectionable, should momentarily judge it worth while to get warm by burning his house down, all that saves him from an act determined by a "compulsion neurosis" is the intellectual realization of what other consequences would ensue with the loss of his house. It is not necessarily a sign of insanity (as in the case cited) to isolate some event projected as an end out of the context of a world of moving changes in which it will in fact take place. But it is at least a sign of immaturity when an individual fails to view his end as also a moving condition of further consequences, thereby treating it as *final* in the sense in which "final" signifies that the course of events has come to a complete stop. Human beings do indulge in such arrests. But to treat them as models for forming a theory of ends is to substitute a manipulation of ideas, abstracted from the contexts in which they arise and function, for the conclusions of observation of concrete facts. It is a sign either of insanity, immaturity, indurated routine, or of a fanaticism that is a mixture of all three. . . .

The objection always brought against the view set forth is that, according to it, valuation activities and judgments are involved in a hopeless *regressus ad infinitum*. If, so it is said, there is no end which is not in turn a means, foresight has no place at which it can stop, and no end-in-view can be formed except by the most arbitrary of acts—an act so arbitrary that it mocks the claim of being a genuine valuation-proposition.

This objection brings us back to the conditions under which desires take shape and foreseen consequences are projected as ends to be reached. These conditions are those of need, deficit, and conflict. Apart from a condition of tension between a person and environing conditions there is, as we have seen, no occasion for evocation of desire for something else; there is nothing to induce the formation of an end, much less the formation of one end rather than any other out of the indefinite number of ends theoretically possible. Control of transformation of active tendencies into a desire in which a particular end-in-view is incorporated, is exercised by the needs or privations of an actual situation as its requirements are disclosed to observation. The "value" of different ends that suggest themselves is estimated or measured by the capacity they exhibit to guide action in making good, *satisfying*, in its literal sense, existing lacks. Here is the factor which cuts short the process of foreseeing and weighing ends-in-view in their function as means. Sufficient unto the day is the evil thereof and sufficient also is the *good* of that which does away with the existing evil. Sufficient because it is the means of instituting a complete situation or an integrated set of conditions.

. . . A physician has to determine the value of various courses of action and their results in the case of a particular patient. He forms ends-in-view having the value that justifies their adoption, on the ground of what his examination discloses is the "matter" or "trouble" with the patient. He estimates the worth of what he undertakes on the ground of its capacity to produce a condition in which these troubles will not exist, in which, as it is ordinarily put, the patient will be "restored to health." He does not have an idea of health as an absolute end-in-itself, an absolute good by which to determine what to do. On the contrary, he forms his general idea of health as an end and a good (value) for the patient on the ground of what his techniques of examination have shown to be the troubles from which patients suffer and the means by which they are overcome. There is no need to deny that a general and abstract conception of health finally develops. But it is the outcome of a great number of definite, empirical inquiries, not an a priori preconditioning "standard" for carrying on inquiries. . . .

• 45 •

THE CRITERION OF TASTE *

George Santayana (1863–1952)

Dogmatism in matters of taste has the same status as dogmatism in other spheres. It is initially justified by sincerity, being a systematic expression of a man's preferences; but it becomes absurd when its basis in a particular disposition is ignored and it pretends to have an absolute or metaphysical scope. Reason, with the order which in every region it imposes on life, is grounded on an animal nature and has no other function than to serve the same; and it fails to exercise its office quite as much when it oversteps its bounds and forgets whom it is serving as when it neglects some part of its legitimate province and serves its master imperfectly, without considering all his interests. . . .

The notorious diversities which human taste exhibits do not become conflicts, and raise no moral problem, until their basis or their function has

* Reprinted with the permission of Charles Scribner's Sons from Reason in Art, pp. 191–207 (ch. 10), by George Santayana. Copyright 1905 Charles Scribner's Sons; renewal copyright 1933. Permission to reprint also granted by Constable and Company Limited, London. See selection 48.

been forgotten, and each has claimed a right to assert itself exclusively. This claim is altogether absurd, and we might fail to understand how so preposterous an attitude could be assumed by anybody did we not remember that every young animal thinks himself absolute, and that dogmatism in the thinker is only the speculative side of greed and courage in the brute. The brute cannot surrender his appetites nor abdicate his primary right to dominate his environment. What experience and reason may teach him is merely how to make his self-assertion well balanced and successful. In the same way taste is bound to maintain its preferences but free to rationalise them. After a man has compared his feelings with the no less legitimate feelings of other creatures, he can reassert his own with more complete authority, since now he is aware of their necessary ground in his nature, and of their affinities with whatever other interests his nature enables him to recognise in others and to co-ordinate with his own.

A criterion of taste is, therefore, nothing but taste itself in its more deliberate and circumspect form. Reflection refines particular sentiments by bringing them into sympathy with all rational life. There is consequently the greatest possible difference in authority between taste and taste, and while delight in drums and eagle's feathers is perfectly genuine and has no cause to blush for itself, it cannot be compared in scope or representative value with delight in a symphony or an epic. The very instinct that is satisfied by beauty prefers one beauty to another; and we have only to question and purge our aesthetic feelings in order to obtain our criterion of taste. This criterion will be natural, personal, autonomous; a circumstance that will give it authority over our own judgment—which is all moral science is concerned about—and will extend its authority over other minds also, in so far as their constitution is similar to ours. In that measure what is a genuine instance of reason in us, others will recognise for a genuine expression of reason in themselves also.

Aesthetic feeling, in different people, may make up a different fraction of life and vary greatly in volume. The more nearly insensible a man is the more incompetent he becomes to proclaim the values which sensibility might have. To beauty men are habitually insensible, even while they are awake and rationally active. Tomes of aesthetic criticism hang on a few moments of real delight and intuition. It is in rare and scattered instants that beauty smiles even on her adorers, who are reduced for habitual comfort to remembering her past favours. An aesthetic glow may pervade experience, but that circumstance is seldom remarked; it figures only as an influence working subterraneously on thoughts and judgments which in themselves take a cognitive or practical direction. Only when the aesthetic ingredient becomes predominant do we exclaim, How beautiful! Ordinarily the pleasures which formal perception gives remain an undistinguished part of our comfort or curiosity.

Taste is formed in those moments when aesthetic emotion is massive and distinct; preferences then grown conscious, judgments then put into words will reverberate through calmer hours; they will constitute prejudices, habits of apperception, secret standards for all other beauties. A period of life in which such intuitions have been frequent may amass tastes and ideals sufficient for the rest of our days. Youth in these matters governs maturity, and while men may develop their early impressions more systematically and find confirmations of them in various quarters, they will seldom look at the world afresh or use new categories in deciphering it. Half our standards come from our first masters, and the other half from our first loves. Never being so deeply stirred again, we remain persuaded that no objects save those we then discovered can have a true sublimity. These high-water marks of aesthetic life may easily be reached under tutelage. It may be some eloquent appreciations read in a book, or some preference expressed by a gifted friend, that may have revealed unsuspected beauties in art or nature; and then, since our own perception was vicarious and obviously inferior in volume to that which our mentor possessed, we shall take his judgments for our criterion, since they were the source and exemplar of all our own. Thus the volume and intensity of some appreciations, especially when nothing of the kind has preceded, makes them authoritative over our subsequent judgments. On those warm moments hang all our cold systematic opinions; and while the latter fill our days and shape our careers it is only the former that are crucial and alive.

A race which loves beauty holds the same place in history that a season of love or enthusiasm holds in an individual life. Such a race has a preeminent right to pronounce upon beauty and to bequeath its judgments to duller peoples. We may accordingly listen with reverence to a Greek judgment on that subject, expecting that what might seem to us wrong about it is the expression of knowledge and passion beyond our range; it will suffice that we learn to live in the world of beauty, instead of merely studying its relics, for us to understand, for instance, that imitation is a fundamental principle in art, and that any rational judgment on the beautiful must be a moral and political judgment, enveloping chance aesthetic feelings and determining their value. What most German philosophers, on the contrary, have written about art and beauty has a minimal importance: it treats artifical problems in a grammatical spirit, seldom giving any proof of experience or imagination. What painters say about painting and poets about poetry is better than lay opinion; it may reveal, of course, some petty jealousy or some partial incapacity, because a special gift often carries with it complementary defects in apprehension; yet what is positive in such judgments is founded on knowledge and avoids the romancing into which litterateurs and sentimentalists will gladly wander. The specific values of art are technical values, more permanent and definite than the adventitious analogies on which a stray observer usually bases his views. Only a technical education can raise judgments on musical compositions above impertinent autobiography. The Japanese know the beauty of flowers, and tailors and dressmakers have the best sense for the fashions. We ask them for suggestions, and if we do not always take their advice, it is not because the fine effects they love are not genuine, but because they may not be effects which we care to produce.

This touches a second consideration, besides the volume and vivacity of feeling, which enters into good taste. What is voluminous may be inwardly confused or outwardly confusing. Excitement, though on the whole and for the moment agreeable, may verge on pain and may be, when it subsides a little, a cause of bitterness. A thing's attractions may be partly at war with its ideal function. In such a case what, in our haste, we call a beauty becomes hateful on a second view, and according to the key of our dissatisfaction we pronounce that effect meretricious, harsh, or affected. These discords appear when elaborate things are attempted without enough art and refinement; they are essentially in bad taste. Rudimentary effects, on the contrary, are pure, and though we may think them trivial when we are expecting something richer, their defect is never intrinsic; they do not plunge us, as impure excitements do, into a corrupt artificial conflict. So wildflowers, plain chant, or a scarlet uniform are beautiful enough; their simplicity is a positive merit, while their crudity is only relative. There is a touch of sophistication and disease in not being able to fall back on such things and enjoy them thoroughly, as if a man could no longer relish a glass of water. Your true epicure will study not to lose so genuine a pleasure. Better forego some artificial stimulus, though that, too, has its charm, than become insensible to natural joys. Indeed, ability to revert to elementary beauties is a test that judgment remains sound.

Vulgarity is quite another matter. An old woman in a blonde wig, a dirty hand covered with jewels, ostentation without dignity, rhetoric without cogency, all offend by an inner contradiction. To like such things we should have to surrender our better intuitions and suffer a kind of dishonour. Yet the elements offensively combined may be excellent in isolation, so that an untrained or torpid mind will be at a loss to understand the critic's displeasure. Oftentimes barbaric art almost succeeds, by dint of splendour, in banishing the sense of confusion and absurdity; for everything, even reason, must bow to force. Yet the impression remains chaotic, and we must be either partly inattentive or partly distressed. Nothing could show better than this alternative how mechanical barbaric art is. Driven by blind impulse or tradition, the artist has worked in the dark. He has dismissed his work without having quite understood it or really justified it to his own mind. It is rather his excretion than his product. Astonished, very likely, at his own fertility, he has thought himself divinely inspired, little knowing that clear reason is the highest and truest of inspirations. Other men, observing his obscure work, have then honoured him for profundity; and so mere bulk or stress or complexity have produced a mystical wonder by which generation after generation may be enthralled. Barbaric art is half necromantic; its ascendancy rests in a certain measure on bewilderment and fraud.

To purge away these impurities nothing is needed but quickened intelligence, a keener spiritual flame. Where perception is adequate, expression is so too, and if a man will only grow sensitive to the various solicitations which anything monstrous combines, he will thereby perceive its monstrosity. Let him but enact his sensations, let him pause to make explicit the confused hints that threaten to stupefy him; he will find that he can follow out each of them only by rejecting and forgetting the others. To free his imagination in any direction he must disengage it from the contrary intent, and so he must either purify his object or leave it a mass of confused promptings. Promptings essentially demand to be carried out, and when once an idea has become articulate it is not enriched but destroyed if it is still identified with its contrary. Any complete expression of a barbarous theme will, therefore, disengage its incompatible elements and turn it into a number of rational beauties.

When good taste has in this way purified and digested some turgid medley, it still has a progress to make. Ideas, like men, live in society. Not only has each a will of its own and an inherent ideal, but each finds itself conditioned for its expression by a host of other beings, on whose co-operation it depends. Good taste, besides being inwardly clear, has to be outwardly fit. A monstrous ideal devours and dissolves itself, but even a rational one does not find an immortal embodiment simply for being inwardly possible and free from contradiction. It needs a material basis, a soil and situation propitious to its growth. This basis, as it varies, makes the ideal vary which is simply its expression; and therefore no ideal can be ultimately fixed in ignorance of the conditions that may modify it. It subsists, to be sure, as an eternal possibility, independently of all further earthly revolutions. Once expressed, it has revealed the inalienable values that attach to a certain form of being, whenever that form is actualised. But its expression may have been only momentary, and that eternal ideal may have no further relevance to the living world. A criterion of taste, however, looks to a social career; it hopes to educate and to judge. In order to be an applicable and a just law, it must represent the interests over which it would preside. . . .

This scope, this representative faculty or wide appeal, is necessary to good taste. All authority is representative; force and inner consistency are gifts on which I may well congratulate another, but they give him no right to speak for me. Either aesthetic experience would have remained a chaos—which it is not altogether—or it must have tended to conciliate certain general human demands and ultimately all those interests which its operation in any way affects. The more conspicuous and permanent a work of art is, the more is such an adjustment needed. A poet or philosopher may be erratic and assure us that he is inspired; if we cannot well gainsay it, we are at least not obliged to read his works. An architect or a sculptor, however, or a public performer of any sort, that thrusts before us a spectacle justified only in his inner consciousness, makes himself a nuisance. A social standard of taste must assert itself here, or else no efficacious and cumulative art can exist at all. Good taste in such matters cannot abstract from tradition, utility, and the temper of the world. It must make itself an interpreter of humanity and think esoteric dreams less beautiful than what the public eye might conceivably admire.

There are various affinities by which art may acquire a representative or classic quality. It may do so by giving form to objects which everybody knows, by rendering experiences that are universal and primary. The human figure, elementary passions, common types and crises of fate—these are facts which pass too constantly through apperception not to have a normal aesthetic value. The artist who can catch that effect in its fulness and simplicity accordingly does immortal work. This sort of art immediately becomes popular; it passes into language and convention so that its aesthetic charm is apparently worn down. The old images after a while hardly stimulate unless they be presented in some paradoxical way; but in that case attention will be diverted to the accidental extravagance, and the chief classic effect will be missed. It is the honourable fate or euthanasia of artistic successes that they pass from the field of professional art altogether and become a portion of human faculty. Every man learns to be to that extent an artist; approved figures and maxims pass current like the words and idioms of a mother-tongue, themselves once brilliant inventions. The lustre of such successes is not really dimmed, however, when it becomes a part of man's daily light; a retrogression from that habitual style or habitual insight would at once prove, by the shock it caused, how precious those ingrained apperceptions continued to be.

Universality may also be achieved, in a more heroic fashion, by art that expresses ultimate truths, cosmic laws, great human ideals. Virgil and Dante are classic poets in this sense, and a similar quality belongs to Greek sculpture and architecture. They may not cause enthusiasm in everybody; but in the end experience and reflection renew their charm; and their greatness, like that of high mountains, grows more obvious with distance. Such eminence is the reward of having accepted discipline and made the mind a clear anagram of much experience. There is a great difference between the depth of expression so gained and richness or realism in details. A supreme work presupposes minute study, sympathy with varied passions, many experiments in expression; but these preliminary things are submerged in it and are not displayed side by side with it, like the foot-notes to a learned work, so that the ignorant may know they have existed. . . .

Human nature, for all its margin of variability, has a substantial core which is invariable, as the human body has a structure which it cannot lose without perishing altogether; for as creatures grow more complex a greater number of their organs become vital and indispensable. Advanced forms will rather die than surrender a tittle of their character; a fact which is the physical basis for loyalty and martyrdom. Any deep interpretation of oneself, or indeed of anything, has for that reason a largely representative truth. Other men, if they look closely, will make the same discovery for themselves. Hence distinction and profundity, in spite of their rarity, are wont to be largely recognised. The best men in all ages keep classic traditions alive. These men have on their side the weight of superior intelligence, and, though they are few, they might even claim the weight of numbers, since the few of all ages, added together, may be more than the many who in any one age follow a temporary fashion. Classic work is nevertheless always national, or at least characteristic of its period, as the classic poetry of each people is that in which its language appears most pure and free. To translate it is impossible; but it is easy to find that the human nature so inimitably expressed in each masterpiece is the same that, under different circumstance, dictates a different performance. The deviations between races and men are not yet so great as is the ignorance of self, the blindness to the native ideal, which prevails in most of them. Hence a great man of a remote epoch is more intelligible than a common man of our own time.

Both elementary and ultimate judgments, then, contribute to a standard of taste; yet human life lies between these limits, and an art which is to be truly adjusted to life should speak also for the intermediate experience. Good taste is indeed nothing but a name for those appreciations which the swelling incidents of life recall and reinforce. Good taste is that taste which is a good possession, a friend to the whole man. It must not alienate him from anything except to ally him to something greater and more fertile in satisfactions. It will not suffer him to dote on things, however seductive, which rob him of some nobler companionship. To have a foretaste of such a loss, and to reject instinctively whatever will cause it, is the very essence of refinement. Good taste comes, therefore, from experience, in the best sense of that word; it comes from having united in one's memory and character the fruit of many diverse undertakings. Mere taste is apt to be bad taste, since it regards nothing but a chance feeling. Every man who pursues an art may be presumed to have some sensibility; the question is whether he has breeding, too, and whether what he stops at is not, in the end, vulgar and offensive. Chance feeling needs to fortify itself with reasons and to find its level in the great world. When it has added fitness to its sincerity, beneficence to its passion, it will have acquired a right to live. Violence and self-justification will not pass muster in a moral society, for vipers possess both, and must nevertheless be stamped out. Citizenship is conferred only on creatures with human and co-operative instincts. A civilised imagination has to understand and to serve the world. . . .

• 46 •

ETHICAL ABSOLUTISM AND ETHICAL RELATIVISM *

Walter T. Stace (1886–)

There is an opinion widely current nowadays in philosophical circles which passes under the name of "ethical relativity." Exactly what this phrase means or implies is certainly far from clear. But unquestionably it stands as a label for the opinions of a group of ethical philosophers whose position is roughly on the extreme left wing among the moral theorizers of the day. And perhaps one may best understand it by placing it in contrast with the opposite kind of extreme view against which, undoubtedly, it has arisen as a protest. For among moral philosophers one may clearly distinguish a left and a right wing. Those of the left wing are the ethical relativists. They are the revolutionaries, the clever young men, the up to date.

* Reprinted from *The Concept of Morals* (New York: The Macmillan Company, 1937), pp. 1–16, 27–28, 46–48, and 53, by kind permission of the author. The title of this selection has been supplied by the editors.

Those of the right wing we may call the ethical absolutists. They are the conservatives and the old-fashioned.

[ETHICAL ABSOLUTISM]

According to the absolutists there is but one eternally true and valid moral code. This moral code applies with rigid impartiality to all men. What is a duty for me must likewise be a duty for you. And this will be true whether you are an Englishman, a Chinaman, or a Hottentot. If cannibalism is an abomination in England or America, it is an abomination in central Africa, notwithstanding that the African may think otherwise. The fact that he sees nothing wrong in his cannibal practices does not make them for him morally right. They are as much contrary to morality for him as they are for us. The only difference is that he is an ignorant savage who does not know this. There is not one law for one man or race of men, another for another. There is not one moral standard for Europeans, another for Indians, another for Chinese. There is but one law, one standard, one morality, for all men. And this standard, this law, is absolute and unvarying.

Moreover, as the one moral law extends its dominion over all the corners of the earth, so too it is not limited in its application by any considerations of time or period. That which is right now was right in the centuries of Greece and Rome, nay, in the very ages of the cave man. That which is evil now was evil then. If slavery is morally wicked today, it was morally wicked among the ancient Athenians, notwithstanding that their greatest men accepted it as a necessary condition of human society. Their opinion did not make slavery a moral good for them. It only showed that they were, in spite of their otherwise noble conceptions, ignorant of what is truly right and good in this matter.

The ethical absolutist recognizes as a fact that moral customs and moral ideas differ from country to country and from age to age. This indeed seems manifest and not to be disputed. We think slavery morally wrong, the Greeks thought it morally unobjectionable. The inhabitants of New Guinea certainly have very different moral ideas from ours. But the fact that the Greeks or the inhabitants of New Guinea think something right does not make it right, even for them. Nor does the fact that we think the same things wrong make them wrong. They are *in themselves* either right or wrong. What we have to do is to discover which they are. What anyone thinks makes no difference. It is here just as it is in matters of physical science. We believe the earth to be a globe. Our ancestors may have thought it flat. This does not show that it *was* flat, and is *now* a globe. What it shows is that men having in other ages been ignorant about the shape of the earth have now learned the truth. So if the Greeks thought slavery morally legitimate, this does not indicate that it was for them and in that age morally legitimate, but rather that they were ignorant of the truth of the matter.

The ethical absolutist is not indeed committed to the opinion that his own, or our own, moral code is the true one. Theoretically at least he might hold that slavery is ethically justifiable, that the Greeks knew better than we do about this, that ignorance of the true morality lies with us and not with them. All that he is actually committed to is the opinion that, whatever the true moral code may be, it is always the same for all men in all ages. His view is not at all inconsistent with the belief that humanity has still much to learn in moral matters. If anyone were to assert that in five hundred years the moral conceptions of the present day will appear as barbarous to the people of that age as the moral conceptions of the middle ages appear to us now, he need not deny it. If anyone were to assert that the ethics of Christianity are by no means final, and will be superseded in future ages by vastly nobler moral ideals, he need not deny this either. For it is of the essence of his creed to believe that morality is in some sense objective, not man-made, not produced by human opinion; that its principles are real truths about which men have to learn—just as they have to learn about the shape of the world—about which they may have been ignorant in the past, and about which therefore they may well be ignorant now.

Thus although absolutism is conservative in the sense that it is regarded by the more daring spirits as an out of date opinion, it is not necessarily conservative in the sense of being committed to the blind support of existing moral ideas and institutions. If ethical absolutists are sometimes conservative in this sense too, that is their personal affair. Such conservatism is accidental, not essential to the absolutist's creed. There is no logical reason, in the nature of the case, why an absolutist should not be a communist, an anarchist, a surrealist, or an upholder of free love. The fact that he is usually none of these things may be accounted for in various ways. But it has nothing to do with the sheer logic of his ethical position. The sole opinion to which he is committed is that whatever is morally right (or wrong)—be it free love or monogamy or slavery or cannibalism or vegetarianism—is morally right (or wrong) for all men at all times.

Usually the absolutist goes further than this. He often maintains, not merely that the moral law is the same for all the men on this planet—which is, after all, a tiny speck in space—but that in some way or in some sense it has application everywhere in the universe. He may express himself by saying that it applies to all "rational beings"—which would apparently include angels and the men on Mars (if they are rational). He is apt to think that the moral law is a part of the fundamental structure of the universe. But with this aspect of absolutism we need not, at the moment, concern ourselves. At present we may think of it as being simply the opinion that there is a single moral standard for all human beings.

[*Historical Causes for the Acceptance of Absolutism.*] This brief and rough sketch of ethical absolutism is intended merely to form a background against which we may the more clearly indicate, by way of contrast, the theory of ethical relativity. Up to the present, therefore, I have not given any of the reasons which the absolutist can urge in favour of his case. It is sufficient for my purpose at the moment to state *what* he believes, without going into the question of *why* he believes it. But before proceeding to our next step—the explanation of ethical relativity—I think it will be helpful to indicate some of the historical causes (as distinguished from logical reasons) which have helped in the past to render absolutism a plausible interpretation of morality as understood by European peoples.

Our civilization is a Christian civilization. It has grown up, during nearly two thousand years, upon the soil of Christian monotheism. In this soil our whole outlook upon life, and consequently all our moral ideas, have their roots. They have been moulded by this influence. The wave of religious scepticism which, during the last half century, has swept over us, has altered this fact scarcely at all. The moral ideas even of those who most violently reject the dogmas of Christianity with their intellects are still Christian ideas. This will probably remain true for many centuries even if Christian theology, as a set of intellectual beliefs, comes to be wholly rejected by every educated person. It will probably remain true so long as our civilization lasts. A child cannot, by changing in later life his intel·lectual creed, strip himself of the early formative moral influences of his childhood, though he can no doubt modify their results in various minor ways. With the outlook on life which was instilled into him in his early days he, in large measure, lives and dies. So it is with a civilization. And our civilization, whatever religious or irreligous views it may come to hold or reject, can hardly escape within its lifetime the moulding influences of its Christian origin. Now ethical absolutism was, in its central ideas, the product of Christian theology.

The connection is not difficult to detect. For morality has been conceived, during the Christian dispensation, as issuing from the will of God. That indeed was its single and all-sufficient source. There would be no point, for the naive believer in the faith, in the philosopher's questions regarding the foundations of morality and the basis of moral obligation. Even to ask such questions is a mark of incipient religious scepticism. For the true believer the author of the moral law is God. What pleases God, what God commands—that is the definition of right. What displeases God, what he forbids, that is the definition of wrong. Now there is, for the Christian monotheist, only one God ruling over the entire universe. And this God is rational, self-consistent. He does not act upon whims. Consequently his will and his commands must be the same everywhere. They will be unvarying for all peoples and in all ages. If the heathen have other moral ideas than ours—inferior ideas—that can only be because they live in ignorance of the true God. If they knew God and his commands, their ethical precepts would be the same as ours.

Polytheistic creeds may well tolerate a number of diverse moral codes. For the God of the western hemisphere might have different views from those entertained by the God of the eastern hemisphere. And the God of the north might issue to his worshippers commands at variance with the commands issued to other peoples by the God of the south. But a monotheistic religion implies a single universal and absolute morality.

This explains why ethical absolutism, until very recently, was not only believed by philosophers but *taken for granted without any argument.* . . .

[ETHICAL RELATIVISM]

We can now turn to the consideration of ethical relativity. . . . The revolt of the relativists against absolutism is, I believe, part and parcel of the general revolutionary tendency of our times. In particular it is a result of the decay of belief in the dogmas of orthodox religion. Belief in absolutism was supported, as we have seen, by belief in Christian monotheism. And now that, in an age of widespread religious scepticism, that support is withdrawn, absolutism tends to collapse. Revolutionary movements are as a rule, at any rate in their first onset, purely negative. They attack and destroy. And ethical relativity is, in its essence, a purely negative creed. It is simply a denial of ethical absolutism. That is why the best way of explaining it is to begin by explaining ethical absolutism. If we understand that what the latter asserts the former denies, then we understand ethical relativity.

Any ethical position which denies that there is a single moral standard which is equally applicable to all men at all times may fairly be called a species of ethical relativity. There is not, the relativist asserts, merely one moral law, one code, one standard. There are many moral laws, codes, standards. What morality ordains in one place or age may be quite different from what morality ordains in another place or age. The moral code of Chinamen is quite different from that of Europeans, that of African savages quite different from both. Any morality, therefore, is relative to the age, the place, and the circumstances in which it is found. It is in no sense absolute.

This does not mean merely—as one might at first sight be inclined to suppose—that the very same kind of action which is *thought* right in one country and period may be *thought* wrong in another. This would be a mere platitude, the truth of which everyone would have to admit. Even the absolutist would admit this—would even wish to emphasize it—since he is well aware that different peoples have different sets of moral ideas, and his whole point is that some of these sets of ideas are false. What the relativist means to assert is, not this platitude, but that the very same kind of action which *is* right in one country and period may *be* wrong in another. And this, far from being a platitude, is a very startling assertion.

It is very important to grasp thoroughly the difference between the two ideas. For there is reason to think that many minds tend to find ethical relativity attractive because they fail to keep them clearly apart. It is so very obvious that moral ideas differ from country to country and from age to age. And it is so very easy, if you are mentally lazy, to suppose that to say this means the same as to say that no universal moral standard exists, —or in other words that it implies ethical relativity. We fail to see that the word "standard" is used in two different senses. It is perfectly true that, in one sense, there are many variable moral standards. We speak of judging a man by the standard of his time. And this implies that different times have different standards. And this, of course, is quite true. But when the word "standard" is used in this sense it means simply the set of moral ideas current during the period in question. It means what people *think* right, whether as a matter of fact it *is* right or not. On the other hand when the absolutist asserts that there exists a single universal moral "standard," he is not using the word in this sense at all. He means by "standard" what *is* right as distinct from what people merely think right. His point is that although what people think right varies in different countries and periods, yet what actually is right is everywhere and always the same. And it follows that when the ethical relativist disputes the position of the absolutist and denies that any universal moral standard exists he too means by "standard" what actually is right. But it is exceedingly easy, if we are not careful, to slip loosely from using the word in the first sense to using it in the second sense; and to suppose that the variability of moral beliefs is the same thing as the variability of what really is moral. And unless we keep the two senses of the word "standard" distinct, we are likely to think the creed of ethical relativity much more plausible than it actually is.

The genuine relativist, then, does not merely mean that Chinamen may think right what Frenchmen think wrong. He means that what is wrong for the Frenchman may *be* right for the Chinaman. And if one enquires how, in those circumstances, one is to know what actually is right in China or in France, the answer comes quite glibly. What is right in China is the same as what people think right in China; and what is right in France is the same as what people think right in France. So that, if you want to know what is moral in any particular country or age all you have to do is to ascertain what are the moral ideas current in that age or country. Those ideas are, *for that age or country*, right. Thus what is morally right is identified with what is thought to be morally right, and the distinction which we made above between these two is simply denied. To put the same thing in another way, it is denied that there can be or ought to be any distinction between the two senses of the word "standard." There is only one kind of standard of right and wrong, namely, the moral ideas current in any particular age or country.

Moral right *means* what people think morally right. It has no other meaning. What Frenchmen think right is, therefore, right *for Frenchmen*. And evidently one must conclude—though I am not aware that relativists are anxious to draw one's attention to such unsavoury but yet absolutely necessary conclusions from their creed—that cannibalism is right for people who believe in it, that human sacrifice is right for those races which practice it, and that burning widows alive was right for Hindus until the British stepped in and compelled the Hindus to behave immorally by allowing their widows to remain alive.

When it is said that, according to the ethical relativist, what is thought right in any social group is right for that group, one must be careful not to misinterpret this. The relativist does not, of course, mean that there actually is an objective moral standard in France and a different objective standard in England, and that French and British opinions respectively give us correct information about these different standards. His point is rather that there are no objectively true moral standards at all. There is no single universal objective standard. Nor are there a variety of local objective standards. All standards are subjective. People's subjective feelings about morality are the only standards which exist.

To sum up. The ethical relativist consistently denies, it would seem, whatever the ethical absolutist asserts. For the absolutist there is a single universal moral standard. For the relativist there is no such standard. There are only local, ephemeral, and variable standards. For the absolutist there are two senses of the word "standard." Standards in the sense of sets of current moral ideas are relative and changeable. But the standard in the sense of what is actually morally right is absolute and unchanging. For the relativist no such distinction can be made. There is only one meaning of the word standard, namely, that which refers to local and variable sets of moral ideas. Or if it is insisted that the word must be allowed two meanings, then the relativist will say that there is at any rate no actual example of a standard in the absolute sense, and that the word as thus used is an empty name to which nothing in reality corresponds; so that the distinction between the two meanings becomes empty and useless. Finally—though this is merely saying the same thing in another way—the absolutist makes a distinction between what actually is right and what is thought right. The relativist rejects this distinction and identifies what is moral with what is thought moral by certain human beings or groups of human beings. . . .

[*Arguments in Favor of Ethical Relativity.*] . . . The first [argument] is that which relies upon the actual varieties of moral "standards" found in the world. It was easy enough to believe in a single absolute morality in older times when there was no anthropology, when all humanity was divided clearly into two groups, Christian peoples and the "heathen." Christian peoples knew and possessed the one true morality. The rest were savages whose moral ideas could be ignored. But all this is changed. Greater knowledge has brought greater tolerance. We can no longer exalt our own morality as alone true, while dismissing all other moralities as false or inferior. The investigations of anthropologists have shown that there exist side by side in the world a bewildering variety of moral codes. On this topic endless volumes have been written, masses of evidence piled up. Anthropologists have ransacked the Melanesian Islands, the jungles of New Guinea, the steppes of Siberia, the deserts of Australia, the forests of central Africa, and have brought back with them countless examples of weird, extravagant, and fantastic "moral" customs with which to confound us. We learn that all kinds of horrible practices are, in this, that, or the other place, regarded as essential to virtue. We find that there is nothing, or next to nothing, which has always and everywhere been regarded as morally good by all men. Where then is our universal morality? Can we, in face of all this evidence, deny that it is nothing but an empty dream?

This argument, taken by itself, is a very weak one. It relies upon a single set of facts—the variable moral customs of the world. But this variability of moral ideas is admitted by both parties to the dispute, and is capable of ready explanation upon the hypothesis of either party. The relativist says that the facts are to be explained by the non-existence of any absolute moral standard. The absolutist says that they are to be explained by human ignorance of what the absolute moral standard is. And he can truly point out that men have differed widely in their opinions about all manner of topics including the subject-matters of the physical sciences—just as much as they differ about morals. And if the various different opinions which men have held about the shape of the earth do not prove that it has no one real shape, neither do the various opinions which they have held about morality prove that there is no one true morality.

Thus the facts can be explained equally plausibly on either hypothesis. There is nothing in the facts themselves which compels us to prefer the relativistic hypothesis to that of the absolutist. And therefore the argument fails to prove the relativist conclusion. If that conclusion is to be established, it must be by means of other considerations.

This is the essential point. But I will add some supplementary remarks. The work of the anthropologists, upon which ethical relativists seem to rely so heavily, has as a matter of fact added absolutely nothing *in principle* to what has always been known about the variability of moral ideas. Educated people have known all along that the Greeks tolerated sodomy, which in modern times has been regarded in some countries as an abominable crime; that the Hindus thought it a sacred duty to burn their widows; that trickery, now thought despicable, was once believed to be a virtue; that terrible torture was thought by our own ancestors only a few centuries ago to be a justifiable weapon of justice; that it was only yesterday that western peoples came to believe that slavery is immoral. Even the ancients knew very well that moral customs and ideas vary—witness the writings of Herodotus. Thus the principle of the variability of moral ideas was well understood long before modern anthropology was ever heard of. Anthropology has added nothing to the knowledge of this principle except a mass of new and extreme examples of it drawn from very remote sources. But to multiply examples of a principle already well known and universally admitted adds nothing to the argument which is built upon that principle. The discoveries of the anthropologists have no doubt been of the highest importance in their own sphere. But in my considered opinion they have thrown no new light upon the special problems of the moral philosopher.

Although the multiplication of examples has no logical bearing on the argument, it does have an immense *psychological* effect upon people's minds. These masses of anthropological learning are impressive. They are propounded in the sacred name of "science." If they are quoted in support of ethical relativity—as they often are—people *think* that they must prove something important. They bewilder and over-awe the simple-minded, batter down their resistance, make them ready to receive humbly the doctrine of ethical relativity from those who have acquired a reputation by their immense learning and their claims to be "scientific." Perhaps this is why so much ado is made by ethical relativists regarding the anthropological evidence. But we must refuse to be impressed. We must discount all this mass of evidence about the extraordinary moral customs of remote peoples. Once we have admitted—as everyone who is instructed must have admitted these last two thousand years without any anthropology at all—the principle that moral ideas vary, all this new evidence adds nothing to the argument. And the argument itself proves nothing for the reasons already given. . . .

[Another] argument in favour of ethical relativity . . . consists in alleging that no one has ever been able to discover upon what foundation an absolute morality could rest, or from what source a universally binding moral code could derive its authority.

If, for example, it is an absolute and unalterable moral rule that all men ought to be unselfish, from whence does this *command* issue? For a command it certainly is, phrase it how you please. There is no difference in meaning between the sentence "You ought to be unselfish" and the sentence "Be unselfish." Now a command implies a commander. An obligation implies some authority which obliges. Who is this commander, what this authority? Thus the vastly difficult question is raised of *the basis of moral obligation*. Now the argument of the relativist would be that it is impossible to find any basis for a universally binding moral law; but that it is quite easy to discover a basis for morality if moral codes are admitted to be variable, ephemeral, and relative to time, place, and circumstance.

. . . I am assuming that it is no longer possible to solve this difficulty by saying naively that the universal moral law is based upon the uniform commands of God to all men. There will be many, no doubt, who will dispute this. But I am not writing for them. I am writing for those who feel the necessity of finding for morality a basis independent of particular religious dogmas. And I shall therefore make no attempt to argue the matter.

The problem which the absolutist has to face, then, is this. The religious basis of the one absolute morality having disappeared, can there be found for it any other, any secular, basis? If not, then it would seem that we cannot any longer believe in absolutism. We shall have to fall back upon belief in a variety of perhaps mutually inconsistent moral codes operating over restricted areas and limited periods. No one of these will be better, or more true, than any other. Each will be good and true for those living in those areas and periods. We shall have to fall back, in a word, on ethical relativity. . . .

[*Arguments Against Ethical Relativity*.] . . . Ethical relativity, in asserting that the moral standards of particular social groups are the only standards which exist, renders meaningless all propositions which attempt to compare these standards with one another in respect of their moral worth. And this is a very serious matter indeed. We are accustomed to think that the moral ideas of one nation or social group may be "higher" or "lower" than those of another. We believe, for example, that Christian ethical ideals are nobler than those of the savage races of central Africa. Probably most of us would think that the Chinese moral standards are higher than those of the inhabitants of New Guinea. In short we habitually compare one civilization with another and judge the sets of ethical ideas to be found in them to be some better, some worse. The fact that such judgments are very difficult to make with any justice, and that they are frequently made on very superficial and prejudiced grounds, has no bearing on the question now at issue. The question is whether such judgments have any *meaning*. We habitually assume that they have.

But on the basis of ethical relativity they can have none whatever. For the relativist must hold that there is no *common* standard which can be applied to the various civilizations judged. Any such comparison of moral standards implies the existence of some superior standard which is applicable to both. And the existence of any such standard is precisely what the relativist denies. According to him the Christian standard is applicable only to Christians, the Chinese standard only to Chinese, the New Guinea standard only to the inhabitants of New Guinea.

What is true of comparisons between the moral standards of different races will also be true of comparisons between those of different ages. It is not unusual to ask such questions as whether the standard of our own day is superior to that which existed among our ancestors five hundred years ago. And when we remember that our ancestors employed slaves, practiced barbaric physical tortures, and burnt people alive, we may be inclined to think that it is. At any rate we assume that the question is one which has meaning and is capable of rational discussion. But if the ethical relativist is right, whatever we assert on this subject must be totally meaningless. For here again there is no common standard which could form the basis of any such judgments.

This in its turn implies that the whole notion of moral *progress* is a sheer delusion. Progress means an advance from lower to higher, from worse to better. But on the basis of ethical relativity it has no meaning to say that the standards of this age are better (or worse) than those of a previous age. For there is no common standard by which both can be measured. . . .

If these arguments are valid, the ethical relativist cannot really maintain that there is anywhere to be found a moral standard binding upon anybody against his will. And he cannot maintain that, even within the social group, there is a common standard as between individuals. And if that is so, then even judgments to the effect that one man is morally better than another become meaningless. All moral valuation thus vanishes. There is nothing to prevent each man from being a rule unto himself. The result will be moral chaos and the collapse of all effective standards. . . .

• 47 •

THE CONTEXT OF MORAL JUDGMENT *

Arthur E. Murphy (1901–)

[I.] THE MEANING OF "PRACTICAL REASON."

" 'Tis not contrary to reason to prefer the destruction of the whole world to the scratching of my finger." In these words and others of similar import, David Hume summed up one of the most important and one of the most disturbing of the doctrines we owe to the development of modern critical philosophy. All of its puzzle, and much of its influence, are due to the fact that it states a substantial truth in a provocative and misleading way, and thus lends to what would otherwise seem to be an indefensible conclusion the support of apparently irrefutable evidence. Is it true or false? The answer depends on what it is understood to say, and that, in turn, on the meaning assigned to the term "reason." If you limit the operations of the mind properly described as "rational" to the tracing out of the implicative relations of ideas, and causal inferences concerning matters of fact, then it will follow that reason, thus employed, can discover nothing in the things it deals with to correspond to what we call their values. It is only when you turn from the object to the subject and survey, not the properties of things themselves, but the "relish" with which they are experienced and enjoyed, that a basis is found for preferring one to another—even if the one be the scratching of a finger and the other destruction of the world. But this "relish" is an affair of feelings and desires, or, in proper eighteenth century terms, of "the passions" and it is these, therefore, that determine what is good or bad, so far, at least, as "good" and

* The greater part of chapter 1, Part II, of *The Uses of Reason.* Copyright 1943 by The Macmillan Company and used with their permission. Compare with selections 40 and 44.

"bad" have an empirically discoverable application. "Reason," identified as above, can tell us whether our estimates of value are logically consistent, and inform us concerning the causal means best suited to further the ends we have in view. The means are properly judged as good, however, only if the end is good, and on this point "reason" has no jurisdiction, for "ultimate ends recommend themselves solely to the affections," or, as a more modern version of the same doctrine would say, to the primary "drives" which determine what the organism desires and on what conditions it can be satisfied. And since the means derive their goodness only from the end they serve, we can see why Hume should conclude that, in the field of morals, "reason is and ought to be the slave of the passions."

What this doctrine says that is true, and will stand the test of critical inspection, is that things are discoverably good or bad, not in their intrinsic characters, but in their capacity to satisfy interests and desires. In Hume's famous instance you may search the geometric properties of a circle as you will, but you will never discover its beauty until you consider it as an object of enjoyment, in its capacity to please aesthetically those who contemplate it. It may be the case, as Miss Millay alleges in a well-known sonnet, that "Euclid alone has looked on Beauty bare," but we shall have to modify the Platonism of this dictum to add that it was not in his capacity as a mathematician that he made this observation. Those less enamoured of the charm of circles than Euclid and Miss Millay can understand the same propositions of geometry and use the same "reason" in exploring their implications. To ask whether, in addition to the beauty that is thus variously enjoyed by appreciative beholders, there is a "real" beauty which inheres in circles quite independently of their capacity to delight aesthetically those who enjoy them—or would enjoy them if their tastes were "developed" in that direction—is to ask a question that we have no means of answering and had better, therefore, leave to those whose interest is literary or edifying rather than philosophical. The value, at least, that *we* find in things and persons is a good that answers to an interest in ourselves, and every command of practical reason, no matter how exalted its pretensions, is cogently addressed only "to whom it may concern." To say, therefore, that reason in morals is "the slave of the passions" *may* mean simply that it is concerned with objects which satisfy desire, and that it is only as affording such satisfaction or capable of doing so that their goodness can responsibly be made out. And, as it is the business of reason, in its practical application, to serve the good, it is *in this sense* its business to serve "the passions" and contribute to their satisfaction. *Apart from* such concern there is no "reason," in the nature of things, to prefer the scratching of a finger to the destruction of the world—or anything to anything else—for the ground of preference, in the possibility of attainable satisfaction, cannot, on this basis, be made out.

But if there is thus a sense in which Hume's statement is true, there is another and no less important one, in which it not merely seems to be, but actually is, false. The burden of the message of the great classical moralists, Greek and Christian alike, was that reason ought not to be, and in a well-ordered life is not, the slave of the passions, but rather controls and directs them to a good, which, apart from its normative influence, they would not have been able to achieve. Did Hume really mean to deny this, as his disciples have denied it since his time? The answer, as in most cases where we are dealing with confused thinking, must be yes and no. As a humane and judicious man he knew how to value what he called the "disinterested" passions, and much of what had traditionally been said of the authority of "reason" in conduct could be restated in his terms, with sympathy taking the place of "reason" and calculation, on a utilitarian basis, operating to liberalize conduct and add foresight to benevolence in a way which, if his terminology did not discourage it, we should naturally describe as rational. Yet the shift in terminology made a real difference, none the less, and one whose effects are still observable. Men do want *ultimate* reasons, and *final* sanctions for conduct, and if they come to believe that there are none, and that the final basis for all our standards of excellence is to be found in "arbitrary" preference and "irrational" instincts, or drives, or will to power, they will be inclined to see in that belief the excuse for arbitrary preferences and irrational claims of a much less innocent sort. There *is* a context in which an arbitrary or irrational action is a wrong action and in which reason is not just an *ad hoc* instrument for finding means to satisfy desires in themselves beyond the range of rational criticism. To suppose that in its use *in this context* the authority of reason was in any way compromised by the Humean discovery that what we are here being reasonable *about* is our desires, and the conditions for their satisfaction, is a mistake, and a disastrous one. Yet it is a mistake that is easily made, once "reason" in general is identified with "reason" in its purely theoretical use, and, in consequence, what is not in *this* sense an affair of reason is handed over to the jurisdiction of "passions" with whose ultimate demands and preferences *mere* reason has nothing to do. Hume, who was in some respects the Bertrand Russell of his time, was at no pains to divorce his theory from this unhappy implication, and later empirical thinkers, encouraged by the prestige of the sciences to limit the properly "objective" and respectable use of reason to the methods of inquiry employed in the physical and social sciences, have for the most part followed in his footsteps. In this way, and with this dubious philosophical benediction, we reach the dichotomy of a reason which has nothing to do with "values," and "values" which, in their *ultimate* basis in non-rational drives, have nothing to do with reason. What it can then mean to be reasonable about values is a further problem to which busy scientists could hardly be expected to give a well-thought-out answer or their popularizers and publicists to take quite seriously. Science, after all, is remaking the world, and will doubtless get around to values in time, if they turn out to be really important.

Philosophers, on the whole, were more far-sighted than this. They saw the necessity, if we are to make sense of morals, of making clear the sense of "reason" in which it properly claims practical authority. The "reason" thus employed will be something other than the purely theoretical faculty which Hume recognized, and its claims will be without cogency save for those who acknowledge the good to which it is directed and the obligations entailed in the pursuit of it. But it will be *reason*, none the less, as distinct from groundless preference or arbitrary demand, and it will be in the name of principles rationally defensible that it speaks. Granting that theoretical reason, dealing with events in space and time in so far as these are causally understandable and predictable, provides no ultimate answer to the question "what ought I to do?" the philosopher therefore looks for further light to *practical* reason, and reaffirms, with its sanction, the truths which he finds that morality requires and science cannot supply. . . .

When I speak hereafter of "practical reason," I shall mean by it the use of reason in the organization of desires and the adjustment of claims in the pursuit of goods judged to be desirable by methods held to be just and proper to that end. Since we are here concerned to discover not merely what does exist but what would be good if it did exist, and is therefore worth accepting as a goal for action, and what is right, fair or just in the sacrifices those associated in a common action are asked to make for it and the rewards they are to receive on its attainment, it is not surprising that considerations will here be pertinent of which neither a physicist, an astronomer, nor an observer of the behavior of rats (a psychologist) would find it necessary to take account in his own somewhat different investigation. If it is stipulated that nothing is within the sphere of reason which their methods do not recognize as relevant or their instruments record, we shall, in this process, have transcended "reason." But we shall not, for all that, have taken leave of our powers of rational discrimination and sound judgment in so doing. On the contrary, we shall find uses for them, which even the most careful observation of rodent behavior could hardly have elicited. Nor shall we be unduly shocked or upset by the discovery that the good thus discerned is one that is relative to the human interests it organizes and articulates, that, in short, it is their good, and that its rational authority lies not in its supposed disclosure of a "reality" outside this context, but in its capacity to bring the desires that operate within it to a level of just and harmonious satisfaction which, by themselves, they could not have discerned. For, while the good it discloses is *their* good, it is not a good which they can set independently of the light which reason thus employed supplies, and reason is not, in consequence, nor should it be, the slave of the passions, though it is, and ought to be, the spokesman for a good in which the passions find their reasonable satisfaction. In trying to see how reason works here and what the differences are between action that, in a moral sense, is right and reasonable and that which is arbitrary and unjust, we shall (fortunately) need no special powers of insight or appreciation vouchsafed only to the elect. Nothing more is needed than reliable knowledge and good will in the understanding and evaluation of matters of public knowledge and issues of common concern. Nothing less, however, will suffice.

[II.] INTEREST AND JUDGMENTS OF VALUE

How can we be rational about values, when the attitude of reason is one of disinterested, unbiased judgment, and the attitude of valuation is one of interest, preference, bias—a way of being *for* some things and *against* others? If to be disinterested, in the sense in which practical reason requires disinterested judgment, was to be unconcerned, while to have a preference for anything rather than anything else was to be biased in its favor, hence *not* disinterested, there would indeed be a fatal incompatibility between reason and the passions, and to talk of practical reason, as we have done, would be a contradiction in terms. Fortunately for us, and for human nature, no such incompatibility exists. But loose and inaccurate thinking has sometimes led men to suppose its existence, and to maintain in consequence that we can only be rational about things we care nothing or very little about, since in these cases only can a "disinterested" and thus a genuinely rational attitude be expected to prevail. We can reach "objective" judgments about the velocity of light, since no very strong emotions are committed in advance to one conclusion rather than another about it; but to be similarly "objective" in instances about which we care greatly is quite out of the question. This conclusion ministers to a number of interests which have more to lose than to gain by the application of reason to human affairs, and it is not surprising that it has enjoyed a certain popularity. Our first task, therefore, will be to clear up the confusion from which it gains its intellectual respectability and, in the process, to locate more precisely the standpoint from which moral judgments are made and the sense in which they can be, and ought to be, disinterested.

We have agreed that all the goods we can identify in experience possess their goodness in their capacity to satisfy interests, wants, desires. None of these interests is antecendently rational, as conforming to the demands of a reality, discerned by reason, which possesses an inherent excellence of its own and to which it is the business of our desires, so far as they are reasonable, to conform. There may be such a reality, but its inherent ex-cellence, whatever it may consist in, from cosmic immensity to plenitude of Being, becomes a value for us only in so far as we can discern in it a good in which our wills, and minds, and hearts are satisfied. And it is with the good that we can discern that practical reason is reasonably concerned.

But while no interest is antecedently rational, and while reason has no criterion for the good outside that which the satisfaction of human wants itself determines, the satisfaction of our wants can come to be a rational process in so far as we judge the claims of each particular interest from the standpoint of an attainable harmony to which each contributes but in which none has exclusive or unqualified authority. If we wanted only one thing, and wanted it unconditionally, there would be no place for the use of reason in the discovery of the good toward which all our efforts should be directed. Reason would then, and rightly, be the slave, not of the passions, but of that one passion to whose unconditional satisfaction our nature was directed. Nothing is more apparent, however, than that we want many things, and that some of these wants conflict. Moreover, there are things we want if we can have them under some conditions that we should rightly reject under others. Until, therefore, we know on what terms our several interests can be jointly satisfied and to what the satisfaction of any one among them would commit us, in relation to the others and the conditions of their satisfaction, we simply do not know what we want. Nor can we find out simply by listing our "fundamental drives" and inviting them to fight it out among themselves for mastery. Men want power, they have a "will to power," and they struggle for power. But unless they are maniacs or Nietzschean supermen, and therefore less or more than human, they want power of certain sorts, under specific conditions, and there are other things they want as well as power, concern for which will qualify the kind of power they go after and the way in which they use it when they get it. And short of special revelation of some sort or other, the only way in which they can reliably find out what sort of power they want and what they want to do with it, is by considering the urge for power in its relation to other urges and the possibility of their joint attainment under the conditions in which action can effectively be carried on. This possibility of satisfaction will stand, relatively to competing present urges, as an ideal, something not now actual but attainable and worth attaining; and it will reasonably have authority over them simply in so far as it expresses what is wanted not blindly or at random but with knowledge of the conditions under which a secure and comprehensive satisfaction can actually be achieved. For this we require not only knowledge of the external world but self-knowledge as well, the kind that Socrates invited his fellow Athenians to seek. The reason that judges, in the light of such knowledge, what is worth seeking, or what is good, is the practical reason we have been looking for. Plato summed up the case for the authority of reason in conduct by saying that the good for man is a mixture, and only reason can reliably judge how, and in what measure, the ingredients in this mixture can rightly be combined. The claim of practical reason could hardly be put more simply or more conclusively.

In what sense is a judgment "disinterested" when it is made from the standpoint of this desirable and possible, hence, relatively to present action, ideal goal? Certainly not in the sense that the good it defines is one about which we are or ought to be unconcerned. What we want such an ideal to provide for us is a *ground* for preference, a way of being for or against competing demands for action *reasonably*, not at all a way of being indifferent or merely neutral concerning them. The notion that only in refusing to commit himself is a man "objective," and hence judicious in matters of conduct, is a current inanity that has done much harm. A practically reasonable man is not one without convictions but one who makes up his mind with a just regard for the merits of the case before him. This presupposes that the case has merits (or demerits), and that these can be found out and fairly assessed. What is required for reasonable judgment is the kind of impartiality which consists in freedom from such *antecedent* commitment to one interest or another as would blind a man to the issues involved, or close his mind to relevant information concerning them, or impede a fair estimate of conflicting claims. There is no doubt that it is in some cases very difficult to be thus impartial. But it is no less evident that we frequently do expect men to manifest such impartiality, and regard it as a prerequisite for responsible fair dealing in social relations.

A selection board is not expected to show its impartiality by refusing to prefer any of the applicants among whom it has to choose to any other, that is, by refusing to make a choice. Nor is it supposed to be lacking in concern for (hence "partiality" to) the good to which an "impartial" selection is supposed to contribute. Quite the contrary. What is expected is that it will not prefer one candidate to another save in so far as that preference can be justified by the merits of the applicants, that is, by their reasonably judged capacity to perform the services required of them for the sake of which judgment is pronounced. There is really no mystery about this, nor is the ability to act thus reasonably in a practical situation ordinarily regarded as something too great to demand of frail human nature. If such a board favored one candidate to another because of his wealth, or family connections, it would be deciding arbitrarily, not because its decision was the expression of an interest, but because the interest in question was not one which could stand inspection in the light of its professed intentions and the end for which it was set up.

In such an instance, the difference between a decision that is just or reasonable and one that is arbitrary, or unreasonable, is not that the one is the expression of an interest and the other not, but that the one contributes to and can be justified by a more comprehensive good, in reference to which it is judged, while the other is in conflict with this good. Those interests which can contribute to such a good are said to be reasonable with respect to it, those that oppose it, irrational. The good itself has no cogency apart from the satisfaction it promises for genuine human wants. If there was no use in selecting candidates on their merits, there would be no sense in condemning those who failed to do so. But it is not to be identified with any of these wants apart from the meaning it takes on as one factor in a more inclusive good. And what it can properly claim, as a member of that order, is not to be settled by its initial urgency or allegedly primitive status, but only by its eventual contribution to that way of living which we prefer when we know what we are doing and what, on the whole, we want. In articulating the structure of this way of living reason is not the slave of the passions, nor their rival in a struggle for power, but the spokesman for a good which is their good, but which, without its aid, they could not have discerned.

I do not suggest, of course, that such rationality always or even usually prevails in human conduct. We do not always choose the highest when we see it, and we often have neither the good sense to see it nor the will to look where it is to be found. Hence conduct is very frequently arbitrary and irrational in ways in which it ought not to be—that is, it falls short of a range and level of satisfaction which was possible to it, if it had had the wit to understand and the will to make the most of its opportunities. What is here important is to make out the kind of difference that reason makes where it does operate, and the good to which it is rightly addressed. This good is not beyond the powers of human nature to achieve; if it were it would not define a relevant ideal. But it is one that is reliably attainable only when human nature develops in a particular way, when the interests

that move men are judged from the standpoint of their eventual collabora-
tion in a comprehensive good, and the knowledge of the good thus identified becomes a factor in the organization of present conduct toward its
effective actualization. Apart from this distinctive aspect of human behavior and the rational use of ideas in the context of activity it defines,
there is no way of making sense of the claims of practical reason. It is not
surprising, therefore, that those who refuse seriously to consider human behavior under this aspect, preferring to reduce it for scientific or other purposes to a congeries of "drives" or reflexes or "frustrations and aggressions,"
have been unable to make sense of these claims. Perhaps it was not their
business to do so. But it is our business, and we intend to pursue it. If
those whose understanding of human nature is restricted, perhaps ad-
visedly, to what can be understood in terms of categories derived from
pathology, physiology and animal behavior will proceed with their own
affairs, there need be no disagreement between us. If, however, they go on
to claim that what they have discovered is "ultimately" all there is in the
human animal and that, in consequence, we are merely fooling ourselves
when we demand "disinterested" behavior of such an organism, we shall
have to reply, with less politeness than pertinence, that on this point they
quite literally do not know what they are talking about.

[III.] MORAL ORDER AND MORAL FREEDOM

We have spoken so far of a comprehensive good in which competing
interests can attain their reasonable satisfaction, finding in it the measure
of fulfilment of which, as elements in an ordered life, they are capable,
and of the role of reason in discovering the nature of this good and making it available, as an ideal, in the organization of present conduct. The
picture thus presented is true as far as it goes. But there is more to practical reason than that. It is not sufficient to talk of a harmony of interests
and a resulting satisfaction. We must go on to ask whose interests are to be
harmonized and from what standpoint, and on what level the satisfaction
is to be achieved. These are old questions, and they are not easy to answer.
Must each man, so far at least as he is reasonable, prefer his own interests to
all others, and regard the good of others simply as a means to the end of
his own satisfaction? And of what sort are these satisfactions to be? Is it
better, as John Stuart Mill declared, to be Socrates dissatisfied than a fool
satisfied? And, if it is, how is this betterness to be made out in terms of
the satisfaction of interests, which we have so far taken as the goal of
reasonable conduct? If we are to understand the use of practical reason,
in its application to moral issues, we must answer these questions; for the
ordering of satisfactions in the good we accept as our ideal will depend

upon our answer, and the reasonable ordering of conduct on the structure of this good.

It is true, indeed it is a truism, that the only interests a man can reasonably be concerned about are his own. But it is no less true, and just as important, to add that he can reasonably be concerned about the interests of others and the claim they make upon him, and can prefer such claims to interests which, if he had had only himself to consider, he would have preferred to satisfy. What the truism says is that he cannot be concerned about the interests of others unless he *is* concerned about them, and unless, in that sense, they are objects of his own interest, in the satisfaction of which he will find at least the satisfaction that comes from getting what one wants even when what one wants, under the circumstances, is the satisfaction of other interests than one's own. This may sound paradoxical, and a paradox has frequently been made of it. But the puzzle arises from a failure to specify the context in which moral judgments are actually made, and the manner in which the preferences that follow such judgment and are guided by it are determined. What a man would want if he had only his own satisfaction to consider is one thing. The interests which, under those circumstances, would reasonably determine his conduct, and the kind of good in which it would eventuate can, with a certain effort of abstractive imagination, be ascertained. If we label such interests *his own* interests and contrast them with the similarly determined interests of others, of which he may have for practical purposes to take account, but only in so far as they serve as instruments or impediments to the satisfaction of "his own" interests as antecedently identified, we shall have a picture of rational conduct in which the end pursued is ego-centric satisfaction and nothing is accounted reasonable in practice that does not serve as a means to this end. It is not a very edifying picture, and it can be used either to justify selfishness as peculiarly rational or to condemn rational action as peculiarly selfish. It has often been used for both purposes. Its plausibilty rests on the dictum that the only good a man can reasonably pursue is that which "his own" concerns or interests dictate, and its fallacious import is seen as soon as it is observed that "his own" has here been defined in terms of a situation which excludes from the start the conditions in which moral problems arise and can significantly be solved.

For it is a manifest fact, though a frequently neglected one, that specifically moral problems arise in just those cases in which a man *is* concerned with the interests and the happiness of others beside himself, either because he values their satisfaction directly as an end worth working for, or because he acknowledges an obligation to respect it. These obligations and values are in this situation *his* concern; they are the objects of his interest; and the good for which he can reasonably work is one in which they must have an appropriate place. To picture them as mere means to a "satisfaction," in which "his own" interests, defined independently of just these concerns, have the dominant place and in respect to which all else functions merely as means, is radically to misrepresent the situation. It is not surprising that the terms of this misrepresentation, masquerading as "rational self-interest," have failed to provide the basis for a sound moral theory.

The object of this concern will, as a rule, be defined by certain approved ways of acting, acknowledged as "right," "fair," or "proper," and felt by the individual to stand as obligations which he is bound to respect in his relations to other people. The keeping of promises, support for aged parents and young children, loyalty to the state and readiness to defend it at grave personal risk in time of war are familiar instances, and there is no society with which we are acquainted, from the most primitive culture to the most developed, in which respect for some such obligations is not a considerable factor in social behavior. To define the good in which men could be satisfied independently of the right ordering of interests in respect to just such obligations would be to define a good which was not their good and in which they could not in fact find satisfaction. It is, therefore, a highly unreasonable procedure, though it is in the name of reason that it is sometimes defended. These rules and obligations are not themselves the product of human reason, save to a minor and limited degree. They include tabus we now regard as cruel and stupid, as well as practices of a more praise-worthy sort. But whether good or bad, from the standpoint of a more reflective morality, they are an essential part of the situation in which men work for the satisfaction of their desires, and they help to determine the structure of any good in which these desires can in fact find satisfaction.

The adjustment of interests that will reasonably satisfy the actual concerns of men must, therefore, have at least the semblance of a moral order —that is, it must be one in which rights and duties are acknowledged and in which decisions, on matters of mutual concern, are regarded as sufficiently warranted only when they can be shown to conform to accredited rules of right action. They may not actually so conform; there is room in such matters for endless hypocrisy and self-deception. And the rules themselves may be blind and arbitrary enough. But so long as they are acknowledged, not merely as threats or commands, conformity to which may or may not be expedient in the furtherance of other interests, but as standards that *ought to be* respected, so that conformity constitutes an obligation which individuals are genuinely concerned to respect, they function as moral rules within the society in question, and men who respect them, in making up their minds, will ask not merely what, on reflection, they want to do, but also, in some instances, what they ought to do. What ought to be done is not necessarily something different from what they antecedently wanted to do. The point is rather that until they have found out what they ought to do, they will not *know* what, on the whole, they want to do. For they want to do what they ought to do, and this is something to be found out, not dictated in advance by the *de facto* urgency of competing interests. There is no doubt, I think, that there are instances in which most men find themselves in this sort of situation. It is no answer to their problem to tell them that they ought to do whatever they want to do, or to "satisfy themselves." That is true enough, so far as it goes, but it will not meet the issue. What they want to do is whatever, under the circumstances, is right and reasonable, and their satisfaction is not to be found short of an adjustment in which other interests than their own demand consideration, not merely as means, but on terms which rules of equity and fair dealing dictate. Practical reason will not have done its work until it has shown us how to meet these situations as reasonably as we can. When Kant insisted that "What ought I to do?" is the basic question for practical reason he was, as usual, keeping his eye on the salient features of the moral situation.

We have, then, the answer to one of the questions asked some pages back. The interests to be harmonized by practical reason are those with which the individual is himself concerned—they could from the nature of the case be no others. But they are those with which he is concerned not merely as a competitive animal or ego-centric calculator of eventual personal rewards, but as a responsible moral agent. As such he can rightly prefer "his own" interests to others only when and in so far as they are entitled to such preference under rules held to be valid not merely for him, but for all those concerned in the moral community. This reasonable preference is by no means the sole or dominant factor in human conduct —nothing could be plainer than that. But it is one factor in it, and a uniquely valuable one. To leave it out when we are estimating the capacities of human nature as a whole is to turn an abstraction, perhaps legitimate for scientific purposes, into an excuse for moral cynicism. And to leave it out when it is moral behavior itself that is under consideration is a kind of blindness of which, in Bradley's phrase, only "a fool or an advanced thinker" could be guilty.

This goes a long way toward answering our second question as well. On what level, it was asked, is the satisfaction which practical reason recommends as a worthy goal for action to be achieved? The satisfactions of the fool are not those of Socrates, but so long as each is satisfied in his own fashion, who is to judge between them? And if one is satisfied and the other not, was not the first the wiser man, at least from a practical point of view? The answer depends, of course, on the value to be placed on the man who is having the satisfaction—the value, that is, of being the kind of man who can be satisfied in that kind of way. For we are concerned not merely with the satisfaction of interests, but of persons, and it is only when we have taken account of what persons are, and what worth they are capable of possessing, that we can rightly estimate their value. . . .

In the context of moral behavior . . . a "person" is an individual with rights and duties, one who can properly be held responsible for what he does because he is capable of assuming or bearing responsibility, of acting in the name and for the sake of interests that are his, not merely as a biological organism, but as a member of a moral order. He is capable, in G. H. Mead's phrase, of "taking the role of the other," that is, of the other members of the social group in which he functions, and judging his own conduct in terms held to be valid alike for all. If this meant only the passive reflection of group pressures in individual conduct, it would fall considerably short of what I mean by personality. It achieves this level, however, when the "other" is generalized to represent the verdict of justice and right reason, and the acceptance of its obligations is an active commitment to a good which the individual acknowledges as his own.

It was in Kant's moral philosophy that the notion of moral personality, and its central place in rational conduct, received classical statement. What he saw clearly was that when men cooperate freely, through their reasonable acknowledgment of mutual responsibilities, as members of "a kingdom of ends," a level of conduct is achieved which is of peculiar value, a moral order which makes sense of much in human nature that without it would remain frustrated and unfulfilled. We may not agree with him that nothing in this world or out of it is good without qualification but a good will, but when we understand ourselves and our purposes we shall find it hard, I think, to deny that good will, as he understood it, is a great good, and that without it many other goods, which men have mistakenly regarded as more important, would lose their worth as well. A "good will," in this usage, is a will freely, and responsibly, directed to the good attainable in such a community, claiming nothing for itself that this common good does not warrant and acknowledging the equal rights of others who are co-workers for its attainment. In Kant's writings this doctrine is hedged around by crabbed distinctions and scholastic complications, but there are sentences in which it comes to splendid expression, as in the great commandment to which every theory of democracy that makes sense must return for its ultimate moral sanction: "So act as to treat humanity, whether in thine own person or that of another, always as an end, never merely as a means."

This dictum is, of course, the categorical, or unconditional moral imperative which Kant regarded as the fundamental principle of all right conduct. It has often been misunderstood by critics, and there are some among the most modern of them who make their inability to understand it an occasion for self-congratulation. Thus Pareto refers to this principle as "a metaphysical entity," which is "still admired by many good souls," and adds that those who "pretend to know what it is . . . can never make it clear to anyone who insists on remaining in touch with reality." If "remaining in touch with reality" means rejecting all ideals which deal with conduct as it ought to be, then this failure is not very difficult to understand. It is, however, remarkably, and even willfully, simple-minded. For Kant was not ignorant of, and had no intention of denying, the fact that "in reality" we constantly use the services of others as means to our own ends, and that it is quite sensible to do so. What he saw was that there is a level of human relationships on which it is possible not *merely* to use men for our own ends but to share with them in purposes that are mutually understood and honored, and that nothing that comes out of such co-operative action is as much worth attaining as the good will and integrity of the men who freely share in it. Humanity—or human nature—at this level of conduct has a dignity or personal worth that accrues to it not just as a means to some further good, but as an end or fulfilment, the actualization of the excellence of which that nature is capable. The injunction to treat humanity, in respect of this capacity in one's own person and that of others, as an end, not merely as a means, does not seem to me incomprehensible or even obscure. Nor do I find it impossible to understand its obvious implication: that those who reduce a humanity capable of such dignity and freedom to a mere instrument for their own ulterior ends are behaving wrongly. For the integrity of free men is beyond price—its worth is not that of an instrument but of an end. And that, I take it, is what the categorical imperative has to tell us. . . .

The notion that social action on such a level is possible and desirable stands, for those who accept it, as an ideal or norm for present action. It does not describe the way in which men always or even usually behave. It represents a good rarely now achieved and perhaps never fully attainable. But without it, and without the possibility it presents of a life lived at some times and in some measure at the height of its human capacities, we should not know what sense to make of other goods to which we are committed and for which we feel very genuine concern. If it is to maintain itself under reasonable examination as a valid ideal for conduct, the possibility it pictures must be a real one—not the "categorical imperative crying in the wilderness" of Santayana's ironic portrayal. It must, that is to say, be reasonably probable that if we acknowledge its claims and act upon them within the limits set by the specific conditions under which action takes place, we can in fact make actual in some measure the goods it promises. No community humanly attainable may in this sense ever be as good as it ideally ought to be; but if concern for what it ought to be is a considerable factor in the direction of policy, it may be considerably better—nearer to what it ought to be—than it would have been if no such ideal had been acknowledged. That is the way in which norms or ideals work in human conduct, when they work at all, and it is the business of practical reason to judge them in their capacity to fulfil this function.

The good thus realized . . . will still be the good for which our *de facto* concerns and interests provide the material, and the satisfaction it promises will have to be one in which they are satisfied. What is claimed here is that when these concerns are judged as those of a responsible self or person nothing short of such a moral order will satisfy them. It is better to be Socrates dissatisfied than a fool satisfied only if one would rather be a Socrates than a fool, and share in the never finished quest for an excellence that fools would hardly feel the lack of. Socrates, too, might have been satisfied with the pleasures of the fool, but he would have had to be a fool to be thus satisfied. "And suppose a man actually is thus satisfied," the objector queries, "how are you going to prove that he is wrong?" For my own part, I should not attempt to do so. If there is nothing in him that rejects that alternative, if he really can be satisfied in it, then for him it is the best available. A fool's paradise may be a paradise indeed, for a fool. But a man in full possession of his faculties could not live well in it. The principle of moral freedom, like any other moral maxim, is addressed, in the last analysis, to whom it may concern. What I do contend, however, and my confidence in the worth of political freedom rests upon it, is that most men under decently human conditions are by no means such fools as social scientists and cynics frequently take them to be, and that, in consequence, the ideal proposed by practical reason for a just ordering of satisfactions in a community in which each man is respected as a person and no one among them serves merely as a tool or instrument to the satisfactions of others is, for them, a relevant and reasonable ideal. The function of reason here is not to report to fallen human nature a good of which it would otherwise have no inkling, but to bring clarity, comprehensiveness and order to concerns already at work and to enable those who follow it to know themselves and what they are trying to do. It cries not, as Santayana suggests, in the wilderness, but in the hearts and minds of men, and there sometimes and to some extent it finds an answer.

[IV.] THE GOOD OF FREEDOM

. . . It is beyond my purpose, as it is beyond my powers, to catalogue the various meanings of the term "freedom," each of which may, in its own context, be legitimate and even enlightening. There is one use of it, however, which is directly relevant to our present interest. A man is said to be morally free when his decision on issues that confront him is his own decision and action consequent upon it the expression of his own will, and when he is prepared to accept the responsibility for both decision and action as his own. That does not mean that his choice is arbitrary, capricious or uncaused. On the contrary, he will normally want to show that he had good ground for deciding as he did, and will adduce his concern to act rightly or fairly and his understanding of what, under the circumstances *was* right and fair, as the determining factors in his decision. If, on the other hand, he was shown that his action had resulted from motives fighting it out for supremacy in his consciousness, the most urgent finally winning out and thereby proving its dominance, he would be inclined to say that, on that showing, it was not *he* who had decided at all, but that the decision was something that happened to him, like a toothache or a broken leg. It is no wonder that psychologists who describe human choices in this fashion can make little sense of the notion of moral freedom. The ideas of moral freedom and moral personality are inextricably bound together. A man is acting freely, in this sense, when he decides and acts for himself, makes up his own mind and acts in his own person. A free decision need not be uncaused or self-caused, as has mistakenly been supposed, but it must be caused by the self and therefore not fully determined apart from the specific contribution which the man *as a self* or person makes to its determination.

In the context of moral action, an individual is or becomes a person in so far as he is capable of giving laws to himself, as Rousseau expressed it. That does not mean that he always acts rightly, or is free only when he so acts. What it means is that he acts in such cases as a self or person, and it is to him in this capacity that the action is properly imputed, not to his body, or his fright in early childhood, or the economic system of which he is a part. All these, no doubt, have helped to make him what he is, but what they have helped to bring into being is not just a healthy or twisted body, or a grown-up but still frightened child, or a human by-product of machine industry, but a person capable of reaching his own decisions and demanding for himself and others the right so to decide. The growth of a self, the achievement of human freedom, is one of the most remarkable things that happen in the world, and it is no wonder that much mystery has been made of it. For those who can "rationalize" a process only by reducing it to its causal antecedents, growth is always a mystery, and there will always, I suppose, be those who insist it does not happen because they cannot find the means to understand it. But it does happen, none the less, and is a mystery only for those who insist on interpreting it in other categories than its own. And when it happens men are free, not because they are uninfluenced by anything outside themselves, or insulated causally from their environment, but because what these causes converge upon is a self that acts in its own person, and for ends that it judges to be, under the conditions which the environment sets, the best attainable.

This is a quite special way in which human beings act, and under special conditions. Of a freedom that should function independently of such a way of acting in such conditions we know so little that metaphysicians are at liberty to speculate about it in almost any manner that they please, and skeptics to deny its existence with impunity. But of the freedom which manifests itself in responsible choice we know a good deal, and it is by no means a matter of indifference what we think or say about it. For when we ask what the good of democracy is, or what the reason for preferring a government that preserves the legal right of its citizens to think and to worship as they will, to its totalitarian rival, we shall hardly get an answer that will stand inspection until we reach the point of saying that it is a good thing to foster the conditions in which men are encouraged to make up their own minds on essential issues, because the kind of people who can and will make up their own minds and take the responsibility for their own actions are the kind of people we want and are determined to be. Nothing that a government can offer its citizens—or subjects—is in the long run worth as much as the character and capacities of men who are men enough to judge it, and themselves, by the best they know and to act as their judgment dictates. No political agency can by legal action create that kind of men. But it can maintain the political conditions under which its citizens have a chance to grow to that stature, and it ought to do so. If any one assures us that he has found out from science, or philosophy, or any other respectable source, that *this* kind of freedom is impossible, or "unreal" or unimportant, we shall want to scrutinize his statements very carefully indeed. We must respect "the facts," wherever we find them, in so far as they *are* facts as they claim to be, and are relevant to the issues we are discussing. . . . We . . . know, at least, what *we* mean by the freedom we value, and why we value it. It is bound up with the capacity for cooperative

action on that level of understanding and good will which we rightly regard as of preeminent human value. We cannot give it up without surrendering with it, not only our right to be respected as persons, but our
self-respect as well. There is no denying that many have made this surrender. What can be questioned is whether, if they still had the capacity
to act as free men, they chose well or wisely in so doing. This is a question
not of psychology, or of political science, or of logical analysis, but of
morals; it concerns the comparative worth of things and persons, and it is
only from a standpoint from which the worth of persons has a meaning
and men are valued for what they are, or can become, rather than for what
can be got out of them, that an unequivocal answer can be given. Those
for whom this standpoint has no cogency and no "reality" will not know
what we are talking about when we say that freedom as we understand it is
more than a political convenience, that it is in fact a spiritual necessity, one
of the things men live by on the only level on which they can with human
dignity consent to live, and that its willful surrender is not just a bargain,
good or bad under varying conditions, but a betrayal. We cannot argue
with them about that, if they have been honest in what they say. But if
they go on to claim that, without understanding this, they are competent
to say what democracy is and what it is worth to those who honor it, they
will be mistaken, nor can the wealth of their factual information com-
pensate here for the poverty of their moral understanding.

The good, then, with which practical reason is concerned, cannot adequately be understood merely as the satisfaction of assorted interests and
drives or, when these conflict, of the most primitive or dominant among
them. The good that is reasonably sought by free men cannot be less than
an *order* of satisfactions, which is also a moral order. You cannot here
judge the worth of the satisfaction apart from the worth of the self that is
satisfied. Nor is the standard that judges the worth of individuals in terms
of their capacity for selfhood in a moral community—a kingdom of ends—
an external and transcendent one, imposed from without upon a human
nature directed to a different good. It is a standard meaningful for those
who can find in it an adequate expression of concerns and aspirations already strongly felt but incapable, apart from the articulation it provides, of
understanding themselves and the conditions of their comprehensive satisfaction. These concerns count as basic, not through their primitive urgency
or pervasiveness throughout the animal kingdom, but through their centrality in the organization of the kind of life in which men can will and act
freely, or as persons. The good they define corresponds, in consequence,
not to what the human animal always and everywhere is, nor to anything
that could be found out about him by psychological tests of backward

children, but to what he can become, and wills to become, when he understands himself and his purposes and can be satisfied with nothing less than the best of which he is capable. It is, in other words, an ideal, and it is in the capacity of human nature, sometimes and under fortunate conditions, to respond to ideals and to act wisely in terms of them, that its cogency is to be sought. It is, once more, not surprising that those who have looked for it elsewhere have failed to find it. . . .

[V.] THE MEANING OF RATIONAL MORALITY

. . . We have been trying in this chapter to specify the context in which and the considerations with respect to which a distinction between good and bad conduct can reasonably be made out. To make this distinction as justly as possible is precisely the task of practical reason, and conduct is reasonable to the extent to which it follows the guidance which, in this matter, a right judgment of the issues of conduct and the worth of the way of living to which they commit us, can supply. To judge wisely of the worth of conduct, we have said, we need to know what we want when we *do* know what we want, when, that is, we adequately understand our own purposes and the conditions of their joint satisfaction. Among these conditions none are more central than those imposed by our concern that rules of fair dealing and equity be observed and that men enjoy not merely what they want, but what they are entitled to. When this concern operates at a distinctively moral level it finds expression in qualities of character which are valued, not only as means to further satisfactions, but as in their own right a fulfilment of the good of which human nature at its best is capable. It is in terms of the worth of persons, thus specified, that the good of freedom can be understood and the centrality of the values bound up with it established. This good, however, is a good of and for individuals who work together in a natural world; it is expressed not in moral self-admiration but in responsible action, and the worth of action is to be determined not only by the excellence of its intention but by the chances that it actually can contribute, more reliably than available alternatives, to the good it professes to seek. No man is as good as he ought to be unless, within the limits of his capacity and condition, he is doing his best, and no man is doing his best unless he has used such intelligence as he has, as well as his "conscience," to guide him in making his action appropriate to and effective in the circumstances of its performance. Bungling is not a moral virtue, and neither is fanaticism. Action that combines good judgment and good will in responsibly shared work for a sharable good comes near enough, for our purposes, to a definition of what we mean by conduct that meets the requirements of rational morality. It is not offered here as a new

identification of "the good," for which moral philosophers have traditionally been searching. There are other goods besides the good of moral conduct; and if moral conduct did not aid in the attainment of these other
goods, its own excellence would be without root or basis in the world. It is
offered simply as an indication of what we are to look for in conduct
whose claim to moral excellence can stand rational examination, and what,
therefore, we are doing when we apply reason significantly in the field of
morals. . . .

• 48 •

CAN WE DISPUTE ABOUT TASTES? *

Monroe C. Beardsley (1915–)

We are assured by an old and often-quoted maxim,** whose authority
is not diminished by its being cast in Latin, that there can be no disputing
about tastes. The chief use of this maxim is in putting an end to disputes
that last a long time and don't appear to be getting anywhere. And for this
purpose it is very efficacious, for it has an air of profound finality, and it
also seems to provide a democratic compromise of a deadlocked issue. If
you can't convince someone that he is wrong, or bring yourself to admit
that he is right, you can always say that neither of you is more wrong than
the other, because nobody can be right.

Remarks that serve to close some people's debates, however, are quite
often just the remarks to start a new one among philosophers. And this
maxim is no exception. It has been given a great deal of thought, some of
it very illuminating; yet there is still something to be learned from further
reflection upon it. Nor is it of small importance to know, if we can, whether
the maxim is true or false, for if it is true we won't waste time in futile
discussion, and if it is false we won't waste opportunities for fruitful discussion.

The question whether tastes are disputable is one to be approached with
wariness. The first thing is to be clear about what it really means. There
are two key words in it that we should pay particular attention to.

* Reprinted from the *Swarthmore College Bulletin*, Alumni Issue, October 1958, with
the kind permission of the author and the editor. Compare with selection 45.
** *De gustibus non est disputandum.*

The first is the word "taste." The maxim is perhaps most readily and least doubtfully applied to taste in its primary sensory meaning: some people like ripe olives, some green; some people like turnips, others cannot abide them; some people will go long distances for pizza pies, others can hardly choke them down. And there are no disputes about olives: we don't find two schools of thought, the Ripe Olive School and the Green Olive School, publishing quarterly journals or demanding equal time on television—probably because there simply isn't much you can say about the relative merits of these comestibles.

But we apply the word "taste," of course, more broadly. We speak of a person's taste in hats and neckties; we speak of his taste in poetry and painting and music. And it is here that the *non disputandum* maxim is most significantly applied. Some people like Auden and others Swinburne, some enjoy the paintings of Jackson Pollock and others avoid them when they can, some people are panting to hear Shostakovitch's latest symphony and others find no music since Haydn really satisfying. In these cases, unlike the olive case, people are generally not at a loss for words: there is plenty you can say about Shostakovitch, pro or con. They talk, all right; they may praise, deplore, threaten, cajole, wheedle, and scream—but, according to the maxim, they do not really dispute.

This brings us, then, to the second key word. What does it mean to say that we cannot *dispute* about tastes in literature, fine arts, and music, even though we can clearly make known our tastes? It certainly doesn't mean that we cannot disagree, or differ in taste: for obviously we do, and not only we but also the acknowledged or supposed experts in these fields. Consider James Gould Cozzens' novel, *By Love Possessed*, which appeared in August, 1957; consult the critics and reviewers to discover whether it is a good novel. Being a serious and ambitious work by a writer of standing, and also a best seller, it provoked unusually forthright judgments from a number of reviewers and critics . . . "Masterpiece . . . brilliant . . . distinguished . . . high order . . . mediocre . . . bad;" that just about covers the spectrum of evaluation.

The International Council of the Museum of Modern Art recently took a large collection of American abstract expressionist paintings on tour in Europe. Its reception was reported in *Time*. In Spain some said, "If this is art, what was it that Goya painted?" and others cheered its "furious vitality" and "renovating spirit." In Italy one newspaper remarked, "It is not painting," but "droppings of paint, sprayings, burstings, lumps, squirts, whirls, rubs and marks, erasures, scrawls, doodles and kaleidoscope backgrounds." In Switzerland it was an "artistic event" that spoke for the genius of American art. And of course all these judgments could be found in this country too.

Not a dispute? Well, what is a dispute? Let us take first the plainest case of a disagreement (no matter what it is about): two people who say, " 'Tis so!" and " 'Taint so!" Let them repeat these words as often as they like, and shout them from the housetops; they still haven't got a dispute going, but merely a contradiction, or perhaps an altercation. But let one person say, " 'Tis so!" and give a *reason* why 'tis so—let him say, "Jones is the best candidate for Senator because he is tactful, honest, and has had much experience in government." And let the other person say, " 'Taint so!" and give a reason why 'taint so—"Jones is not the best candidate, because he is too subservient to certain interests, indecisive and wishy-washy in his own views, and has no conception of the United States' international responsibilities." *Then* we have a dispute—that is, a disagreement in which the parties give reasons for their contentions. Of course this is not all there is to it; the dispute has just begun. But we see how it might continue, each side giving further reasons for its own view, and questioning whether the reasons given by the other are true, relevant, and compelling.

It is this kind of thing that counts as a dispute about the possibility of getting to the moon, about American intervention in the Middle East, about a Supreme Court decision, or anything else. And if we can dispute about these things, why not about art?

But here is where the *non disputandum* maxim would draw the line. We do not speak (or not without irony) about people's tastes in Senatorial candidates or missile policies (if the President replied to critics by saying, "Well, your taste is for speeding up the missile program and spending money, but that's not to my taste," we would feel he ought to back up his opinion more than that). Nor do we speak of tastes in international affairs, or laws, or constitutions. And that seems to be because we believe that judgments on these matters can be, and ought to be, based on good reasons—not that they always are, of course. To prefer a democratic to a totalitarian form of government is *not* just a matter of taste, though to like green olives better than ripe olives is a matter of taste, and we don't require the green olive man to rise and give his reasons, or even to *have* reasons. What kind of reasons could he have? "Green olives are better because they are green" would not look like much of a reason to the ripe olive devotee.

The question, then, is whether a preference for Picasso or Monteverdi is more like a preference for green olives or like a preference for a Senatorial candidate: is it *arguable?* can it be *reasoned?*

When we read what critics and reviewers have to say about the things they talk about, we cannot doubt that they do not merely praise or blame, but defend their judgments by giving reasons, or what they claim to be reasons. The judgments of *By Love Possessed* . . . are supplied with arguments, some of them with long arguments dealing in detail with the plot, style, characterization, structure, underlying philosophy, attitudes towards Catholics, Jews, and Negroes, and other aspects of the novel. Collect a number of these reviews together and it certainly *reads* like a dispute. Or here is one person who says, "Mozart's Quintet in E Flat Major for Piano and Winds (K. 452) is a greater piece of music than Beethoven's Quintet in E Flat Major for Piano and Winds (Op. 16) because it has greater melodic invention, subtlety of texture, a more characteristic scoring for the wind instruments, and a more expressive slow movement." And here is his friend, who replies, "The Beethoven quintet is greater because it has richer sonority, greater vigor and vitality, and a more powerful dynamic spirit." There's a dispute, or something that looks very much like one.

But according to the Aesthetic Skeptic—if I may choose this convenient name for the upholder of the "no disputing" doctrine—this is an illusion. The apparent reasons are not genuine reasons, or cannot be compelling reasons, like the ones we find in other fields. For in the last analysis they rest upon sheer liking or disliking, which is not susceptible of rational discussion. The defender of the Mozart Quintet, for example, seems to be trying to prove his point, but what he is actually doing (says the Skeptic) is better put this way: "*If* you like subtle texture and expressiveness in slow movements, *then* you (like me) will prefer the Mozart quintet." But what if his friend cares more for vigor and vitality? Then the so-called "argument" is bound to leave him cold. He can only reply, "*If* you like vigor and vitality, as I do, *then* you would prefer the Beethoven quintet." But this is no longer a dispute; they are talking completely at cross purposes, not even contradicting each other.

The Aesthetic Skeptic would analyze all apparent disputes among critics in these terms: the critic can point out features of the novel, the abstract expressionist painting, the quintet for winds, but when he does this he is taking for granted, what may not be true, that you happen to like these features. You can't, says the Skeptic, argue anybody into liking something he doesn't like, and that's why there's no disputing about tastes; all disputes are in the end useless.

Now this view, which I have here stated in a fairly rough way, can be worked out into a sophisticated and impressive position, and if it is mistaken, as I believe it is, its mistakes are not childish or simple-minded. Consequently, I cannot pretend to give here an adequate treatment of it. But I should like to consider briefly some of the difficulties in Aesthetic

Skepticism, as I see it, and point out the possibility of an alternative theory.

The Skeptical theory takes people's likes and dislikes as ultimate and unappealable facts about them; when two people finally get down to saying "I like X" and "I don't like X" (be it the flavor of turnip or subtlety of texture in music), there the discussion has to end, there the dispute vanishes. But though it is true that you can't change a disliking into a liking by arguments, that doesn't imply that you can't change it at all, or that we cannot argue whether or not it *ought* to be changed. . . . Appreciation isn't something you do if you just decide to. But the fact remains that one person can give reasons to another why he would be better off if he *could* enjoy music or painting that he now abhors, and sometimes the other person can set about indirectly, by study and enlarged experience, to change his own tastes, or, as we say, to improve them. There is not just your taste and mine, but better and worse taste; and this doesn't mean just that I have a taste for my taste, but not yours—I might in fact have a distaste for the limitations of my own taste (though that is a queer way to put it). It is something like a person with deep-rooted prejudices, to which he has been conditioned from an early age; perhaps he cannot quite get rid of them, no matter how he tries, and yet he may acknowledge in them a weakness, a crippling feature of his personality, and he may resolve that he will help his children grow up free from them.

The Skeptic does not allow for the possibility that we might give reasons why a person would be better off if he liked or disliked *By Love Possessed* in the way, and to the degree, that it deserves to be liked or disliked. Sometimes, I think, he really holds that it would not be worth the trouble. After all, what does it matter whether people like green olives or ripe olives? We can obtain both in sufficient supply, and nothing much depends upon it as far as the fate of the world is concerned. That's another reason why we ordinarily don't speak of Senatorial candidates as a matter of taste—unless we want to be disparaging, as when people speak of the President's choice in Secretaries of State, to imply that he has no good reason for his choice. It does matter who is Senator, or Secretary of State—it matters a great deal. But what about music, painting, and literature? . . .

Now of course, if we are thinking of our two musical disputants about the relative merits of the two quintets, this is a dispute we may safely leave alone. Both quintets are of such a high order that it perhaps doesn't matter enormously which we decide to rank higher than the other, though there's no harm in trying to do this, if we wish. But the question about *By Love Possessed* is whether it is a "masterpiece" or "bad"; and the question about the paintings is whether they ought to be shown abroad at all. It may not matter so very much whether a person on the whole admires Mozart or Beethoven more, but what if he cannot make up his mind between Mozart and Strauss, or between Beethoven and Shostakovitch?

The fact is that the prevailing level of taste in the general public matters a great deal to me, for it has a great deal to do with determining what I shall have the chance to read, what movies will be filmed, shown, or censored, what music will be played most availably on the radio, what plays will be performed on television. And it has a great deal to do with what composers and painters and poets will do, or whether some of them will do anything at all. But more than that, even: if I am convinced that the kind of experiences that can only be obtained by access to the greatest works is an important ingredient of the richest and most fully-developed human life, then do I not owe it to others to try to put that experience within their reach, or them within its reach? It might be as important to them as good housing, good medical and dental care, or good government.

But here is another point at which the Skeptic feels uneasy. Isn't it undemocratic to go around telling other people that they have crude tastes— wouldn't it be more in keeping with our laissez-faire spirit of tolerance, and less reminiscent of totalitarian absolutism and compulsion, to let others like and enjoy what they like and enjoy? Isn't this their natural right?

There are too many confusions in this point of view to clear them all up briefly. But some of them are worth sorting out. Of course it is a person's right to hear the music he enjoys, provided it doesn't bother other people too much. But it is no invasion of his right, if he is willing to consider the problem, to try to convince him that he should try to like other things that appear to deserve it. . . .

The distinction that many Skeptics find it hard to keep in mind is this: I may hold that there *is* a better and a worse in music and novels without at all claiming that *I know for certain* which are which. Those critics and reviewers who pronounced their judgments on *By Love Possessed* are not necessarily dogmatic because they deny that it's all a matter of taste (even though some of them were more positive than they had a right to be). They believe that some true and reasonable judgment of the novel is in principle possible, and that objective critics, given time and discussion, could in principle agree, or come close to agreeing, on it. But they do not have to claim infallibility—people can be mistaken about novels, as they can about anything else. Works of art are complicated. There need be nothing totalitarian about literary criticism, and there is nothing especially democratic in the view that nobody is wrong because there is no good or bad to be wrong about.

It would help us all, I think, to look at the problem of judging works of art in a more direct way. These judgments, as can easily be seen in any random collection of reviews, go off in so many directions that it sometimes seems that the reviewers are talking about different things. We must keep our eye on the object—the painting, the novel, the quintet. Because the composer's love affairs were in a sorry state at the time he was composing, people think that the value of the music must somehow be connected with this circumstance. Because the painter was regarding his model while he painted, people think that the value of the painting must depend on some relation to the way she really looked, or felt. Because the novelist is known to be an anarchist or a conservative, people think that the value of the novel must consist partly in its fidelity to these attitudes. Now, of course, when we approach a work of art, there are many kinds of interest that we can take in it, as well as in its creator. But when we are trying to judge it *as* a work of art, rather than as biography or social criticism or something else, there is a central interest that ought to be kept in view.

A work of art, whatever its species, is an object of some kind—something somebody made. And the question is whether it was worth making, what it is good for, what can be done with it. In this respect it is like a tool. Tools of course are production goods, instrumental to other instruments, whereas paintings and musical compositions and novels are consumption goods, directly instrumental to some sort of experience. And their own peculiar excellence consists, I believe, in their capacity to afford certain valuable kinds and degrees of aesthetic experience. Of course they do not yield this experience to those who cannot understand them, just as a tool is of no use to one who has not the skill to wield it. But we do not talk in the Skeptical way about tools: we do not say that the value of a hammer is all a matter of taste, some people having a taste for hammering nails, some not. No, the value resides in its capability to drive the nail, given a hand and arm with the right skill, and if the need should arise. And this value it would have, though unrealized, even if the skill were temporarily lost.

So with works of art, it seems to me. Their value is what they can do to and for us, if we are capable of having it done. And for those who do not, or not yet, have this capacity, it is not a simple fact that they do not, but a misfortune, and the only question is whether, or to what extent, it can be remedied. It is because this question sometimes has a hopeful answer that we dispute, and must dispute, about tastes. When the political disputant gives his reasons for supporting one Senatorial candidate over another, he cites facts about that candidate that he knows, from past experience, justify the hope of a good performance—the hope that the candidate, once elected, will do what a Senator is supposed to do, well. When the critic gives his reasons for saying that a work of art is good or bad, he is not, as the Skeptic claims, trying to guess whom it will please or displease; he is pointing out those features of the work—its qualities, structure, style, and so on—that are evidence of the work's ability or inability to provide qualified readers, listeners, or viewers, with a deep aesthetic experience.

PART VII

POLITICAL PHILOSOPHY

• 49 •

MORALITY AND POLITICS *
Immanuel Kant (1724–1804)

. . . True politics can never take a step, without having previously rendered homage to morality; united with this, it is no longer a difficult or complicated art; morality cuts the knot which politics is incapable of untying, whenever they are in opposition to each other. The rights of man ought to be religiously respected, even if sovereigns in maintaining them should have to make the greatest sacrifices. One cannot compromise here between right and utility; politics must bend the knee before morality. But by this means it may also expect insensibly to attain to an eminence, where it will shine with an immortal glory. . . .

When I represent to myself, according to the usage of the lawyers, the public right, in all its habitual associations with the relations of the individuals of a state, and of states among themselves; if I then make an abstraction of all the material of right, there still remains to me a form, which is essential to it, that of publicity. Without publicity there can be no justice, for justice can be conceived of only as being able to be rendered public, and there would then no longer be right, since right is founded only on justice. Each juridical claim ought to be capable of being made public; and as it is very easy to judge in each case, if the principles of one who acts would bear publicity, this possibility itself may commodiously serve as a purely intellectual criterion, in order to discover by reason alone, the injustice of a juridical claim.

I understand by the material of civil and public right, all that experience alone can make us add to its idea (such as, for instance, the pretended wickedness of human nature, which necessarily requires constraint). Let us abstract from all that, and we shall then have a transcendental formula of public right:

All the actions, relative to the right of another, whose maxims are not capable of publicity, are unjust.

* Appendix II (and the last paragraph of Appendix I) of *Perpetual Peace* (1795), with a few minor omissions, in the original (anonymous) translation of 1796, as revised by the editors. The title of this selection has been supplied by the editors. Compare with selection 41.

This principle is not only moral, and essential to the doctrine of virtue; it is likewise juridical and equally respects the right of men. For a maxim which I dare not divulge, without defeating my own ends, which absolutely requires secrecy in order to succeed, and which I cannot publicly avow, without arming all others against my projects; such a maxim can owe only to the injustice with which it menaces others, the infallible and universal opposition of which reason forsees the absolute necessity.

Furthermore, this principle is merely negative; it only serves for the detection of what is contrary to the rights of others. Like an axiom, it is certain without demonstration; and it is easily applied, as may be seen from the following applications of it.

1. In civil law a question occurs, considered as very difficult of solution, which the transcendental principle of publicity immediately decides; i.e. do a people act consistently with right, in shaking off by rebellion the yoke of a tyrant? The rights of the people are violated; but no wrong is done to the tyrant by dethroning him; that is beyond a doubt. It is nonetheless true, that the subjects are in the highest degree wrong in pursuing their right in this manner, and that they cannot complain of injustice, if, subdued in the struggle, they afterwards suffer in consequence thereof the severest punishments.

If one wishes to decide the question by a dogmatic deduction of rights, one will argue a long time for and against; but our transcendental principle of public right frees us from all these difficulties.

According to this principle, a people would ask itself, prior to the institution of the social contract, whether, on a given occasion, it dare publish the design it might entertain of revolting. It is manifest that if, in founding a constitution, a people reserved to itself the condition of being able, in a supposed case, to employ force against its chief, it would assume a legitimate power over him; but then the chief would cease to be chief; or if it wished to make this condition a clause of the constitution, this would be impossible, and the people would fail of its end. The injustice of rebellion then is manifest, inasmuch as publicity would render the maxim which permits it impracticable; as a consequence it would be necessary to keep it secret. Now, it would not be thus with the chief of the state; he can boldly declare that he will inflict the punishment of death upon every author of revolt even when the conspirators might imagine that the chief has first violated the fundamental law of the civil constitution; the chief must enjoy an irresistible and inviolable power, since he could not have the right to command each, if he had not the power to protect each against the others. For feeling himself invested with this power, he has no longer to fear acting hostily to his own views in making his maxims public. A consequence not less evident of this principle is, that if the people succeed in its revolt, the chief, re-entering into the class of subjects, would not then be entitled to begin a new rebellion, in order to re-ascend the throne; nor need he fear being summoned to render an account of his preceding administration.

2. The right of nations supposes a juridical state; for being a public right, it includes already in its notion the declaration of rights which the general will assigns to each. This juridical state ought to result from an antecedent pact, founded, not upon the laws of constraint, like the civil pact, but upon a free and permanent association, such as a federation of states. . . .

In the state of nature, and without a sort of juridical state, which might unite among themselves the diverse physical and moral persons, there can exist only individual right. Now, it is equally evident, that there exists between politics and morality, which have respect to right, an opposition easily removed, if one applies thereto the principle of publicity. I suppose, however, that the federation of nations will have for its object only the maintenance of peace, and not of conquests. The following are the problems in which politics are at variance with morality, and their solution.

a. When one state has promised aid to another, the cession of some province, or subsidies, and the like, the question may arise whether it can retract its promise, in case the safety of the state be endangered, by pretending to consider itself under a double point of view; sometimes as sovereign, free from all responsibility towards the state; sometimes as first public functionary, accountable to its fellow citizens, so that it may retract in this last character engagements entered into in the first.

But if a state, or its chief, rendered this maxim public, all others would naturally avoid treating therewith, or would associate with one another in order to resist its pretensions; which proves that politics, with all its cunning, would of itself, in practising sincerity, defeat its object; and consequently the maxim in question must be unjust.

b. If a power has become formidable by its acquisitions, dare it admit that it will, because it can, oppress others; and have the powers of the second order a right to attack it conjointly, without their having been injured by it? A state which should openly declare this maxim, would only augment the evil, instead of extinguishing it. For the superior power would anticipate the less, and the association of others is only a feeble reed, incapable of resisting any one who well understands the *divide et impera*.* This maxim of politics, rendered notorious, necessarily annihilates of itself its effect, and consequently it is unjust.

* The maxim "divide and govern."

c. When a small state is so situated as to hamper, between the parts of a great state, the communication necessary to its preservation, is not the greater authorized to subject the other, or to incorporate it into itself?

It is easy to perceive, that it ought well to guard against suffering this maxim to be made public before the execution; for, either the small states would form betimes defensive alliances, or other great powers would dispute the prey. Publicity then would render this maxim impracticable; a certain indication that it is unjust. It may likewise be unjust in a very high degree. For, however small the object of an injustice may be, the injustice itself may be very great. . . .

Here then is a characteristic by which we are able to recognize the non-conformity of a maxim of politics to the morality which has relation to right; i.e. the incompatibility of maxims of public right with publicity. It concerns us now to know the conditions under which these maxims *accord* with the right of nations. For it cannot be inferred conversely from the publicity of a maxim that it is just, since no one has need of concealing his plans when he possesses a decided superiority of power.

The first condition necessary to render the public right possible is, in general, the existence of a juridical order. Now . . . there is no other juridical state compatible with the liberty of states, than the federative association for the sole maintenance of peace. The agreement of politics with morality can take place then only by means of a similar association, founded upon intellectual principles of right, and this is consequently necessary. All politics is founded upon this legal federalism, otherwise it is only a refinement of injustice. The jesuits have no casuistry more subtle than has this false policy. It has, first, mental reservations, ambiguities which it knows how adroitly to slip into public treaties, in order to be able afterwards to explain them to its advantage; as, for instance, the distinction between the status quo *de fait et de droit* (in fact and in right). Again, it has probabilism, in attributing hostile intentions to others, and imagining that its probable superiority of power gives it a right to undermine other peaceable states. Lastly, it has its philosophical sin, in regarding it as a very pardonable fault, and perhaps even as a blessing to mankind, that great states should swallow up the lesser ones.

Morality itself is the specious pretext of all these maxims, whose various branches political duplicity knows how to employ to its own ends. Benevolence is a duty as well as respect for the rights of man; but the former is only a conditional duty, while the latter is absolutely necessary. One must be sure of having never violated the latter, before one may give one's self up to the sweet sentiment of benevolence. Politics easily accords with morality, in the former sense of benevolence, in order to be able to abandon the rights of men to their superiors; but as to morality, in the sense of establishing the rights of man, instead of prostrating itself before it, as it ought, politics finds it convenient to combat it and dispute with it all reality, preferring to reduce all duties to benevolence. Now this artifice of gloomy politics would be soon unmasked by the publicity of its maxims, which philosophers would give to open day, if it possessed but the courage to allow them the publication of their principles.

In this view, I propose another transcendental and affirmative principle of public right, whose formula would be:

All maxims which, in order to have their effect, stand in need of publicity, agree with politics and morality combined.

For, if they cannot produce their effect only as far as they are notorious, they must accord with the general end of the public—happiness; consequently they are reconcilable with politics, which is occupied in conceiving a state of things, with which each may be satisfied. And if this end can be attained only by the publicity of the maxims which are proposed, i.e. in removing from them all that is subject to distrust, they must also be conformable to the rights of the public: the only point of union at which the particular ends of all can be made to meet. . . .

• 50 •

THE DANGERS OF MAJORITY RULE *

John C. Calhoun (1782–1850)

[I. THE RIGHT OF SUFFRAGE]

. . . What I propose is . . . to explain on what principles government must be formed in order to resist by its own interior structure—or to use a single term, *organism*—the tendency to abuse of power. . . .

There is but one way in which this can possibly be done, and that is by such an organism as will furnish the ruled with the means of resisting successfully this tendency on the part of the rulers to oppression and abuse. Power can only be resisted by power—and tendency by tendency. Those who exercise power and those subject to its exercise—the rulers and the ruled—stand in antagonistic relations to each other. The same constitution

* Excerpted from *A Disquisition on Government*, published posthumously in 1853. The title of this selection has been supplied by the editors. Compare Part V with selection 53.

of our nature which leads rulers to oppress the ruled—regardless of the object for which government is ordained—will, with equal strength, lead the ruled to resist when possessed of the means of making peaceable and effective resistance. Such an organism, then, as will furnish the means by which resistance may be systematically and peaceably made on the part of the ruled to oppression and abuse of power on the part of the rulers is the first and indispensable step toward *forming* a constitutional government. And as this can only be effected by or through the right of suffrage—the right on the part of the ruled to choose their rulers at proper intervals and to hold them thereby responsible for their conduct—the responsibility of the rulers to the ruled, through the right of suffrage, is the indispensable and primary principle in the *foundation* of a constitutional government. When this right is properly guarded, and the people sufficiently enlightened to understand their own rights and the interests of the community and duly to appreciate the motives and conduct of those appointed to make and execute the laws, it is all-sufficient to give to those who elect effective control over those they have elected.

I call the right of suffrage the indispensable and primary principle, for it would be a great and dangerous mistake to suppose, as many do, that it is, of itself, sufficient to form constitutional governments. . . . So far from being, of itself, sufficient—however well guarded it might be and however enlightened the people—it would, unaided by other provisions, leave the government as absolute as it would be in the hands of irresponsible rulers; and with a tendency, at least as strong, toward oppression and abuse of its power, as I shall next proceed to explain.

The right of suffrage, of itself, can do no more than give complete control to those who elect over the conduct of those they have elected. In doing this, it accomplishes all it possibly can accomplish. This is its aim —and when this is attained, its end is fulfilled. It can do no more, however enlightened the people or however extended or well guarded the right may be. The sum total, then, of its effects, when most successful, is to make those elected the true and faithful representatives of those who elected them—instead of irresponsible rulers, as they would be without it; and thus, by converting it into an agency, and the rulers into agents, to divest government of all claims to sovereignty and to retain it unimpaired to the community. But it is manifest that the right of suffrage in making these changes transfers, in reality, the actual control over the government from those who make and execute the laws of the body of the community and thereby places the powers of the government as fully in the mass of the community as they would be if they, in fact, had assembled, made, and executed the laws themselves without the intervention of representatives or agents. The more perfectly it does this, the more perfectly it accomplishes its ends; but in doing so, it only changes the seat of authority without counteracting, in the least, the tendency of the government to oppression and abuse of its powers.

If the whole community had the same interests so that the interests of each and every portion would be so affected by the action of the government that the laws which oppressed or impoverished one portion would necessarily oppress and impoverish all others—or the reverse—then the right of suffrage, of itself, would be all-sufficient to counteract the tendency of the government to oppression and abuse of its powers, and, of course, would form, of itself, a perfect constitutional government. The interest of all being the same, by supposition, as far as the action of the government was concerned, all would have like interests as to what laws should be made and how they should be executed. All strife and struggle would cease as to who should be elected to make and execute them. The only question would be, who was most fit, who the wisest and most capable of understanding the common interest of the whole. This decided, the election would pass off quietly and without party discord, as no one portion could advance its own peculiar interest without regard to the rest by electing a favorite candidate.

But such is not the case. On the contrary, nothing is more difficult than to equalize the action of the government in reference to the various and diversified interests of the community; and nothing more easy than to pervert its powers into instruments to aggrandize and enrich one or more interests by oppressing and impoverishing the others; and this, too, under the operation of laws couched in general terms and which, on their face, appear fair and equal. Nor is this the case in some particular communities only. It is so in all—the small and the great, the poor and the rich—irrespective of pursuits, productions, or degrees of civilization; with, however, this difference, that the more extensive and populous the country, the more diversified the condition and pursuits of its population; and the richer, more luxurious, and dissimilar the people, the more difficult is it to equalize the action of the government, and the more easy for one portion of the community to pervert its powers to oppress and plunder the other.

Such being the case, it necessarily results that the right of suffrage, by placing the control of the government in the community, must, from the same constitution of our nature which makes government necessary to preserve society, lead to conflict among its different interests—each striving to obtain possession of its powers as the means of protecting itself against the others or of advancing its respective interests regardless of the interests of others. For this purpose, a struggle will take place between the various interests to obtain a majority in order to control the government. If no one interest be strong enough, of itself, to obtain it, a combination will be formed between those whose interests are most alike—each conceding something to the others until a sufficient number is obtained to make a majority. The process may be slow and much time may be required before a compact, organized majority can be thus formed, but formed it will be in time, even without preconcert or design, by the sure workings of that principle or constitution of our nature in which government itself originates. When once formed, the community will be divided into two great parties, a major and minor, between which there will be incessant struggles on the one side to retain, and on the other to obtain the majority and, thereby, the control of the government and the advantages it confers. . . .

As, then, the right of suffrage, without some other provision, cannot counteract this tendency of government, the next question for consideration is, What is that other provision? . . .

[II. THE CONCURRENT MAJORITY]

. . . It is manifest that this provision must be of a character calculated to prevent any one interest or combination of interests from using the powers of government to aggrandize itself at the expense of the others. Here lies the evil: and just in proportion as it shall prevent, or fail to prevent it, in the same degree it will effect, or fail to effect, the end intended to be accomplished. There is but one certain mode in which this result can be secured, and that is by the adoption of some restriction or limitation which shall so effectually prevent any one interest or combination of interests from obtaining the exclusive control of the government as to render hopeless all attempts directed to that end. There is, again, but one mode in which this can be effected, and that is by taking the sense of each interest or portion of the community which may be unequally and injuriously affected by the action of the government separately, through its own majority or in some other way by which its voice may be fairly expressed, and to require the consent of each interest either to put or to keep the government in action. This, too, can be accomplished only in one way, and that is by such an organism of the government—and, if necessary for the purpose, of the community also—as will, by dividing and distributing the powers of government, give to each division or interest, through its appropriate organ, either a concurrent voice in making and executing the laws or a veto on their execution. It is only by such an organism that the assent of each can be made necessary to put the government in motion, or the power made effectual to arrest its action when put in motion; and it is only by the one or the other that the different interests, orders, classes, or portions into which the community may be divided can be protected, and all conflict and struggle between them prevented—by rendering it impossible to put or to keep it in action without the concurrent consent of all.

Such an organism as this, combined with the right of suffrage, constitutes, in fact, the elements of constitutional government. The one, by rendering those who make and execute the laws responsible to those on whom they operate, prevents the rulers from oppressing the ruled; and the other, by making it impossible for any one interest or combination of interests . . . of the community to obtain exclusive control, prevents any one of them from oppressing the other. It is clear that oppression and abuse of power must come, if at all, from the one or the other quarter. From no other can they come. It follows that the two, suffrage and proper organism combined, are sufficient to counteract the tendency of government to oppression and abuse of power and to restrict it to the fulfillment of the great ends for which it is ordained.

In coming to this conclusion I have assumed the organism to be perfect and the different interests, portions, or classes of the community to be sufficiently enlightened to understand its character and object, and to exercise, with due intelligence, the right of suffrage. To the extent that either may be defective, to the same extent the government would fall short of fulfilling its end. But this does not impeach the truth of the principles on which it rests. In reducing them to proper form, in applying them to practical uses, all elementary principles are liable to difficulties, but they are not, on this account, the less true or valuable. Where the organism is perfect, every interest will be truly and fully represented, and of course the whole community must be so. It may be difficult, or even impossible, to make a perfect organism; but, although this be true, yet even when, instead of the sense of each and of all, it takes that of a few great and prominent interests only, it would still, in a great measure, if not altogether, fulfill the end intended by a constitution. For in such case it would require so large a portion of the community, compared with the whole, to concur or acquiesce in the action of the government that the number to be plundered would be too few and the number to be aggrandized too many to afford adequate motives to oppression and the abuse of its powers. Indeed, however imperfect the organism, it must have more or less effect in diminishing such tendency.

It may be readily inferred, from what has been stated, that the effect of organism is neither to supersede nor diminish the importance of the right of suffrage, but to aid and perfect it. The object of the latter is to collect the sense of the community. The more fully and perfectly it accomplishes this, the more fully and perfectly it fulfills its end. But the most it can do, of itself, is to collect the sense of the greater number; that is, of the stronger interests or combination of interests, and to assume this to be the sense of the community. It is only when aided by a proper organism that it can collect the sense of the entire community, of each and all its interests; of each, through its appropriate organ, and of the whole through all of them united. This would truly be the sense of the entire community, for whatever diversity each interest might have within itself—as all would have the same interest in reference to the action of the government—the individuals composing each would be fully and truly represented by its own majority or appropriate organ, regarded in reference to the other interests. In brief, every individual of every interest might trust, with confidence, its majority or appropriate organ against that of every other interest.

It results, from what has been said, that there are two different modes in which the sense of the community may be taken: one, simply by the right of suffrage, unaided; the other, by the right through a proper organism. Each collects the sense of the majority. But one regards numbers only and considers the whole community as a unit having but one common interest throughout, and collects the sense of the greater number of the whole as that of the community. The other, on the contrary, regards interests as well as numbers—considering the community as made up of different and conflicting interests, as far as the action of the government is concerned—and takes the sense of each through its majority or appropriate organ, and the united sense of all as the sense of the entire community. The former of these I shall call the numerical or absolute majority, and the latter, the concurrent or constitutional majority. I call it the constitutional majority because it is an essential element in every constitutional government, be its form what it may. So great is the difference, politically speaking, between the two majorities that they cannot be confounded without leading to great and fatal errors; and yet the distinction between them has been so entirely overlooked that when the term "majority" is used in political discussions, it is applied exclusively to designate the numerical—as if there were no other. . . .

The first and leading error which naturally arises from overlooking the distinction referred to is to confound the numerical majority with the people, and this so completely as to regard them as identical. This is a consequence that necessarily results from considering the numerical as the only majority. All admit that a popular government, or democracy, is the government of the people, for the terms imply this. A perfect government of the kind would be one which would embrace the consent of every citizen or member of the community; but as this is impracticable in the opinion of those who regard the numerical as the only majority and who can perceive no other way by which the sense of the people can be taken, they are compelled to adopt this as the only true basis of popular government, in contradistinction to governments of the aristocractical or monarchical form. Being thus constrained, they are, in the next place, forced to regard the numerical majority as in effect the entire people; that is, the greater part as the whole, and the government of the greater part as the government of the whole. It is thus the two come to be confounded and a part made identical with the whole. And it is thus also that all the rights, powers, and immunities of the whole people come to be attributed to the numerical majority—and, among others, the supreme, sovereign authority of establishing and abolishing governments at pleasure. . . .

If the numerical majority were really the people, and if to take its sense truly were to take the sense of the people truly, a government so constituted would be a true and perfect model of a popular constitutional government; and every departure from it would detract from its excellence. But as such is not the case, as the numerical majority, instead of being the people, is only a portion of them, such a government, instead of being a true and perfect model of the people's government, that is, a people self-governed, is but the government of a part over a part, the major over the minor portion. . . .

. . . I shall next proceed to explain, more fully, why the concurrent majority is . . . to give to each interest or portion of the community a negative on the others. It is this mutual negative among its various conflicting interests which invests each with the power of protecting itself, and places the rights and safety of each where only they can be securely placed, under its own guardianship. Without this there can be no systematic, peaceful, or effective resistance to the natural tendency of each to come into conflict with the others; and without this there can be no constitution. It is this negative power—the power of preventing or arresting the action of the government, be it called by what term it may, veto, interposition, nullification, check, or balance of power—which in fact forms the constitution. They are all but different names for the negative power. In all its forms, and under all its names, it results from the concurrent majority. Without this there can be no negative, and without a negative, no constitution. The assertion is true in reference to all constitutional governments, be their forms what they may. It is, indeed, the *negative* power which makes the constitution, and the *positive* which makes the government. The one is the power of acting, and the other the power of preventing or arresting action. The two, combined, make constitutional governments.

But as there can be no constitution without the negative power, and no negative power without the concurrent majority, it follows necessarily that, where the numerical majority has the sole control of the government, there can be no constitution, as constitution implies limitation or restriction—and, of course, is inconsistent with the idea of sole or exclusive power. And hence the numerical, unmixed with the concurrent, majority necessarily forms, in all cases, absolute government.

It is, indeed, the single or *one power* which excludes the negative and constitutes absolute government, and not the *number* in whom the power is vested. The numerical majority is as truly a *single power*, and excludes the negative as completely as the absolute government of one or of the few. The former is as much the absolute government of the democratic or popular form as the latter of the monarchical or aristocratical. It has, accordingly, in common with them the same tendency to oppression and abuse of power.

Constitutional governments, of whatever form, are, indeed, much more similar to each other in their structure and character than they are, respectively, to the absolute governments, even of their own class. All constitutional governments, of whatever class they may be, take the sense of the community by its parts—each through its appropriate organ—and regard the sense of all its parts as the sense of the whole. They all rest on the right of suffrage and the responsibility of ruler, directly or indirectly. On the contrary, all absolute governments, of whatever form, concentrate power in one uncontrolled and irresponsible individual or body whose will is regarded as the sense of the community. And hence the great and broad distinction between governments is not that of the one, the few, or the many, but of the constitutional and the absolute.

From this there results another distinction which, although secondary in its character, very strongly marks the difference between these forms of government. I refer to their respective conservative principle—that is, the principle by which they are upheld and preserved. This principle in constitutional governments is *compromise*; and in absolute governments is *force.* . . .

[III. FORCE AND COMPROMISE]

. . . Absolute governments, of all forms, exclude all other means of resistance to their authority than that of force, and, of course, leave no other alternative to the governed but to acquiesce in oppression, however great it may be, or to resort to force to put down the government. But the dread of such a resort must necessarily lead the government to prepare to meet force in order to protect itself, and hence, of necessity, force becomes the conservative principle of all such governments.

On the contrary, the government of the concurrent majority, where the organism is perfect, excludes the possibility of oppression by giving to each interest, or portion, or order—where there are established classes—the means of protecting itself by its negative against all measures calculated to advance the peculiar interests of others at its expense. Its effect, then, is to cause the different interests, portions, or orders, as the case may be, to desist from attempting to adopt any measure calculated to promote the prosperity of one, or more, by sacrificing that of others; and thus to force them to unite in such measures only as would promote the prosperity of all, as the only means to prevent the suspension of the action of the government, and, thereby, to avoid anarchy, the greatest of all evils. It is by means of such authorized and effectual resistance that oppression is prevented and the necessity of resorting to force superseded in governments of the concurrent majority; and hence compromise, instead of force, becomes their conservative principle. . . .

. . . The numerical majority will divide the community, let it be ever so homogeneous, into two great parties which will be engaged in perpetual struggles to obtain the control of the government . . . The great importance of the object at stake must necessarily form strong party attachments and party antipathies—attachments on the part of the members of each to their respective parties through whose efforts they hope to accomplish an object dear to all; and antipathies to the opposite party, as presenting the only obstacle to success.

In order to have a just conception of their force it must be taken into consideration that the object to be won or lost appeals to the strongest passions of the human heart—avarice, ambition, and rivalry. It is not then wonderful that a form of government which periodically stakes all its honors and emoluments as prizes to be contended for should divide the community into two great hostile parties; or that party attachments, in the progress of the strife, should become so strong among the members of each respectively as to absorb almost every feeling of our nature, both social and individual; or that their mutual antipathies should be carried to such an excess as to destroy, almost entirely, all sympathy between them and to substitute in its place the strongest aversion. Nor is it surprising that under their joint influence the community should cease to be the common center of attachment or that each party should find that center only in itself. It is thus that in such governments devotion to party becomes stronger than devotion to country—the promotion of the in-

terests of party more important than the promotion of the common good
of the whole, and its triumph and ascendency objects of far greater solici-
tude than the safety and prosperity of the community. It is thus also that
the numerical majority, by regarding the community as a unit and having,
as such, the same interests throughout all its parts, must, by its necessary
operation, divide it into two hostile parts waging, under the forms of
law, incessant hostilities against each other.

The concurrent majority, on the other hand, tends to unite the most
opposite and conflicting interests and to blend the whole in one common
attachment to the country. By giving to each interest, or portion, the
power of self-protection, all strife and struggle between them for ascendency
is prevented, and thereby not only every feeling calculated to weaken the
attachment to the whole is suppressed, but the individual and the social
feelings are made to unite in one common devotion to country. Each sees
and feels that it can best promote its own prosperity by conciliating the
good will and promoting the prosperity of the others. And hence there
will be diffused throughout the whole community kind feelings between
its different portions and, instead of antipathy, a rivalry amongst them to
promote the interests of each other, as far as this can be done consistently
with the interest of all. Under the combined influence of these causes,
the interests of each would be merged in the common interests of the
whole; and thus the community would become a unit by becoming the
common center of attachment of all its parts. And hence, instead of
faction, strife, and struggle for party ascendency, there would be patriotism,
nationality, harmony, and a struggle only for supremacy in promoting the
common good of the whole.

But the difference in their operation, in this respect, would not end here.
Its effects would be as great in a moral as I have attempted to show they
would be in a political point of view. Indeed, public and private morals
are so nearly allied that it would be difficult for it to be otherwise. That
which corrupts and debases the community politically must also corrupt
and debase it morally. The same cause which in governments of the
numerical majority gives to party attachments and antipathies such force
as to place party triumph and ascendency above the safety and prosperity of
the community will just as certainly give them sufficient force to over-
power all regard for truth, justice, sincerity, and moral obligations of every
description. It is, accordingly, found that, in the violent strifes between
parties for the high and glittering prize of governmental honors and emoluments, falsehood, injustice, fraud, artifice, slander, and breach of faith are
freely resorted to as legitimate weapons, followed by all their corrupting
and debasing influences.

In the government of the concurrent majority, on the contrary, the same cause which prevents such strife as the means of obtaining power, and which makes it the interest of each portion to conciliate and promote the interests of the others, would exert a powerful influence toward purifying and elevating the character of the government and the people, morally as well as politically. The means of acquiring power—or, more correctly, influence—in such governments would be the reverse. Instead of the vices by which it is acquired in that of the numerical majority, the opposite virtues—truth, justice, integrity, fidelity, and all others by which respect and confidence are inspired—would be the most certain and effectual means of acquiring it. . . .

[IV. SECURITY AND LIBERTY]

If the two be compared in reference to the ends for which government is ordained, the superiority of the government of the concurrent majority will not be less striking. These, as has been stated, are twofold: to protect and to perfect society. But to preserve society, it is necessary to guard the community against injustice, violence, and anarchy within, and against attacks from without. If it fail in either, it would fail in the primary end of government and would not deserve the name.

To perfect society, it is necessary to develop the faculties, intellectual and moral, with which man is endowed. But the mainspring to their development, and, through this, to progress, improvement, and civilization, with all their blessings, is the desire of individuals to better their condition. For this purpose liberty and security are indispensable. Liberty leaves each free to pursue the course he may deem best to promote his interest and happiness, as far as it may be compatible with the primary end for which government is ordained, while security gives assurance to each that he shall not be deprived of the fruits of his exertions to better his condition. These combined give to this desire the strongest impulse of which it is susceptible. For to extend liberty beyond the limits assigned would be to weaken the government and to render it incompetent to fulfill its primary end—the protection of society against dangers, internal and external. The effect of this would be insecurity; and of insecurity, to weaken the impulse of individuals to better their condition and thereby retard progress and improvement. On the other hand, to extend the powers of the government so as to contract the sphere assigned to liberty would have the same effect, by disabling individuals in their efforts to better their condition.

Herein is to be found the principle which assigns to power and liberty their proper spheres and reconciles each to the other under all circumstances. For if power be necessary to secure to liberty the fruits of its exertions, liberty, in turn, repays power with interest—by increased population, wealth, and other advantages which progress and improvement bestow on the community. By thus assigning to each its appropriate sphere, all conflicts between them cease, and each is made to cooperate with and assist the other in fulfilling the great ends for which government is ordained. . . .

But some communities require a far greater amount of power than others to protect them against anarchy and external dangers; and, of course, the sphere of liberty in such must be proportionally contracted. The causes calculated to enlarge the one and contract the other are numerous and various. Some are physical, such as open and exposed frontiers surrounded by powerful and hostile neighbors. Others are moral, such as the different degrees of intelligence, patriotism, and virtue among the mass of the community, and their experience and proficiency in the art of self-government. Of these, the moral are by far the most influential. A community may possess all the necessary moral qualifications in so high a degree as to be capable of self-government under the most adverse circumstances, while, on the other hand, another may be so sunk in ignorance and vice as to be incapable of forming a conception of liberty or of living, even when most favored by circumstances, under any other than an absolute and despotic government.

The principle in all communities, according to these numerous and various causes, assigns to power and liberty their proper spheres. To allow liberty, in any case, a sphere of action more extended than this assigns would lead to anarchy, and this, probably, in the end to a contraction instead of an enlargement of its sphere. Liberty, then, when forced on a people unfit for it, would, instead of a blessing, be a curse, as it would in its reaction lead directly to anarchy—the greatest of all curses. No people, indeed, can long enjoy more liberty than that to which their situation and advanced intelligence and morals fairly entitle them. If more than this be allowed, they must soon fall into confusion and disorder—to be followed, if not by anarchy and despotism, by a change to a form of government more simple and absolute, and therefore better suited to their condition. And hence, although it may be true that a people may not have as much liberty as they are fairly entitled to and are capable of enjoying, yet the reverse is unquestionably true—that no people can long possess more than they are fairly entitled to.

Liberty, indeed, though among the greatest of blessings, is not so great as that of protection, inasmuch as the end of the former is the progress and improvement of the race, while that of the latter is its preservation and perpetuation. And hence, when the two come into conflict, liberty must, and ever ought, to yield to protection, as the existence of the race is of greater moment than its improvement.

It follows, from what has been stated, that it is a great and dangerous error to suppose that all people are equally entitled to liberty. It is a reward to be earned, not a blessing to be gratuitously lavished on all alike—a reward reserved for the intelligent, the patriotic, the virtuous and deserving, and not a boon to be bestowed on a people too ignorant, degraded, and vicious to be capable either of appreciating or of enjoying it. Nor is it any disparagement to liberty that such is and ought to be the case. On the contrary, its greatest praise, its proudest distinction, is that all-wise Providence has reserved it as the noblest and highest reward for the development of our faculties, moral and intellectual. A reward more appropriate than liberty could not be conferred on the deserving, nor a punishment inflicted on the undeserving more just than to be subject to lawless and despotic rule. This dispensation seems to be the result of some fixed law; and every effort to disturb or defeat it, by attempting to elevate a people in the scale of liberty above the point to which they are entitled to rise, must ever prove abortive and end in disappointment. The progress of a people rising from a lower to a higher point in the scale of liberty is necessarily slow; and by attempting to precipitate, we either retard or permanently defeat it.

[V. EQUALITY AND LIBERTY]

There is another error, not less great and dangerous, usually associated with the one which has just been considered. I refer to the opinion that liberty and equality are so intimately united that liberty cannot be perfect without perfect equality.

That they are united to a certain extent, and that equality of citizens, in the eyes of the law, is essential to liberty in a popular government, is conceded. But to go further and make equality of *condition* essential to liberty would be to destroy both liberty and progress. The reason is that inequality of condition, while it is a necessary consequence of liberty, is at the same time indispensable to progress. In order to understand why this is so, it is necessary to bear in mind that the mainspring to progress is the desire of individuals to better their condition, and that the strongest impulse which can be given to it is to leave individuals free to exert themselves in the manner they may deem best for that purpose, as far at least as it can be done consistently with the ends for which government is ordained, and to secure to all the fruits of their exertions. Now, as individuals differ greatly from each other in intelligence, sagacity, energy, perseverance, skill, habits of industry and economy, physical power, position and opportunity—the necessary effect of leaving all free to exert themselves to better their condition must be a corresponding inequality between those who may possess these qualities and advantages in a high degree and those who may be deficient in them. The only means by which this result can be prevented are either to impose such restrictions on the exertions of those who may possess them in a high degree as will place them on a level with those who do not, or to deprive them of the fruits of their exertions. But to impose such restrictions on them would be destructive of liberty, while to deprive them of the fruits of their exertions would be to destroy the desire of bettering their condition. It is, indeed, this inequality of condition between the front and rear ranks, in the march of progress, which gives so strong an impulse to the former to maintain their position, and to the latter to press forward into their files. This gives to progress its greatest impulse. To force the front rank back to the rear or attempt to push forward the rear into line with the front, by the interposition of the government, would put an end to the impulse and effectually arrest the march of progress.

These great and dangerous errors have their origin in the prevalent opinion that all men are born free and equal—than which nothing can be more unfounded and false. It rests upon the assumption of a fact which is contrary to universal observation, in whatever light it may be regarded. It is, indeed, difficult to explain how an opinion so destitute of all sound reason ever could have been so extensively entertained unless we regard it as being confounded with another which has some semblance of truth, but which, when properly understood, is not less false and dangerous. I refer to the assertion that all men are equal in the state of nature, meaning by a state of nature a state of individuality supposed to have existed prior to the social and political state, and in which men lived apart and independent of each other. If such a state ever did exist, all men would have been, indeed, free and equal in it; that is, free to do as they pleased and exempt from the authority or control of others—as, by supposition, it existed anterior to society and government. But such a state is purely hypothetical. It never did nor can exist, as it is inconsistent with the preservation and perpetuation of the race. It is, therefore, a great misnomer to call it "the state of nature." Instead of being the natural state of man, it is, of all conceivable states, the most opposed to his nature—most repugnant to his feelings and most incompatible with his wants. His natural state is the social and political, the one for which his Creator made him, and the only one in which he can preserve and perfect his race. As, then, there never was such a state as the so-called state of nature, and never can be, it follows that men, instead of being born in it, are born in the social and political state; and of course, instead of being born free and equal, are born subject, not only to parental authority, but to the laws and institutions of the country where born and under whose protection they draw their first breath. . . .

[VI. CONCLUSION]

Such are the many and striking advantages of the concurrent over the numerical majority. Against the former but two objections can be made. The one is that it is difficult of construction . . . and the other that it would be impracticable to obtain the concurrence of conflicting interests where they were numerous and diversified, or, if not, that the process for this purpose would be too tardy to meet with sufficient promptness the many and dangerous emergencies to which all communities are exposed. . . .

The diversity of opinion is usually so great on almost all questions of policy that it is not surprising, on a slight view of the subject, it should be thought impracticable to bring the various conflicting interests of a community to unite on any one line of policy, or that a government founded on such a principle would be too slow in its movements and too weak in its foundation to succeed in practice. But plausible as it may seem at the first glance, a more deliberate view will show that this opinion is erroneous. It is true that, when there is no urgent necessity, it is difficult to bring those who differ to agree on any one line of action. Each will naturally insist on taking the course he may think best, and, from pride of opinion, will be unwilling to yield to others. But the case is different when there is an urgent necessity to unite on some common course of action, as reason and experience both prove. When something *must* be done, and when it can be done only by the united consent of all, the necessity of the case will force to a compromise, be the case of that necessity what it may. On all questions of acting, necessity, where it exists, is the overruling motive; and where, in such cases, compromise among the parties is an indispensable condition to acting, it exerts an overruling influence in predisposing them to acquiesce in some one opinion or course of action. Experience furnishes many examples in confirmation of this important truth. . . .

• 51 •

AUTHORITY AND SOCIETY *

Alexis de Tocqueville (1805–1859)

At different periods dogmatical belief is more or less common. It arises in different ways, and it may change its object and its form; but under no circumstances will dogmatical belief cease to exist, or, in other words, men will never cease to entertain some opinions on trust, and without discussion. If every one undertook to form all his own opinions, and to seek for truth by isolated paths struck out by himself alone, it would follow that no considerable number of men would ever unite in any common belief.

But obviously without such common belief no society can prosper— say, rather, no society can exist; for without ideas held in common, there is no common action, and without common action there may still be men, but there is no social body. In order that society should exist, and, *a fortiori*, that a society should prosper, it is required that all the minds of the citizens should be rallied and held together by certain predominant ideas; and this cannot be the case unless each of them sometimes draws his opinions from the common source, and consents to accept certain matters of belief already formed.

If I now consider man in his isolated capacity, I find that dogmatical belief is not less indispensable to him in order to live alone, than it is to enable him to co-operate with his fellows. If man were forced to demonstrate for himself all the truths of which he makes daily use, his task would never end. He would exhaust his strength in preparatory demonstrations, without ever advancing beyond them. As, from the shortness of his life, he has not the time, nor, from the limits of his intelligence, the capacity, to accomplish this, he is reduced to take upon trust a number of facts and opinions which he has not had either the time or the power to verify for himself, but which men of greater ability have sought out, or which the world adopts. On this groundwork he raises for himself the structure of his own thoughts; he is not led to proceed in this manner by choice, but is constrained by the inflexible law of his condition. There is no philosopher

* From Book I, chapter 2, of the second volume of *Democracy in America* (1840); in the translation by Henry Reeve, as edited by Francis Bowen (1862). The title of this selection has been supplied by the editors. Compare with selections 6, 13, and 52.

of so great parts in the world, but that he believes a million of things on the faith of other people, and supposes a great many more truths than he demonstrates.

This is not only necessary, but desirable. A man who should undertake to inquire into everything for himself, could devote to each thing but little time and attention. His task would keep his mind in perpetual unrest, which would prevent him from penetrating to the depth of any truth, or of grappling his mind firmly to any conviction. His intellect would be at once independent and powerless. He must therefore make his choice from amongst the various objects of human belief, and adopt many opinions without discussion, in order to search the better into that smaller number which he sets apart for investigation. It is true, that whoever receives an opinion on the word of another, does so far enslave his mind, but it is a salutary servitude which allows him to make a good use of freedom.

A principle of authority must then always occur, under all circumstances, in some part or other of the moral and intellectual world. Its place is variable, but a place it necessarily has. The independence of individual minds may be greater, or it may be less: unbounded it cannot be. Thus the question is, not to know whether any intellectual authority exists in the ages of democracy, but simply where it resides and by what standard it is to be measured. . . .

When the ranks of society are unequal, and men unlike one another in condition, there are some individuals wielding the power of superior intelligence, learning, and enlightenment, whilst the multitude are sunk in ignorance and prejudice. Men living at these aristocratic periods are therefore naturally induced to shape their opinions by the standard of a superior person, or superior class of persons, whilst they are averse to recognize the infallibility of the mass of the people.

The contrary takes place in ages of equality. The nearer the people are drawn to the common level of an equal and similar condition, the less prone does each man become to place implicit faith in a certain man or a certain class of men. But his readiness to believe the multitude increases, and opinion is more than ever mistress of the world. Not only is common opinion the only guide which private judgment retains amongst a democratic people, but amongst such a people it possesses a power infinitely beyond what it has elsewhere. At periods of equality, men have no faith in one another, by reason of their common resemblance; but this very resemblance gives them almost unbounded confidence in the judgment of the public; for it would not seem probable, as they are all endowed with equal means of judging, but that the greater truth should go with the greater number.

When the inhabitant of a democratic country compares himself individually with all those about him, he feels with pride that he is the equal of any one of them; but when he comes to survey the totality of his fellows, and to place himself in contrast with so huge a body, he is instantly overwhelmed by the sense of his own insignificance and weakness. The same equality which renders him independent of each of his fellow-citizens, taken severally, exposes him alone and unprotected to the influence of the greater number. The public has therefore, among a democratic people, a singular power, which aristocratic nations cannot conceive of; for it does not persuade to certain opinions, but it enforces them, and infuses them into the intellect by a sort of enormous pressure of the minds of all upon the reason of each.

In the United States, the majority undertakes to supply a multitude of ready-made opinions for the use of individuals, who are thus relieved from the necessity of forming opinions of their own. Everybody there adopts great numbers of theories, on philosophy, morals, and politics, without inquiry, upon public trust; and if we look to it very narrowly, it will be perceived that religion herself holds sway there much less as a doctrine of revelation than as a commonly received opinion.

The fact that the political laws of the Americans are such that the majority rules the community with sovereign sway, materially increases the power which that majority naturally exercises over the mind. For nothing is more customary in man than to recognize superior wisdom in the person of his oppressor. This political omnipotence of the majority in the United States doubtless augments the influence which public opinion would obtain without it over the minds of each member of the community; but the foundations of that influence do not rest upon it. They must be sought for in the principle of equality itself, not in the more or less popular institutions which men living under that condition may give themselves. The intellectual dominion of the greater number would probably be less absolute amongst a democratic people governed by a king, than in the sphere of a pure democracy, but it will always be extremely absolute; and by whatever political laws men are governed in the ages of equality, it may be foreseen that faith in public opinion will become a species of religion there, and the majority its ministering prophet.

Thus intellectual authority will be different, but it will not be diminished; and far from thinking that it will disappear, I augur that it may readily acquire too much preponderance, and confine the action of private judgment within narrower limits than are suited either to the greatness or the happiness of the human race. In the principle of equality I very clearly discern two tendencies; the one leading the mind of every man to untried thoughts, the other which would prohibit him from thinking at all. And I perceive how, under the dominion of certain laws, democracy would extinguish that liberty of the mind to which a democratic social condition is favorable; so that, after having broken all the bondage once imposed on it by ranks or by men, the human mind would be closely fettered to the general will of the greatest number.

If the absolute power of a majority were to be substituted, by democratic nations, for all the different powers which checked or retarded overmuch the energy of individual minds, the evil would only have changed character. Men would not have found the means of independent life; they would simply have discovered (no easy task) a new physiognomy of servitude. There is,—and I cannot repeat it too often,—there is here matter for profound reflection to those who look on freedom of thought as a holy thing, and who hate not only the despot, but despotism. For myself, when I feel the hand of power lie heavy on my brow, I care but little to know who oppresses me; and I am not the more disposed to pass beneath the yoke because it is held out to me by the arms of a million of men.

• 52 •

DEMOCRACY AS A WAY OF LIFE *

John Dewey (1859–1952)

. . . Democracy is much broader than a special political form, a method of conducting government, of making laws and carrying on governmental administration by means of popular suffrage and elected officers. It is that, of course. But it is something broader and deeper than that. The political and governmental phase of democracy is a means, the best means so far found, for realizing ends that lie in the wide domain of human relationships and the development of human personality. It is, as we often say, though perhaps without appreciating all that is involved in the saying, a way of life, social and individual. The key-note of democracy as a way of life may be expressed, it seems to me, as the necessity for the participation of every mature human being in formation of the values that regulate

* Reprinted in part from *School and Society*, April 3, 1937, by permission of The Society for the Advancement of Education, Inc. The title of this selection has been supplied by the editors. Compare with selection 54.

the living of men together: which is necessary from the standpoint of both the general social welfare and the full development of human beings as individuals.

Universal suffrage, recurring elections, responsibility of those who are in political power to the voters, and the other factors of democratic government are means that have been found expedient for realizing democracy as the truly human way of living. They are not a final end and a final value. They are to be judged on the basis of their contribution to the end. It is a form of idolatry to erect means into the end which they serve. Democratic political forms are simply the best means that human wit has devised up to a special time in history. But they rest back upon the idea that no man or limited set of men is wise enough or good enough to rule others without their consent; the positive meaning of this statement is that all those who are affected by social institutions must have a share in producing and managing them. The two facts that each one is influenced in what he does and enjoys and in what he becomes by the institutions under which he lives, and that therefore he shall have, in a democracy, a voice in shaping them, are the passive and active sides of the same fact.

The development of political democracy came about through substitution of the method of mutual consultation and voluntary agreement for the method of subordination of the many to the few enforced from above. Social arrangements which involve fixed subordination are maintained by coercion. The coercion need not be physical. There have existed, for short periods, benevolent despotisms. But coercion of some sort there has been; perhaps economic, certainly psychological and moral. The very fact of exclusion from participation is a subtle form of suppression. It gives individuals no opportunity to reflect and decide upon what is good for them. Others who are supposed to be wiser and who in any case have more power decide the question for them and also decide the methods and means by which subjects may arrive at the enjoyment of what is good for them. This form of coercion and suppression is more subtle and more effective than is overt intimidation and restraint. When it is habitual and embodied in social institutions, it seems the normal and natural state of affairs. The mass usually become unaware that they have a claim to a development of their own powers. Their experience is so restricted that they are not conscious of restriction. It is part of the democratic conception that they as individuals are not the only sufferers, but that the whole social body is deprived of the potential resources that should be at its service. The individuals of the submerged mass may not be very wise. But there is one thing they are wiser about than anybody else can be, and that is where the shoe pinches, the troubles they suffer from.

The foundation of democracy is faith in the capacities of human nature; faith in human intelligence and in the power of pooled and cooperative experience. It is not belief that these things are complete but that if given a show they will grow and be able to generate progressively the knowledge and wisdom needed to guide collective action. Every autocratic and authoritarian scheme of social action rests on a belief that the needed intelligence is confined to a superior few, who because of inherent natural gifts are endowed with the ability and the right to control the conduct of others; laying down principles and rules and directing the ways in which they are carried out. It would be foolish to deny that much can be said for this point of view. It is that which controlled human relations in social groups for much the greater part of human history. The democratic faith has emerged very, very recently in the history of mankind. Even where democracies now exist, men's minds and feelings are still permeated with ideas about leadership imposed from above, ideas that developed in the long early history of mankind. After democratic political institutions were nominally established, beliefs and ways of looking at life and of acting that originated when men and women were externally controlled and subjected to arbitrary power, persisted in the family, the church, business and the school, and experience shows that as long as they persist there, political democracy is not secure.

Belief in equality is an element of the democratic credo. It is not, however, belief in equality of natural endowments. Those who proclaimed the idea of equality did not suppose they were enunciating a psychological doctrine, but a legal and political one. All individuals are entitled to equality of treatment by law and in its administration. Each one is affected equally in quality if not in quantity by the institutions under which he lives and has an equal right to express his judgment, although the weight of his judgment may not be equal in amount when it enters into the pooled result to that of others. In short, each one is equally an individual and entitled to equal opportunity of development of his own capacities, be they large or small in range. Moreover, each has needs of his own, as significant to him as those of others are to them. The very fact of natural and psychological inequality is all the more reason for establishment by law of equality of opportunity, since otherwise the former becomes a means of oppression of the less gifted.

While what we call intelligence be distributed in unequal amounts, it is the democratic faith that it is sufficiently general so that each individual has something to contribute, whose value can be assessed only as enters into the final pooled intelligence constituted by the contributions of all. Every authoritarian scheme, on the contrary, assumes that its value may be assessed by some *prior* principle, if not of family and birth or race and color or possession of material wealth, then by the position and rank a person occupies in the existing social scheme. The democratic faith in equality is the faith that each individual shall have the chance and opportunity to contribute whatever he is capable of contributing and that the value of his contribution be decided by its place and function in the organized total of similar contributions, not on the basis of prior status of any kind whatever.

I have emphasized in what precedes the importance of the effective release of intelligence in connection with personal experience in the democratic way of living. I have done so purposely because democracy is so often and so naturally associated in our minds with freedom of *action*, forgetting the importance of freed intelligence which is necessary to direct and to warrant freedom of action. Unless freedom of individual action has intelligence and informed conviction back of it, its manifestation is almost sure to result in confusion and disorder. The democratic idea of freedom is not the right of each individual to *do* as he pleases, even if it be qualified by adding "provided he does not interfere with the same freedom on the part of others." While the idea is not always, not often enough, expressed in words, the basic freedom is that of freedom of *mind* and of whatever degree of freedom of action and experience is necessary to produce freedom of intelligence. The modes of freedom guaranteed in the Bill of Rights are all of this nature: Freedom of belief and conscience, of expression of opinion, of assembly for discussion and conference, of the press as an organ of communication. They are guaranteed because without them individuals are not free to develop and society is deprived of what they might contribute.

. . . There is some kind of government, of control, wherever affairs that concern a number of persons who act together are engaged in. It is a superficial view that holds government is located in Washington and Albany. There is government in the family, in business, in the church, in every social group. There are regulations, due to custom if not to enactment, that settle how individuals in a group act in connection with one another.

It is a disputed question of theory and practice just how far a democratic political government should go in control of the conditions of action within special groups. At the present time, for example, there are those who think the federal and state governments leave too much freedom of independent action to industrial and financial groups, and there are others who think the government is going altogether too far at the present time. I do not need to discuss this phase of the problem, much less to try to settle it. But it must be pointed out that if the methods of regulation and administration in vogue in the conduct of secondary social groups are non-democratic, whether directly or indirectly or both, there is bound to be an unfavorable reaction back into the habits of feeling, thought and action of citizenship in the broadest sense of that word. The way in which any organized social interest is controlled necessarily plays an important part in forming the dispositions and tastes, the attitudes, interests, purposes and desires, of those engaged in carrying on the activities of the group. For illustration, I do not need to do more than point to the moral, emotional and intellectual effect upon both employers and laborers of the existing industrial system. Just what the effects specifically are is a matter about which we know very little. But I suppose that every one who reflects upon the subject admits that it is impossible that the ways in which activities are carried on for the greater part of the waking hours of the day; and the way in which the share of individuals are involved in the management of affairs in such a matter as gaining a livelihood and attaining material and social security, can not but be a highly important factor in shaping personal dispositions; in short, forming character and intelligence.

In the broad and final sense all institutions are educational in the sense that they operate to form the attitudes, dispositions, abilities and disabilities that constitute a concrete personality. The principle applies with special force to the school. For it is the main business of the family and the school to influence directly the formation and growth of attitudes and dispositions, emotional, intellectual and moral. Whether this educative process is carried on in a predominantly democratic or non-democratic way becomes, therefore, a question of transcendent importance not only for education itself but for its final effect upon all the interests and activities of a society that is committed to the democratic way of life. Hence, if the general tenor of what I have said about the democratic ideal and method is anywhere near the truth, it must be said that the democratic principle requires that every teacher should have some regular and organic way in which he can, directly or through representatives democratically chosen, participate in the formation of the controlling aims, methods and materials of the school of which he is a part. . . .

. . . Absence of participation tends to produce lack of interest and concern on the part of those shut out. The result is a corresponding lack of effective responsibility. Automatically and unconsciously, if not consciously, the feeling develops, "This is none of our affair; it is the business of those at the top; let that particular set of Georges do what needs to be done." The countries in which autocratic government prevails are just those in which there is least public spirit and the greatest indifference to matters of general as distinct from personal concern. Can we expect a different kind of psychology to actuate teachers? Where there is little power, there is correspondingly little sense of positive responsibility. It is enough to do what one is told to do sufficiently well to escape flagrant unfavorable notice. About larger matters, a spirit of passivity is engendered. In some cases, indifference passes into evasion of duties when not directly under the eye of a supervisor; in other cases, a carping, rebellious spirit is engendered. A sort of game is instituted between teacher and supervisor like that which went on in the old-fashioned schools between teacher and pupil. Other teachers pass on, perhaps unconsciously, what they feel to be arbitrary treatment received by them to their pupils.

The argument that teachers are not prepared to assume the responsibility of participation deserves attention, with its accompanying belief that natural selection has operated to put those best prepared to carry the load in the positions of authority. Whatever the truth in this contention, it still is also true that incapacity to assume the responsibilities involved in having a voice in shaping policies is bred and increased by conditions in which that responsibility is denied. I suppose there has never been an autocrat, big or little, who did not justify his conduct on the ground of the unfitness of his subjects to take part in government. I would not compare administrators to political autocrats. Upon the whole, what exists in the schools is more a matter of habit and custom than it is of any deliberate autocracy. But, as was said earlier, habitual exclusion has the effect of reducing a sense of responsibility for what is done and its consequences. What the argument for democracy implies is that the best way to produce initiative and constructive power is to exercise it. Power, as well as interest, comes by use and practice. Moreover, the argument from incapacity proves too much. If it is so great as to be a permanent bar, then teachers can not be expected to have the intelligence and skill that are necessary to execute the directions given them. The delicate and difficult task of developing character and good judgment in the young needs every stimulus and inspiration possible. It is impossible that the work should not be better done when teachers have that understanding of what they are doing that comes from having shared in forming its guiding ideas. . . .

The fundamental beliefs and practices of democracy are now challenged as they never have been before. In some nations they are more than challenged. They are ruthlessly and systematically destroyed. Everywhere there are waves of criticism and doubt as to whether democracy can meet pressing problems of order and security. The causes for the destruction of political democracy in countries where it was nominally established are complex. But of one thing I think we may be sure. Wherever it has fallen it was too exclusively political in nature. It had not become part of the bone and blood of the people in daily conduct of its life. Democratic forms were limited to Parliament, elections and combats between parties. What is happening proves conclusively, I think, that unless democratic habits of thought and action are part of the fiber of a people, political democracy is insecure. It can not stand in isolation. It must be buttressed by the presence of democratic methods in all social relationships. The relations that exist in educational institutions are second only in importance in this respect to those which exist in industry and business, perhaps not even to them.

I recur then to the idea that the particular question discussed is one phase of a wide and deep problem. I can think of nothing so important in this country at present as a rethinking of the whole problem of democracy and its implications. Neither the rethinking nor the action it should produce can be brought into being in a day or year. The democratic idea itself demands that the thinking and activity proceed cooperatively. . . .

• 53 •

LIBERTY AND EQUALITY *

R. H. Tawney (1880–)

Liberty and equality have usually in England been considered antithetic; and, since fraternity has rarely been considered at all, the famous trilogy has been easily dismissed as a hybrid abortion. Equality implies the deliberate acceptance of social restraints upon individual expansion. It involves the prevention of sensational extremes of wealth and power by public action for the public good. If liberty means, therefore, that every individual shall be free, according to his opportunities, to indulge without limit his appetite for either, it is clearly incompatible, not only with economic and social, but with civil and political, equality, which also prevent the strong exploiting to the full the advantages of their strength, and, indeed, with any habit of life save that of the Cyclops. But freedom for the pike is death for the minnows. It is possible that equality is to be con-

* Chapter V, section 2 of *Equality* (4th ed., 1952). Footnotes have been deleted. Reprinted by permission of the publishers, George Allen & Unwin, Ltd., London. Published in the United States by The Macmillan Company, New York. Compare with Part V of selection 50.

trasted, not with liberty, but only with a particular interpretation of it.

The test of a principle is that it can be generalized, so that the advantages of applying it are not particular, but universal. Since it is impossible for every individual, as for every nation, simultaneously to be stronger than his neighbours, it is a truism that liberty, as distinct from the liberties of special persons and classes, can exist only in so far as it is limited by rules, which secure that freedom for some is not slavery for others. The spiritual energy of human beings, in all the wealth of their infinite diversities, is the end to which external arrangements, whether political or economic, are merely means. Hence institutions which guarantee to men the opportunity of becoming the best of which they are capable are the supreme political good, and liberty is rightly preferred to equality, when the two are in conflict. The question is whether, in the conditions of modern society, they conflict or not. It is whether the defined and limited freedom, which alone can be generally enjoyed, is most likely to be attained by a community which encourages violent inequalities, or by one which represses them.

Inequality of power is not necessarily inimical to liberty. On the contrary, it is the condition of it. Liberty implies the ability to act, not merely to resist. Neither society as a whole, nor any group within it, can carry out its will except through organs; and, in order that such organs may function with effect, they must be sufficiently differentiated to perform their varying tasks, of which direction is one and execution another. But, while inequality of power is the condition of liberty, since it is the condition of any effective action, it is also a menace to it, for power which is sufficient to use is sufficient to abuse. Hence, in the political sphere, where the danger is familiar, all civilized communities have established safeguards, by which the advantages of differentiation of function, with the varying degrees of power which it involves, may be preserved, and the risk that power may be tyrannical, or perverted to private ends, averted or diminished. They have endeavoured, for example, as in England, to protect civil liberty by requiring that, with certain exceptions, the officers of the State shall be subject to the ordinary tribunals, and political liberty by insisting that those who take decisions on matters affecting the public shall be responsible to an assembly chosen by it. The precautions may be criticized as inadequate, but the need for precautions is not to-day disputed. It is recognized that political power must rest ultimately on consent, and that its exercise must be limited by rules of law.

The dangers arising from inequalities of economic power have been less commonly recognized. They exist, however, whether recognized or not. For the excess or abuse of power, and its divorce from responsibility, which results in oppression, are not confined to the relations which arise between men as members of a state. They are not a malady which is peculiar to political systems, as was typhus to slums, and from which other departments of life can be regarded as immune. They are a disease, not of political organization, but of organization. They occur, in the absence of preventive measures, in political associations, because they occur in all forms of association in which large numbers of individuals are massed for collective action. The isolated worker may purchase security against exploitation at the cost of poverty, as the hermit may avoid the corruptions of civilization by foregoing its advantages. But, as soon as he is associated with his fellows in a common undertaking, his duties must be specified and his rights defined; and, in so far as they are not, the undertaking is impeded. The problem of securing a livelihood ceases to be merely economic, and becomes social and political. The struggle with nature continues, but on a different plane. Its efficiency is heightened by co-operation. Its character is complicated by the emergence of the question of the terms on which co-operation shall take place.

In an industrial civilization, when its first phase is over, most economic activity is corporate activity. It is carried on, not by individuals, but by groups, which are endowed by the State with a legal status, and the larger of which, in size, complexity, specialization of functions and unity of control, resemble less the private enterprise of the past than a public department. As far as certain great industries are concerned, employment must be found in the service of these corporations, or not at all. Hence the mass of mankind pass their working lives under the direction of a hierarchy, whose heads define, as they think most profitable, the lines on which the common enterprise is to proceed, and determine, subject to the intervention of the State and voluntary organizations, the economic, and to a considerable, though diminishing, extent, the social environment of their employees. Possessing the reality of power, without the decorative trappings —unless, as in England is often the case, it thinks it worth while to buy them—this business oligarchy is the effective aristocracy of industrial nations, and the aristocracy of tradition and prestige, when such still exists, carries out its wishes and courts its favours. In such conditions, authority over human beings is exercised, not only through political, but through economic, organs. The problem of liberty, therefore, is necessarily concerned, not only with political, but also with economic, relations.

It is true, of course, that the problems are different. But to suppose that the abuses of economic power are trivial, or that they are automatically prevented by political democracy, is to be deceived by words. Freedom is always, no doubt, a matter of degree; no man enjoys all the requirements of full personal development, and all men possess some of them. It is not only compatible with conditions in which all men are fellow-servants, but would find in such conditions its most perfect expression. What it excludes is a society where only some are servants, while others are masters.

For, whatever else the idea involves, it implies at least, that no man shall be amenable to an authority which is arbitrary in its proceedings, exorbitant in its demands, or incapable of being called to account when it abuses its office for personal advantage. In so far as his livelihood is at the mercy of an irresponsible superior, whether political or economic, who can compel his reluctant obedience by *force majeure,** whose actions he is unable to modify or resist, save at the cost of grave personal injury to himself and his dependents, and whose favour he must court, even when he despises it, he may possess a profusion of more tangible blessings, from beer to motor-bicycles, but he cannot be said to be in possession of freedom. In so far as an economic system grades mankind into groups, of which some can wield, if unconsciously, the force of economic duress for their own profit or convenience, whilst others must submit to it, its effect is that freedom itself is similarly graded. Society is divided, in its economic and social relations, into classes which are ends, and classes which are instruments. Like property, with which in the past it has been closely connected, liberty becomes the privilege of a class, not the possession of a nation.

Political principles resemble military tactics; they are usually designed for a war which is over. Freedom is commonly interpreted in England in political terms, because it was in the political arena that the most resounding of its recent victories were won. It is regarded as belonging to human beings as citizens, rather than to citizens as human beings; so that it is possible for a nation, the majority of whose members have as little influence on the decisions that determine their economic destinies as on the motions of the planets, to applaud the idea with self-congratulatory gestures of decorous enthusiasm, as though history were of the past, but not of the present. If the attitude of the ages from which it inherits a belief in liberty had been equally ladylike, there would have been, it is probable, little liberty to applaud.

For freedom is always relative to power, and the kind of freedom which at any moment it is most urgent to affirm depends on the nature of the power which is prevalent and established. Since political arrangements may be such as to check excesses of power, while economic arrangements permit or encourage them, a society, or a large part of it, may be both politically free and economically the opposite. It may be protected against

* greater force.

arbitrary action by the agents of government, and be without the security against economic oppression which corresponds to civil liberty. It may possess the political institutions of an advanced democracy, and lack the will and ability to control the conduct of those powerful in its economic affairs, which is the economic analogy of political freedom.

The extension of liberty from the political to the economic sphere is evidently among the most urgent tasks of industrial societies. It is evident also, however, that, in so far as this extension takes place, the traditional antithesis between liberty and equality will no longer be valid. As long as liberty is interpreted as consisting exclusively in security against oppression by the agents of the State, or as a share in its government, it is plausible, perhaps, to dissociate it from equality; for, though experience suggests that, even in this meagre and restricted sense, it is not easily maintained in the presence of extreme disparities of wealth and influence, it is possible for it to be enjoyed, in form at least, by pauper and millionaire. Such disparities, however, though they do not enable one group to become the political master of another, necessarily cause it to exercise a preponderant influence on the economic life of the rest of society.

Hence, when liberty is construed, realistically, as implying, not merely a minimum of civil and political rights, but securities that the economically weak will not be at the mercy of the economically strong, and that the control of those aspects of economic life by which all are affected will be amenable, in the last resort, to the will of all, a large measure of equality, so far from being inimical to liberty, is essential to it. In conditions which impose co-operative, rather than merely individual, effort, liberty is, in fact, equality in action, in the sense, not that all men perform identical functions or wield the same degree of power, but that all men are equally protected against the abuse of power, and equally entitled to insist that power shall be used, not for personal ends, but for the general advantage. Civil and political liberty obviously imply, not that all men shall be members of parliament, cabinet ministers, or civil servants, but the absence of such civil and political inequalities as enable one class to impose its will on another by legal coercion. It should be not less obvious that economic liberty implies, not that all men shall initiate, plan, direct, manage, or administer, but the absence of such economic inequalities as can be used as a means of economic constraint.

The danger to liberty which is caused by inequality varies with differences of economic organization and public policy. When the mass of the population are independent producers, or when, if they are dependent on great undertakings, the latter are subject to strict public control, it may be absent or remote. It is seen at its height when important departments of economic activity are the province of large organizations, which, if they do not themselves, as sometimes occurs, control the State, are sufficiently powerful to resist control by it. Among the numerous interesting phenomena which impress the foreign observer of American economic life, not the least interesting is the occasional emergence of industrial enterprises which appear to him, and, indeed, to some Americans, to have developed the characteristics, not merely of an economic undertaking, but of a kind of polity. Their rule may be a mild and benevolent paternalism, lavishing rest-rooms, schools, gymnasia, and guarantees for constitutional behaviour on care-free employees; or it may be a harsh and suspicious tyranny. But, whether as amiable as Solon, or as ferocious as Lycurgus, their features are cast in a heroic mould. Their gestures are those of the sovereigns of little commonwealths rather than of mere mundane employers.

American official documents have, on occasion, called attention to the tendency of the bare stem of business to burgeon, in a favourable environment, with almost tropical exuberance, so that it clothes itself with functions that elsewhere are regarded as belonging to political authorities. The corporations controlled by six financial groups, stated the Report of the United States Commission on Industrial Relations some twenty years ago, employ 2,651,684 wage-earners, or 440,000 per group. Some of these companies own, not merely the plant and equipment of industry, but the homes of the workers, the streets through which they pass to work, and the halls in which, if they are allowed to meet, their meetings must be held. They employ private spies and detectives, private police and, sometimes, it appears, private troops, and engage, when they deem it expedient, in private war. While organized themselves, they forbid organization among their employees, and enforce their will by evicting malcontents from their homes, and even, on occasion, by the use of armed force. In such conditions business may continue in its modesty, since its object is money, to describe itself as business; but, in fact, it is a tyranny. "The main objection to the large corporation," remarks Mr. Justice Brandeis, who, as a judge of the Supreme Court, should know the facts, "is that it makes possible—and in many cases makes inevitable—the exercise of industrial absolutism." Property in capital, thus inflated and emancipated, acquires attributes analogous to those of property in land in a feudal society. It carries with it the disposal, in fact, if not in law, of an authority which is quasi-governmental. Its owners possess what would have been called in the ages of darkness a private jurisdiction, and their relations to their dependents, though contractual in form, resemble rather those of ruler and subject than of equal parties to a commercial venture. The liberty which they defend against the encroachments of trade unionism and the State is most properly to be regarded, not as freedom, but as a franchise.

The conventional assertion that inequality is inseparable from liberty is obviously, in such circumstances, unreal and unconvincing; for the existence of the former is a menace to the latter, and the latter is most likely to be secured by curtailing the former. It is true that in England, where three generations of trade unionism and state intervention have done something to tame it, the exercise of economic power is, at ordinary times, less tyrannical than it once was. It still remains, nevertheless, a formidable menace to the freedom of common men. The pressure of such power is felt by the consumer, when he purchases necessaries which, directly or indirectly, are controlled by a monopoly. It is felt in the workshop, where, within the limits set by industrial legislation and collective agreements, the comfort and amenity of the wage-earners' surroundings, the discipline and tone of factory life, the security of employment and methods of promotion, the recruitment and dismissal of workers, the degree to which successive relays of cheap juvenile labour are employed, the opportunity to secure consideration for grievances, depend ultimately upon the policy pursued by a board of directors, who may have little love, indeed, for their shareholders, but who represent, in the last resort, their financial interests, and who, in so far as they are shareholders themselves, are necessarily judges in their own cause.

The effects of such autocracy are even graver in the sphere of economic strategy, which settles the ground upon which these tactical issues are fought out, and, in practice, not infrequently determines their decision before they arise. In such matters as the changes in organization most likely to restore prosperity to an embarrassed industry, and, therefore, to secure a tolerable livelihood to the workers engaged in it; methods of averting or meeting a depression; rationalization, the closing of plants and the concentration of production; the sale of a business on which a whole community depends or its amalgamation with a rival—not to mention the critical field of financial policy, with its possibilities, not merely of watered capital and of the squandering in dividends of resources which should be held as reserves, but of a sensational redistribution of wealth and widespread unemployment as a result of decisions taken by bankers—the diplomacy of business, like that of governments before 1914, is still commonly conducted over the heads of those most affected by it. The interests of the public, as workers and consumers, may receive consideration when these matters are determined; but the normal organization of economic life does not offer reliable guarantee that they will be considered. Nor can it plausibly be asserted that, if they are not, those aggrieved can be certain of any redress.

Power over the public is public power. It does not cease to be public merely because private persons are permitted to buy and sell, own and bequeath it, as they deem most profitable. To retort that its masters are themselves little more than half-conscious instruments, whose decisions register and transmit the impact of forces that they can neither anticipate nor control, though not wholly unveracious, is, nevertheless, superficial. The question is not whether there are economic movements which elude human control, for obviously there are. It is whether the public possesses adequate guarantees that those which are controllable are controlled in the general interest, not in that of a minority. Like the gods of Homer, who were subject themselves to a fate behind the fates, but were not thereby precluded from interfering at their pleasure in the affairs of men, the potentates of the economic world exercise discretion, not, indeed, as to the situation which they will meet, but as to the manner in which they will meet it. They hold the initiative, have such freedom to manoeuvre as circumstances allow, can force an issue or postpone it, and, if open conflict seems inevitable or expedient, can choose, as best suits themselves, the ground where it shall take place.

"Even if socialism were practicable without the destruction of freedom," writes Lord Lothian, "would there be any advantage in converting the whole population into wage or salary earners, directed by the relatively few, also salaried, officials, who by ability, or promotion, or 'pull,' could work their way to the top of the political machine or the permanent bureaucracy? . . . Is not that community the best, and, in the widest sense of the word, the most healthy, which has the largest proportion of citizens who have the enterprise, and energy, and initiative, to create new things and new methods for themselves, and not merely to wait to carry out the orders of somebody 'higher up'?" In view of the practice, of some parts, at least, of the business world, the less said about "pull," perhaps, the better. But how true in substance! And how different the liner looks from the saloon-deck and the stoke-hold! And how striking that the conditions which Lord Lothian deplores as a hypothetical danger should be precisely those which ordinary men experience daily as an ever-present fact!

For, in England at any rate, as a glance at the Registrar-General's reports would have sufficed to show him, not only the majority of the population, but the great majority, are to-day "wage or salary earners," who, for quite a long time, have been "directed by the relatively few," and who, if they did not "wait to carry out the orders of somebody higher up," would be sent about their business with surprising promptitude. Unless Lord

Lothian proposes to abolish, not only a particular political doctrine, but banks, railways, coal-mines and cotton-mills, the question is not whether orders shall be given, but who shall give them; whether there shall be guarantees that they are given in the general interest; and whether those to whom they are given shall have a reasonable security that, when their welfare is at stake, their views will receive an unbiased consideration.

Freedom may be, as he insists, more important than comfort. But is a miner, who is not subject to a bureaucracy, or at least, to a bureaucracy of the kind which alarms Lord Lothian, conspicuously more free than a teacher, who is? If a man eats bread made of flour produced to the extent of forty per cent by two milling combines and meat supplied by an international meat trust, and lives in a house built of materials of which twenty-five per cent are controlled by a ring, and buys his tobacco from one amalgamation, and his matches from another, while his wife's sewing-thread is provided by a third, which has added eight millionaires to the national roll of honour in the last twenty years, is he free as a consumer? Is he free as a worker, if he is liable to have his piece-rates cut at the discretion of his employer, and, on expressing his annoyance, to be dismissed as an agitator, and to be thrown on the scrap-heap without warning because his employer has decided to shut down a plant, or bankers to restrict credit, and to be told, when he points out that the industry on which his livelihood depends is being injured by mismanagement, that his job is to work, and that the management in question will do his thinking for him? And if, in such circumstances, he is but partially free as a consumer and a worker, is not his freedom as a citizen itself also partial, rather than, as Lord Lothian would desire, unqualified and complete?

Lord Lothian is misled as to liberty, because he has omitted to consider the bearing upon it of another phenomenon, the phenomenon of inequality. The truth is that, when the economic scales are so unevenly weighted, to interpret liberty as a political principle, which belongs to one world, the world of politics and government, while equality belongs—if, indeed, it belongs anywhere—to another world, the world of economic affairs, is to do violence to realities. Governments, it is true, exercise powers of a great and special kind, and freedom requires that they should be held strictly to account. But the administration of things is not easily distinguished, under modern conditions of mass organization, from the control of persons, and both are in the hands, to some not inconsiderable degree, of the minority who move the levers of the economic mechanism. The truth of the matter is put by Professor Pollard in his admirable study, *The Evolution of Parliament*. "There is only one solution," he writes, "of the problem of liberty, and it lies in equality. . . . Men vary in physical strength; but so far as their social relations go that inequality has been abolished. . . . Yet there must have been a period in social evolution when this refusal to permit the strong man to do what he liked with his own physical strength seemed, at least to the strong, an outrageous interference with personal liberty. . . . There is, in fact, no more reason why a man should be allowed to use his wealth or his brain than his physical strength as he likes. . . . The liberty of the weak depends upon the restraint of the strong, that of the poor upon the restraint of the rich, and that of the simpler-minded upon the restraint of the sharper. Every man should have this liberty and no more, to do unto others as he would that they should do unto him; upon that common foundation rest liberty, equality, and morality."

• 54 •

FALLACIES IN POLITICAL THINKING *

C. D. Broad (1887–)

I want to discuss and illustrate . . . certain fallacies which we are all very liable to commit in our thinking about political and social questions. Perhaps "thinking" is rather too high-sounding a name to attach to the mental processes which lie behind most political talk. It is at any rate thinking of a very low grade, for a considerable proportion of such discussion in Press and Parliament and private conversation hardly rises above the intellectual level of disputes between boys at a preparatory school.

The first fallacy which I will consider is this. There is a very natural tendency for a person to base his judgments about present trends and future prospects on the quite recent history of a quite small part of the world, in particular on what has happened in his own country during his own and perhaps his parents' lifetime. Now the features which he notices in this restricted segment of space-time, and which he makes the basis of his political and social judgments, may depend on a concatenation of circumstances which have seldom occurred before, are unlikely to happen again, and perhaps never existed outside a small area. This may well lead

* From "Some Common Fallacies in Political Thinking," an essay that originally appeared in *Philosophy*, vol. XXV (April 1950), and was reprinted in Professor Broad's *Religion, Philosophy and Psychical Research*, 1953. Reprinted by permission of the author, the Royal Institute of Philosophy, and Routledge & Kegan Paul Ltd., London. The title of this selection has been supplied by the editors.

to an unjustified optimism or an equally unjustified pessimism, and in any case to ill-founded judgments.

. . . Consider an example of this fallacy which is common both to Americans and Englishmen. This is the very usual belief that what we know as "democracy" is a suitable article for export and a form of government which all and sundry could and should adopt. For my part I prefer to avoid the word "democracy" altogether, for it has become little more than an emotive noise with the minimum of cognitive meaning. What in practice it means for us is roughly this. It means that legislation and administration are subject to the control of a representative assembly, chosen at fairly frequent intervals by almost universal suffrage exercised by an electorate organized into two nearly equal political parties. It is assumed that the electors record their votes and that the representatives conduct their discussions without serious interference from the executive or from powerful individuals or groups. It is further assumed that the magistrates hold their offices independently of the executive, the representative assembly, and the electorate; and that they habitually make their judicial decisions, even in matters which directly concern the government, in accordance with existing law and without being subject to pressure either from the executive or the populace.

Now I am not concerned to discuss the merits and defects of this form of government. What I do wish to emphasize is that it presupposes a certain very special kind of historical background and contemporary conditions; that these are absent in the greater part of the world; and that there is not the faintest reason to believe that it is a practicable form of government for most peoples at most times. Even if it be, as I think it probably is, in the abstract a less undesirable form of government than most of the known alternatives, it does not follow that it is the best form for those peoples in whom the necessary conditions for its success are lacking. It may be better to have a worse kind of government, suited to one's traditions and situation and national character, than a better kind imported from abroad which is a grotesque misfit. . . .

So far as I am aware, this kind of government has never worked even moderately well except in Great Britain, Scandinavia, Holland, Belgium, and Switzerland, and in those non-European lands which were first peopled by emigrants from certain of these parts of Europe and are now occupied by their descendants. It is difficult to say with confidence that it has worked decently in France, and one can say with certainty that it has been a fiasco in central, eastern, and south-eastern Europe. One hardly knows whether to laugh or to weep at the naïvety of the common American belief that it is a suitable system of government to impose upon Japan; and our own talk of "educating Germany for democracy" seems to me little less ludicrous. . . .

. . . An instance of this fallacy which is probably common not only to Englishmen and Americans, but also to most Western Europeans . . . consists in taking as normal the peculiarly favourable economic conditions which prevailed in Europe from about 1850 to 1930, and assuming that, apart from occasional set-backs, they will continue and even grow more favourable. If I am not mistaken, that relatively fortunate economic situation, and the marked rise in the standard of refinement, decency and humanity which it made possible, depended on very special conditions which seem unlikely to recur in the foreseeable future. For a short period the resources of food and raw materials available to Europeans increased at a much greater rate than the population which could exert an effective demand upon them. This happened through the rapid exploitation of the virgin lands of America, Australia and Africa, and the simultaneous development on a vast scale of methods of cheap and quick transport and of cold storage. As a part of this unusually favourable situation huge numbers of men and women were able to relieve the pressure of population in Europe by emigrating and settling in these empty fertile lands, where their labours not only supported themselves but also produced a surplus for those whom they had left at home. I do not see how anything closely parallel to this can happen again to Western Europeans. On the other hand, the population of these new lands has grown and will continue to grow. Their demands for food and raw materials will increase, and so too will their power of producing cheaply and efficiently all the manufactured goods that they need. They will thus have less and less to export to Europe and less and less inducement to take European manufactured goods in exchange. So far from the economic conditions which prevailed in the world during the lives of our grandfathers and fathers being normal, they may be compared to a tidal wave which has left Western Europe in general and England in particular stranded high and dry on a shelf on the face of a cliff, from which it is impossible to climb up and hard to climb down without disaster.

I could easily give other examples of this fallacy of taking temporary and local conditions as permanent and world-wide and basing one's political judgments and actions on that assumption. But it is time to mention and illustrate other common fallacies. I shall take next a bunch of them which it will be convenient to group together under the name of "causal fallacies," because they all involve a reference to causation though some of them involve other notions beside.

Quite apart from all metaphysical questions, the notion of cause is a complex one which needs a fairly elaborate and subtle logical analysis. It would be inappropriate to enter in detail into this here and now; it will suffice for our present purpose to say that the statement that C causes E sometimes means that C is a *necessary* though perhaps not sufficient condition of E, sometimes that C is a *sufficient* though not perhaps necessary condition of E, and sometimes that C is a set of conditions which are *severally necessary and jointly sufficient* to produce E. Now popular talk about this causing that does not clearly distinguish these alternatives. It is very common, e.g., to start from the fact, which may be quite trivial and even tautologous, that C causes E in the sense that it is a necessary condition of E; then to take for granted that C causes E in the important and doubtful sense that it is necessary and sufficient to produce E; and then to infer various far-reaching practical conclusions from this.

An example is the assertion, often made with a great flourish of trumpets by pacifists, that armaments cause war. Since war involves, by definition, a conflict between the armed forces of nations, it is a tautological proposition that armaments are a necessary condition of wars. From this nothing follows except the platitude that, if all nations simultaneously disarmed and remained disarmed, there would be no more wars. This does not give the slightest guidance as to what a particular nation should do, if it is practically certain that at least one fairly strong nation will retain its armaments. It is obvious that there are situations in which a diminution of armaments by a certain nation or group of nations increases the chances of war, whilst an increase in their armaments diminishes it. . . .

Another common causal fallacy may be called for shortness the "extrapolation fallacy." . . . It is known or reasonably conjectured that a change in a certain direction has produced predominantly good results. It is then uncritically assumed that further doses of change in that direction will produce still further predominantly good results, and that it is desirable to administer these additional doses as soon as possible. It is forgotten that almost any change involves at least some loss in some respects as well as gain in others, and that it often produces certain positive evils which would otherwise not have existed. The gains may well overbalance the losses, and the main positive goods may well be greater than the collateral positive evils, until the process has gone a certain length; but the losses and the collateral evils may begin to predominate if it is carried further. Again, even if it be desirable on the whole to continue a certain process further in the same direction, it is often most undesirable to do so with the maximum possible speed. People who would benefit from a slow development, to each phase of which they had time to adapt themselves or to adapt their children, may be merely bewildered and demoralized if the pace becomes too hot for them.

All this is admirably illustrated by the transition from handicraft to large-scale mechanized production and the continued application of new scientific discoveries and techniques to the conditions of daily life. Up to a point there is clearly an enormous gain in handing over to machines much of the heavy drudgery of human work, in making possible the rapid transport of goods and persons over long distances, and producing and distributing food, clothing and other necessities and even luxuries on a scale which would otherwise have been impossible. But it is plain that there are great and increasing disadvantages to be set against this. The most obvious, and the one which lies not far at the back of the minds of all of us nowadays, is the almost unlimited power of destruction which the later developments of this process have put into the hands of individuals and communities much below the level of intellectual, moral and political development at which they can be trusted not to misuse it. I have little doubt that any benefits which mankind may have derived from the invention of the internal combustion engine are heavily outweighed by the fact that it has made the bombing aeroplane and the submarine warship possible and actual. It would be platitudinous to enlarge on the disasters with which mankind is threatened by the most untimely discovery of a means of releasing atomic energy.

I suspect that the only recent advances of applied science on which we can still on balance congratulate ourselves are in the regions of biology and medicine. But we must not forget that each branch of science and technology is so intimately linked with all the others that the advances which we welcome would be impossible without the conditions which have led to those which we deplore. It is the same great tree which bears the poisonous berries, the refreshing fruits, and the healing balsams, and it may even happen that some of its poisons are an essential ingredient in some of its wholesome products. (Cf., e.g. the use of the products of atomic disintegration as tracer elements in medical research.)

In this connection it may be worth while to note the following fact. Sometimes the development of a certain social trend leads to results which almost all decent and sensible people deplore. Yet the development of that trend in any one society may make that community so powerful in relation to others that they are compelled to follow suit and to impose it on themselves if they will not be rendered impotent and perhaps have it and even worse things imposed on them by others. Large-scale industrialization and the great increase of urban population which accompanies it are a case in point. This is a development from which a nation with a reasonably small well-distributed population and a comfortable balance between agriculture, fishery, manufacture, etc., might well pray to be delivered. But those nations in which such a development takes place become so powerful from a military and economic standpoint that they can and do dictate the conditions of life to all the others. . . .

Industrialization has already destroyed and continues to destroy natural beauty on a vast scale. But there seems good reason to think that it has begun to undermine itself by destroying the natural fertility of the soil and the natural balance of plant and animal life over huge areas of the earth. Nor is this the only way in which its inordinate development cuts away the branch on which it sits. I would venture to suggest that it engenders a psychological condition which in the long run may well be fatal to it. What I have in mind is this. As the organization of industry becomes more complex the connection of individual diligence and efficiency with economic or social reward becomes more and more remote. So, too, does the connection of individual slackness and incompetence with economic or social disadvantage. The remoteness of this connection tends to be increased still further by the methods of taxation and the social welfare legislation which are characteristic of communities in which the balance of political power is in the hands of the wage-drawers. Now there is no evidence for, and much evidence against, the view that the average person under normal conditions will work hard and strive to be efficient in intrinsically uninteresting tasks when not under the stimulus of direct economic or social advantage or disadvantage to himself or his family. A rapidly decreasing number of wage-drawers still have the habit of working hard and efficiently as a kind of hangover from an earlier and simpler social system and the customs and standards of values which accompanied it. A few persons will always do so because they are made that way. A considerable number will do so for short periods under the stress of some crisis which appeals strongly to certain social feelings, e.g. when their country is visibly in danger of immediate defeat in war, or when a revolution is taking place or a new system which appeals to their emotions has lately been set up. But I see no reason whatever to believe that any but very direct and visible motives of economic gain or loss to themselves or their families can be trusted to call forth continued efficient work at dull tasks in most men at most times. Yet the system will not provide a high standard of living and leisure unless it can call forth steady continuous effort in the employees while they are at work, and enterprise and inventiveness and readiness to take risks on the part of the directors, whether they be private individuals or State officials.

I find it hard to believe that the communists have discovered any permanently effective alternative to the direct economic incentives which
are now ceasing to operate in Western Europe and will probably in time
cease to do so in America. At the moment they enjoy all the advantages of
a religious revival combined with such a crisis-mentality as evoked prodigious efforts in England in 1940. Even so, this has to be supplemented by
the daily terror of the concentration camp and the political witch trials,
and has to be stimulated by increasingly strident propaganda, in which
self-adulation and anti-foreign war scares are mingled in a welter of nonsense and mendacity which can rarely have been equalled in the long history of human folly and wickedness. If these things have to be done in the
green leaf, what will be done in the dry when the Church Militant shall
have become the Church Triumphant? I cannot but suppose that even
Slavs eventually become inured to this stuff, and that it will become less
and less effective as a stimulant in the dull, daily, irritating round of work
in factory and field and mine. Then nothing will remain but naked terror,
and I doubt whether this is an efficient method of stimulating production
in the long run and on a large scale. I wonder what proportion of the
populations behind the iron curtain even now are occupied as policemen,
prison warders, *agents provocateurs*, and in the hundred-and-one other
non-productive tasks involved in building the New Jerusalem.

For these reasons, quite apart from the high probability of a catastrophic
upset in the near future through atomic and bacteriological warfare, I suspect that industrialism, like fermentation, generates by-products which
gradually check its development and might even bring it to a not very
stable state of equilibrium. I cannot pretend to shed many tears over this.
I do not view with any enthusiasm a millennium in which there would be
no square inch of the earth's surface that did not stink of petrol and humanity and re-echo with the blare of the wireless loud-speaker discoursing
mechanical music, enunciating platitude or nonsense, and ingeminating
hatred.

It is high time to turn now to another common causal fallacy, viz. that
which has been called *post hoc ergo propter hoc*. From the nature of the
case it is extremely difficult to say with any high degree of reasonable confidence whether a certain factor did or did not contribute to an important
extent to cause a certain other factor in social or political phenomena. This
is because it is practically impossible to isolate the facts to be investigated,
to find really parallel cases, to devise and perform experiments intended to
answer definite questions, and so on. But fools cannot be restrained from
rushing in where logicians fear to tread; and, if some fairly outstanding
social phenomenon A immediately preceded some other fairly outstand-

ing phenomenon *B* in some part of the world at some period in history, they will promptly generalize and conclude that *A* is necessary and sufficient to produce *B*. It will be entertaining to consider some examples of this.

I have heard it cited as an instance of the truth of Karl Marx's economic theories that they enabled him to prophecy that great wars would happen with frequency in the Western world, that they would be increasingly destructive, and so on, and that we have seen this prophecy abundantly fulfilled. As if wars had not been a regular occurrence in the history of Europe and the rest of the world throughout recorded time; as if they had not always been waged with the maximum resources available at the time to the belligerents; and as if those resources had not enormously increased through industrialization and applied science. How can any particular theory be verified by foretelling what could have been foretold with confidence on almost any theory or on no theory at all?

Another example concerns "democracy" in the Western sense of that word. It is often said by political speakers and writers in England and America that the superior efficiency of our system of government is shown by the fact that we defeated the non-democratic Germans in two great wars. The fact is that Germany came within an ace of defeating us, and that in both wars we had as an important ally Russia, a country which was in 1914 and is now at the opposite pole to all that we understand by democracy. The really relevant factors were that Germany, by stupid diplomacy, blundered into war with too many strong nations at once; that England was an island and the United States far too remote to be attacked; and that the combined industrial resources of these two countries, if once they were given time and opportunity to deploy them, were enormously greater than those of Germany. It should be added that nothing but the imbecility of the governments of England, France and the United States, due to their dependence on the votes of ignorant and ostrich-like electors, who wanted nothing but a quiet life and would not read the signs of the times nor listen to those who could, made it possible for Germany to re-arm and indulge in a second world-war after its defeat in the first. I think it might fairly be said that the main achievement of Western democracy between the two wars was to prevent those who knew what ought to be done from doing it in the economic and the military spheres and in that of international relations.

A consequence of fallacies of this kind is that what may roughly be called "parliamentary government" has acquired a prestige among peoples who have never experienced it and are most unlikely to be able to practise it successfully, which makes them eager to adopt something that looks like it whenever they emerge from tutelage. We have seen plenty of examples of this in central, southern and south-eastern Europe, and we are now witnessing more and bigger ones in the near and the far East. A little later on I fully expect to see a similar result arising from similar causes in connection with the communist system as practised by Russia and its satellites. It seems to me that the fact is that under almost any imaginable system of government which was not completely imbecile North America would have become one of the wealthiest and most powerful communities in the world. Under almost any imaginable system of government, not completely imbecile, the Russian empire, with its vast and as yet hardly scratched natural resources, will become at least equally wealthy and powerful. In the one case the credit has gone to the system which happened to prevail in North America, in the other it will no doubt go to the system which happens to prevail in Russia. We shall be told, and many of us will believe, that this immense wealth and power is "due to" communism, just as we have been told and many of us believe that it was "due to" democracy in the Western sense. In each case there is very little rational ground for believing that the system of government is much more than a fly on the wheel. Any government which kept internal order over these vast empty rich territories and avoided defeat and invasion, and which either allowed individuals or companies to exploit the natural resources or undertook that exploitation itself on a large scale, would secure much the same spectacular results in these exceptionally favourable conditions.

I will consider one other causal fallacy, which often leads to governments or individuals being unfairly blamed or extravagantly praised. Suppose that there is a critical situation in which a government or a leading statesman has a choice of one or other of a comparatively few practically possible alternative courses of action, A, B and C, including among these the possible alternative of doing nothing and letting events take their course. Alternative A is chosen, and we will suppose that the state of affairs which ensues is admittedly much worse than that which immediately preceded the decision. Then it is very common to hold that a wrong decision was made, and to blame severely the individual or the government which made it. Now of course such a judgment may be justified in some cases. But in most cases a whole nest of fallacies is involved. In the first place, even if a different decision would have had a more fortunate sequel, it does not follow that the maker of the actual decision was blameworthy. Before we can decide this we must know whether, in the situation in which he was placed and with the information which was available to him at the time, he might reasonably have been expected to see that the consequences would be much worse than those of some other alternative which he might reasonably have been expected to contemplate as possible. The mere fact, if it be a fact, that *we* can see all this *after* the event may have very little bearing on this question.

Secondly, the mere fact that the state of affairs which followed the choice of alternative A was much worse than that which preceded it is not sufficient evidence that the decision was mistaken. It may be that the ensuing state of affairs would have been much worse than the preceding *whichever* of the alternatives had been adopted, and that the results of adopting any other would have been still worse than those of adopting A. Men find it very hard to admit that there are situations in which *all* possible alternative developments will be changes for the worse, and where the wisest decision that can be made will do no more than minimize the inevitably ensuing evil. Suppose that we tacitly and unjustifiably assume that there are no such situations. Then we shall automatically conclude that there *must* have been some alternative open to the maker of the decision which would have averted the evils which in fact ensued and would not have been followed by still greater evils. And so we shall judge that the actual decision was mistaken. But there is no reason whatever to accept this premise, and therefore there is no reason to accept any such judgment as a conclusion from it.

It is on such grounds as these, e.g., that the decision of the British Cabinet to go to war with Germany in 1914, or the agreement made by Mr. Chamberlain with Hitler at Munich, has been confidently asserted by many persons to have been unwise and to have redounded to the discredit of those concerned. Naturally I express no opinion here on the *truth* or *falsity* of these judgments. What I do contend is this. Most of those who make them with so much confidence have not begun to realize how many questions would have to be raised and settled before they had a shadow of justification for their assertions. Moreover, some of these questions can never be answered even approximately, for they involve conjectures about the consequences which would have followed if other alternatives had been chosen.

The last fallacy that I shall consider is of a very different kind. It is more trivial than those which I have noticed above; but it is so common and has such an inhibiting effect on many worthy persons that it seems desirable to mention and expose it. It is this. A citizen of country A condemns some contemporary public action or institution in another country B. Thereupon a fellow-citizen gets up and says 'We did the same,' and produces in support of his assertion some public action which was taken or some institution which existed at some time in the history of their common fatherland. This is supposed by many to provide some kind of answer to the criticism on this action or institution in the foreign country. At any rate it is often felt to be relevant and embarrassing by the critic himself, and the fear that such remarks might justifiably be made often prevents scrupulous persons from condemning publicly incidents in foreign countries which they cannot but deeply disapprove in private.

It is obvious that there must be a number of suppressed premisses at the back of such an argument, and when one tries to make them explicit one sees that it is so hopelessly confused that nothing coherent can be made of it. I think we should all admit that a person ought to feel, and very often will feel, uncomfortable if it can be shown that at the same time he strongly condemns x and approves or tolerates y when the only relevant difference between x and y is that the former occurs in a foreign country and the latter in his own. Even this, however, would not show that he is mistaken in condemning x. The fact that a man is inconsistent in his judgments or his emotions does not show that a particular one judgment is false or a particular one emotion is misdirected. Sin is not less sinful when it is Satan who condemns it; and he has the advantage of expert knowledge. But suppose, as is very often the case, that a man not only condemns x in the foreign country but also quite consistently condemns similar actions and institutions in the history of his own country. Why on earth should the fact that something similar to what he condemns in another country exists or has existed in his own be thought to show that it is not worthy of condemnation? And, if he equally condemns similar acts or institutions in the history of his own country, why on earth should he feel embarrassed or diffident in publicly condemning them when they exist in a foreign country? Is bestial cruelty in contemporary Russian labour-camps any less evil because there was bestial cruelty in English slave-ships in the eighteenth century? And must an Englishman, who deplores that incident in English history and whose ancestors abolished that evil after a long and arduous Parliamentary struggle, hang his head in embarrassed silence and refrain from calling slavery and cruelty by their name when practised on a vast scale by foreign countries which claim to be the moral leaders of mankind?

I have assumed so far, for the sake of argument, that there really is something in one's own country which is closely or exactly parallel to that which one condemns in another country, and I have shown that even on that assumption this method of rebutting or silencing criticism is logically worthless. But in nine cases out of ten the alleged parallel will not survive a moment's critical inspection. Often it is merely verbal, as it would be, e.g., if one said that England made use of concentration camps in the latter stages of the Boer war and therefore Englishmen have no right to criticize the use of concentration camps by Germany or Russia. Often the only parallel which can be found to a present-day practice in a foreign country is something which formerly existed in one's own and has long since been abolished there by the efforts of reformers and is now condemned by everyone. Any attempt, e.g., to regard the harsh treatment of factory workers and of paupers in England in the early nineteenth century as a relevant parallel to present-day slave-labour in Russia and its satellites would be open to this criticism. The upshot of the matter is that I should advise anyone to whom this kind of argument is addressed either to pay no attention whatever to it or to answer the fool who uses it according to his own folly.

It is time for me to bring my paper to an end. It is not a cheerful paper, for I do not find mankind in their social and political relationships a cheerful subject to contemplate. Gibbon, who knew something of history, described it as mainly a record of the crimes, the follies, and the misfortunes of mankind. I see no reason to think that it will be fundamentally different in this respect in future from what it has been in the past. I suspect that there will always be, as there have always been, relatively infrequent and not very persistent oases of prosperity and culture in a desert of penury, ignorance and unthinking brutality. And at every stage any experienced and intelligent statesman will have occasion to repeat Axel Oxenstierna's words to his son: "Behold, my son, with how little wisdom the world is governed!"

BIOGRAPHICAL NOTES

These notes are intended to be no more than brief identifications of the authors represented in this book. In most cases, the writings that are cited here are in addition to those from which selections have been taken for this volume.

SAINT ANSELM (selection 29) was an Italian churchman, and served as archbishop of Canterbury from 1093 to 1109. He is most famous for his defense of the Church against King Henry I of England. Philosophically his fame rests on his devising the Ontological Argument for the existence of God, which is included in this volume. His most important works are the *Monologium* and the *Proslogium*.

SAINT THOMAS AQUINAS (selection 30 and Part IV of selection 20) is generally regarded as the greatest of Medieval philosophers. He was born in Italy but spent most of his life in Paris, where he enjoyed great fame and influence. He attempted to reconcile the doctrines of Plato and Aristotle with the doctrines of the Catholic Church. His most important works are the *Summa Contra Gentiles* and the *Summa Theologica*. Detailed accounts of his life and philosophy can be found in *St. Thomas Aquinas* by G. K. Chesterton, and *The Philosophy of St. Thomas Aquinas* by Etienne Gilson.

ARISTOTLE (selections 4, 19, 20, and 39), along with Socrates and Plato, is one of the three major figures of ancient philosophy. He was a student of Plato's, but later founded his own school, the Lyceum. At one time he served as tutor to Alexander the Great. His influence on later philosophy, literature, and science is equalled only by Plato's. Medieval philosophers held him in such esteem that for centuries he was known as The Philosopher. He is known as the founder of logic, and his classification of the sciences has endured, in its main outlines, down to the present day. Author of many works, including the *Organon, Physics, Metaphysics, Nicomachean Ethics, Politics, Poetics, Rhetoric,* and *On the Heavens.* See *Aristotle,* by W. D. Ross, for an account of his life and philosophy.

MONROE CURTIS BEARDSLEY (selection 48) was born in Connecticut and educated at Yale University. He has taught philosophy at Mt. Holyoke College, Yale University, and, since 1947, at Swarthmore College. Author of *Practical Logic, Theme and Form* (co-author), and *Aesthetics*.

JEREMY BENTHAM (selection 42) was one of the outstanding English philosophers and political theorists of the 19th century. Educated at Oxford, he studied for the law, but devoted his life to the analysis and attempts at reform of political and legal institutions. He was the outstanding advocate of Utilitarianism, which attracted to it many British liberals, including John Stuart Mill, and was the leader of the reform movement based on this philosophy. He wrote much, but published little. Among his works are *A Fragment on Government, Comment on the Commentaries, The Theory of Legislation, The Theory of Fictions, Deontology,* and *The Limits of Jurisprudence Defined* (some of which were published posthumously).

GEORGE BERKELEY (selection 21) is frequently regarded as the founder of Modern Idealism. Irish by birth, he was educated at Trinity College, Dublin. Along with John Locke and David Hume, he was one of the three most famous representatives of British empiricism. Before he was 30 he had written his most famous and controversial works, which have exerted an extensive influence. He became an Anglican clergyman, and was appointed Bishop of Cloyne. Spent three years in Rhode Island, 1729 to 1732, in an abortive attempt to found a university to educate the Colonial and Indian youth of America. Author of many works, including *An Essay Towards a New Theory of Vision, Three Dialogues between Hylas and Philonous, Alciphron, De Motu,* and *Siris.*

MAX BLACK (selection 8) was born in Russia but raised in England, receiving his education at Cambridge University, the University of Goettingen, and the University of London, from which he received a Ph.D. in 1939. Taught for a time at the Institute of Education in London, and came to the United States in 1940. Has taught philosophy at the Universities of Illinois and Washington, and is at present Sage Professor of Philosophy at Cornell University, where he has been since 1946. Has been an editor of the *Journal of Symbolic Logic* and *The Philosophical Review.* Author of *The Nature of Mathematics, Critical Thinking, Language and Philosophy,* and *Problems of Analysis,* and edited *Philosophical Analysis* (1950).

CHARLIE DUNBAR BROAD (selection 54) is one of the most distinguished of living English philosophers. Taught in a number of British universities, and from 1933 to 1953 was Knightsbridge Professor of Moral Philosophy at the University of Cambridge. In addition to writing extensively in many areas of philosophy, he has been for many years actively interested in problems of Psychical Research. Author, among other works, of *Perception, Physics and Reality; The Mind and its Place in Nature; Examination of McTaggart's Philosophy; Five Types of Ethical Theory;* and *Ethics and the History of Philosophy.*

JOHN CALDWELL CALHOUN (selection 50) was born in South Carolina and educated at Yale University. He served as Congressman from South Carolina (1811–1817), Secretary of War (1817–25) under Monroe, and Vice President of the United States under John Quincy Adams (1825–29) and Andrew Jackson (1829–1832). Served as a Senator from South Carolina for many years, and became known as the outstanding spokesman for the South, States' Rights, and Nullification. Author of the posthumous *Discourse on the Constitution and Government of the United States*. His papers have been collected in six volumes by R. K. Cralle.

C. ARTHUR CAMPBELL (selection 28) was born in Scotland, and educated at the Universities of Oxford and Glasgow. He has taught philosophy at the University College, Bangor, Wales, and has been since 1938 Professor of Logic and Rhetoric in the University of Glasgow. Author of *Scepticism and Construction*, and *On Selfhood and Godhood* (Gifford Lectures, 1957), in addition to numerous contributions to philosophical journals.

WILLIAM KINGDON CLIFFORD (selection 14) was born and raised in England and educated at the Universities of Cambridge and London. In 1868 he was elected a Fellow of Trinity College, Cambridge, and in 1871 he was appointed Professor of Applied Mathematics and Mechanics at University College, London. His brilliant career was ended by death at the early age of 34. Author of *Elements of Dynamic*, and the posthumously published *Mathematical Papers*, and *The Common Sense of the Exact Sciences* (completed by Karl Pearson, 1885).

MORRIS RAPHAEL COHEN (selections 6 and 37) was born in Russia, came to the United States at the age of 12, and was educated at the College of the City of New York, Columbia University, and Harvard University. He taught mathematics and then philosophy at City College for 36 years, and then for a few years at the University of Chicago, and was known as one of the great teachers of his time. His books include *Reason and Nature*, *Law and the Social Order*, *A Preface to Logic*, *The Meaning of Human History*, *Reason and Law*, *American Thought*, and the autobiographical *A Dreamer's Journey*.

IRVING MARMER COPI (selections 9 and 10) was born in Minnesota and received his education at the University of Michigan, from which he received a Ph.D. in 1948. Has taught philosophy at the University of Illinois, and is presently Professor of Philosophy at the University of Michigan, where he has taught since 1948. Has been a Guggenheim Fellow, a Fellow of the Fund for the Advancement of Education, and a Research Associate at the University of California. Author of *Symbolic Logic* and numerous articles in philosophical journals.

CLARENCE SEWARD DARROW (selection 26) was born in Ohio, and lived in Chicago a good many years. Practiced law for over fifty years, and became known as an outstanding criminal and trial lawyer. He was an outspoken agnostic and opponent of capital punishment. Author of a novel, *Farmington*, and of *A Persian Pearl and Other Essays*, *An Eye for an Eye*, *The Prohibition Mania*, and many other writings on social and economic questions.

RENÉ DESCARTES (selection 11) was a French philosopher who is often regarded as "the father of modern philosophy." In addition to his philosophical works, he contributed to mathematics (where he founded analytic geometry) and various sciences. In philosophy, his writings have been of major importance in epistemology and metaphysics. These include *A Discourse on Method*, *The Principles of Philosophy*, *Treatise on the Passions of the Soul*, and *Rules for the Direction of the Mind*.

JOHN DEWEY (selections 44 and 52) was born and raised in Vermont, and taught philosophy at the Universities of Michigan, Minnesota, and Chicago, and from 1904 to 1929 at Columbia University. He traveled widely, took part in several experiments in educational reform, and wrote a large number of books, including *Democracy and Education*, *Essays in Experimental Logic*, *Reconstruction in Philosophy*, *Human Nature and Conduct*, *Experience and Nature*, *The Public and its Problems*, *The Quest for Certainty*, *Philosophy and Civilization*, *Art as Experience*, *Logic: The Theory of Inquiry*, and *Freedom and Culture*. An account of his life, and a discussion of his philosophy, may be found in *The Philosophy of John Dewey*, ed. by P. A. Schilpp.

CURT JOHN DUCASSE (selection 3) was born in France, and was educated at the University of Washington and Harvard University. He has taught philosophy at a number of colleges and universities throughout the United States, and has been Professor of Philosophy at Brown University since 1929. He has written extensively in many areas of philosophy. His principal interests are in metaphysics, theory of knowledge, philosophy of religion, and psychical research. Author, among other works, of *The Philosophy of Art*; *Philosophy as a Science*; *Nature, Mind, and Death*; *Art, the Critics, and You*; and *A Philosophical Scrutiny of Religion*.

HUGH ELLIOT (selection 27) was a distinguished British philosopher of science. He was educated at Eton and Cambridge. His interest in aviation led to his untimely death in a plane crash in 1930. Author of *Modern Science and the Illusions of Professor Bergson*, *Herbert Spencer*, and *Human Character*.

FRIEDRICH ENGELS (selection 25), together with Karl Marx, was the founder of Dialectical Materialism, the theoretical basis of modern

Communism. After meeting Marx in 1844, he devoted his life to organizing revolutionary movements and writing on the theory of Socialism. In 1848 he and Marx collaborated in writing the influential *Communist Manifesto*. His major writings include *The Condition of the Working Class in England in 1844*; *Landmarks of Scientific Socialism*; *The Origin of the Family, Private Property, and the State*; and *Anti-Dühring*. He also edited the second and third volumes of Marx's *Das Kapital*.

PAUL HENRI THYRY, BARON D'HOLBACH (selection 32) was one of the famous French Encyclopedists. Known as a defender of naturalism and materialism and as an opponent of Christianity. He was guillotined during the French Revolution. His best known work is *System of Nature*.

DAVID HUME (selections 12, 22, 31, and 40), one of the greatest philosophical intellects of all time, was born in Scotland and educated at Edinburgh. One of the three outstanding British empiricists, along with Locke and Berkeley. Much of modern philosophy may be regarded as an attempt to answer his defense of philosophical skepticism, and his philosophical influence, aided by the beauty of his style, remains strong to this day. He never held an academic post, though he was for a time librarian at the University of Edinburgh, when he wrote his famous *History of England*. Author, among other works, of *An Enquiry Concerning the Principles of Morals*; *Essays, Literary, Moral and Political*; *An Abstract of a Treatise on Human Nature*; and *Political Discourses*. Many insights into his thought and character can be obtained from his *Letters* (published 1932).

WILLIAM JAMES (selections 33 and 34), son of the theologian Henry James and brother of the novelist Henry James, became one of the most widely-read and influential thinkers of his day. He was born in New York City and received his education at Harvard University, where he started teaching in 1872 as a lecturer on anatomy and physiology, and then in 1880 as a psychologist and philosopher. Author, among other works, of *Principles of Psychology*, *The Varieties of Religious Experience*, *A Pluralistic Universe*, *The Meaning of Truth*, and of the posthumous *Some Problems in Philosophy* and *Essays in Radical Empiricism*. For an account of his life and thought, see R. B. Perry, *The Thought and Character of William James*.

CYRIL EDWIN MITCHINSON JOAD (selection 16) was one of the best known of contemporary British philosophers, having written forty-six books on philosophy and related subjects during his career. He was educated at the University of Oxford and served in the British Civil Service and Ministry of Labour from 1914 to 1930. In 1930 he became head of the Philosophy Department at Birkbeck College, University of London, a post he held until his retirement in 1946. His many writings include *Philosophies of the World, Guide to Philosophy, Guide to Modern Wickedness, God and Evil, The Recovery of Belief, A Restatement of Christian Philosophy, Common Sense Ethics,* and *A Critique of Logical Positivism.*

IMMANUEL KANT (selections 41 and 49), one of the greatest thinkers of all time, was born and lived in Königsberg, Germany, where he was educated. Lectured at the University of Königsberg in philosophy and various sciences starting in 1755, and in 1770 became Professor of Logic and Metaphysics. Author of numerous works, including *Critique of Pure Reason, Critique of Practical Reason, Critique of Judgment, Natural History and Theory of the Heavens, Religion within the Limits of Reason Alone, Prolegomena to any Future Metaphysics,* and *Metaphysics of Morals.* See A. D. Lindsay, *Kant.*

JOHN STUART MILL (selections 5, 23, 24, and 43), son of James Mill, spent much of his life in the employ of the East India Company, and was for a term a member of Parliament. He has become known as the outstanding liberal thinker of the 19th century, and his work has acquired classic significance in a number of fields. He was the author, among other works, of *Principles of Political Economy, On Liberty, Representative Government, The Subjection of Women, Utilitarianism, Examination of Sir William Hamilton's Philosophy, August Comte and Positivism,* and *Dissertations and Discussions.* His unique and amazing education, administered by his father, is described in his *Autobiography* (1873).

WILLIAM PEPPERELL MONTAGUE (selection 15) was born in Massachusetts and educated at Harvard. He taught philosophy at Columbia University from 1903 until his retirement in 1947. He was one of the leaders of the Neo-Realist school of American philosophy. His works include *Belief Unbound; The Ways of Things; Knowledge, Nature, and Value;* and *Great Visions of Philosophy.*

ARTHUR EDWARD MURPHY (selections 17 and 47) was born in Ithaca, N.Y., and received his education at the University of California. Has taught philosophy at the Universities of California, Chicago, Illinois, and Washington, and at Brown and Cornell Universities, and is at present Professor of Philosophy at the University of Texas. Delivered the Carus Lectures in 1954. Co-editor of *Essays in Political Theory,* co-author of *Philosophy in American Education,* contributor to *American Scholarship in the Twentieth Century,* and has been editor of *The Philosophical Review.* Author of the forthcoming *The Theory of Practical Reason,* and of numerous articles in philosophical and other periodicals.

ERNEST NAGEL (selection 6) was born in Czechoslovakia but raised in the United States, and was educated at the College of the City of New York and Columbia University. He is presently Dewey Professor of Philosophy at Columbia University. He has twice been a Guggenheim Fellow, and has been an editor of the *Journal of Philosophy* and the *Journal of Symbolic Logic*. He is the author of *Principles of the Theory of Probability, Logic of Measurement, Sovereign Reason, Logic Without Metaphysics, Gödel's Proof* (with James R. Newman), and *The Structure of Science.*

MAX CARL OTTO (selection 36) was born in Germany but raised in the United States and received his education at the University of Wisconsin. He also attended the Universities of Chicago and Heidelberg. He taught philosophy at the University of Wisconsin from 1910 until his retirement in 1947. He was known as one of the outstanding teachers in the mid-west. Co-author of *Philosophy in American Education* and author of *Things and Ideals, Natural Law and Human Hopes,* and *The Human Enterprise.* A number of his writings have been collected in a book entitled *Science and the Moral Life.*

CHARLES SANDERS PEIRCE (selection 13) was born in Massachusetts and educated at Harvard University, where he was lecturer in Philosophy 1864–65 and 1869–70. His only other formal teaching was at Johns Hopkins University from 1879 to 1884. Worked with the United States Coast and Geodetic Survey for 30 years. Died in dire poverty at Milford, Pennsylvania. Peirce is known as the founder of pragmatism. He wrote voluminously, though he published little, and the only book he published in his lifetime was *Photometric Research* (1878). His major philosophical writings are gathered in *Collected Papers,* in 8 volumes, edited by Hartshorne, Weiss, and Burks, and a selection from them in *Chance, Love, and Logic,* ed. by M. R. Cohen.

PLATO (selections 18 and 38) was one of the three outstanding philosophers of ancient Greece, and one of the most famous and influential philosophers of all time. He was a student of Socrates, and the founder of the Academy, which is reputed to be the first university, and is the most famous school of ancient times. His philosophical writings are in the form of dialogues, which are known not only for their philosophical merit, but for their literary style and, in some cases, their dramatic interest. Socrates is the major character in many of these dialogues and, since Socrates himself left no writings, these dialogues provide us with our main source of information about his philosophy. Some of these dialogues are the *Gorgias, Protagoras, Parmenides, Theaetetus, Sophist, Symposium, Philebus, Phaedrus, Timaeus, Euthyphro, Apology, Crito,* and *Laws.* See A. E. Taylor, *Plato: The Man and His Work.*

ARTHUR KENYON ROGERS (selection 2) taught philosophy from 1900 to 1920 at Butler University, the University of Missouri, and Yale University. He retired from teaching at the age of 52 in order to devote himself to writing, and was the author of A *Student's History of Philosophy, English and American Philosophy since 1800, Morals in Review, A Theory of Ethics, What is Truth?, The Socratic Problem,* and *Ethics and Moral Tolerance,* and contributed to *Essays in Critical Realism.*

GEORGE SANTAYANA (selections 35 and 45) was born in Spain and came to the United States at the age of 9. He was educated at Harvard University, and taught philosophy there from 1889 to 1912, when he retired to live in Europe, living for a while in England, and spending the last years of his life in retirement in a convent in Italy. Author, among other works, of *The Sense of Beauty, Interpretations of Poetry and Religion, Winds of Doctrine, Egotism in German Philosophy, Character and Opinion in the United States, Soliloquies in England and Later Soliloquies, Dialogues in Limbo, Platonism and the Spiritual Life, Realms of Being* (4 vols.), *Dominations and Powers,* several books of *Poems,* the novel *The Last Puritan,* and the autobiographical *Persons and Places* (3 volumes).

JOHN SOMERVILLE (selection 7) was born in New York City and educated at Columbia University. Has taught philosophy at the College of the City of New York, Columbia University, Stanford University, and the College of the Pacific, and is currently Professor of Philosophy at Hunter College of the City of New York, where he has taught philosophy since 1939. Author of *Soviet Philosophy, The Way of Science,* and *The Philosophy of Peace,* in addition to numerous articles in philosophical and other periodicals.

WALTER TERENCE STACE (selection 46) is Emeritus Professor of Philosophy at Princeton University. Born in England, he was educated there, and in Scotland and Ireland. He served for twenty-two years with the British Civil Service in Ceylon, and began teaching at Princeton in 1932. Author, among other works, of *The Theory of Knowledge and Existence, Religion and the Modern Mind, Time and Eternity, The Philosophy of Hegel, Critical History of Greek Philosophy, The Gate of Silence,* and *The Destiny of Western Man.*

RICHARD HENRY TAWNEY (selection 53) was born in Calcutta, India, and educated at Rugby and at Balliol College, Oxford. Was prominent for a number of years in the Workers Educational Association, was a Fellow of Balliol College, Oxford, and for many years Professor of Economic History at the University of London. Author of *The Acquisitive Society, Religion and the Rise of Capitalism, Land and Labour in China,* and *The Attack and Other Papers.*

ALEXIS DE TOCQUEVILLE (selection 51) was a French statesman and writer. He was prominent for a time in French politics, and was for a short time (in 1849) minister of foreign affairs. His *Democracy in America*, written after an official mission to the United States to study the American penal system, was the first systematic account of American government and institutions, and has become a classic of its kind. Author of *L'Ancien Régime et la Révolution* and of the posthumous *Recollections*. His writings have been edited in 9 volumes by H. G. de Beaumont.

ALFRED NORTH WHITEHEAD (selection 1) was born in England and educated at the University of Cambridge, and taught, first mathematics and then philosophy, at Cambridge and the University of London. In 1924 he came to the United States to become Professor of Philosophy at Harvard University, a post he held until his retirement in 1937. He has written extensively, in an elegant style, in mathematics, philosophy, and education, and had one of the greatest mathematical and speculative minds of the 20th century. Co-author of *Principia Mathematica*, and author, among other works, of *A Treatise on Universal Algebra*, *The Concept of Nature*, *The Principles of Natural Knowledge*, *The Principle of Relativity*, *Science and the Modern World*, *Religion in the Making*, *Process and Reality*, *Adventures of Ideas*, and *Modes of Thought*.

BIBLIOGRAPHY

The student who is interested in doing further reading on the topics covered in this volume will find the following books of interest. In general, works from which selections have been taken for this book are not listed here. Those especially recommended for beginners are marked with an asterisk.

THE HISTORY OF PHILOSOPHY

Boas, George: *Dominant Themes of Modern Philosophy* (1957)
Burnet, John: *Early Greek Philosophy* (1892)
Copleston, F. C.: *History of Philosophy* (6 Volumes, 1946–60)
Durant, Will: *The Story of Philosophy** (1926)
Jones, W. T.: *A History of Western Philosophy** (2 Volumes, 1952)
Randall, John Herman: *The Making of the Modern Mind* (1926)
Rogers, A. K.: *A Student's History of Philosophy** (1932)
Sorley, W. R.: *A History of English Philosophy** (1937)
Ueberweg, Friedrich: *A History of Philosophy from Thales to the Present Time* (trans. G. S. Morris, 2 Volumes, 1876)
Weber, Alfred: *History of Philosophy* (trans. F. Thilly, 1898)
Windelband, Wilhelm: *A History of Philosophy* (trans. J. H. Tufts, 1901)

I. THE NATURE AND USES OF PHILOSOPHY

Ayer, A. J., and others: *Revolution in Philosophy* (1956)
Collingwood, R. G.: *An Essay on Philosophical Method* (1933)
Dewey, John: *Reconstruction in Philosophy* (1920)
Ducasse, C. J.: *Philosophy as a Science* (1941)
Ewing, A. C.: *The Fundamental Questions of Philosophy** (1951)
Grene, Marjorie: *Dreadful Freedom: A Critique of Existentialism* (1948)
James, William: *Some Problems of Philosophy** (1911)
Johnstone, Henry W., Jr.: *Philosophy and Argument* (1960)
Murphy, A. E., and others: *Philosophy in American Education* (1945)
Randall, J. H., and Buchler, J.: *Philosophy: An Introduction** (1942)
Sidgwick, Henry: *Philosophy: Its Scope and Relations** (1902)
Sinclair, A.: *An Introduction to Philosophy* (1944)

II. LOGIC AND PHILOSOPHY OF SCIENCE

CLASSICS

Aristotle: *Prior Analytics*
   Posterior Analytics

Bacon, Francis: *Novum Organum*
Johnson, W. E.: *Logic* (3 Volumes)
Keynes, John Maynard: *A Treatise on Probability*
Keynes, John Neville: *Studies and Exercises in Formal Logic*
Whately, Richard: *Elements of Logic**

RECENT WORKS

Beardsley, Monroe: *Practical Logic** (1950)
Bernard, Claude: *An Introduction to the Study of Experimental Medicine* (trans. H. C. Greene, 1927)
Black, Max: *Critical Thinking** (1952)
Campbell, Norman: *What Is Science?** (1921)
Cohen, Morris: *Reason and Nature* (1931)
Dewey, John: *Logic: The Theory of Inquiry* (1938)
Duhem, Pierre: *The Aim and Structure of Physical Theory* (trans. P. P. Wiener, 1954)
Feigl, H., and Brodbeck, M.: *Readings in the Philosophy of Science* (1953)
Kemeny, John: *A Philosopher Looks at Science** (1959)
Kneale, W. C.: *Probability and Induction* (1949)
Poincaré, Henri: *The Foundations of Science* (trans. G. B. Halsted, 1913)
Ramsperger, Albert G.: *Philosophies of Science** (1942)
Ruby, Lionel: *The Art of Making Sense: A Guide to Logical Thinking** (1954)
Russell, Bertrand: *Introduction to Mathematical Philosophy* (1913)
Stebbing, Susan: *Thinking to Some Purpose** (1939)
Strawson, P. F.: *Introduction to Logical Theory* (1952)
Thouless, Robert: *Straight and Crooked Thinking** (1930)
Toulmin, Stephen: *The Philosophy of Science* (1953)
                    The Uses of Argument (1958)
Whitehead, Alfred North: *An Introduction to Mathematics** (1911)
                    Science and the Modern World (1926)

III. THEORY OF KNOWLEDGE

CLASSICS

Berkeley, George: *Dialogues between Hylas and Philonous**
Kant, Immanuel: *Critique of Pure Reason*
Locke, John: *An Essay Concerning Human Understanding*
Plato: *Meno**
        Theaetetus
Reid, Thomas: *Essays on the Intellectual Powers of Man*

RECENT WORKS

Ayer, A. J.: *The Problem of Knowledge* (1956)
Hobhouse, L. T.: *The Theory of Knowledge* (1896)

BIBLIOGRAPHY 393

Joachim, Harold H.: *The Nature of Truth* (1906)
Laird, John: *Knowledge, Belief, and Opinion* (1930)
Lovejoy, Arthur O.: *The Revolt against Dualism* (1930)
Moore, G. E.: *Philosophical Studies* (1922)
  Philosophical Papers (1959)
Price, H. H.: *Perception* (1932)
Prichard, H. A.: *Knowledge and Perception* (1950)
Rogers, A. K.: *What Is Truth?* (1923)
Russell, Bertrand: *The Problems of Philosophy** (1912)
  Our Knowledge of the External World (1914)
Woozley, A. D.: *Theory of Knowledge** (1949)

IV. METAPHYSICS

CLASSICS

Aristotle: *Metaphysics*
Hegel, G. W. F.: *The Phenomenology of Mind*
Kant, Immanuel: *Prolegomena to any Future Metaphysics*
Leibniz, Gottfried Wilhelm: *Monadology*
Plato: *The Republic**
  Timaeus
Spinoza, Benedict: *Ethics*

RECENT WORKS

Alexander, Samuel: *Space, Time, and Deity* (1920)
Ayer, A. J.: *Language, Truth and Logic* (1936)
Broad, C. D.: *The Mind and Its Place in Nature* (1925)
Collingwood, R. G.: *An Essay on Metaphysics* (1940)
Dewey, John: *Experience and Nature* (1925)
Ducasse, C. J.: *Nature, Mind, and Death* (1951)
Lewis, C. I.: *Mind and the World Order* (1929)
Pap, Arthur: *Elements of Analytic Philosophy** (1949)
Russell, Bertrand: *Mysticism and Logic* (1917)
Ryle, Gilbert: *The Concept of Mind* (1949)
Sartre, Jean-Paul: *Existentialism** (1948)
Taylor, A. E.: *Elements of Metaphysics* (1903)
Whiteley, C. H.: *An Introduction to Metaphysics** (1950)
Wisdom, John: *Problems of Mind and Matter* (1934)

V. PHILOSOPHY OF RELIGION

CLASSICS

Augustine, St.: *City of God*
Butler, Joseph: *The Analogy of Religion*

Kant, Immanuel: *Religion within the Limits of Reason Alone*
Paley, William: *View of the Evidences of Christianity*

RECENT WORKS

Bronstein, D. J., and Shulweis, H. M., eds.: *Approaches to the Philosophy of Religion** (1954)
Bergson, Henri: *The Two Sources of Morality and Religion* (1935)
Burtt, E. A.: *Types of Religious Philosophy** (1939)
Dewey, John: *A Common Faith** (1934)
Ducasse, C. J.: *A Philosophical Scrutiny of Religion** (1953)
Garnett, A. C.: *Religion and the Moral Life** (1955)
James, William: *Varieties of Religious Experience* (1902)
MacGregor, Geddes: *Introduction to Religious Philosophy** (1959)
Paton, H. J.: *The Modern Predicament* (1955)
Pratt, J. B.: *The Religious Consciousness* (1920)
Russell, Bertrand: *Religion and Science** (1935)
Stace, Walter T.: *Religion and the Modern Mind** (1952)
Whitehead, Alfred North: *Religion in the Making* (1926)

VI. ETHICS AND VALUES

A. *Ethics*

CLASSICS

Aristotle: *Eudemian Ethics*
Butler, Joseph: *Sermons on Human Nature*
Hume, David: *An Inquiry Concerning the Principles of Morals*
Mill, John Stuart: *Utilitarianism**
Selby-Bigge, L. A., ed.: *British Moralists*
Sidgwick, Henry: *The Methods of Ethics*

RECENT WORKS

Albee, Ernest: *A History of English Utilitarianism* (1901)
Baier, Kurt: *The Moral Point of View* (1958)
Brandt, Richard: *Ethical Theory* (1959)
Broad, C. D.: *Five Types of Ethical Theory** (1930)
Dewey, John: *Human Nature and Conduct* (1922)
Dewey, J., and Tufts, J. H.: *Ethics** (1910)
Garnett, A. C.: *Ethics: A Critical Introduction** (1960)
Garvin, Lucius: *A Modern Introduction to Ethics** (1953)
Nowell-Smith, P. H.: *Ethics* (1954)
Paulsen, Friedrich: *A System of Ethics** (trans. F. Thilly, 1899)
Rogers, A. K.: *Morals in Review** (1927)
Sidgwick, Henry: *Outlines of the History of Ethics* (6th ed. revised, 1931)
Singer, M. G.: *Generalization in Ethics* (1961)
Stevenson, C. L.: *Ethics and Language* (1943)

Toulmin, Stephen: *The Place of Reason in Ethics* (1950)
Williams, Glanville: *The Sanctity of Life and the Criminal Law* (1958)

B. Aesthetics

CLASSICS

Aristotle: *Poetics*
Kant, Immanuel: *The Critique of Aesthetic Judgment*
Plato: *Ion*
    Phaedrus
    Symposium
Tolstoy, Lev. N.: *What Is Art?*

RECENT WORKS

Beardsley, Monroe: *Aesthetics* (1958)
Bosanquet, Bernard: *A History of Aesthetic* (1892)
Carritt, E. F.: *The Theory of Beauty* (1914)
Ducasse, C. J.: *Art, the Critics, and You** (1944)
Gilbert, K., and Kuhn, H.: *History of Esthetics* (2nd ed., 1953)
Gotshalk, D. W.: *Art and the Social Order** (1947)
Langer, Susanne K.: *Philosophy in a New Key* (1942)
                Feeling and Form (1953)
Rader, Melvin M., ed.: *A Modern Book of Esthetics** (3rd ed., 1959)
Santayana, George: *The Sense of Beauty* (1896)
Vivas, E., and Krieger, M.: *The Problems of Aesthetics* (1953)
Weitz, Morris, ed.: *Problems in Aesthetics* (1959)

VII. POLITICAL PHILOSOPHY

CLASSICS

Aristotle: *Politics*
Bentham, Jeremy: *A Fragment on Government*
Green, T. H.: *Lectures on the Principles of Political Obligation*
Hobbes, Thomas: *Leviathan*
         De Cive
Locke, John: *Second Treatise on Civil Government*
Mill, John Stuart: *On Liberty**
             Representative Government
Plato: *The Republic**
    The Statesman
    The Laws
Rousseau, Jean Jacques: *The Social Contract*

RECENT WORKS

Bosanquet, Bernard: *The Philosophical Theory of the State* (1899)
Cairns, Huntington: *Legal Philosophy from Plato to Hegel* (1949)

Cohen, Morris R.: *Law and the Social Order* (1933)
Collingwood, R. G.: *The New Leviathan* (1942)
Dewey, John: *The Public and Its Problems** (1927)
Hobhouse, L. T.: *The Elements of Social Justice** (1922)
                The Metaphysical Theory of the State (1918)
Hook, Sidney: *Reason, Social Myths and Democracy* (1940)
Mabbott, J. D.: *The State and the Citizen** (1948)
Mackenzie, John S.: *An Introduction to Social Philosophy** (2nd ed., 1895)
Popper, Karl: *The Open Society and Its Enemies* (1945)
Pound, Roscoe: *An Introduction to the Philosophy of Law* (1922)
Sabine, George H.: *A History of Political Theory* (1937)
Sidgwick, Henry: *The Elements of Politics** (1891)
Tawney, R. H.: *The Acquisitive Society ** (1921)
Weldon, T. D.: *The Vocabulary of Politics* (1953)
Willoughby, W. W.: *Social Justice* (1900)

CHRONOLOGICAL TABLE OF CONTENTS